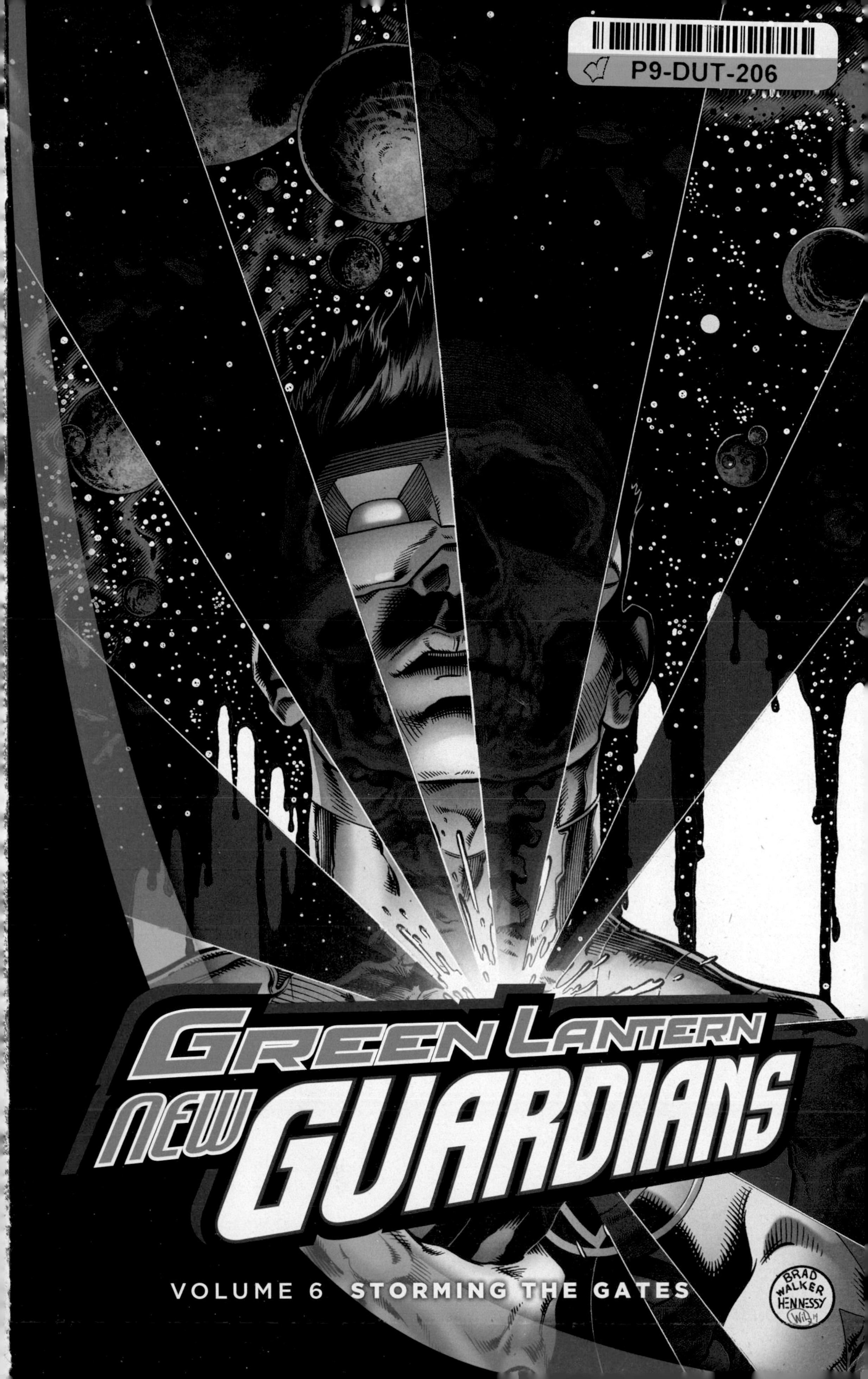
GREEN LANTERN
NEW GUARDIANS
VOLUME 6 STORMING THE GATES
BRAD WALKER HENNESSY

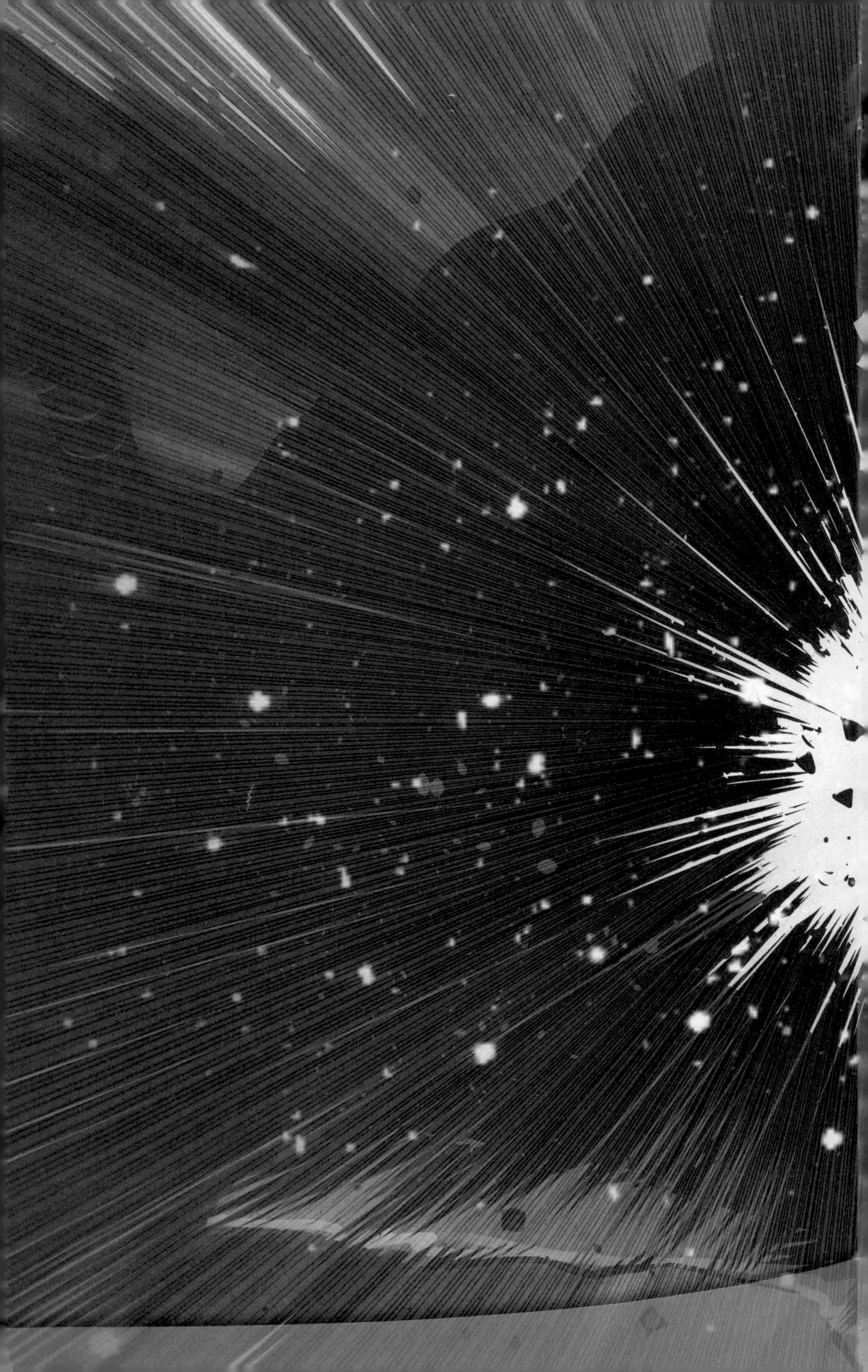

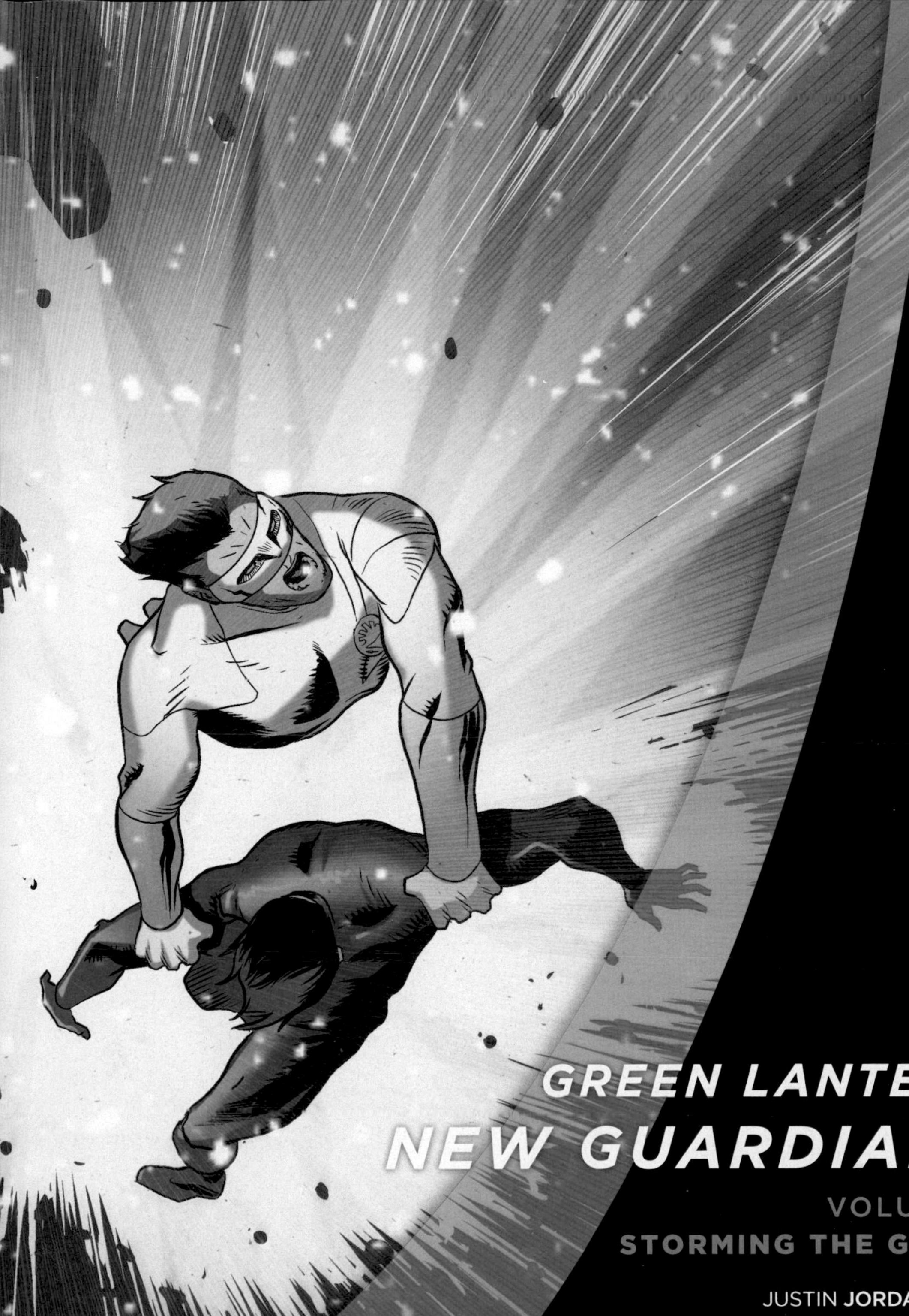

GREEN LANTERN
NEW GUARDIANS

VOLUME 6
STORMING THE GATES

JUSTIN **JORDAN** writer

DIOGENES **NEVES** MARC **DEERING**
BRAD **WALKER** ANDREW **HENNESSY**
ROBIN **RIGGS** RODNEY **BUCHEMI**
DANIEL **HENRIQUES** RONAN **CLIQUET**
ROGE **ANTONIO** artists

WIL **QUINTANA** ANDREW **DALHOUSE** colorists

DAVE **SHARPE** TAYLOR **ESPOSITO** letterers

DIOGENES **NEVES** MARC **DEERING** WIL **QUINTANA** collection cover artists

MATT IDELSON Editor – Original Series   DARREN SHAN Associate Editor – Original Series
JEB WOODARD Group Editor - Collected Editions   LIZ ERICKSON Editor   ROBBIE BIEDERMAN Publication Design

BOB HARRAS Senior VP – Editor-in-Chief, DC Comics

DIANE NELSON President   DAN DIDIO and JIM LEE Co-Publishers
GEOFF JOHNS Chief Creative Officer   AMIT DESAI Senior VP – Marketing & Global Franchise Management
NAIRI GARDINER Senior VP – Finance   SAM ADES VP – Digital Marketing   BOBBIE CHASE VP –Talent Development
MARK CHIARELLO Senior VP – Art, Design & Collected Editions   JOHN CUNNINGHAM VP – Content Strategy
ANNE DEPIES VP – Strategy Planning & Reporting   DON FALLETTI VP – Manufacturing Operations
LAWRENCE GANEM VP – Editorial Administration & Talent Relations   ALISON GILL Senior VP – Manufacturing & Operations
HANK KANALZ Senior VP – Editorial Strategy & Administration   JAY KOGAN VP – Legal Affairs
DEREK MADDALENA Senior VP – Sales & Business Development   DAN MIRON VP – Sales Planning & Trade Development
NICK NAPOLITANO VP – Manufacturing Administration   CAROL ROEDER VP – Marketing
EDDIE SCANNELL VP – Mass Account & Digital Sales   SUSAN SHEPPARD VP – Business Affairs
COURTNEY SIMMONS Senior VP – Publicity & Communications   JIM (SKI) SOKOLOWSKI VP – Comic Book Specialty & Newsstand Sales

GREEN LANTERN - NEW GUARDIANS VOLUME 6: STORMING THE GATES

Published by DC Comics. Compilation Copyright © 2015 DC Comics. All Rights Reserved.

Originally published in single magazine form in GREEN LANTERN: NEW GUARDIANS 35-40 © 2014, 2015 DC Comics. All Rights Reserved.
All characters, their distinctive likenesses and related elements featured in this publication are trademarks of DC Comics.
The stories, characters and incidents featured in this publication are entirely fictional.
DC Comics does not read or accept unsolicited ideas, stories or artwork.

DC Comics, 4000 Warner Blvd., Burbank, CA 91522
A Warner Bros. Entertainment Company.
Printed by RR Donnelley, Owensville, MO, USA. 7/17/15. First Printing.

ISBN: 978-1-4012-5477-3

SUSTAINABLE FORESTRY INITIATIVE
Certified Chain of Custody
20% Certified Forest Content,
80% Certified Sourcing
www.sfiprogram.org
SFI-01042
APPLIES TO TEXT STOCK ONLY

Library of Congress Cataloging-in-Publication Data

Jordan, Justin, author.
Green Lantern: New Guardians. Volume 6 / Justin Jordan, writer ; Brad
Walker, artist.
pages cm. — (The New 52!)
ISBN 978-1-4012-5477-3 (paperback)
1. Graphic novels. 2. Superhero comic books, strips, etc. I.
Walker, Brad (Comic book artist) illustrator. II. Title.
PN6728.G74J694 2015
741.5'973—dc23
2015008040

THE **LIFE** EQUATION IS **BEYOND** YOU, MORTAL. IT IS FOR THE **GODS ALONE** TO WIELD.

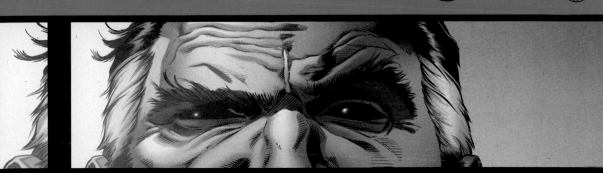

GODHEAD: ACT I, PART IV: TRUST

JUSTIN JORDAN writer BRAD WALKER penciller ANDREW HENNESSY with ROBIN RIGGS inkers WIL QUINTANA colorist DAVE SHARPE letterer
cover art by WALKER, HENNESSY and QUINTANA

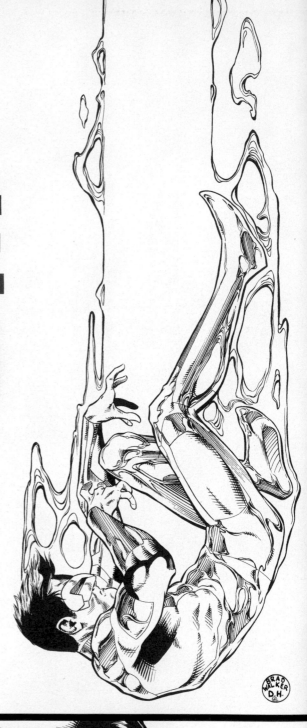

"THE LIFE EQUATION IS BEYOND YOU, MORTAL. IT IS FOR THE GODS ALONE TO WIELD.

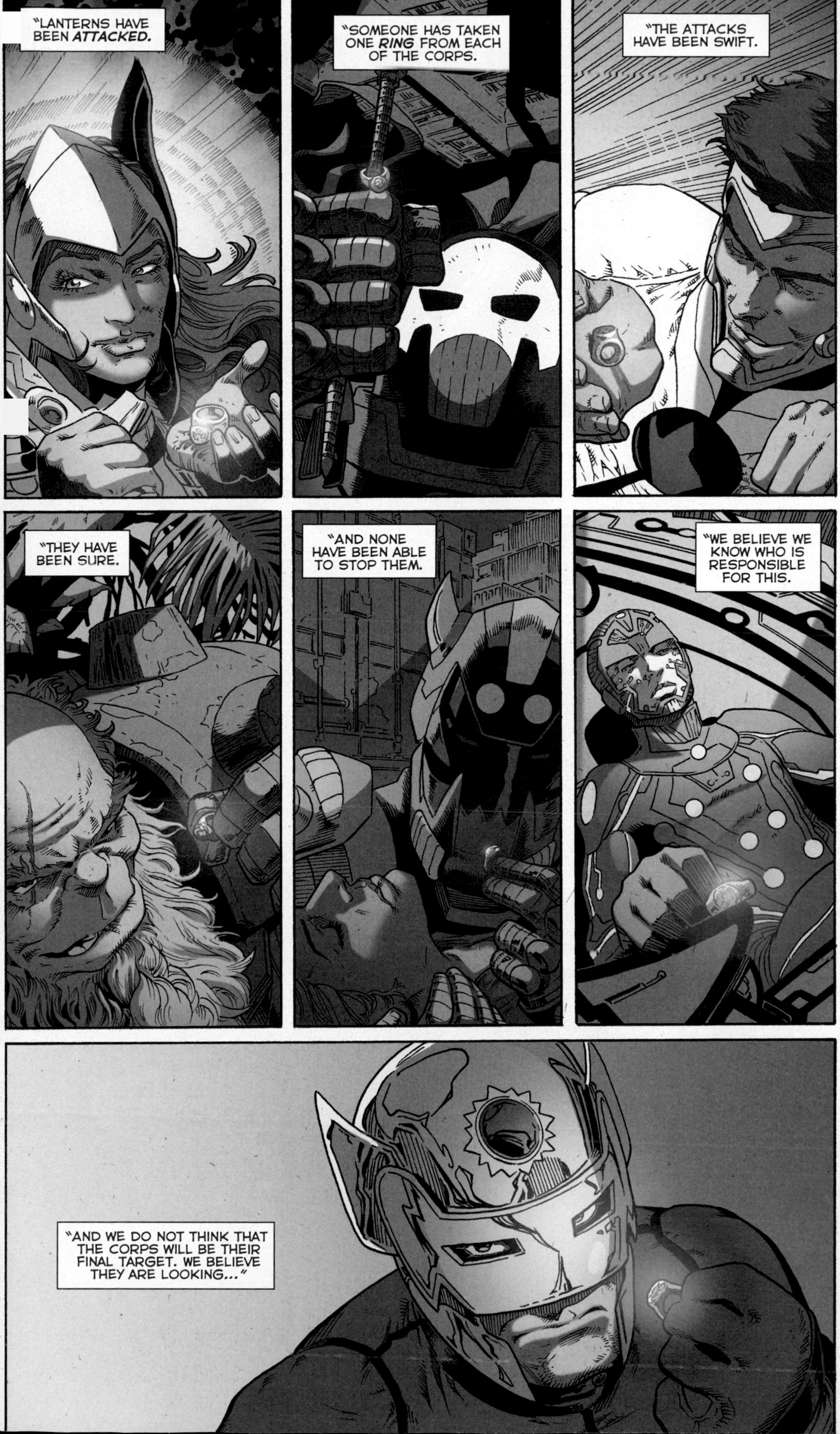
"LANTERNS HAVE BEEN ATTACKED.
"SOMEONE HAS TAKEN ONE RING FROM EACH OF THE CORPS.
"THE ATTACKS HAVE BEEN SWIFT.
"THEY HAVE BEEN SURE.
"AND NONE HAVE BEEN ABLE TO STOP THEM.
"WE BELIEVE WE KNOW WHO IS RESPONSIBLE FOR THIS.
"AND WE DO NOT THINK THAT THE CORPS WILL BE THEIR FINAL TARGET. WE BELIEVE THEY ARE LOOKING..."

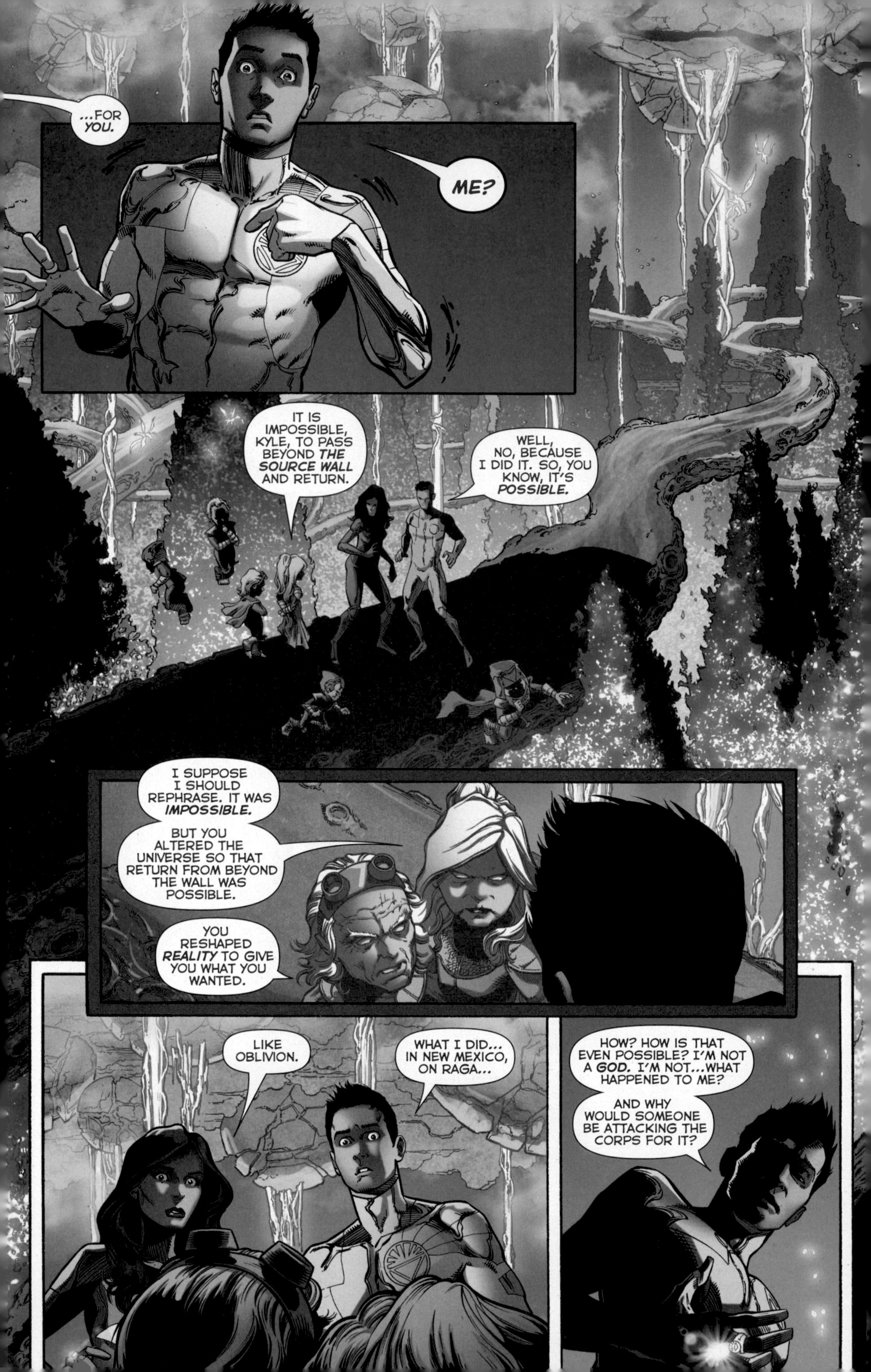
...FOR YOU.
ME?
IT IS IMPOSSIBLE, KYLE, TO PASS BEYOND THE SOURCE WALL AND RETURN.
WELL, NO, BECAUSE I DID IT. SO, YOU KNOW, IT'S POSSIBLE.
I SUPPOSE I SHOULD REPHRASE. IT WAS IMPOSSIBLE.
BUT YOU ALTERED THE UNIVERSE SO THAT RETURN FROM BEYOND THE WALL WAS POSSIBLE.
YOU RESHAPED REALITY TO GIVE YOU WHAT YOU WANTED.
LIKE OBLIVION.
WHAT I DID... IN NEW MEXICO, ON RAGA...
HOW? HOW IS THAT EVEN POSSIBLE? I'M NOT A GOD. I'M NOT...WHAT HAPPENED TO ME?
AND WHY WOULD SOMEONE BE ATTACKING THE CORPS FOR IT?

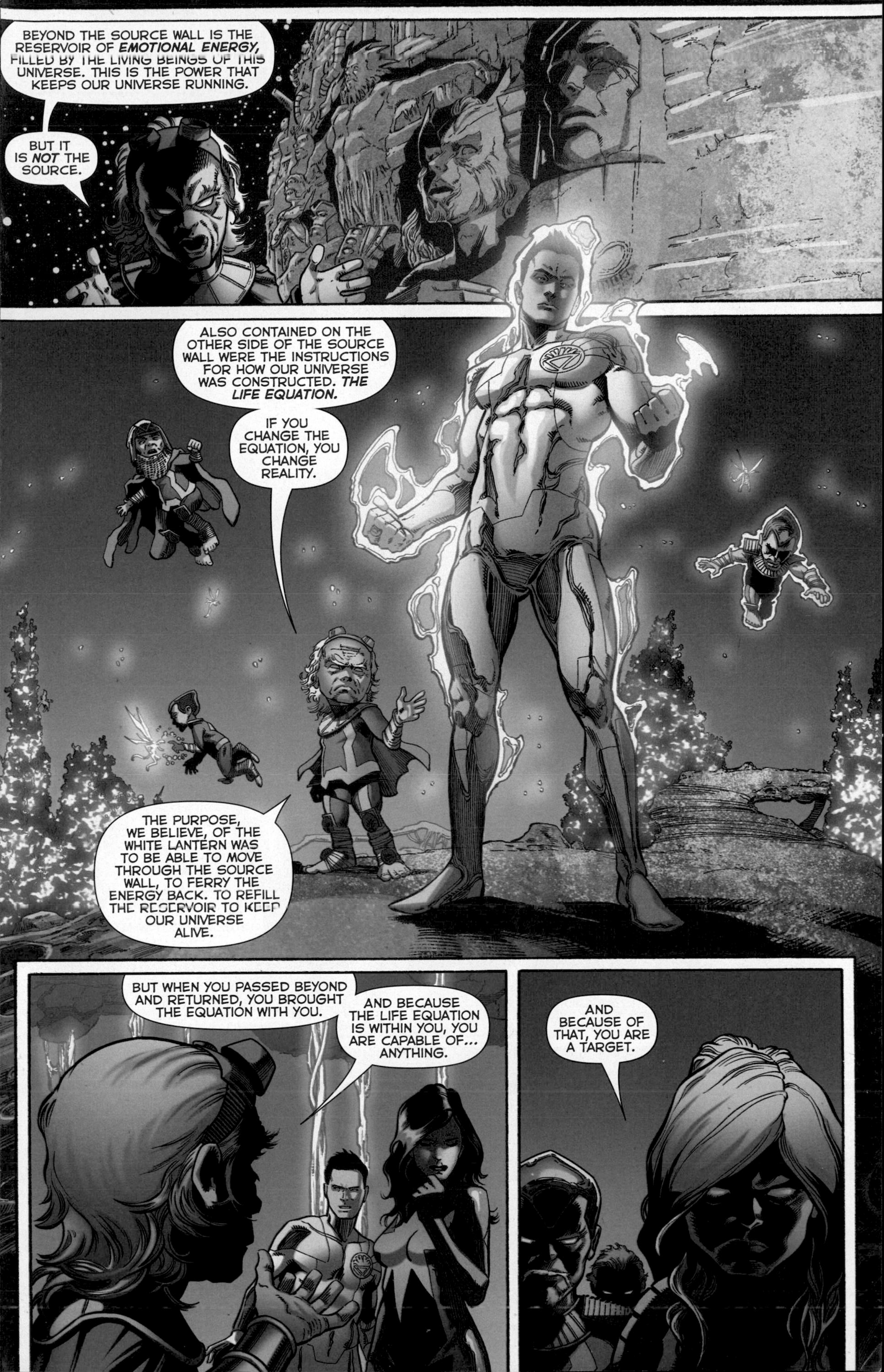
BEYOND THE SOURCE WALL IS THE RESERVOIR OF *EMOTIONAL ENERGY,* FILLED BY THE LIVING BEINGS OF THIS UNIVERSE. THIS IS THE POWER THAT KEEPS OUR UNIVERSE RUNNING.
BUT IT IS *NOT* THE SOURCE.
ALSO CONTAINED ON THE OTHER SIDE OF THE SOURCE WALL WERE THE INSTRUCTIONS FOR HOW OUR UNIVERSE WAS CONSTRUCTED. *THE LIFE EQUATION.*
IF YOU CHANGE THE EQUATION, YOU CHANGE REALITY.
THE PURPOSE, WE BELIEVE, OF THE WHITE LANTERN WAS TO BE ABLE TO MOVE THROUGH THE SOURCE WALL, TO FERRY THE ENERGY BACK. TO REFILL THE RESERVOIR TO KEEP OUR UNIVERSE ALIVE.
BUT WHEN YOU PASSED BEYOND AND RETURNED, YOU BROUGHT THE EQUATION WITH YOU.
AND BECAUSE THE LIFE EQUATION IS WITHIN YOU, YOU ARE CAPABLE OF... ANYTHING.
AND BECAUSE OF THAT, YOU ARE A TARGET.

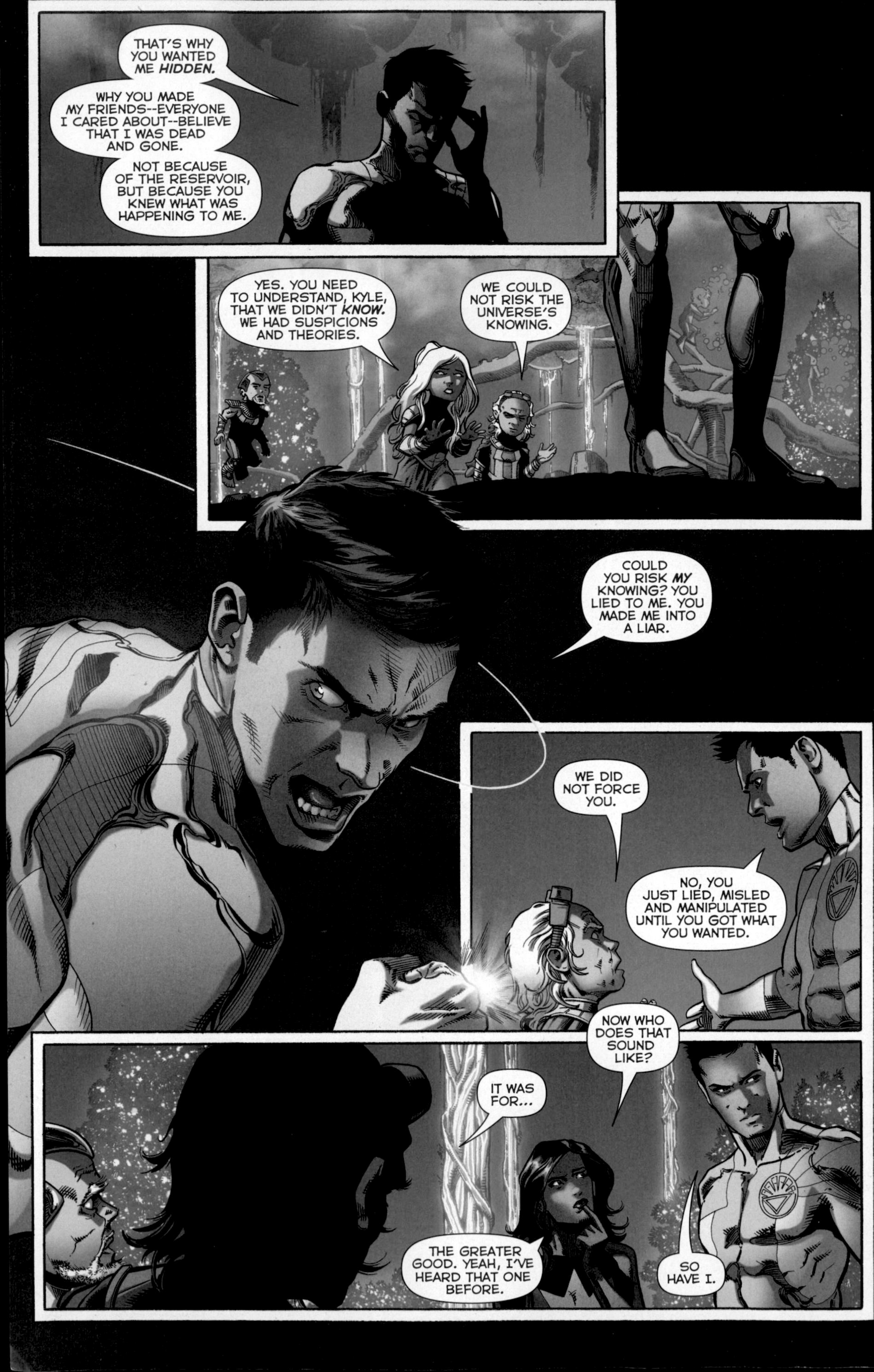
THAT'S WHY YOU WANTED ME *HIDDEN.*
WHY YOU MADE MY FRIENDS--EVERYONE I CARED ABOUT--BELIEVE THAT I WAS DEAD AND GONE.
NOT BECAUSE OF THE RESERVOIR, BUT BECAUSE YOU KNEW WHAT WAS HAPPENING TO ME.
YES. YOU NEED TO UNDERSTAND, KYLE, THAT WE DIDN'T *KNOW.* WE HAD SUSPICIONS AND THEORIES.
WE COULD NOT RISK THE UNIVERSE'S KNOWING.
COULD YOU RISK *MY* KNOWING? YOU LIED TO ME. YOU MADE ME INTO A LIAR.
WE DID NOT FORCE YOU.
NO, YOU JUST LIED, MISLED AND MANIPULATED UNTIL YOU GOT WHAT YOU WANTED.
NOW WHO DOES THAT SOUND LIKE?
IT WAS FOR...
THE GREATER GOOD. YEAH, I'VE HEARD THAT ONE BEFORE.
SO HAVE I.

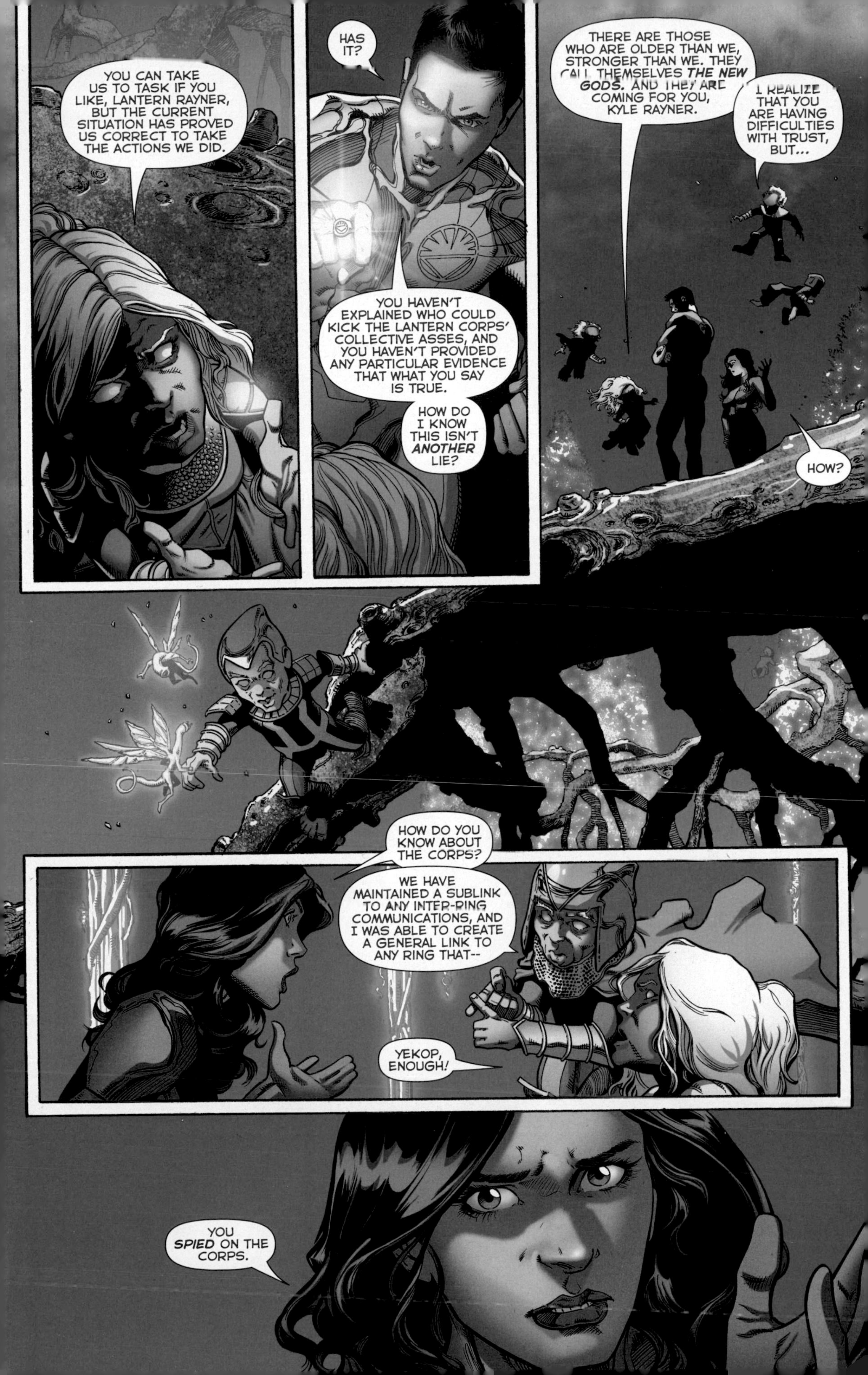
YOU CAN TAKE US TO TASK IF YOU LIKE, LANTERN RAYNER, BUT THE CURRENT SITUATION HAS PROVED US CORRECT TO TAKE THE ACTIONS WE DID.
HAS IT?
YOU HAVEN'T EXPLAINED WHO COULD KICK THE LANTERN CORPS' COLLECTIVE ASSES, AND YOU HAVEN'T PROVIDED ANY PARTICULAR EVIDENCE THAT WHAT YOU SAY IS TRUE.
HOW DO I KNOW THIS ISN'T ANOTHER LIE?
THERE ARE THOSE WHO ARE OLDER THAN WE, STRONGER THAN WE. THEY CALL THEMSELVES THE NEW GODS. AND THEY ARE COMING FOR YOU, KYLE RAYNER.
I REALIZE THAT YOU ARE HAVING DIFFICULTIES WITH TRUST, BUT...
HOW?
HOW DO YOU KNOW ABOUT THE CORPS?
WE HAVE MAINTAINED A SUBLINK TO ANY INTER-RING COMMUNICATIONS, AND I WAS ABLE TO CREATE A GENERAL LINK TO ANY RING THAT--
YEKOP, ENOUGH!
YOU SPIED ON THE CORPS.

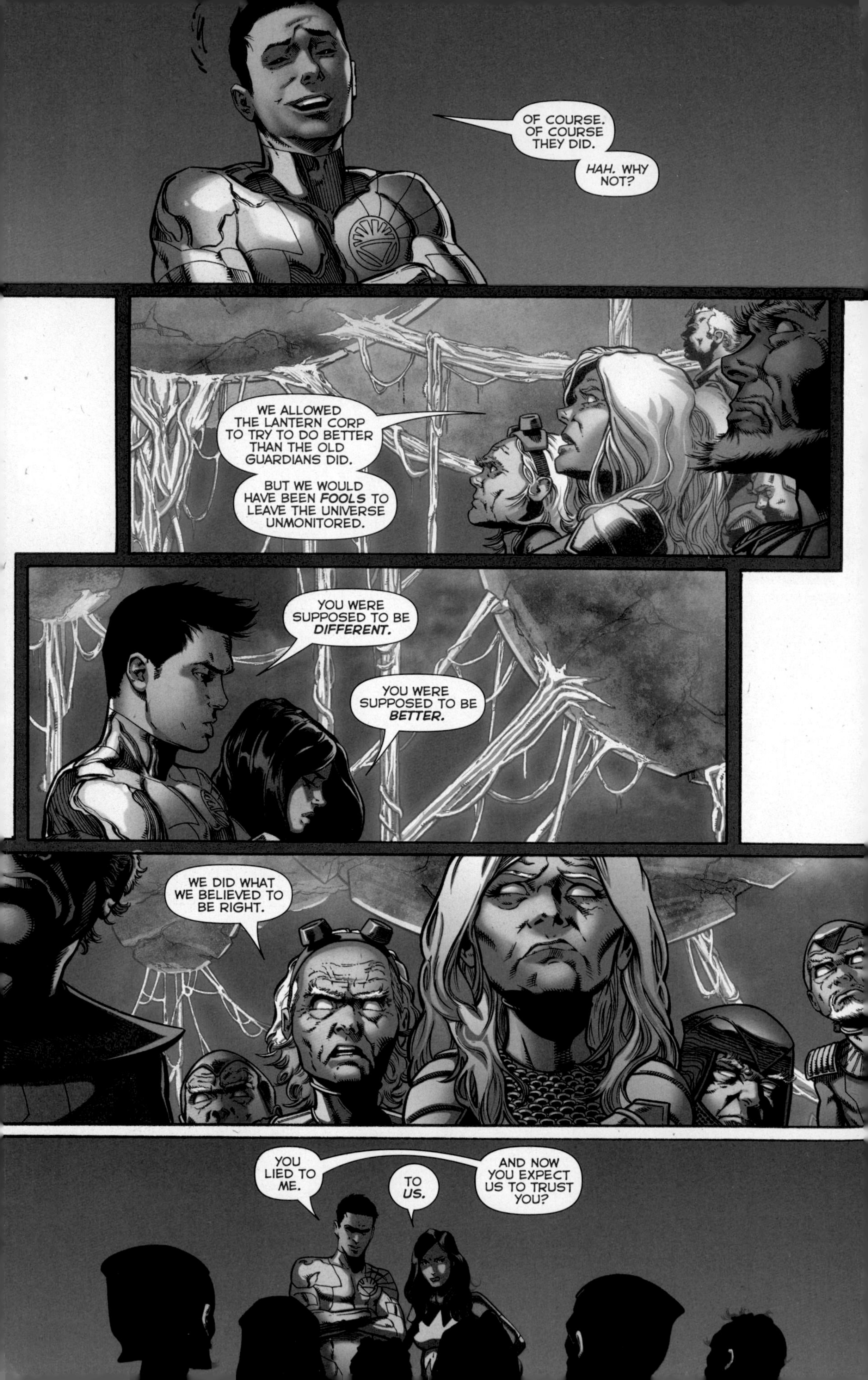
OF COURSE. OF COURSE THEY DID.
HAH. WHY NOT?
WE ALLOWED THE LANTERN CORP TO TRY TO DO BETTER THAN THE OLD GUARDIANS DID.
BUT WE WOULD HAVE BEEN ***FOOLS*** TO LEAVE THE UNIVERSE UNMONITORED.
YOU WERE SUPPOSED TO BE ***DIFFERENT.***
YOU WERE SUPPOSED TO BE ***BETTER.***
WE DID WHAT WE BELIEVED TO BE RIGHT.
YOU LIED TO ME.
TO ***US.***
AND NOW YOU EXPECT US TO TRUST YOU?

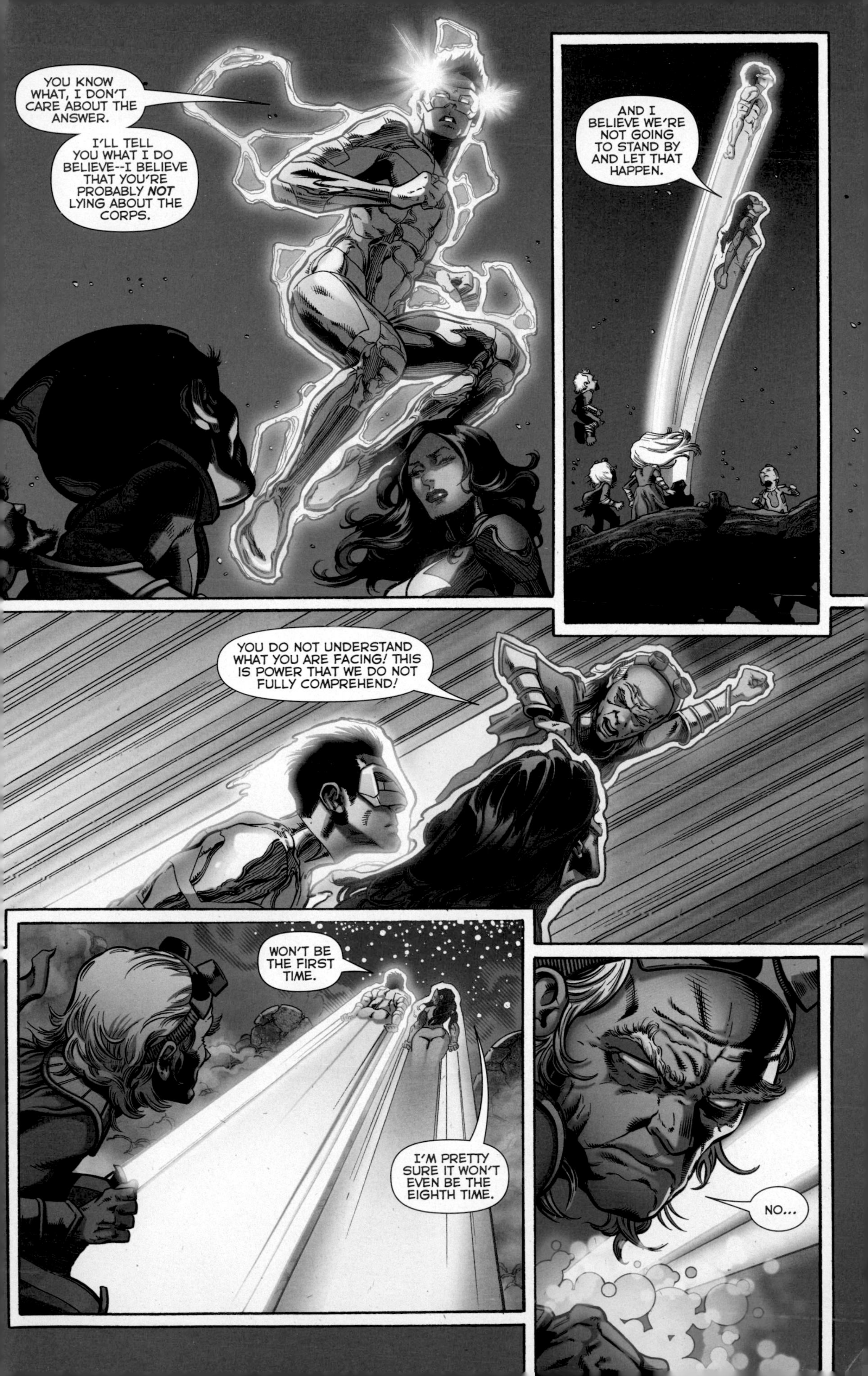
YOU KNOW WHAT, I DON'T CARE ABOUT THE ANSWER.
I'LL TELL YOU WHAT I DO BELIEVE--I BELIEVE THAT YOU'RE PROBABLY **NOT** LYING ABOUT THE CORPS.
AND I BELIEVE WE'RE NOT GOING TO STAND BY AND LET THAT HAPPEN.
YOU DO NOT UNDERSTAND WHAT YOU ARE FACING! THIS IS POWER THAT WE DO NOT FULLY COMPREHEND!
WON'T BE THE FIRST TIME.
I'M PRETTY SURE IT WON'T EVEN BE THE EIGHTH TIME.
NO...

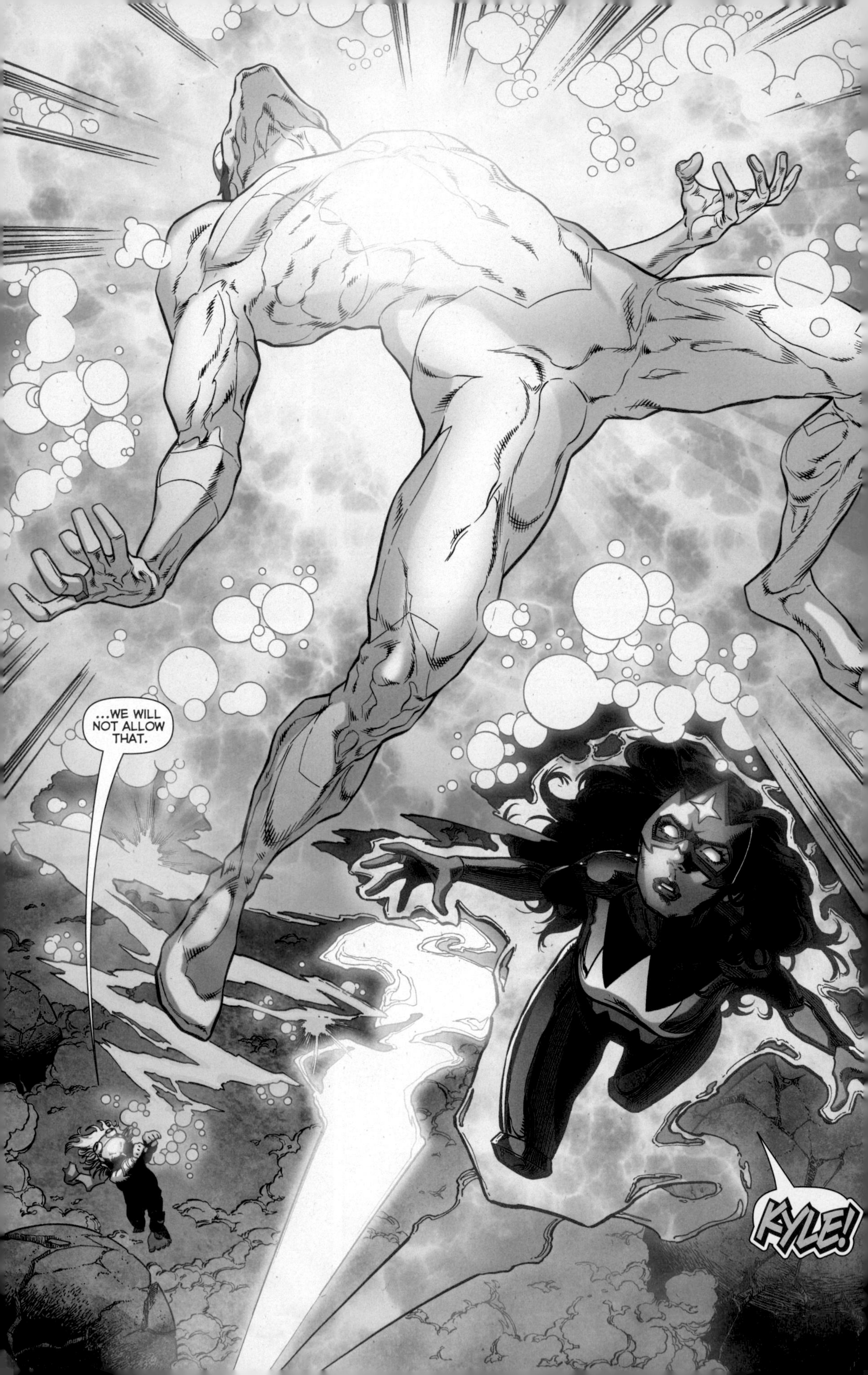
...WE WILL NOT ALLOW THAT.
KYLE!

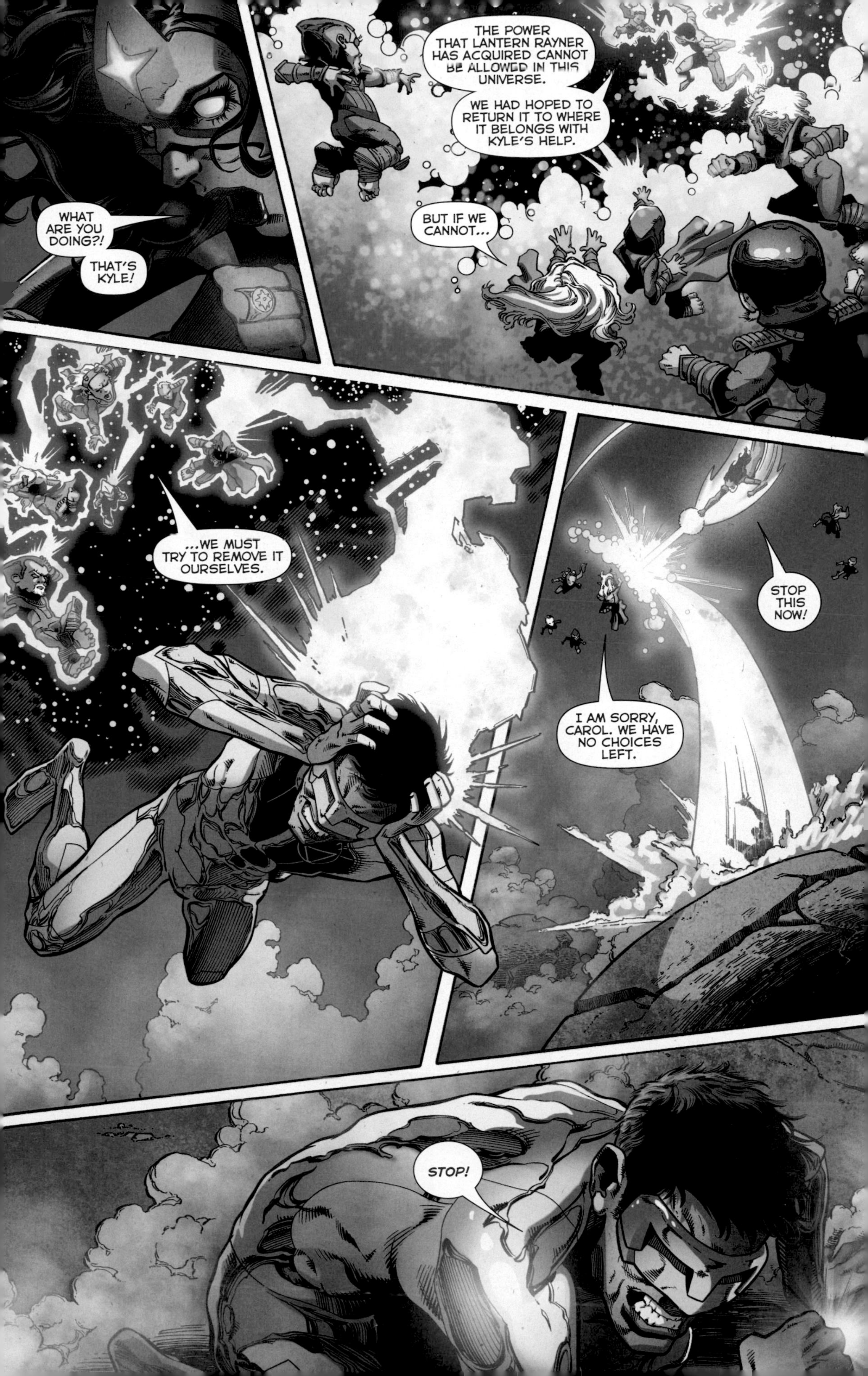
WHAT ARE YOU DOING?!
THAT'S KYLE!
THE POWER THAT LANTERN RAYNER HAS ACQUIRED CANNOT BE ALLOWED IN THIS UNIVERSE.
WE HAD HOPED TO RETURN IT TO WHERE IT BELONGS WITH KYLE'S HELP.
BUT IF WE CANNOT...
...WE MUST TRY TO REMOVE IT OURSELVES.
STOP THIS NOW!
I AM SORRY, CAROL. WE HAVE NO CHOICES LEFT.
STOP!

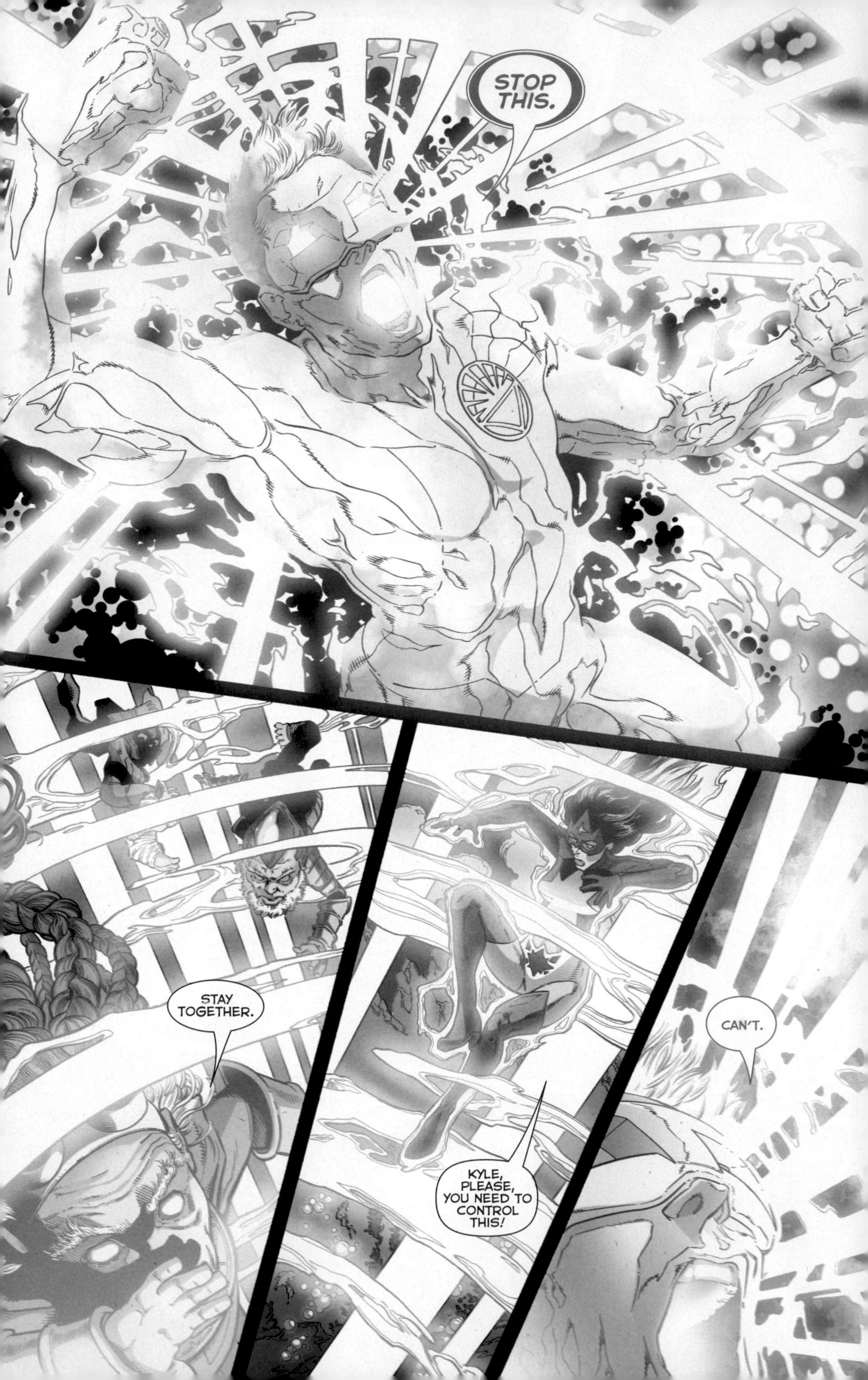
STOP THIS.
STAY TOGETHER.
KYLE, PLEASE, YOU NEED TO CONTROL THIS!
CAN'T.

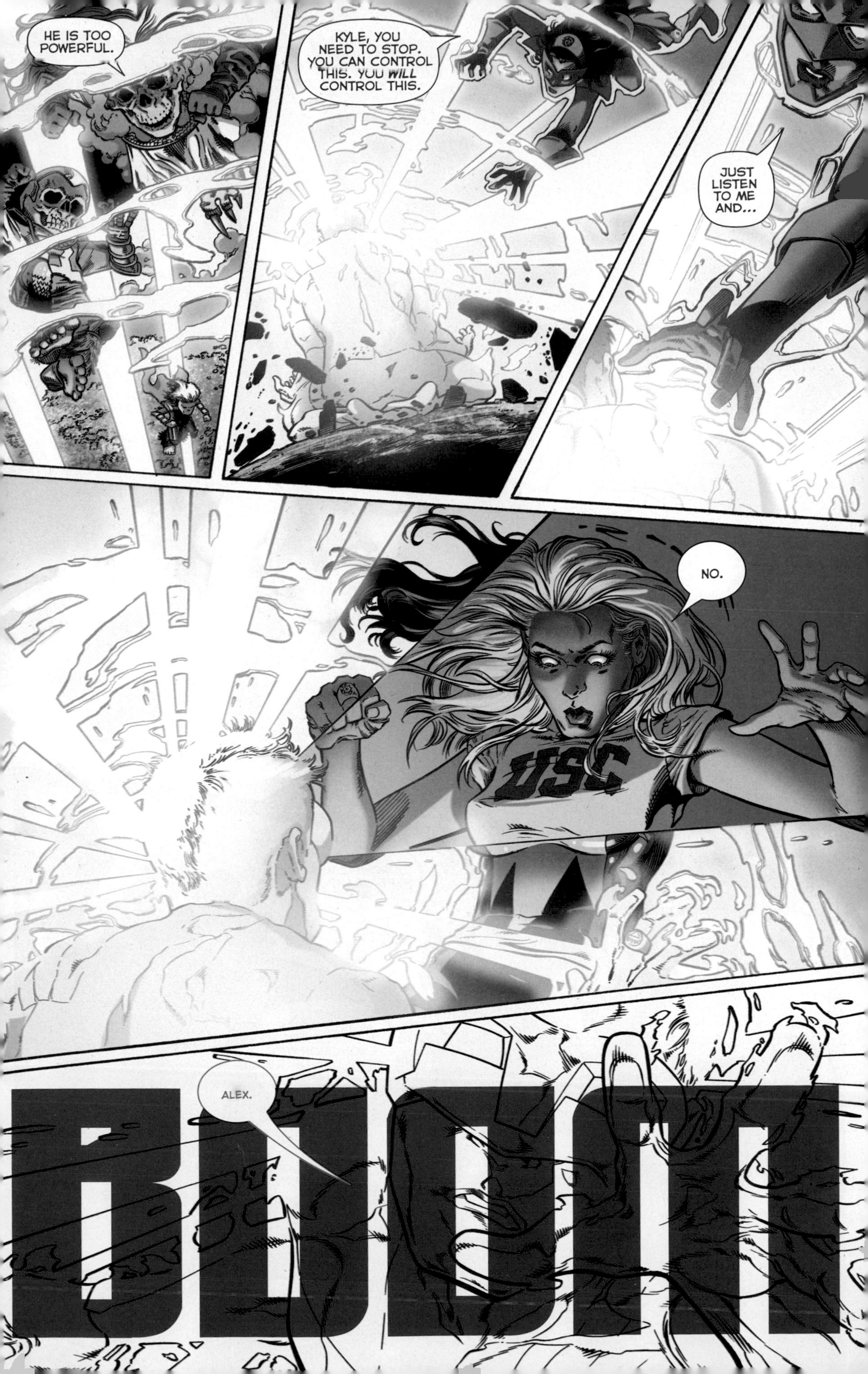
HE IS TOO POWERFUL.
KYLE, YOU NEED TO STOP. YOU CAN CONTROL THIS. YOU *WILL* CONTROL THIS.
JUST LISTEN TO ME AND...
NO.
ALEX.
BOOM

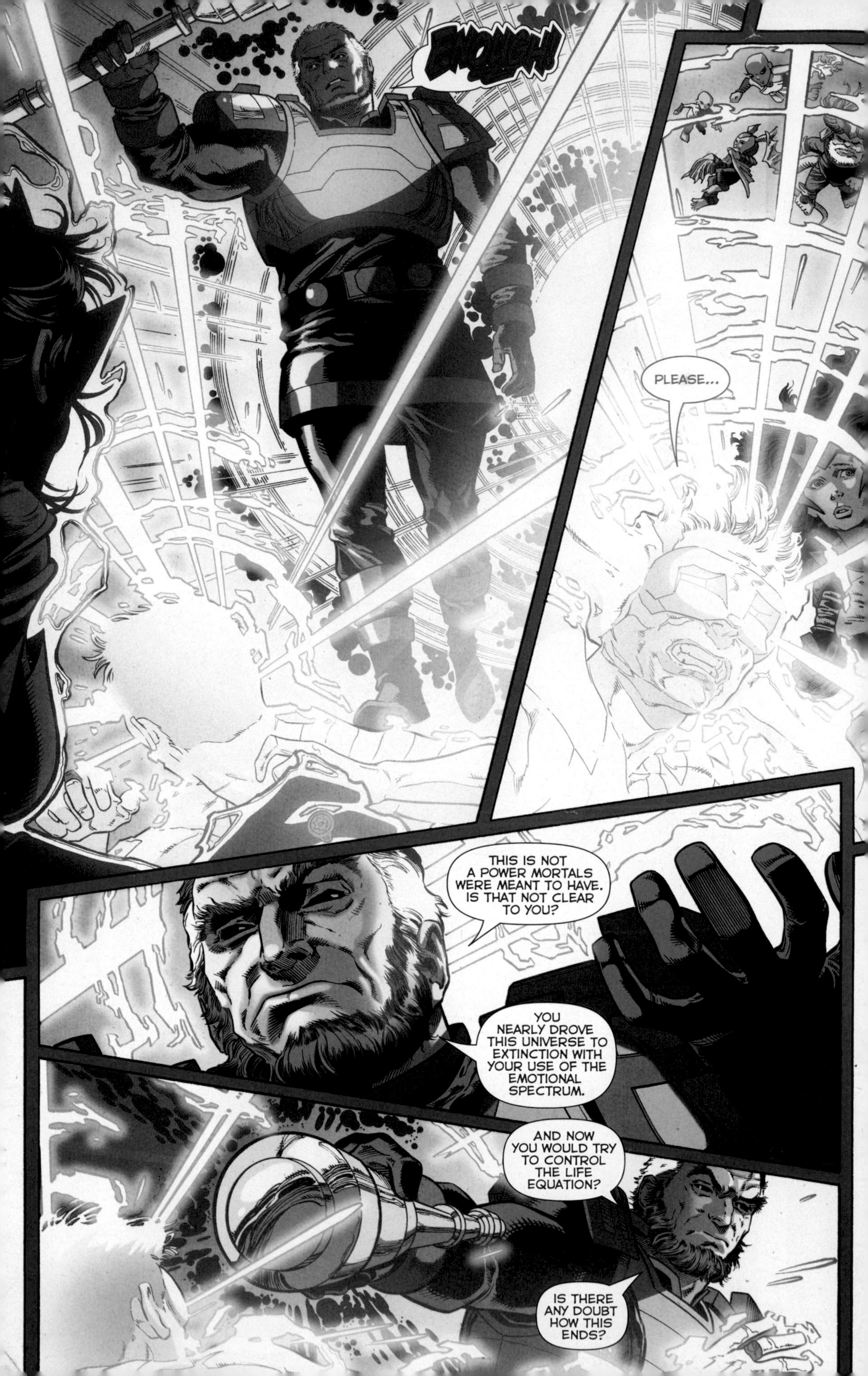
ENOUGH!
PLEASE...
THIS IS NOT A POWER MORTALS WERE MEANT TO HAVE. IS THAT NOT CLEAR TO YOU?
YOU NEARLY DROVE THIS UNIVERSE TO EXTINCTION WITH YOUR USE OF THE EMOTIONAL SPECTRUM.
AND NOW YOU WOULD TRY TO CONTROL THE LIFE EQUATION?
IS THERE ANY DOUBT HOW THIS ENDS?

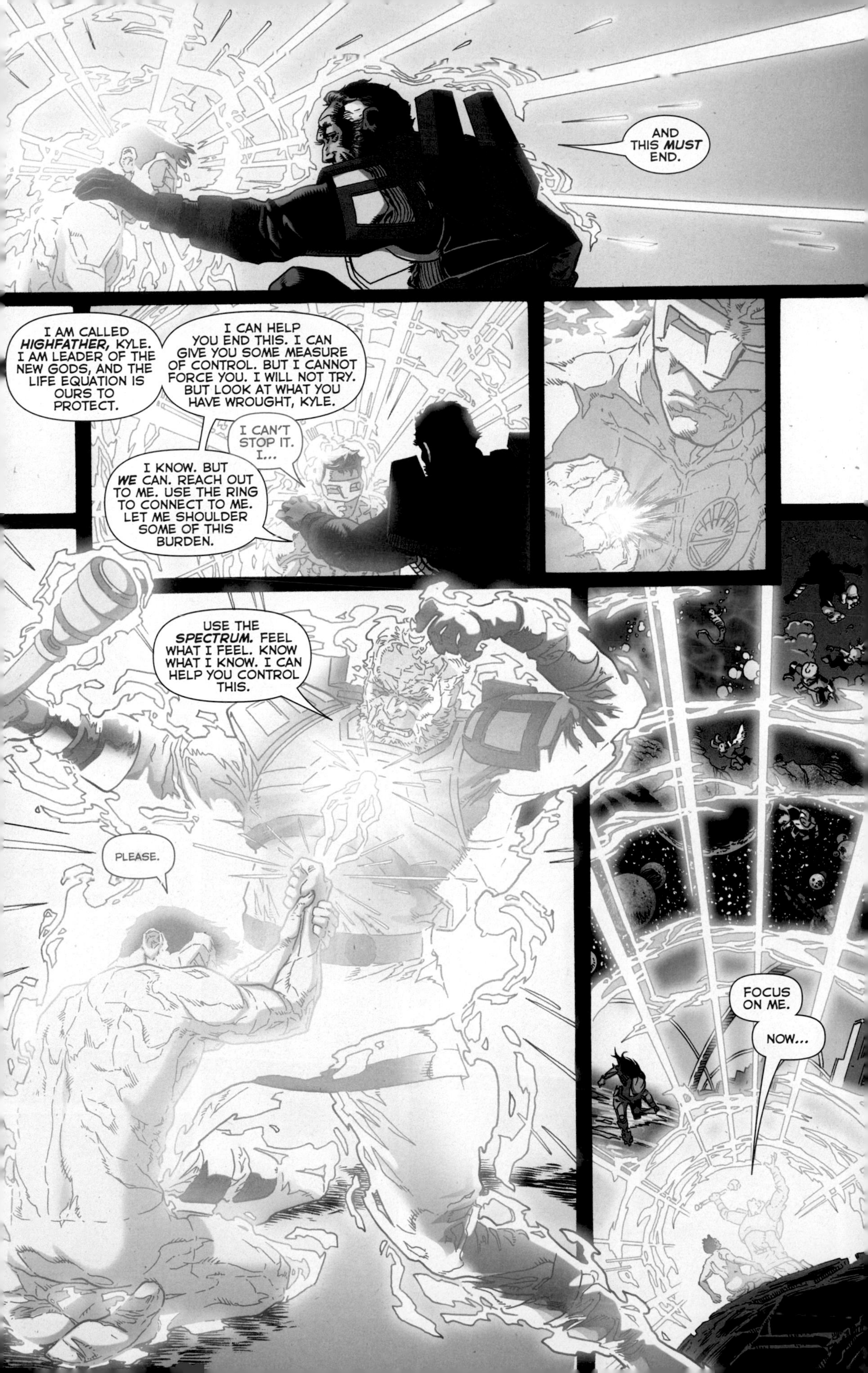
AND THIS MUST END.
I AM CALLED HIGHFATHER, KYLE. I AM LEADER OF THE NEW GODS, AND THE LIFE EQUATION IS OURS TO PROTECT.
I CAN HELP YOU END THIS. I CAN GIVE YOU SOME MEASURE OF CONTROL. BUT I CANNOT FORCE YOU. I WILL NOT TRY. BUT LOOK AT WHAT YOU HAVE WROUGHT, KYLE.
I CAN'T STOP IT. I...
I KNOW. BUT WE CAN. REACH OUT TO ME. USE THE RING TO CONNECT TO ME. LET ME SHOULDER SOME OF THIS BURDEN.
USE THE SPECTRUM. FEEL WHAT I FEEL. KNOW WHAT I KNOW. I CAN HELP YOU CONTROL THIS.
PLEASE.
FOCUS ON ME.
NOW...

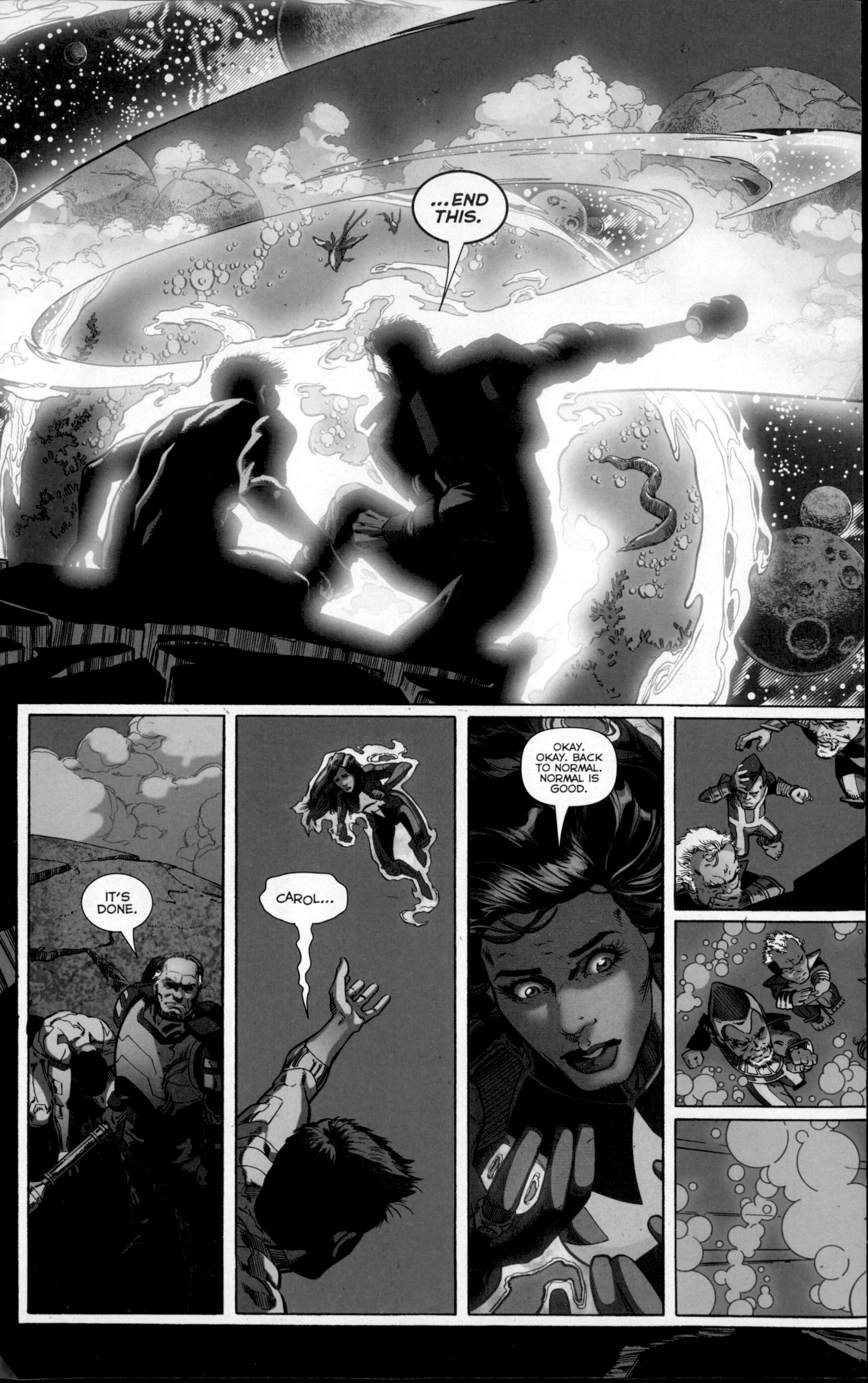
...END THIS.
IT'S DONE.
CAROL...
OKAY. OKAY. BACK TO NORMAL. NORMAL IS GOOD.

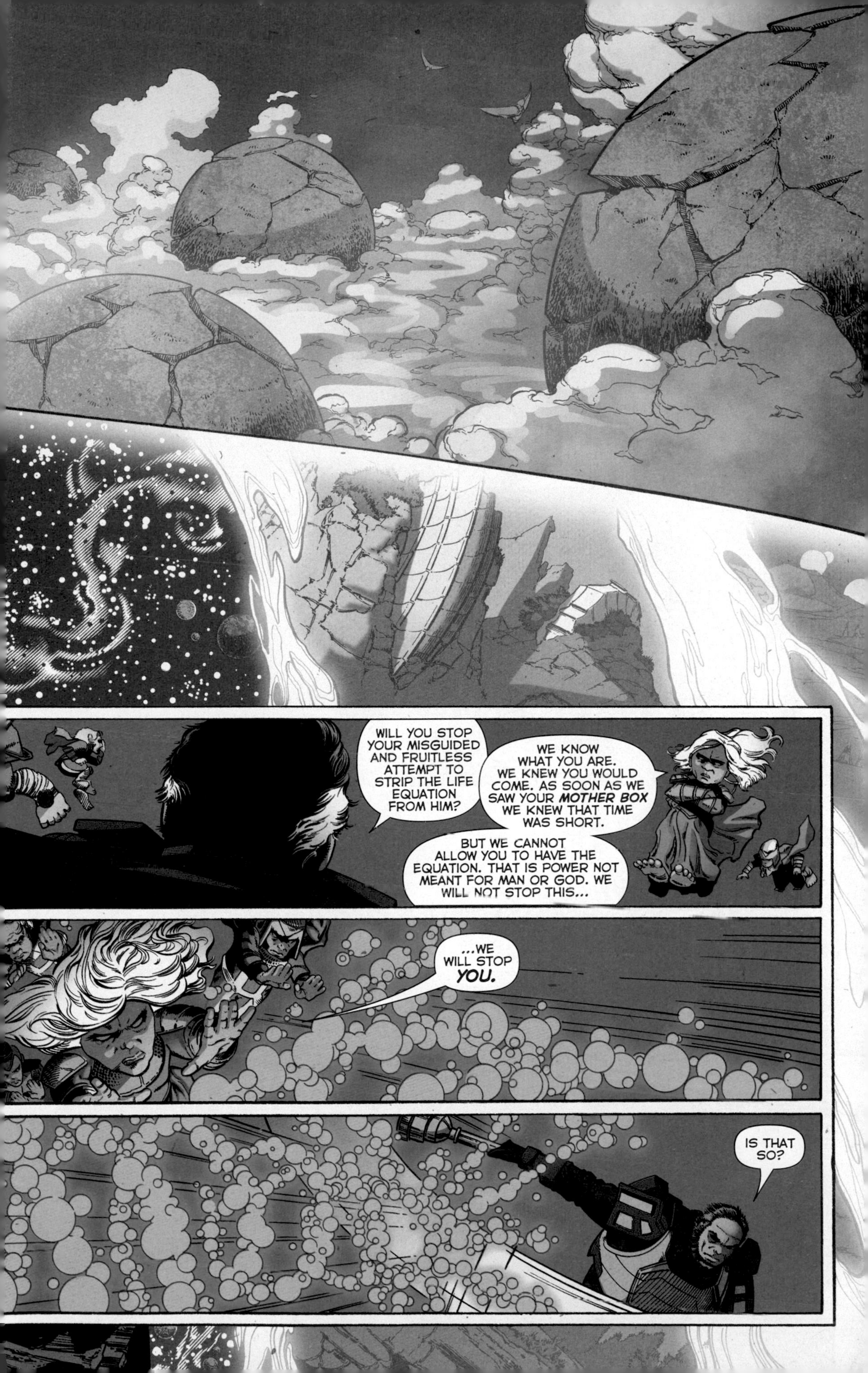
WILL YOU STOP YOUR MISGUIDED AND FRUITLESS ATTEMPT TO STRIP THE LIFE EQUATION FROM HIM?
WE KNOW WHAT YOU ARE. WE KNEW YOU WOULD COME. AS SOON AS WE SAW YOUR MOTHER BOX WE KNEW THAT TIME WAS SHORT.
BUT WE CANNOT ALLOW YOU TO HAVE THE EQUATION. THAT IS POWER NOT MEANT FOR MAN OR GOD. WE WILL NOT STOP THIS...
...WE WILL STOP YOU.
IS THAT SO?

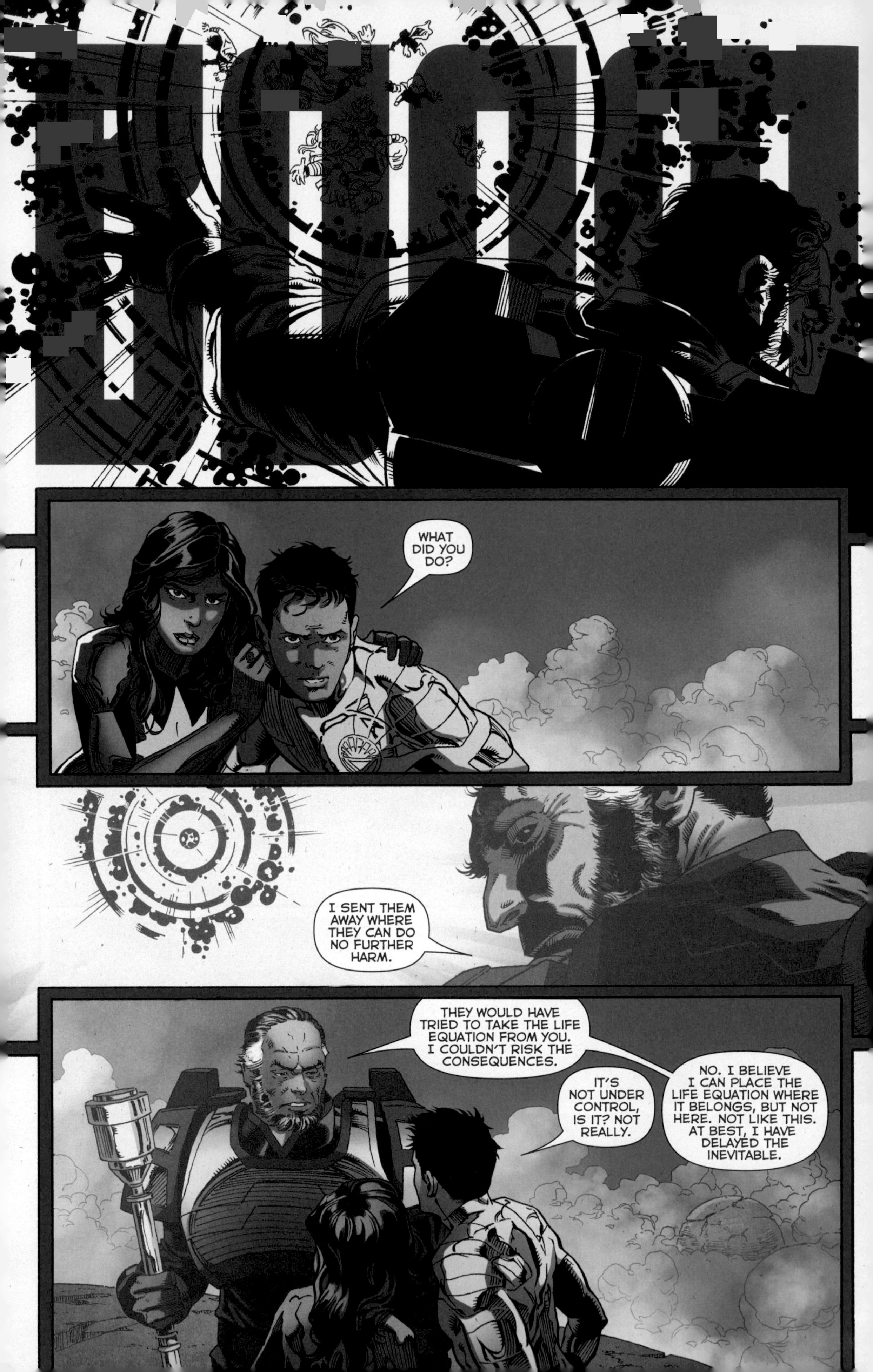
WHAT DID YOU DO?
I SENT THEM AWAY WHERE THEY CAN DO NO FURTHER HARM.
THEY WOULD HAVE TRIED TO TAKE THE LIFE EQUATION FROM YOU. I COULDN'T RISK THE CONSEQUENCES.
IT'S NOT UNDER CONTROL, IS IT? NOT REALLY.
NO. I BELIEVE I CAN PLACE THE LIFE EQUATION WHERE IT BELONGS, BUT NOT HERE. NOT LIKE THIS. AT BEST, I HAVE DELAYED THE INEVITABLE.

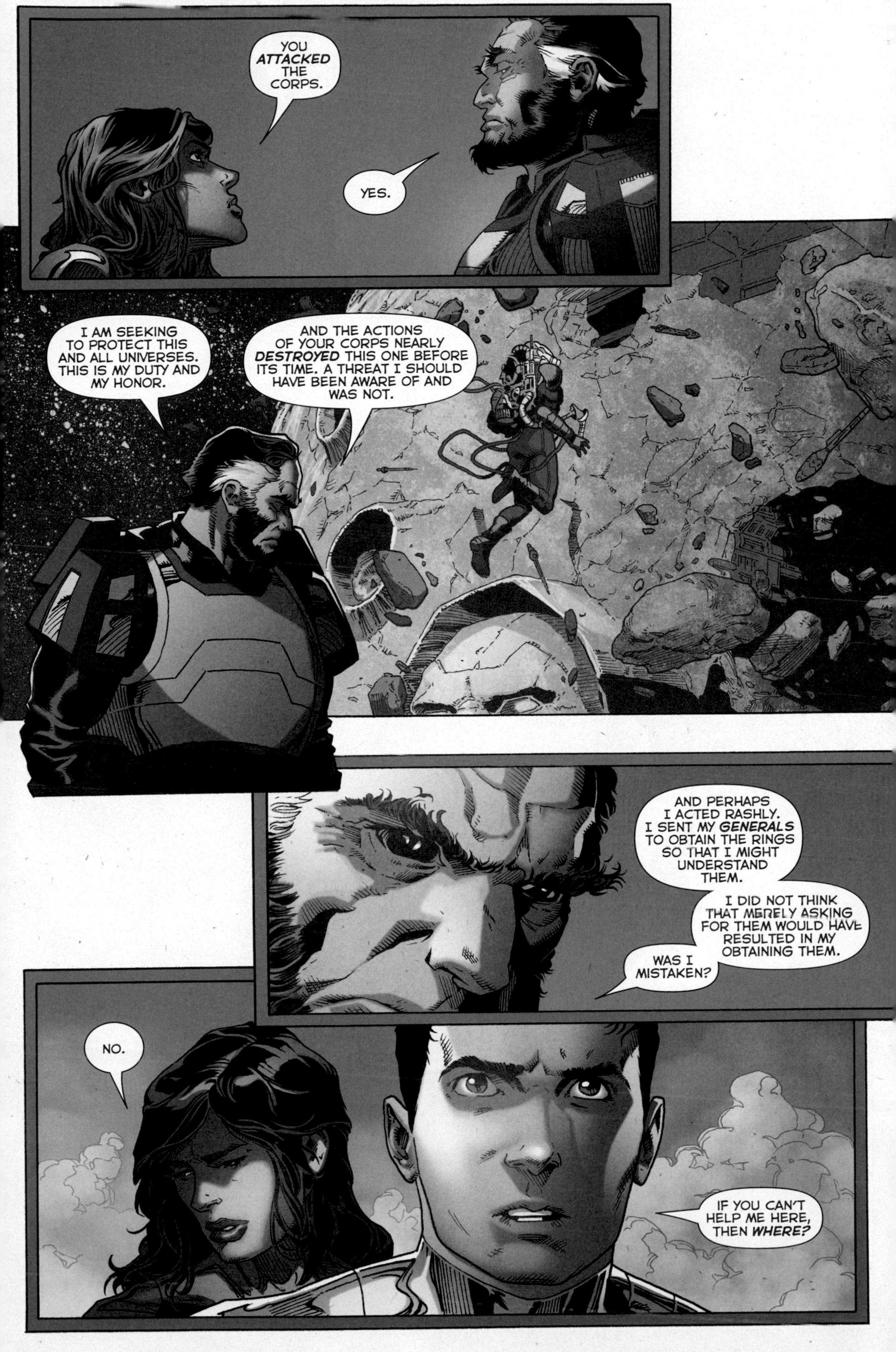
YOU ATTACKED THE CORPS.
YES.
I AM SEEKING TO PROTECT THIS AND ALL UNIVERSES. THIS IS MY DUTY AND MY HONOR.
AND THE ACTIONS OF YOUR CORPS NEARLY DESTROYED THIS ONE BEFORE ITS TIME. A THREAT I SHOULD HAVE BEEN AWARE OF AND WAS NOT.
AND PERHAPS I ACTED RASHLY. I SENT MY GENERALS TO OBTAIN THE RINGS SO THAT I MIGHT UNDERSTAND THEM.
I DID NOT THINK THAT MERELY ASKING FOR THEM WOULD HAVE RESULTED IN MY OBTAINING THEM.
WAS I MISTAKEN?
NO.
IF YOU CAN'T HELP ME HERE, THEN WHERE?

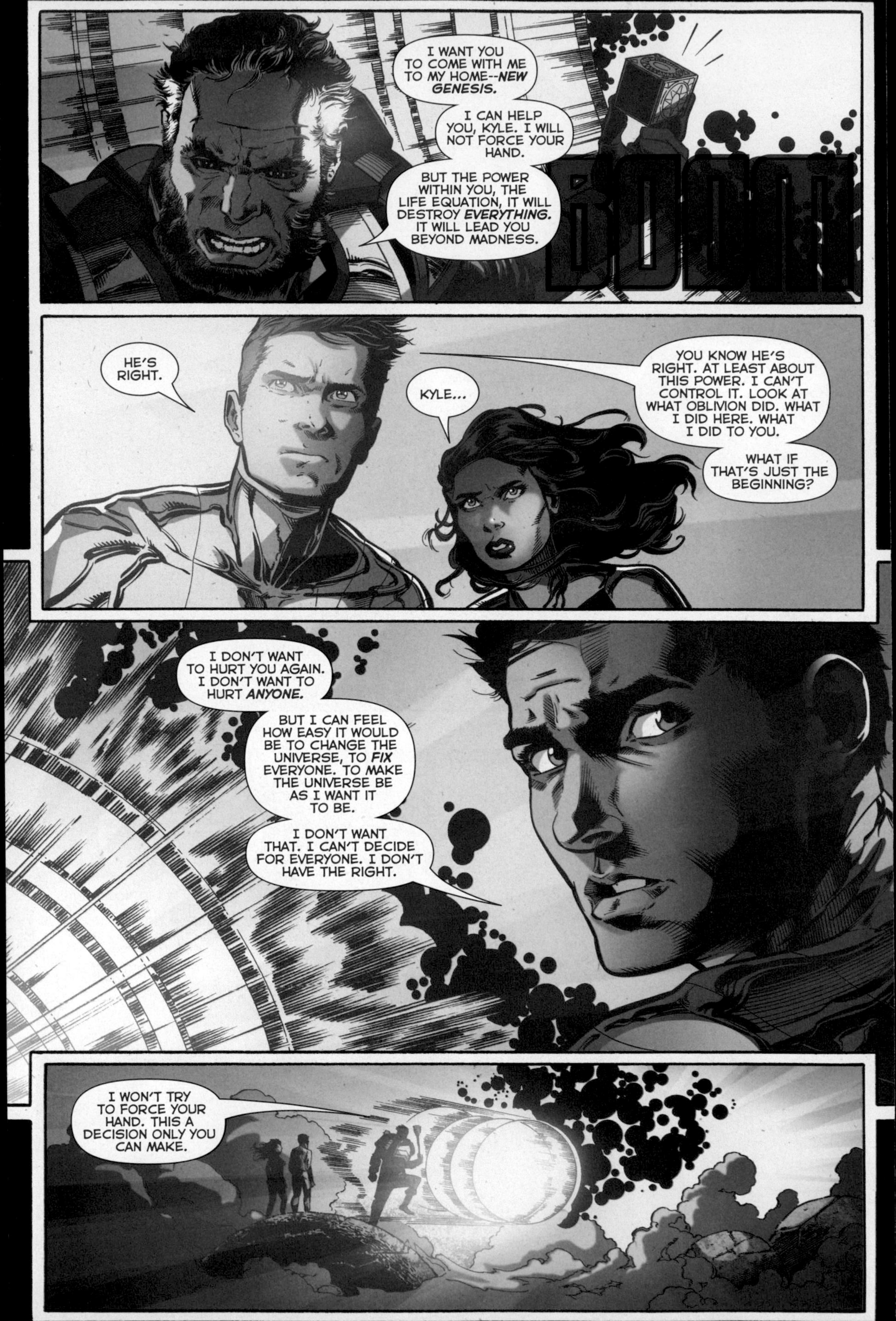
I WANT YOU TO COME WITH ME TO MY HOME--*NEW GENESIS.*
I CAN HELP YOU, KYLE. I WILL NOT FORCE YOUR HAND.
BUT THE POWER WITHIN YOU, THE LIFE EQUATION, IT WILL DESTROY *EVERYTHING.* IT WILL LEAD YOU BEYOND MADNESS.
BOOM
HE'S RIGHT.
KYLE...
YOU KNOW HE'S RIGHT. AT LEAST ABOUT THIS POWER. I CAN'T CONTROL IT. LOOK AT WHAT OBLIVION DID. WHAT I DID HERE. WHAT I DID TO YOU.
WHAT IF THAT'S JUST THE BEGINNING?
I DON'T WANT TO HURT YOU AGAIN. I DON'T WANT TO HURT *ANYONE.*
BUT I CAN FEEL HOW EASY IT WOULD BE TO CHANGE THE UNIVERSE, TO *FIX* EVERYONE. TO MAKE THE UNIVERSE BE AS I WANT IT TO BE.
I DON'T WANT THAT. I CAN'T DECIDE FOR EVERYONE. I DON'T HAVE THE RIGHT.
I WON'T TRY TO FORCE YOUR HAND. THIS A DECISION ONLY YOU CAN MAKE.

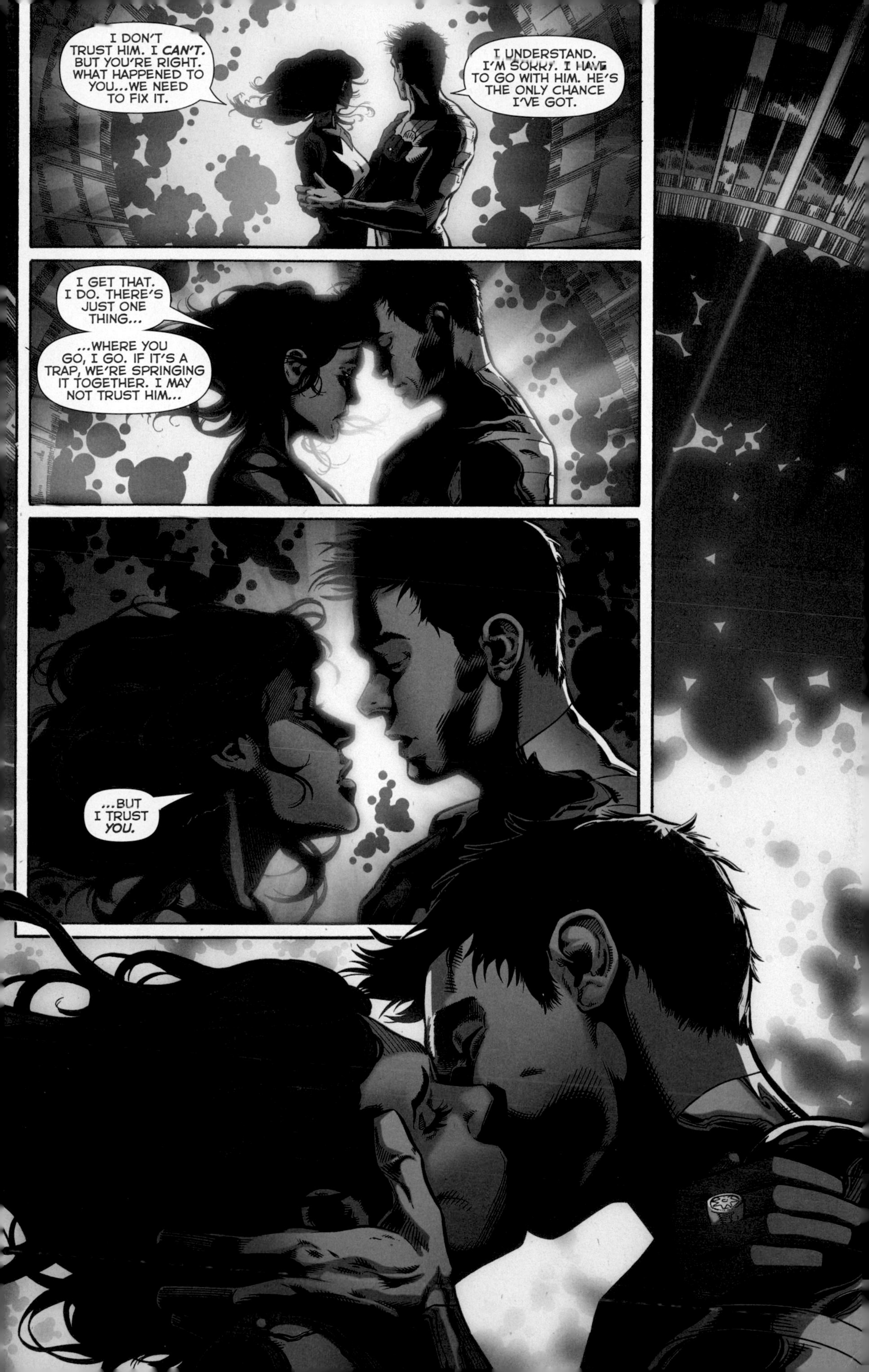
I DON'T TRUST HIM. I *CAN'T.* BUT YOU'RE RIGHT. WHAT HAPPENED TO YOU...WE NEED TO FIX IT.
I UNDERSTAND. I'M SORRY. I HAVE TO GO WITH HIM. HE'S THE ONLY CHANCE I'VE GOT.
I GET THAT. I DO. THERE'S JUST ONE THING...
...WHERE YOU GO, I GO. IF IT'S A TRAP, WE'RE SPRINGING IT TOGETHER. I MAY NOT TRUST HIM...
...BUT I TRUST *YOU.*

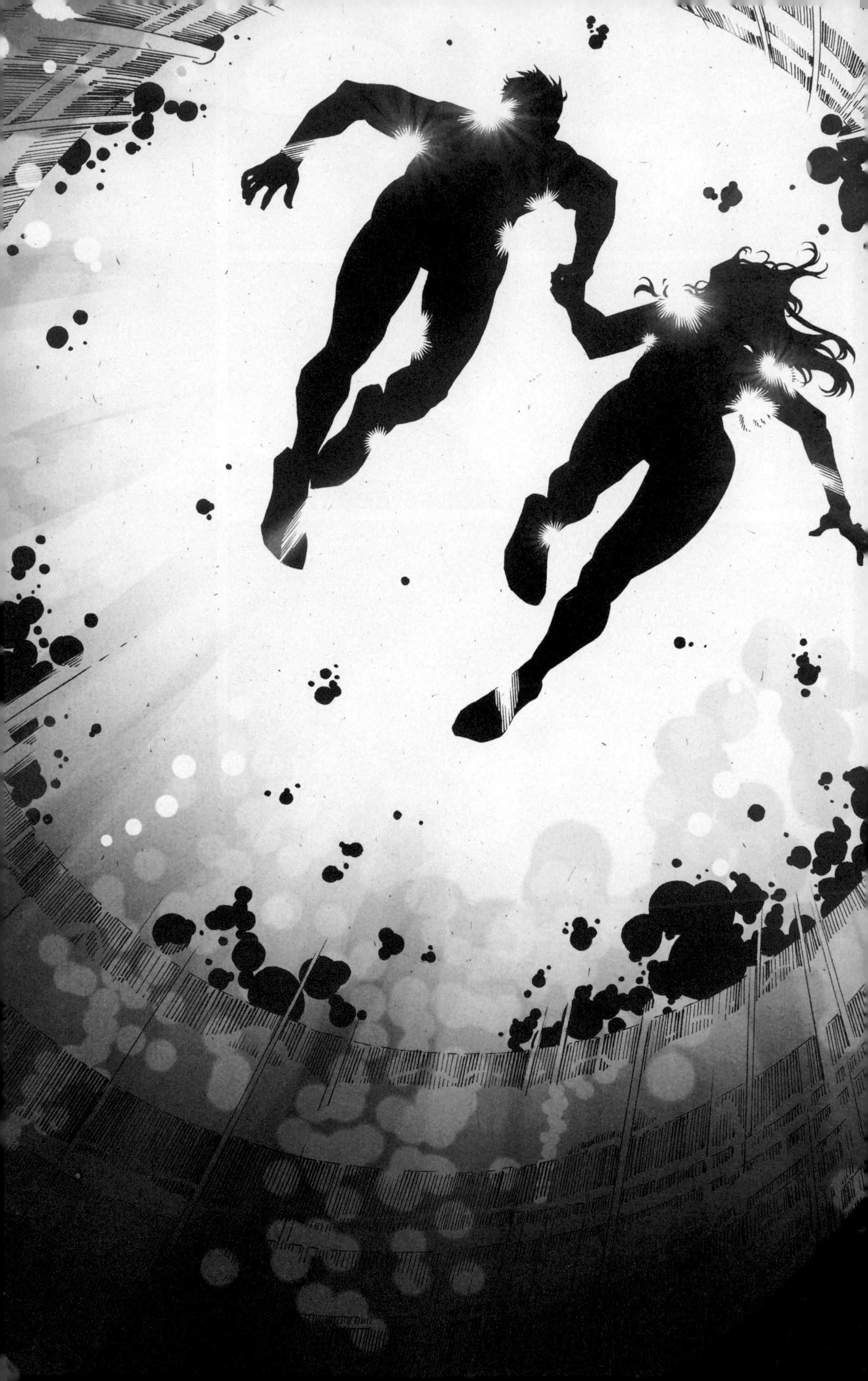

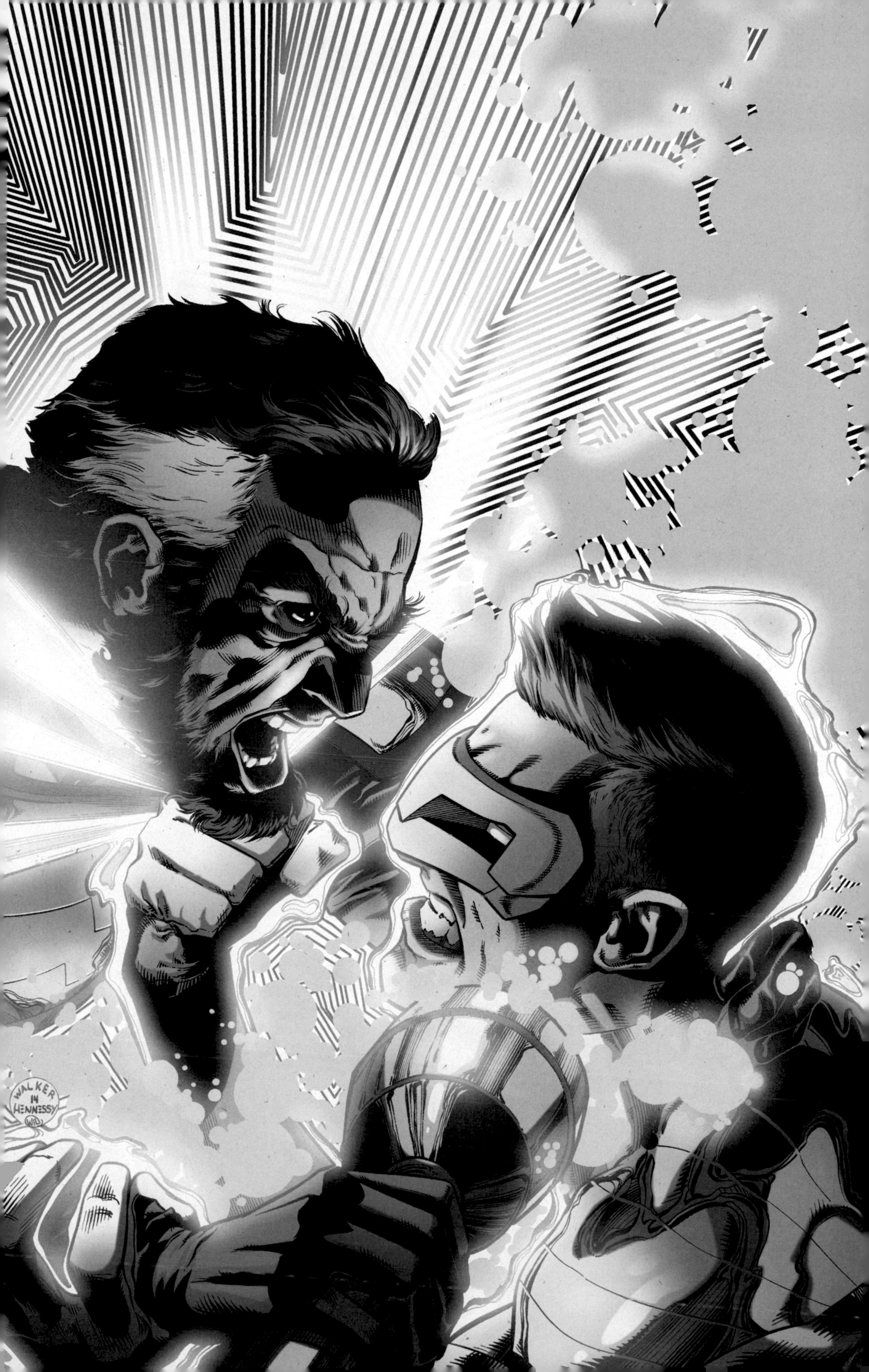
WALKER
14
HENNESSY

GODHEAD: ACT II, PART III: BEST LAID PLANS

JUSTIN JORDAN writer DIOGENES NEVES penciller MARC DEERING inker WIL QUINTANA colorist TAYLOR ESPOSITO letterer

cover art by WALKER, HENNESSY and QUINTANA

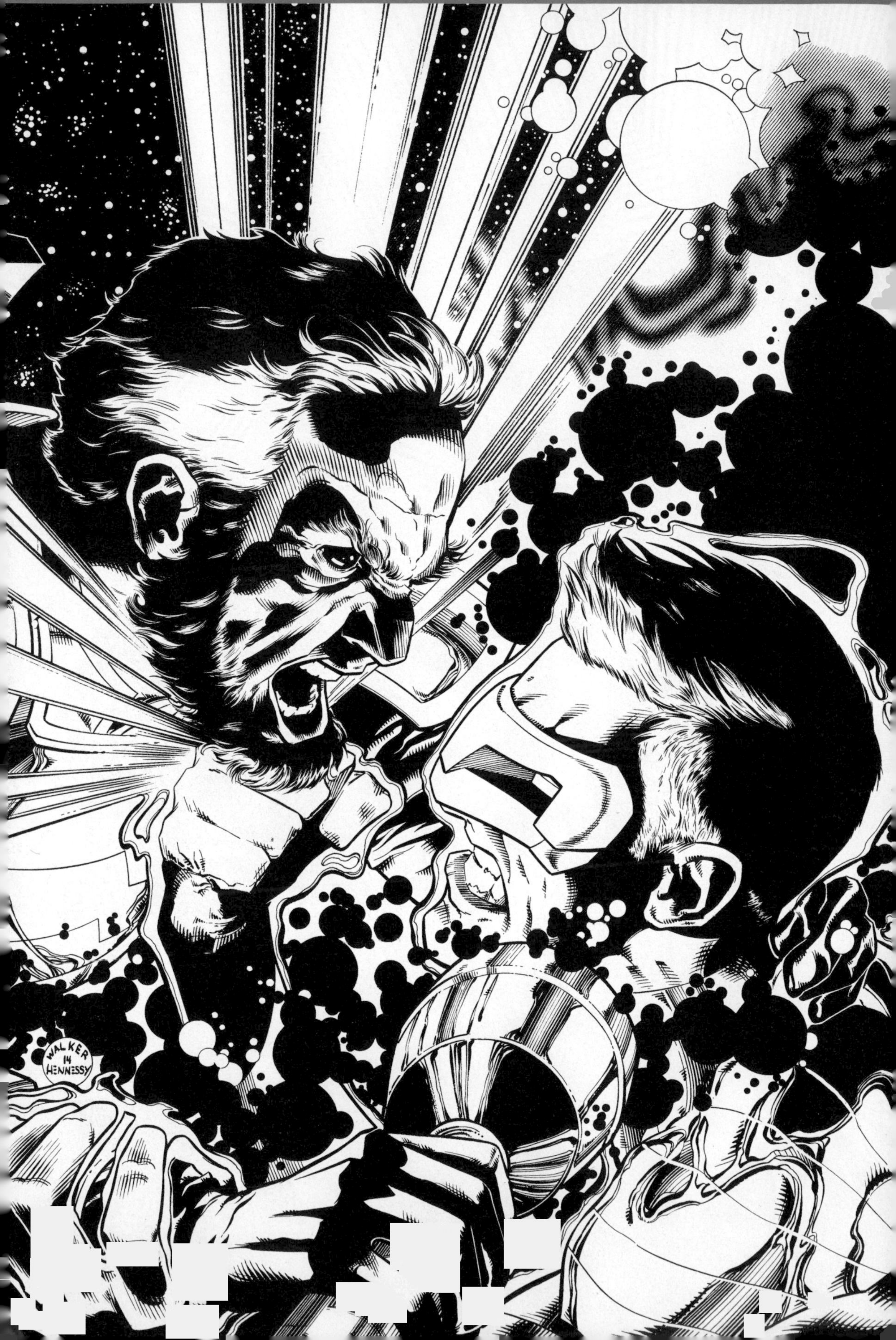
WALKER 14 HENNESSY

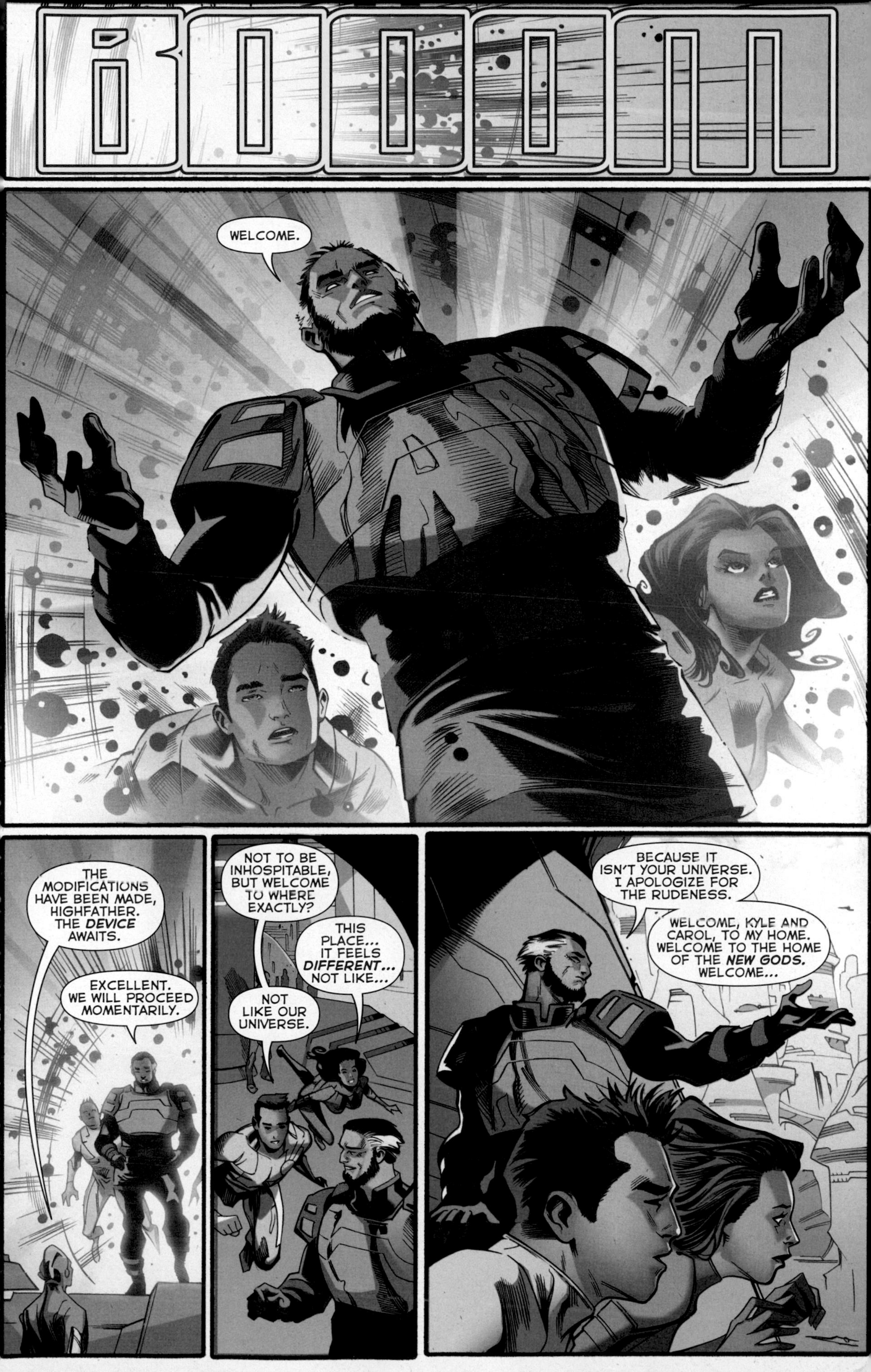
BOOOOM
WELCOME.
THE MODIFICATIONS HAVE BEEN MADE, HIGHFATHER. THE *DEVICE* AWAITS.
EXCELLENT. WE WILL PROCEED MOMENTARILY.
NOT TO BE INHOSPITABLE, BUT WELCOME TO WHERE EXACTLY?
THIS PLACE... IT FEELS *DIFFERENT*... NOT LIKE...
NOT LIKE OUR UNIVERSE.
BECAUSE IT ISN'T YOUR UNIVERSE. I APOLOGIZE FOR THE RUDENESS.
WELCOME, KYLE AND CAROL, TO MY HOME. WELCOME TO THE HOME OF THE *NEW GODS.* WELCOME...

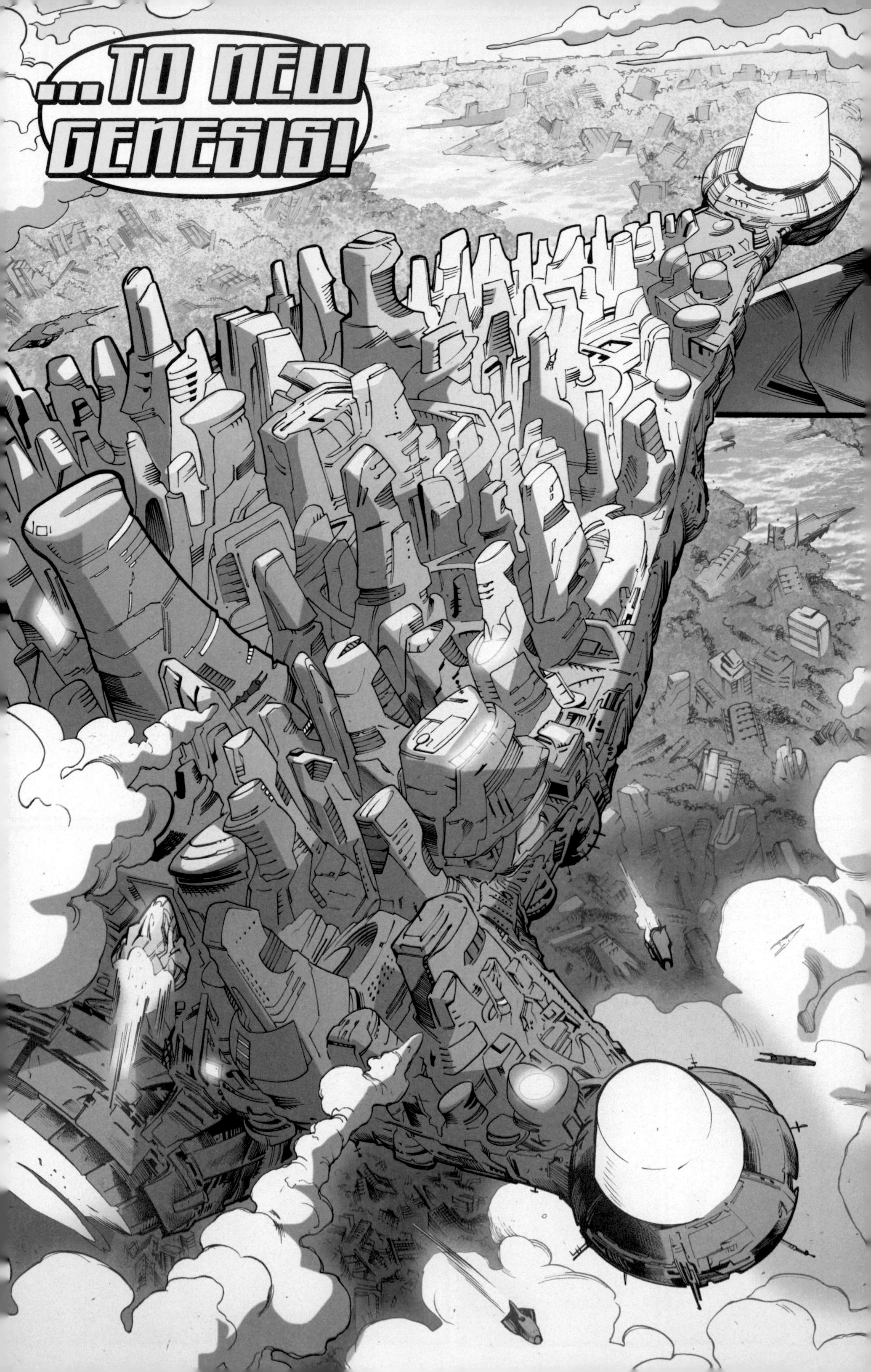
...TO NEW GENESIS!

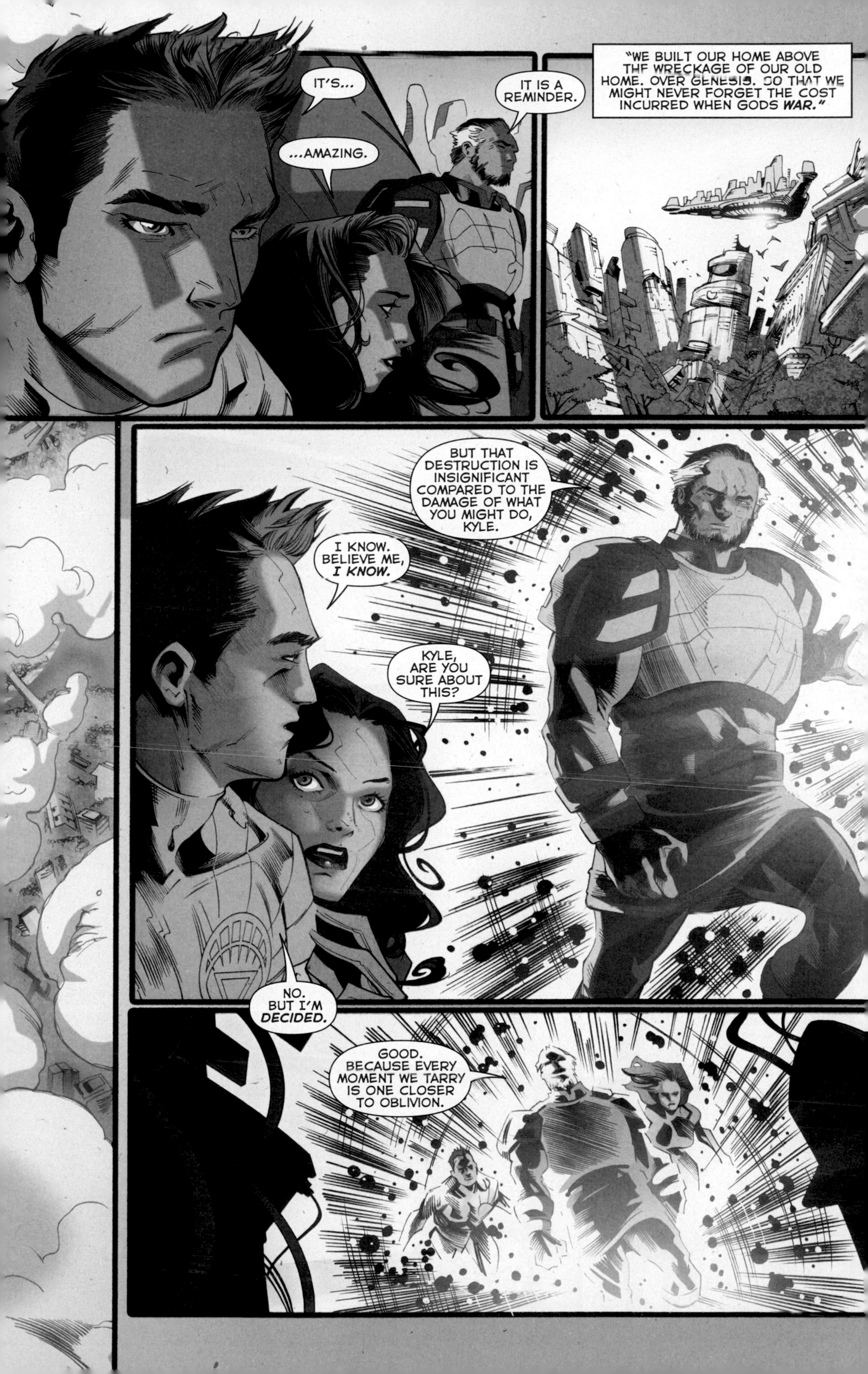
IT'S...
...AMAZING.
IT IS A REMINDER.
"WE BUILT OUR HOME ABOVE THE WRECKAGE OF OUR OLD HOME. OVER GENESIS. SO THAT WE MIGHT NEVER FORGET THE COST INCURRED WHEN GODS WAR."
BUT THAT DESTRUCTION IS INSIGNIFICANT COMPARED TO THE DAMAGE OF WHAT YOU MIGHT DO, KYLE.
I KNOW. BELIEVE ME, I KNOW.
KYLE, ARE YOU SURE ABOUT THIS?
NO. BUT I'M DECIDED.
GOOD. BECAUSE EVERY MOMENT WE TARRY IS ONE CLOSER TO OBLIVION.

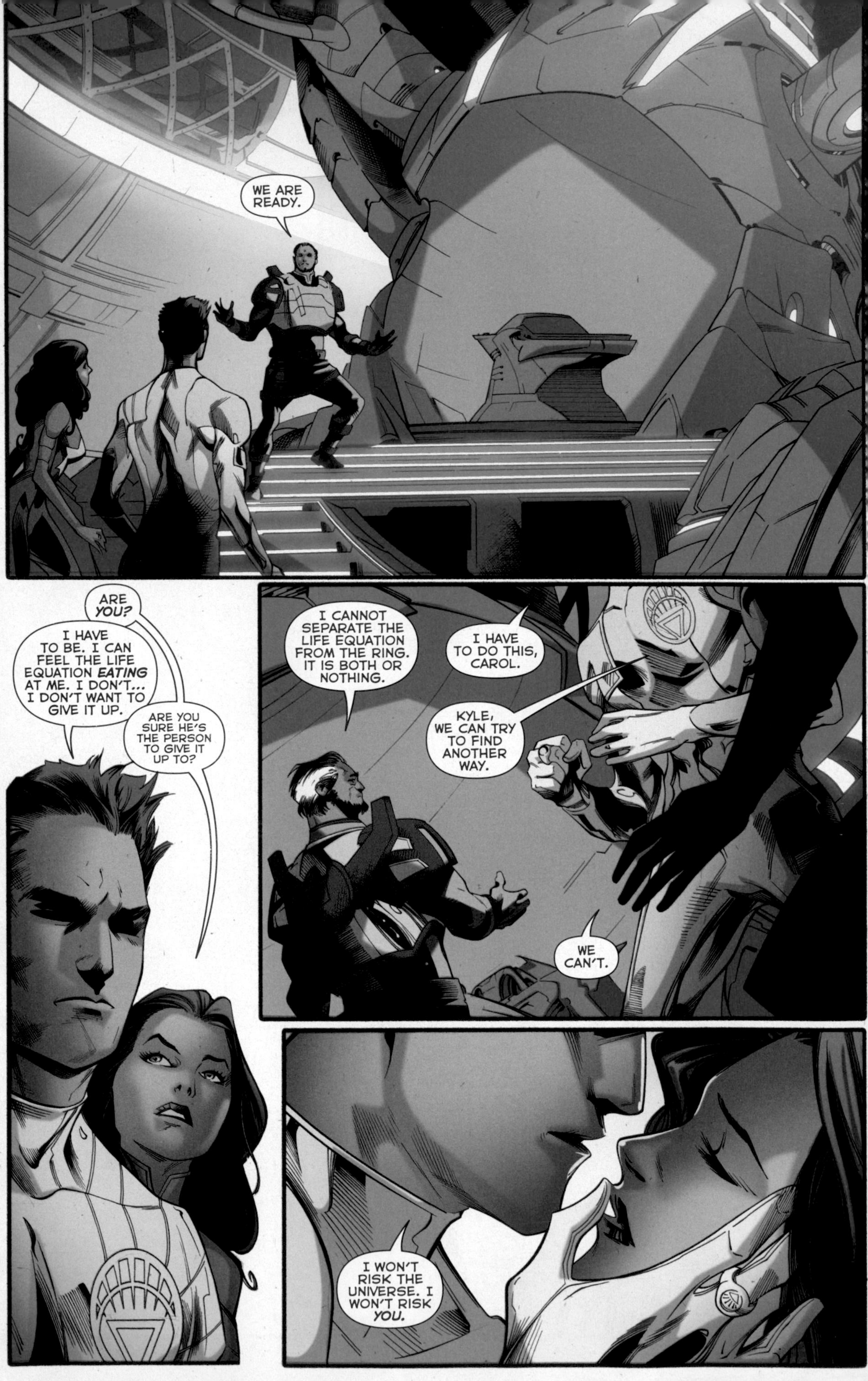
WE ARE READY.
ARE YOU?
I HAVE TO BE. I CAN FEEL THE LIFE EQUATION EATING AT ME. I DON'T... I DON'T WANT TO GIVE IT UP.
ARE YOU SURE HE'S THE PERSON TO GIVE IT UP TO?
I CANNOT SEPARATE THE LIFE EQUATION FROM THE RING. IT IS BOTH OR NOTHING.
I HAVE TO DO THIS, CAROL.
KYLE, WE CAN TRY TO FIND ANOTHER WAY.
WE CAN'T.
I WON'T RISK THE UNIVERSE. I WON'T RISK YOU.

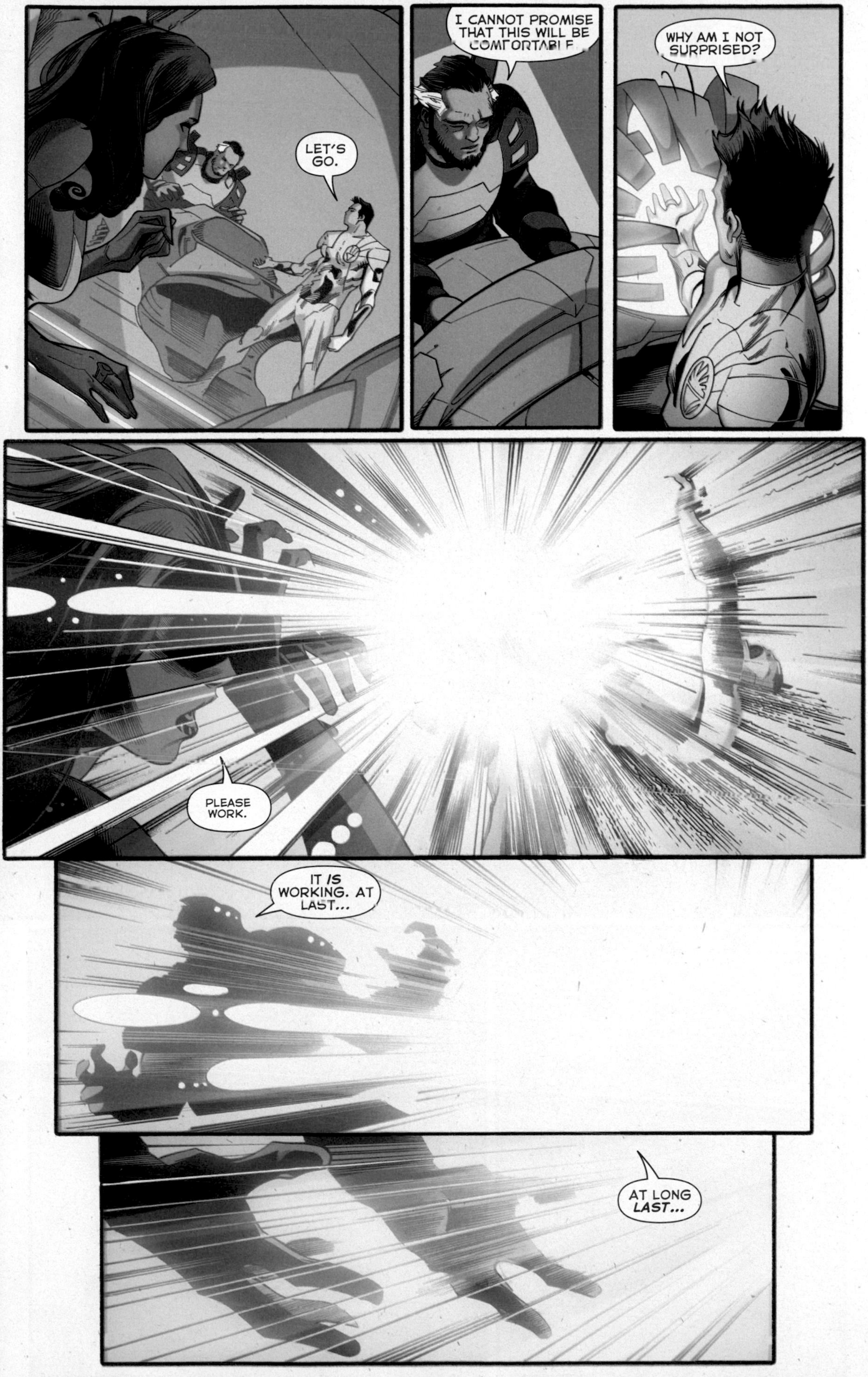
LET'S GO.
I CANNOT PROMISE THAT THIS WILL BE COMFORTABLE.
WHY AM I NOT SURPRISED?
PLEASE WORK.
IT *IS* WORKING. AT LAST...
AT LONG *LAST*...

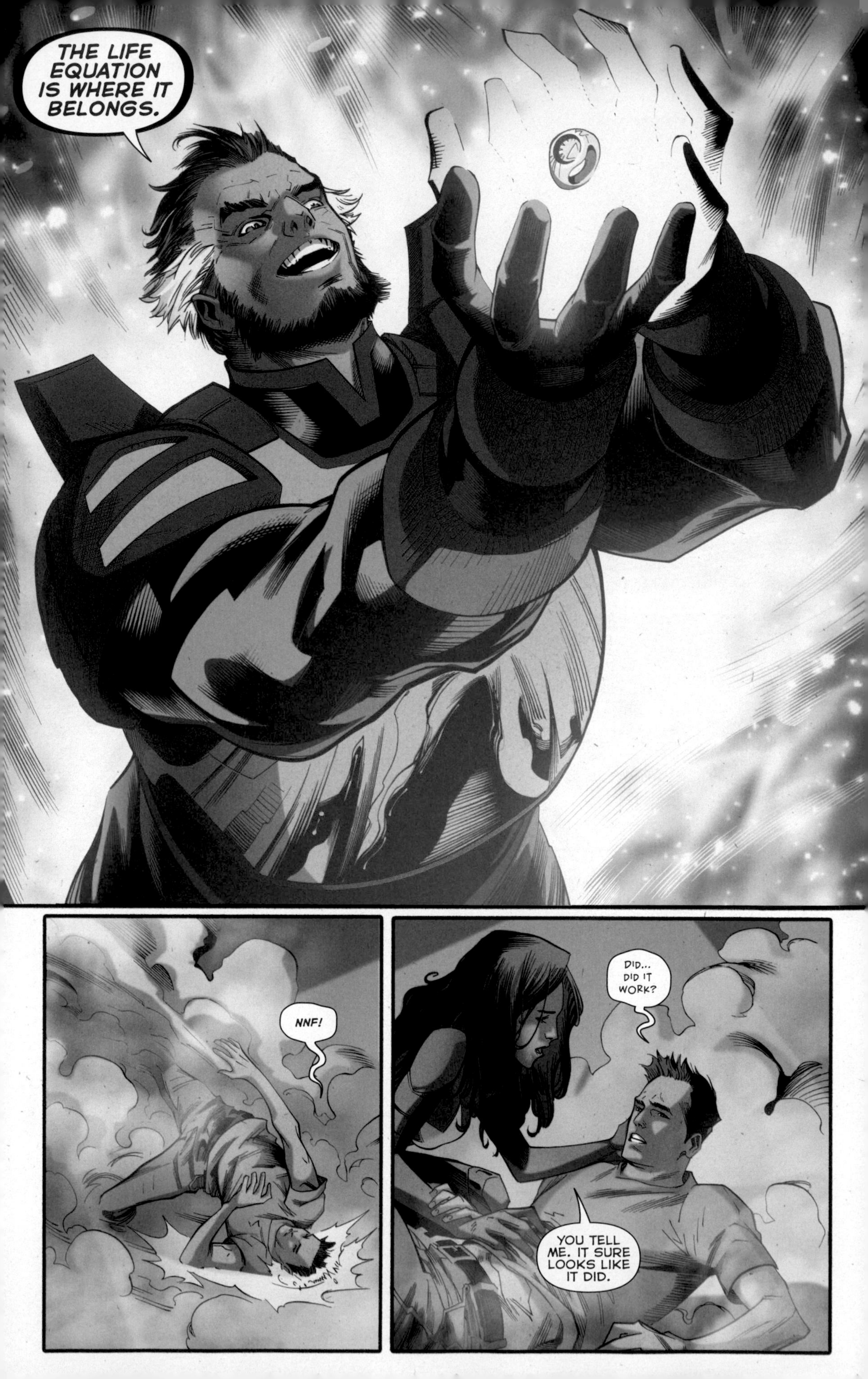
THE LIFE EQUATION IS WHERE IT BELONGS.
NNF!
DID... DID IT WORK?
YOU TELL ME. IT SURE LOOKS LIKE IT DID.

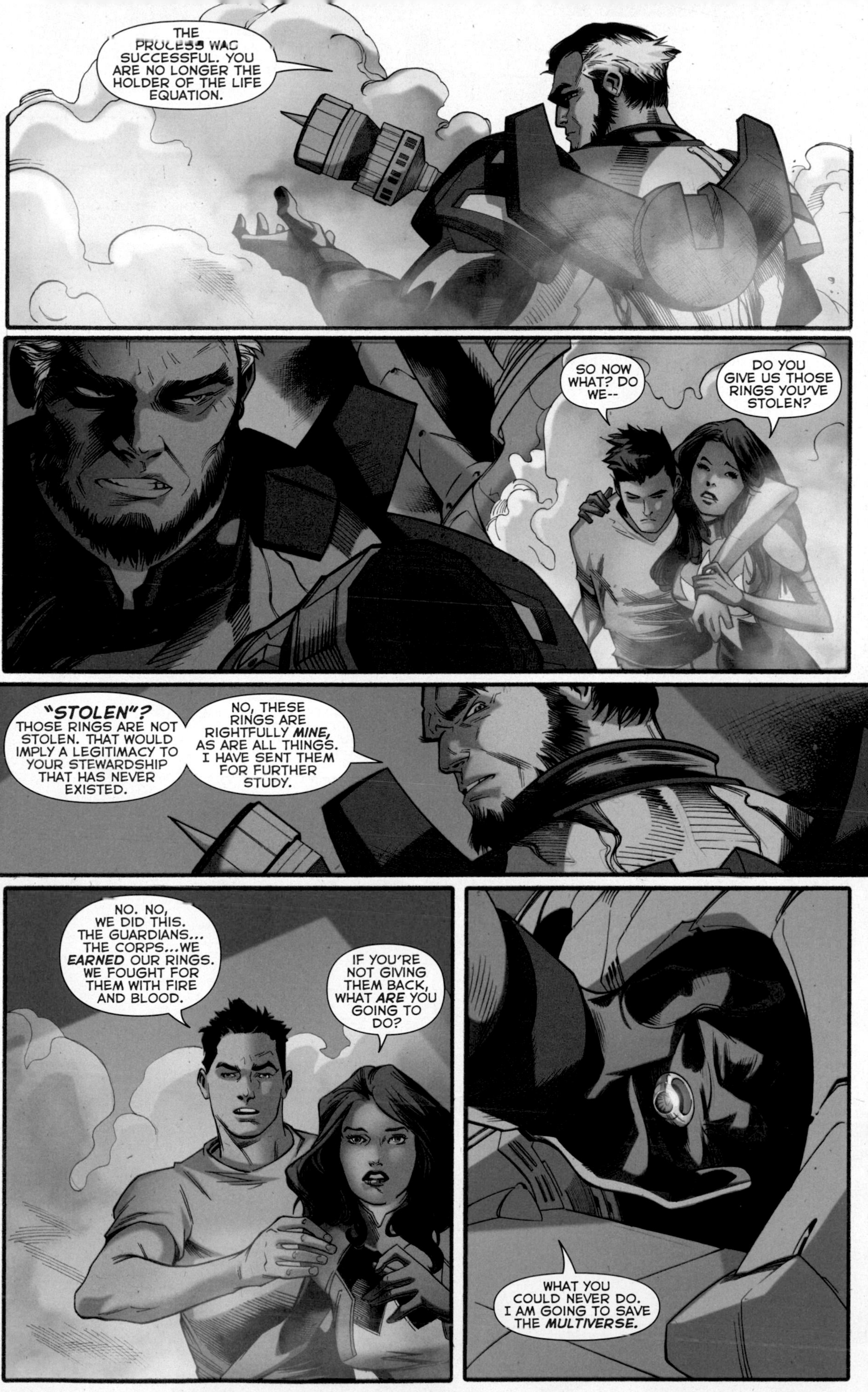
THE PROCESS WAS SUCCESSFUL. YOU ARE NO LONGER THE HOLDER OF THE LIFE EQUATION.
SO NOW WHAT? DO WE--
DO YOU GIVE US THOSE RINGS YOU'VE STOLEN?
"STOLEN"? THOSE RINGS ARE NOT STOLEN. THAT WOULD IMPLY A LEGITIMACY TO YOUR STEWARDSHIP THAT HAS NEVER EXISTED.
NO, THESE RINGS ARE RIGHTFULLY MINE, AS ARE ALL THINGS. I HAVE SENT THEM FOR FURTHER STUDY.
NO. NO, WE DID THIS. THE GUARDIANS... THE CORPS...WE EARNED OUR RINGS. WE FOUGHT FOR THEM WITH FIRE AND BLOOD.
IF YOU'RE NOT GIVING THEM BACK, WHAT ARE YOU GOING TO DO?
WHAT YOU COULD NEVER DO. I AM GOING TO SAVE THE MULTIVERSE.

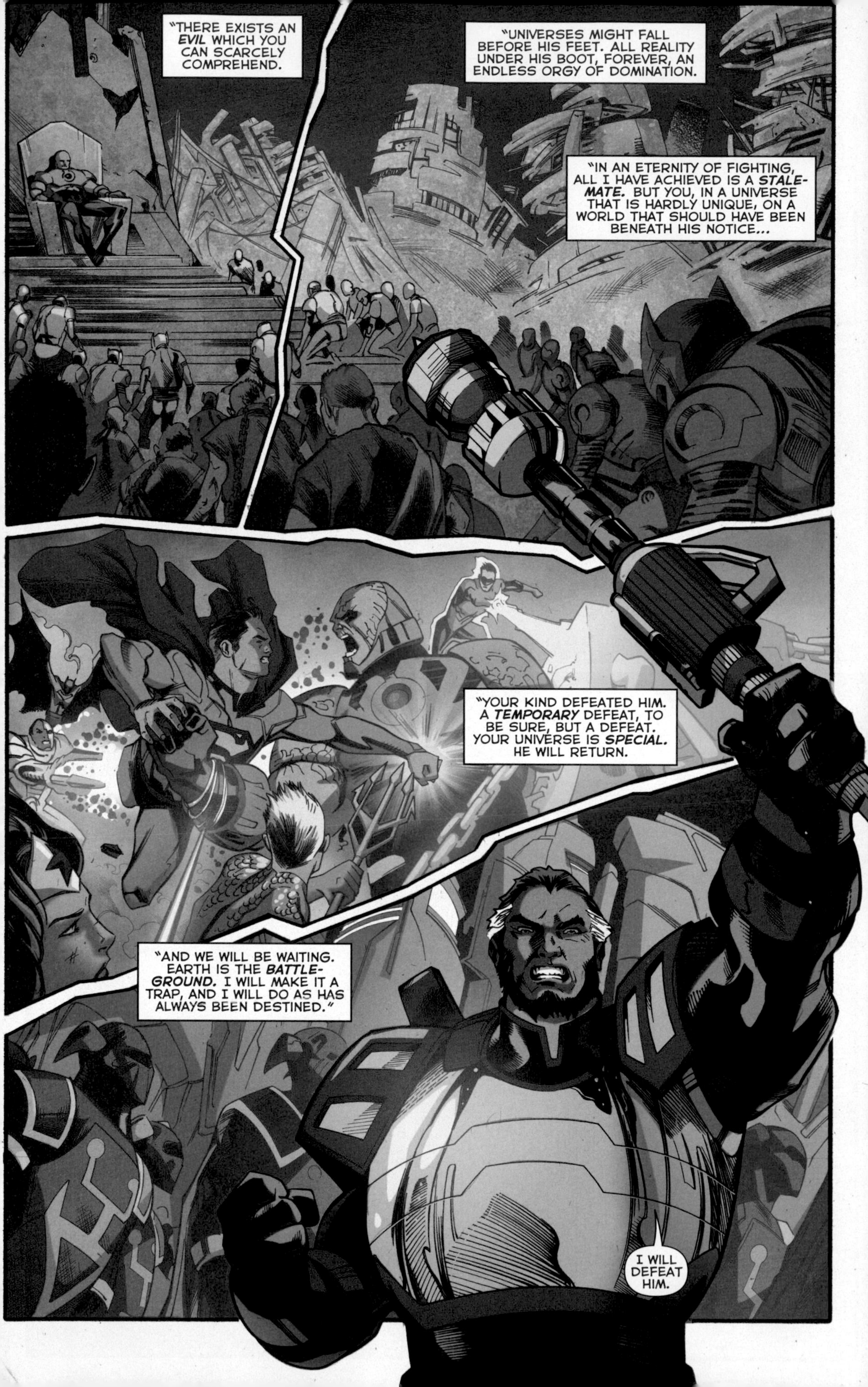
"THERE EXISTS AN EVIL WHICH YOU CAN SCARCELY COMPREHEND.
"UNIVERSES MIGHT FALL BEFORE HIS FEET. ALL REALITY UNDER HIS BOOT, FOREVER, AN ENDLESS ORGY OF DOMINATION.
"IN AN ETERNITY OF FIGHTING, ALL I HAVE ACHIEVED IS A STALEMATE. BUT YOU, IN A UNIVERSE THAT IS HARDLY UNIQUE, ON A WORLD THAT SHOULD HAVE BEEN BENEATH HIS NOTICE...
"YOUR KIND DEFEATED HIM. A TEMPORARY DEFEAT, TO BE SURE, BUT A DEFEAT. YOUR UNIVERSE IS SPECIAL. HE WILL RETURN.
"AND WE WILL BE WAITING. EARTH IS THE BATTLEGROUND. I WILL MAKE IT A TRAP, AND I WILL DO AS HAS ALWAYS BEEN DESTINED."
I WILL DEFEAT HIM.

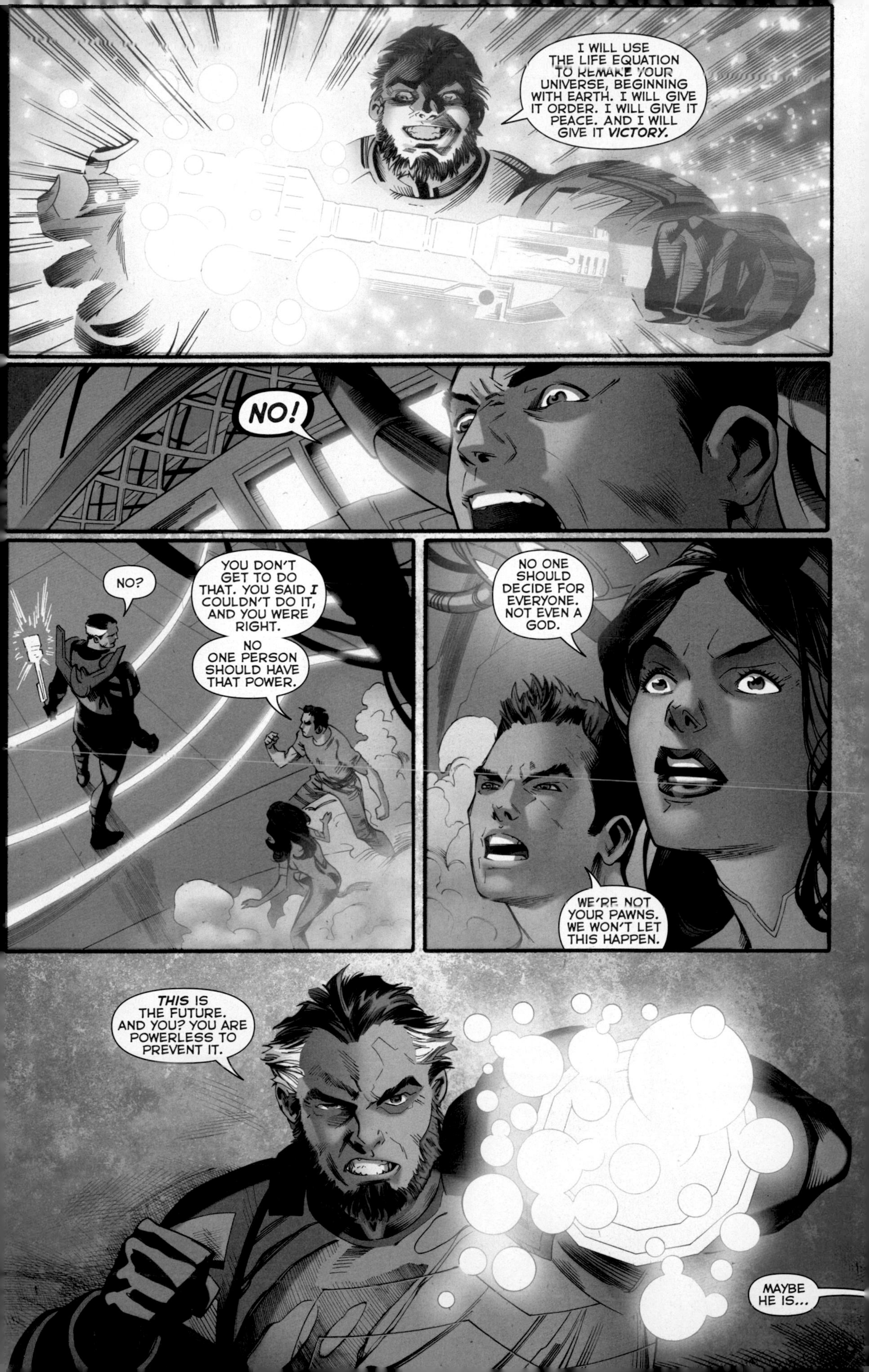

I WILL USE THE LIFE EQUATION TO REMAKE YOUR UNIVERSE, BEGINNING WITH EARTH. I WILL GIVE IT ORDER. I WILL GIVE IT PEACE. AND I WILL GIVE IT VICTORY.
NO!
NO?
YOU DON'T GET TO DO THAT. YOU SAID I COULDN'T DO IT, AND YOU WERE RIGHT.
NO ONE PERSON SHOULD HAVE THAT POWER.
NO ONE SHOULD DECIDE FOR EVERYONE. NOT EVEN A GOD.
WE'RE NOT YOUR PAWNS. WE WON'T LET THIS HAPPEN.
THIS IS THE FUTURE. AND YOU? YOU ARE POWERLESS TO PREVENT IT.
MAYBE HE IS...

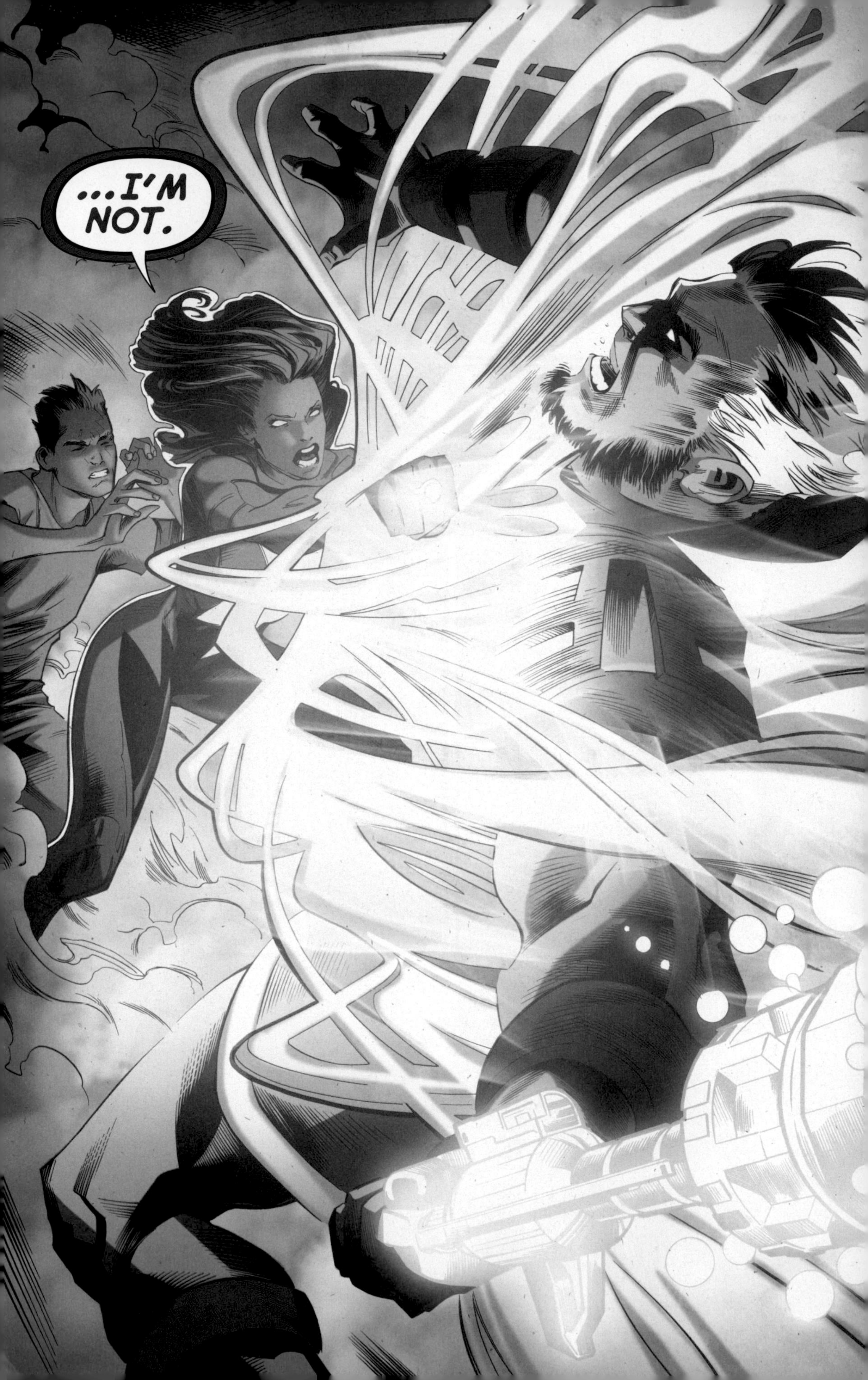
...I'M NOT.

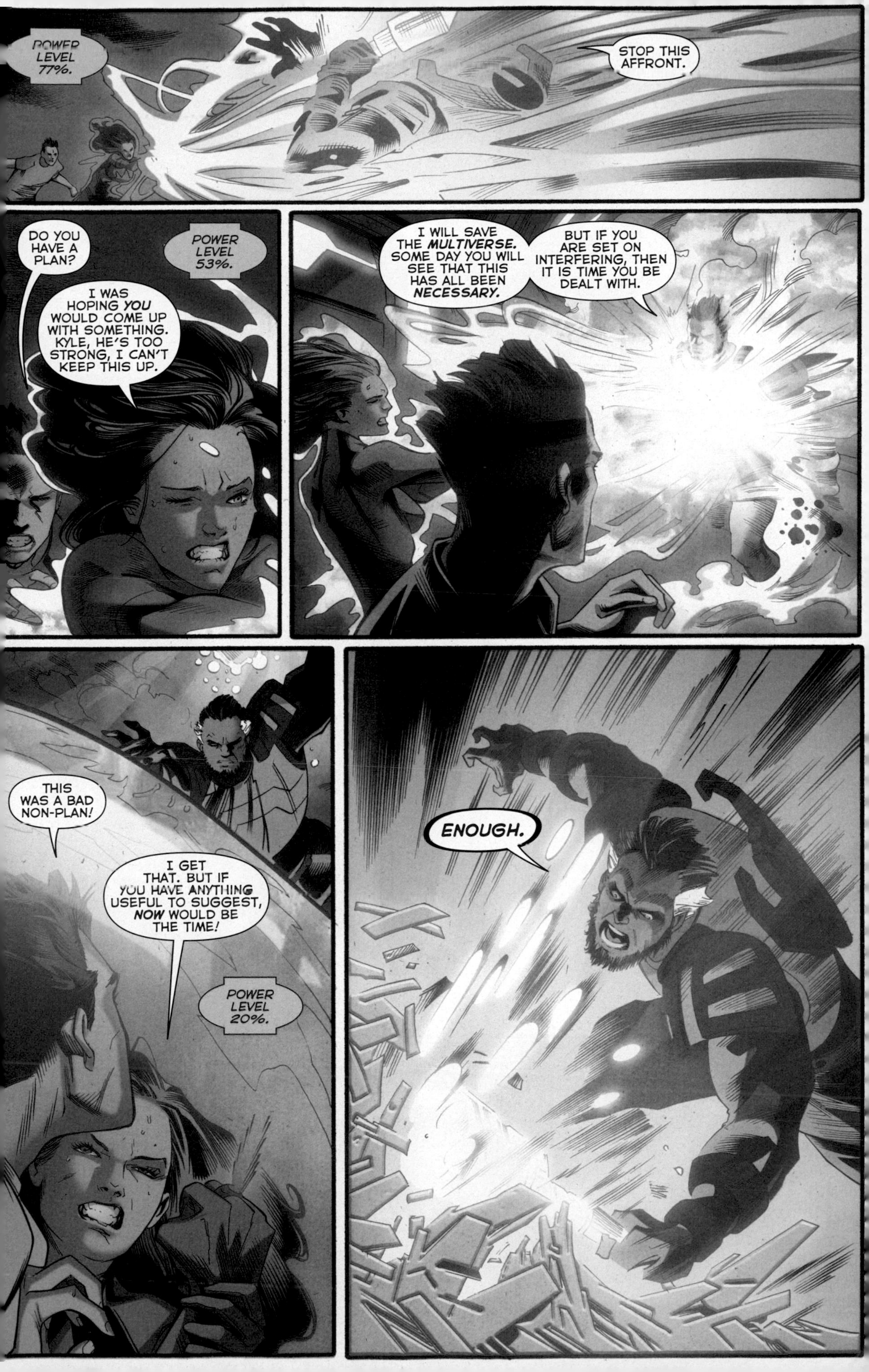
POWER LEVEL 77%.
STOP THIS AFFRONT.
DO YOU HAVE A PLAN?
POWER LEVEL 53%.
I WAS HOPING YOU WOULD COME UP WITH SOMETHING. KYLE, HE'S TOO STRONG, I CAN'T KEEP THIS UP.
I WILL SAVE THE MULTIVERSE. SOME DAY YOU WILL SEE THAT THIS HAS ALL BEEN NECESSARY.
BUT IF YOU ARE SET ON INTERFERING, THEN IT IS TIME YOU BE DEALT WITH.
THIS WAS A BAD NON-PLAN!
I GET THAT. BUT IF YOU HAVE ANYTHING USEFUL TO SUGGEST, NOW WOULD BE THE TIME!
POWER LEVEL 20%.
ENOUGH.

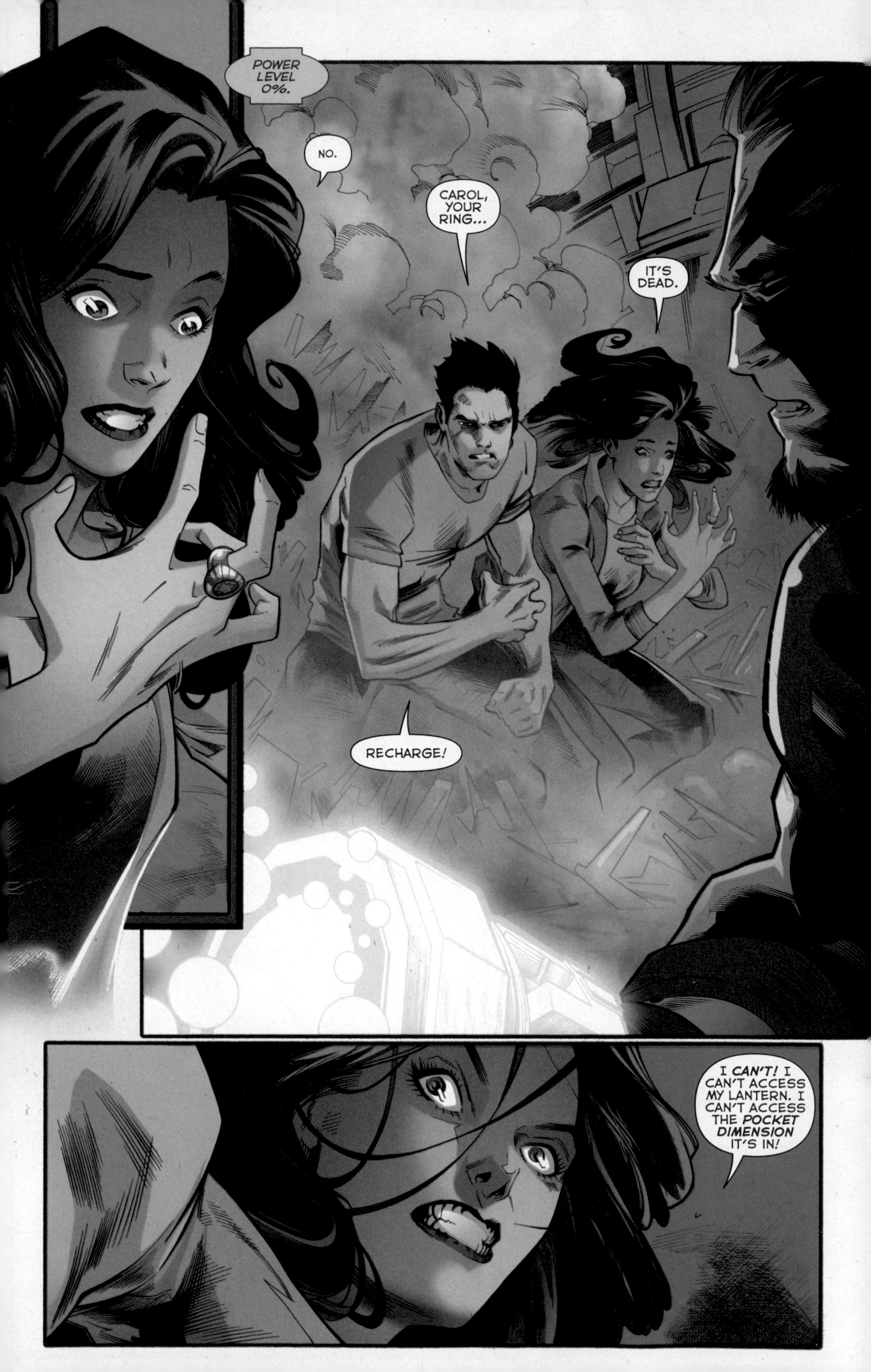
POWER LEVEL 0%.
NO.
CAROL, YOUR RING...
IT'S DEAD.
RECHARGE!
I *CAN'T!* I CAN'T ACCESS MY LANTERN. I CAN'T ACCESS THE *POCKET DIMENSION* IT'S IN!

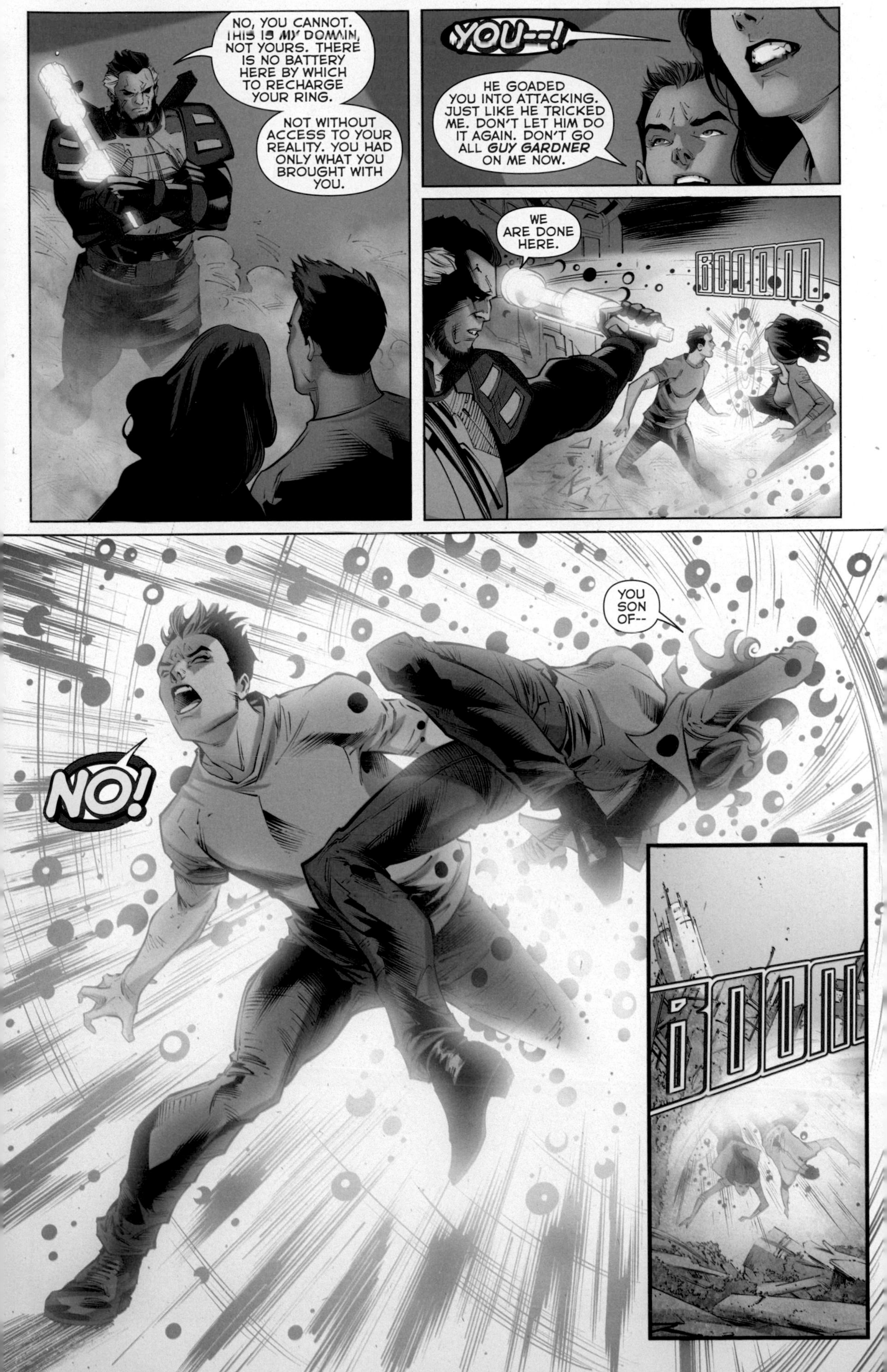
NO, YOU CANNOT. THIS IS MY DOMAIN, NOT YOURS. THERE IS NO BATTERY HERE BY WHICH TO RECHARGE YOUR RING.
NOT WITHOUT ACCESS TO YOUR REALITY. YOU HAD ONLY WHAT YOU BROUGHT WITH YOU.
YOU--!
HE GOADED YOU INTO ATTACKING. JUST LIKE HE TRICKED ME. DON'T LET HIM DO IT AGAIN. DON'T GO ALL GUY GARDNER ON ME NOW.
WE ARE DONE HERE.
BOOOM
YOU SON OF--
NO!

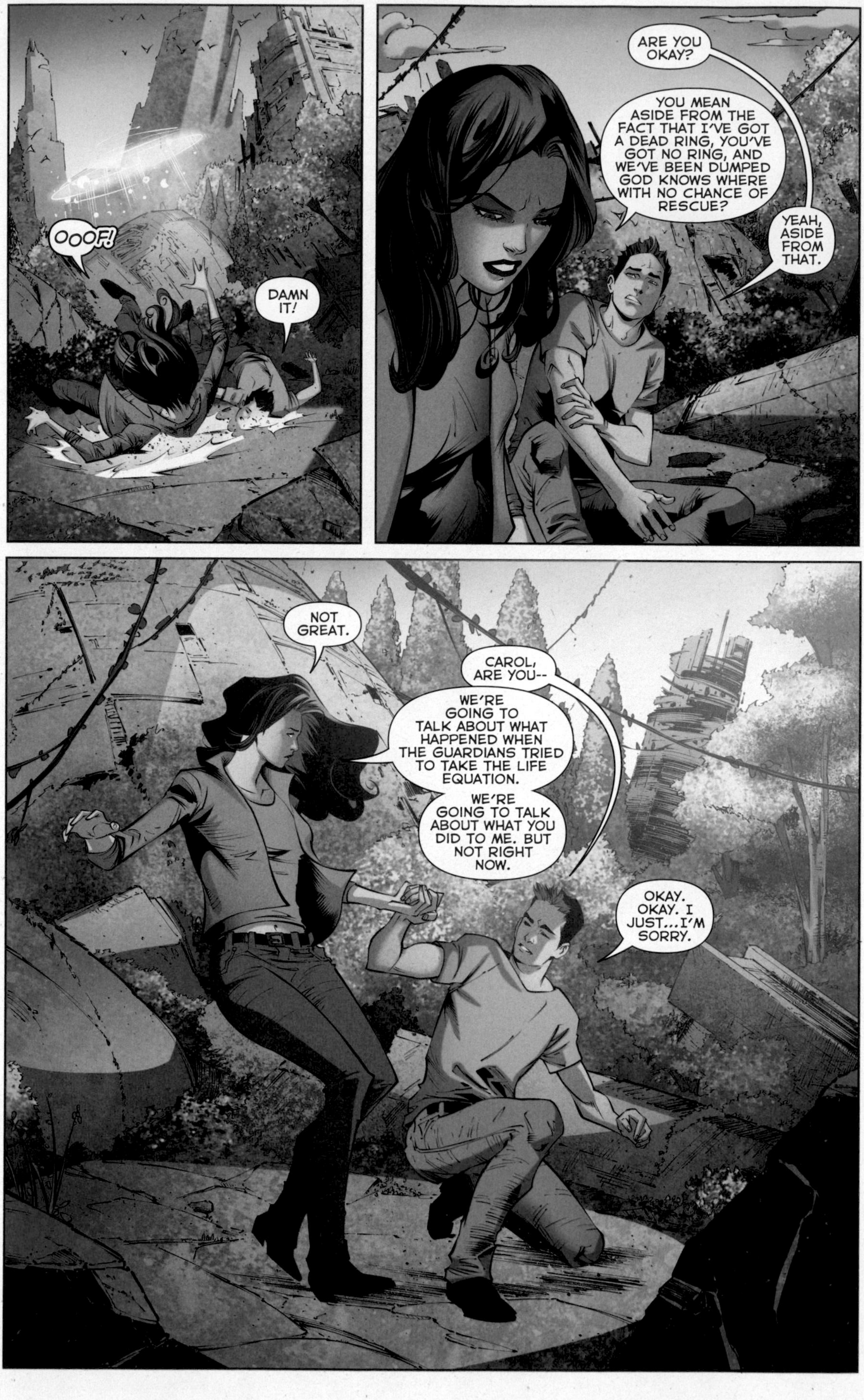
OOOF!
DAMN IT!
ARE YOU OKAY?
YOU MEAN ASIDE FROM THE FACT THAT I'VE GOT A DEAD RING, YOU'VE GOT NO RING, AND WE'VE BEEN DUMPED GOD KNOWS WHERE WITH NO CHANCE OF RESCUE?
YEAH, ASIDE FROM THAT.
NOT GREAT.
CAROL, ARE YOU--
WE'RE GOING TO TALK ABOUT WHAT HAPPENED WHEN THE GUARDIANS TRIED TO TAKE THE LIFE EQUATION.
WE'RE GOING TO TALK ABOUT WHAT YOU DID TO ME. BUT NOT RIGHT NOW.
OKAY. OKAY. I JUST...I'M SORRY.

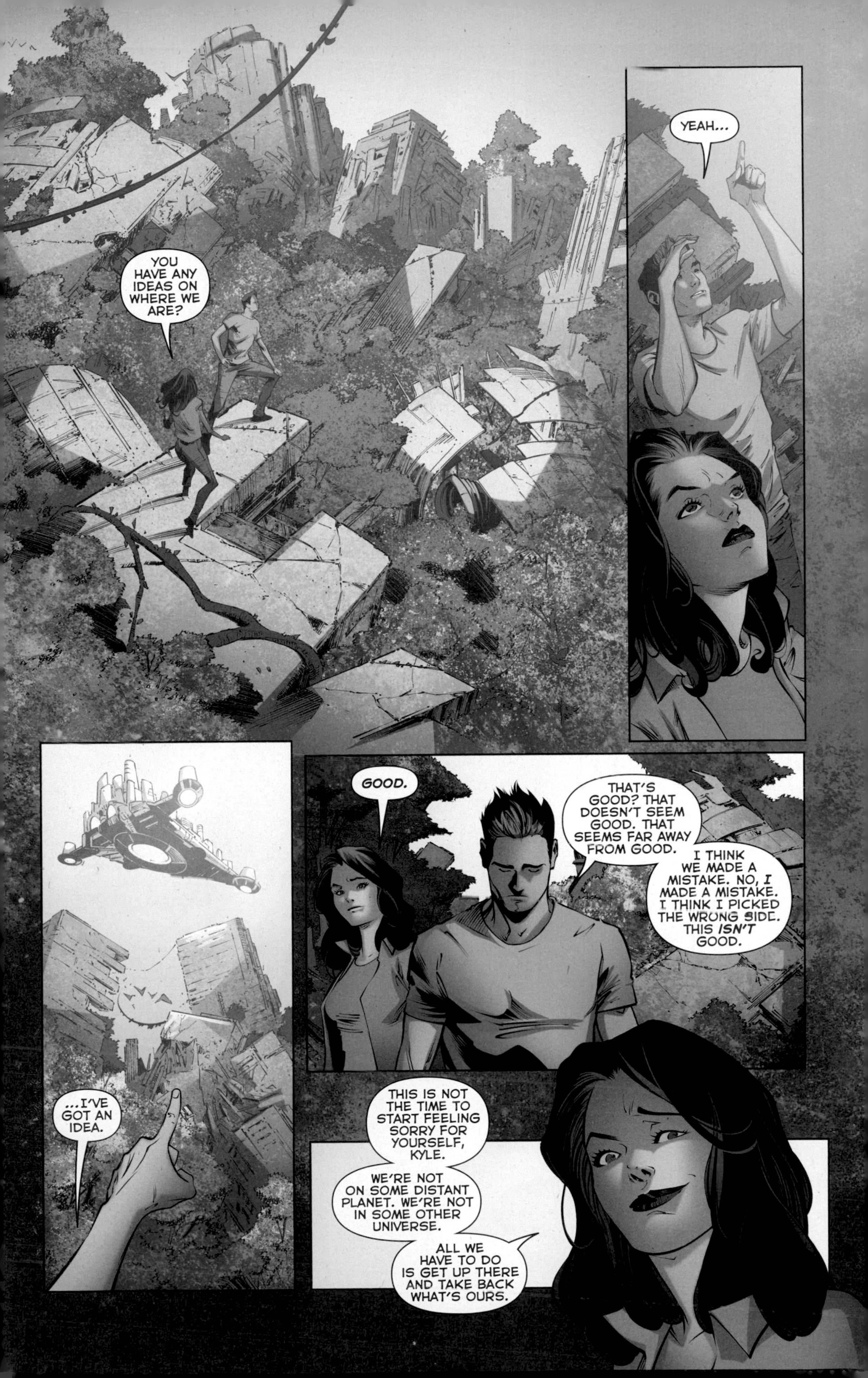
YOU HAVE ANY IDEAS ON WHERE WE ARE?
YEAH...
...I'VE GOT AN IDEA.
GOOD.
THAT'S GOOD? THAT DOESN'T SEEM GOOD. THAT SEEMS FAR AWAY FROM GOOD.
I THINK WE MADE A MISTAKE. NO, I MADE A MISTAKE. I THINK I PICKED THE WRONG SIDE. THIS ISN'T GOOD.
THIS IS NOT THE TIME TO START FEELING SORRY FOR YOURSELF, KYLE.
WE'RE NOT ON SOME DISTANT PLANET. WE'RE NOT IN SOME OTHER UNIVERSE.
ALL WE HAVE TO DO IS GET UP THERE AND TAKE BACK WHAT'S OURS.

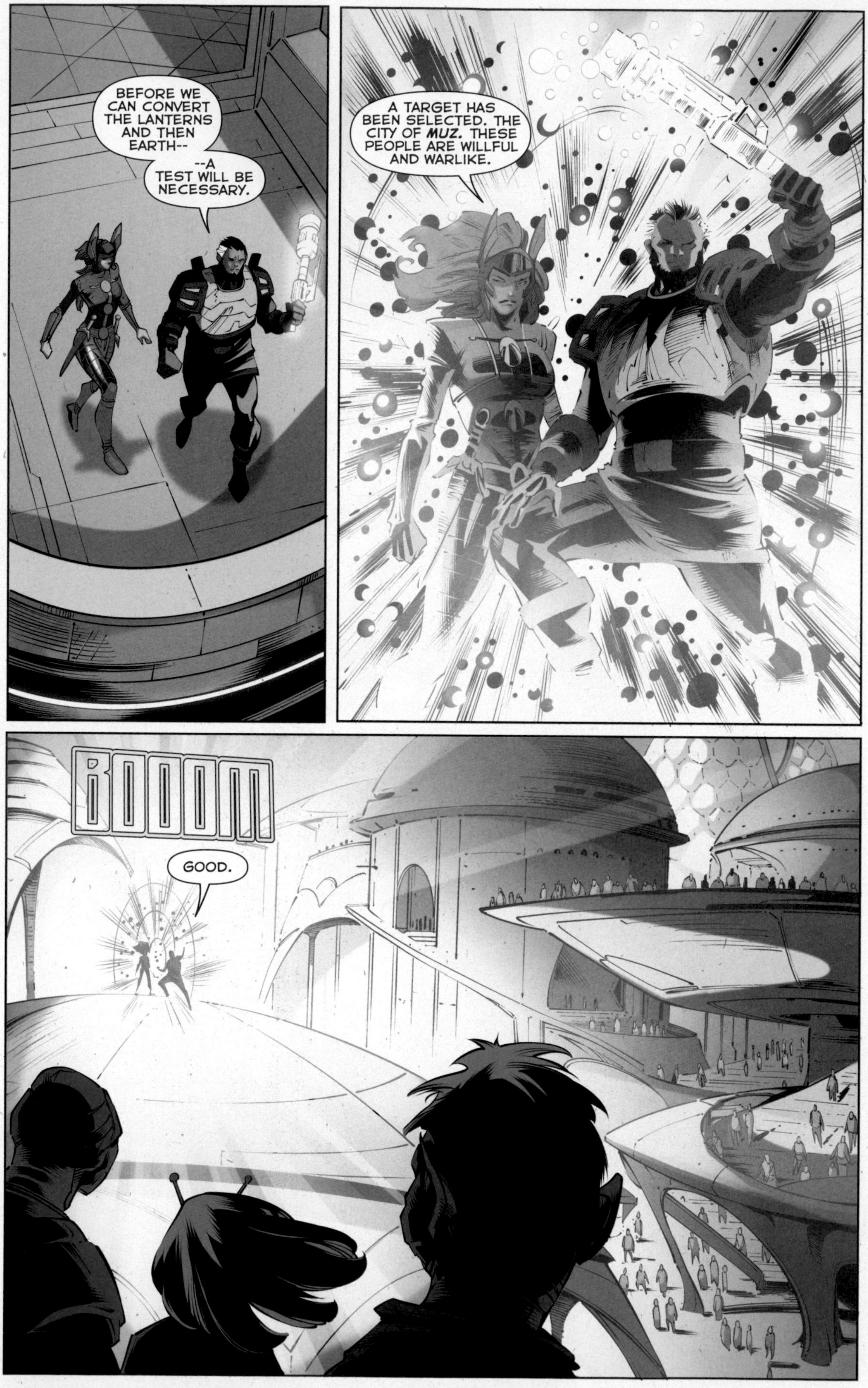
BEFORE WE CAN CONVERT THE LANTERNS AND THEN EARTH--
--A TEST WILL BE NECESSARY.
A TARGET HAS BEEN SELECTED. THE CITY OF MUZ. THESE PEOPLE ARE WILLFUL AND WARLIKE.
BOOOM
GOOD.

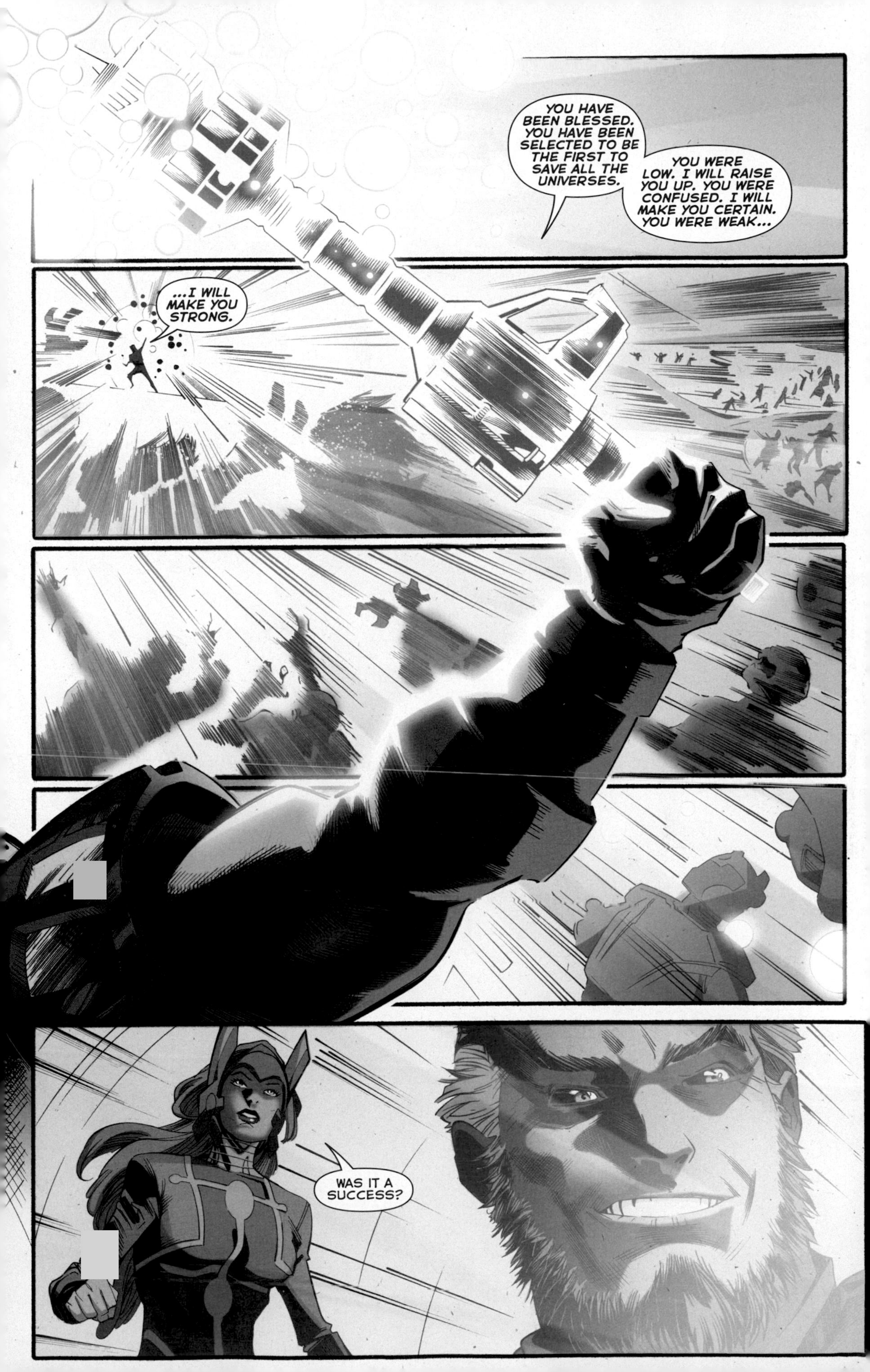
YOU HAVE BEEN BLESSED. YOU HAVE BEEN SELECTED TO BE THE FIRST TO SAVE ALL THE UNIVERSES.
YOU WERE LOW. I WILL RAISE YOU UP. YOU WERE CONFUSED. I WILL MAKE YOU CERTAIN. YOU WERE WEAK...
...I WILL MAKE YOU STRONG.
WAS IT A SUCCESS?

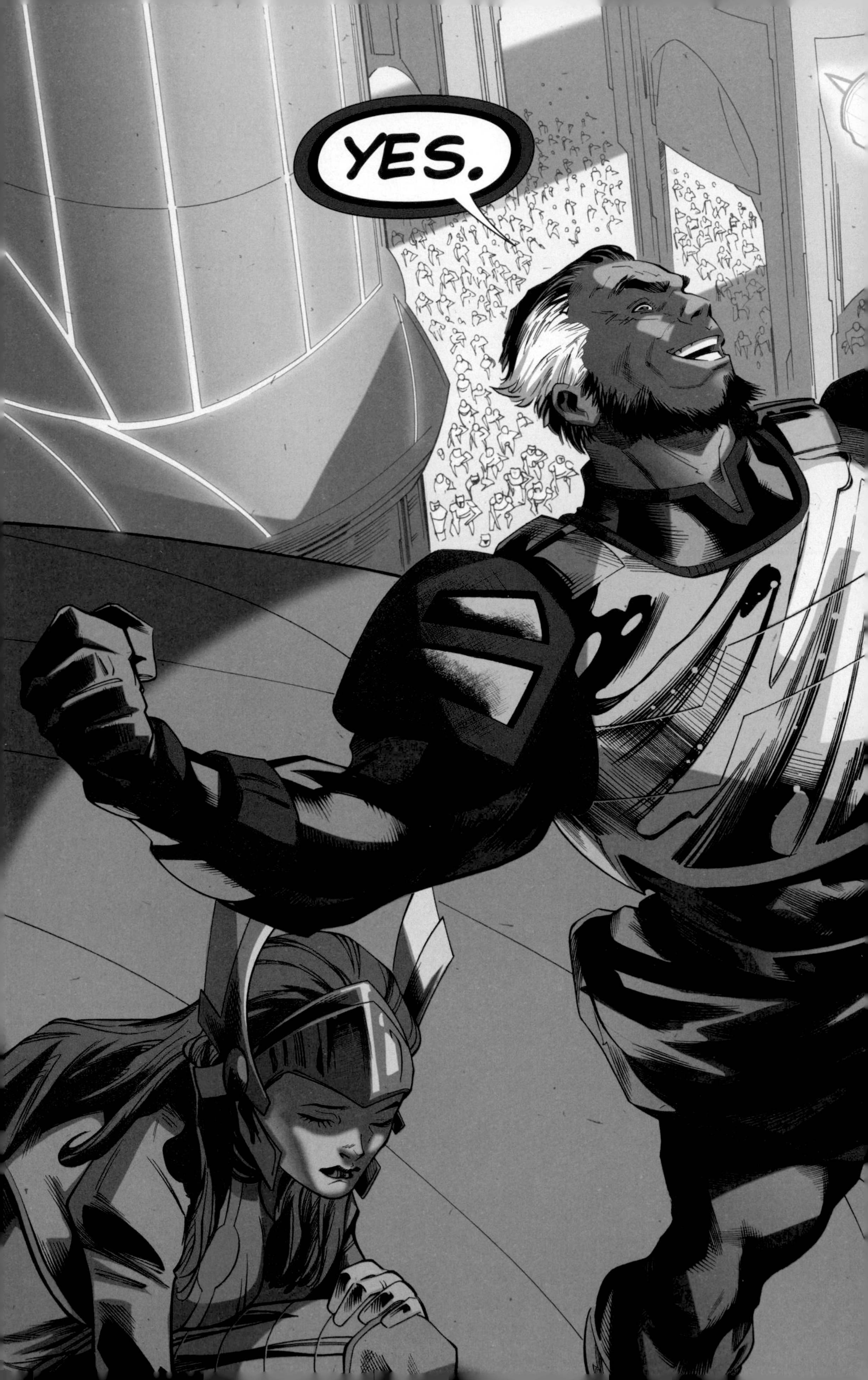
YES.

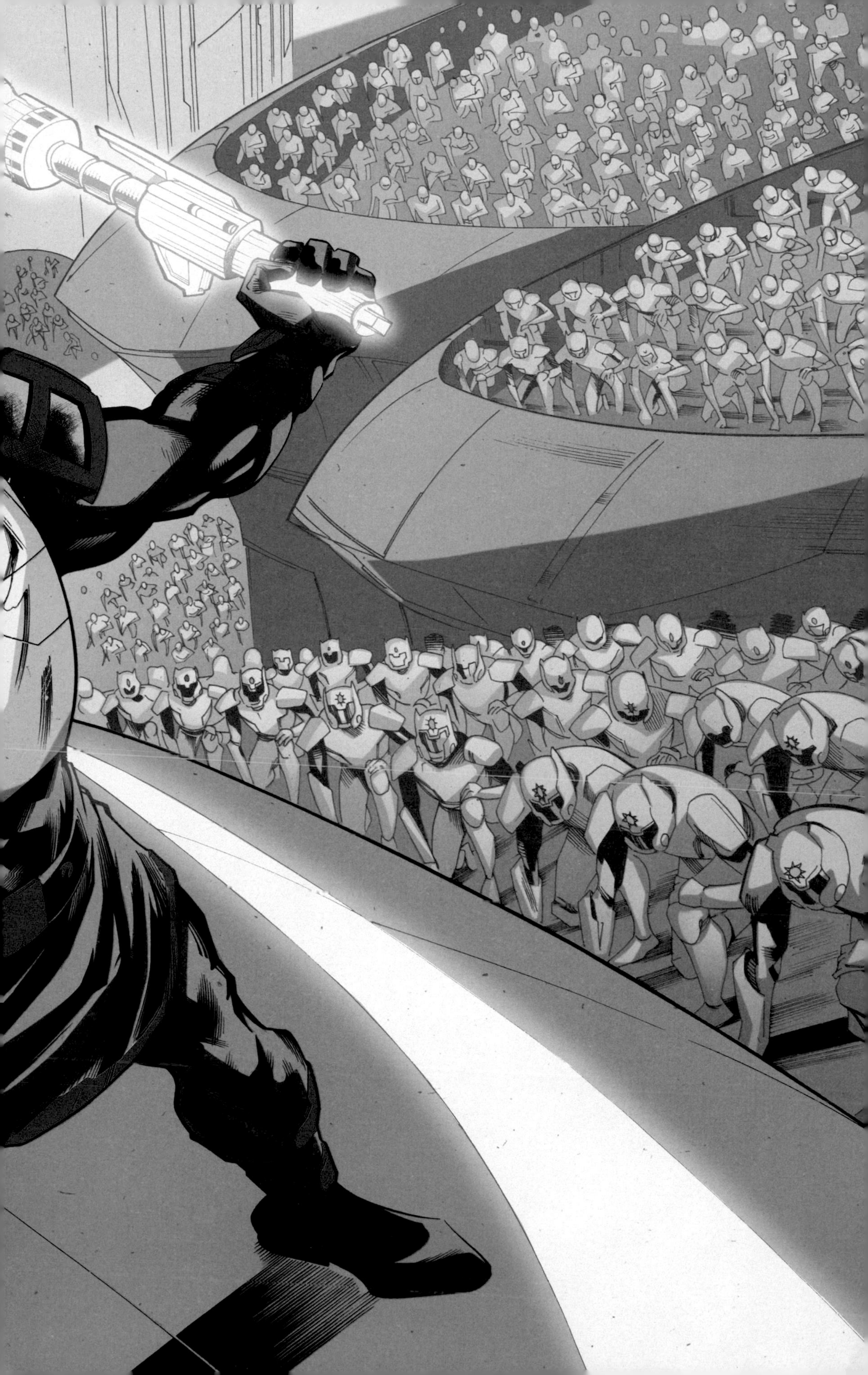

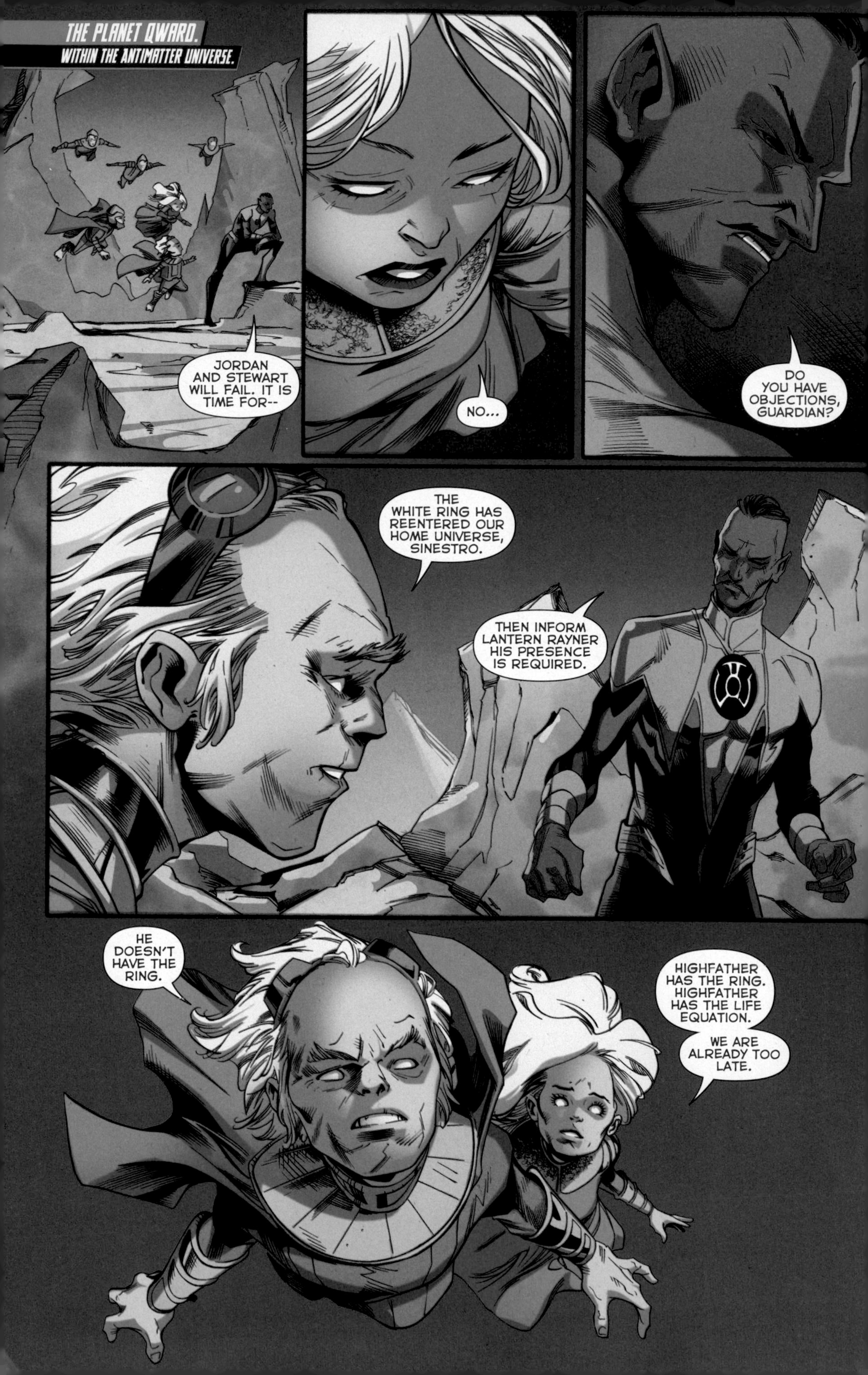
THE PLANET QWARD.
WITHIN THE ANTIMATTER UNIVERSE.
JORDAN AND STEWART WILL FAIL. IT IS TIME FOR--
NO...
DO YOU HAVE OBJECTIONS, GUARDIAN?
THE WHITE RING HAS REENTERED OUR HOME UNIVERSE, SINESTRO.
THEN INFORM LANTERN RAYNER HIS PRESENCE IS REQUIRED.
HE DOESN'T HAVE THE RING.
HIGHFATHER HAS THE RING. HIGHFATHER HAS THE LIFE EQUATION.
WE ARE ALREADY TOO LATE.

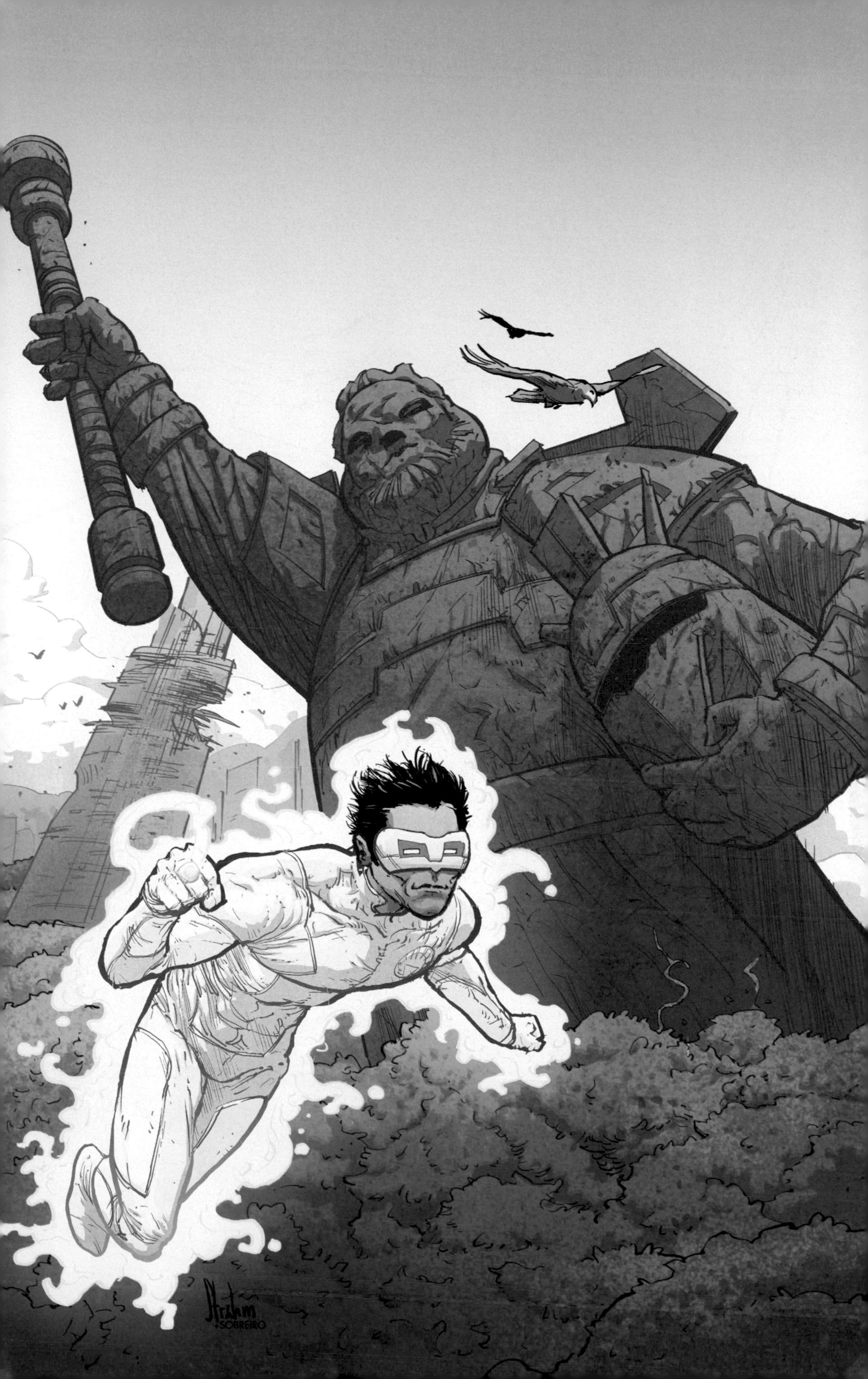

GODHEAD: ACT III, PART III: STORMING THE GATES

JUSTIN JORDAN writer **DIOGENES NEVES RODNEY BUCHEMI** pencillers **MARC DEERING RODNEY BUCHEMI DANIEL HENRIQUES** inkers **ANDREW DALHOUSE** colorist **TAYLOR ESPOSITO** letterer cover art by **KYLE STRAHM** and **FELIPE SOBREIRO**

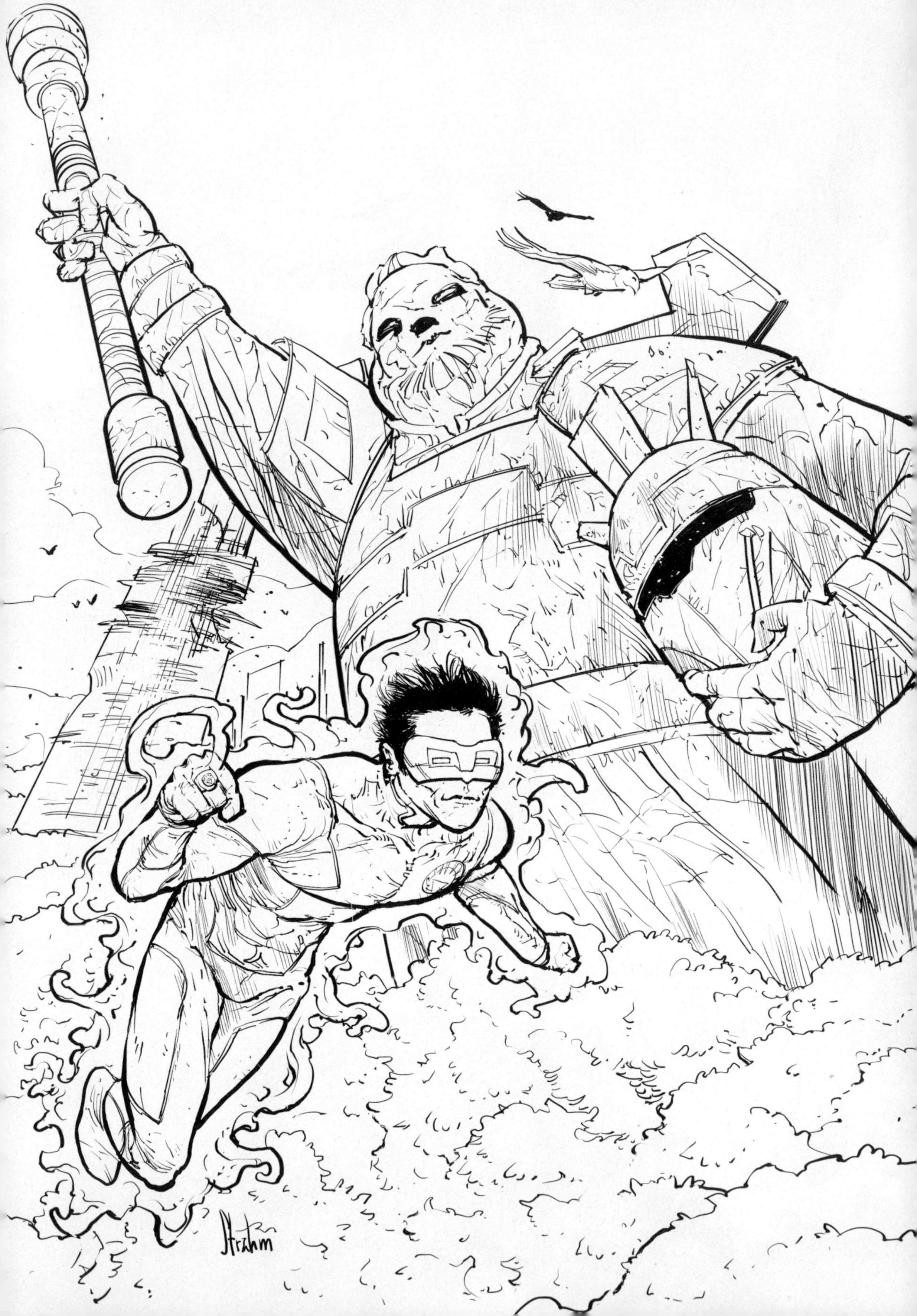
Strahm

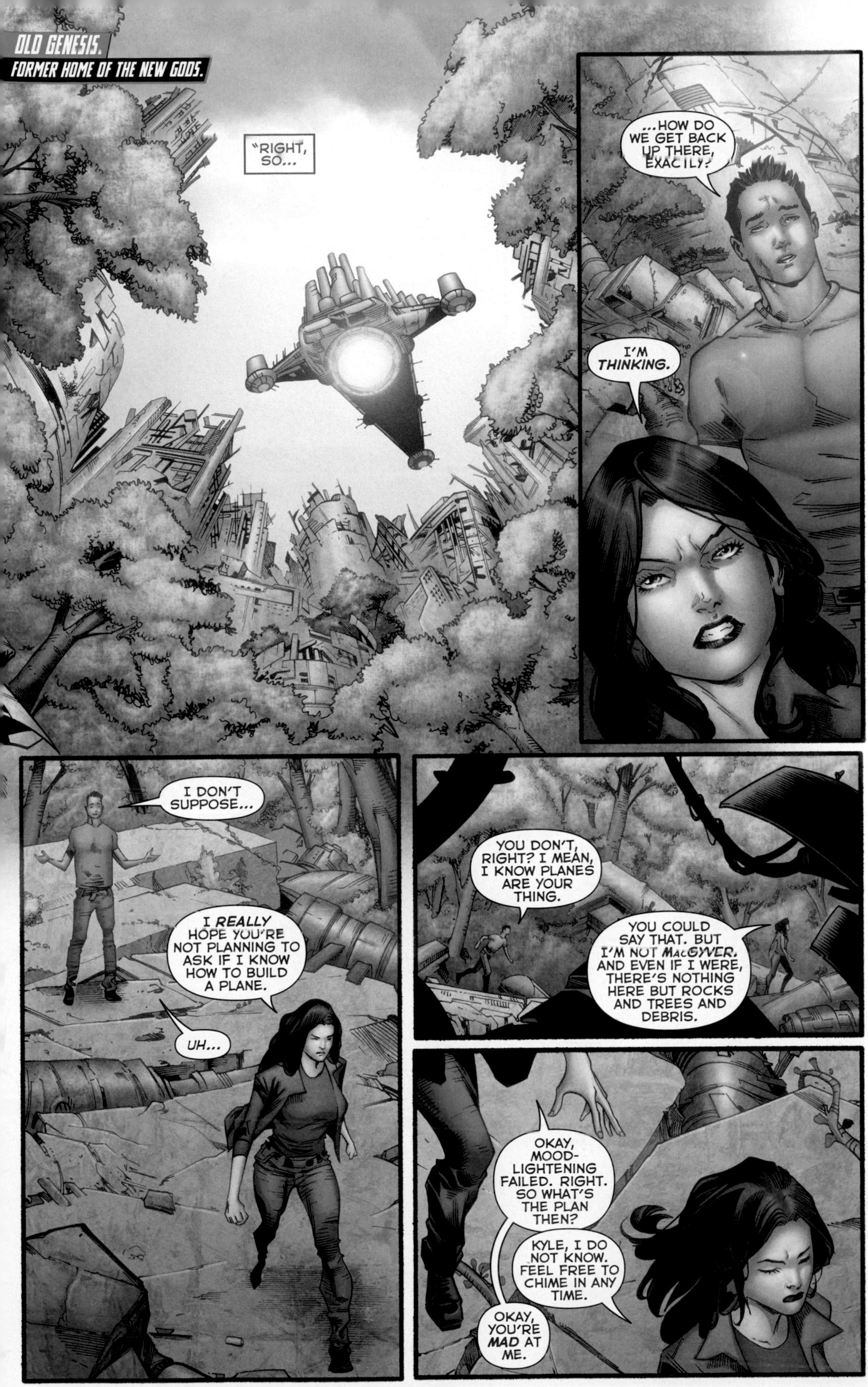
OLD GENESIS.
FORMER HOME OF THE NEW GODS.
"RIGHT, SO...
...HOW DO WE GET BACK UP THERE, EXACTLY?
I'M *THINKING*.
I DON'T SUPPOSE...
I *REALLY* HOPE YOU'RE NOT PLANNING TO ASK IF I KNOW HOW TO BUILD A PLANE.
UH...
YOU DON'T, RIGHT? I MEAN, I KNOW PLANES ARE YOUR THING.
YOU COULD SAY THAT. BUT I'M NOT *MacGYVER*. AND EVEN IF I WERE, THERE'S NOTHING HERE BUT ROCKS AND TREES AND DEBRIS.
OKAY, MOOD-LIGHTENING FAILED. RIGHT. SO WHAT'S THE PLAN THEN?
KYLE, I DO NOT KNOW. FEEL FREE TO CHIME IN ANY TIME.
OKAY, YOU'RE *MAD* AT ME.

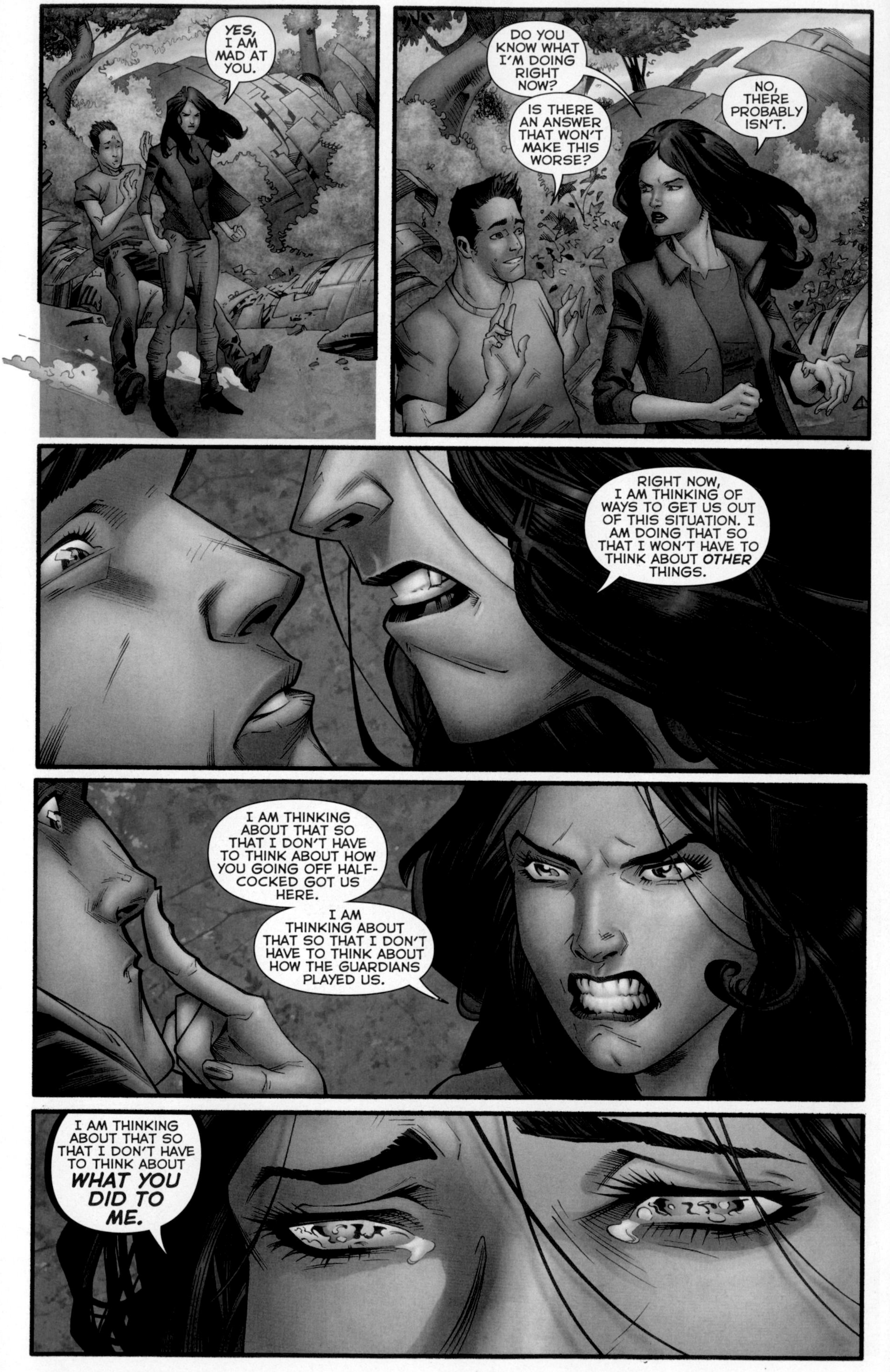
YES, I AM MAD AT YOU.
DO YOU KNOW WHAT I'M DOING RIGHT NOW?
IS THERE AN ANSWER THAT WON'T MAKE THIS WORSE?
NO, THERE PROBABLY ISN'T.
RIGHT NOW, I AM THINKING OF WAYS TO GET US OUT OF THIS SITUATION. I AM DOING THAT SO THAT I WON'T HAVE TO THINK ABOUT OTHER THINGS.
I AM THINKING ABOUT THAT SO THAT I DON'T HAVE TO THINK ABOUT HOW YOU GOING OFF HALF-COCKED GOT US HERE.
I AM THINKING ABOUT THAT SO THAT I DON'T HAVE TO THINK ABOUT HOW THE GUARDIANS PLAYED US.
I AM THINKING ABOUT THAT SO THAT I DON'T HAVE TO THINK ABOUT WHAT YOU DID TO ME.

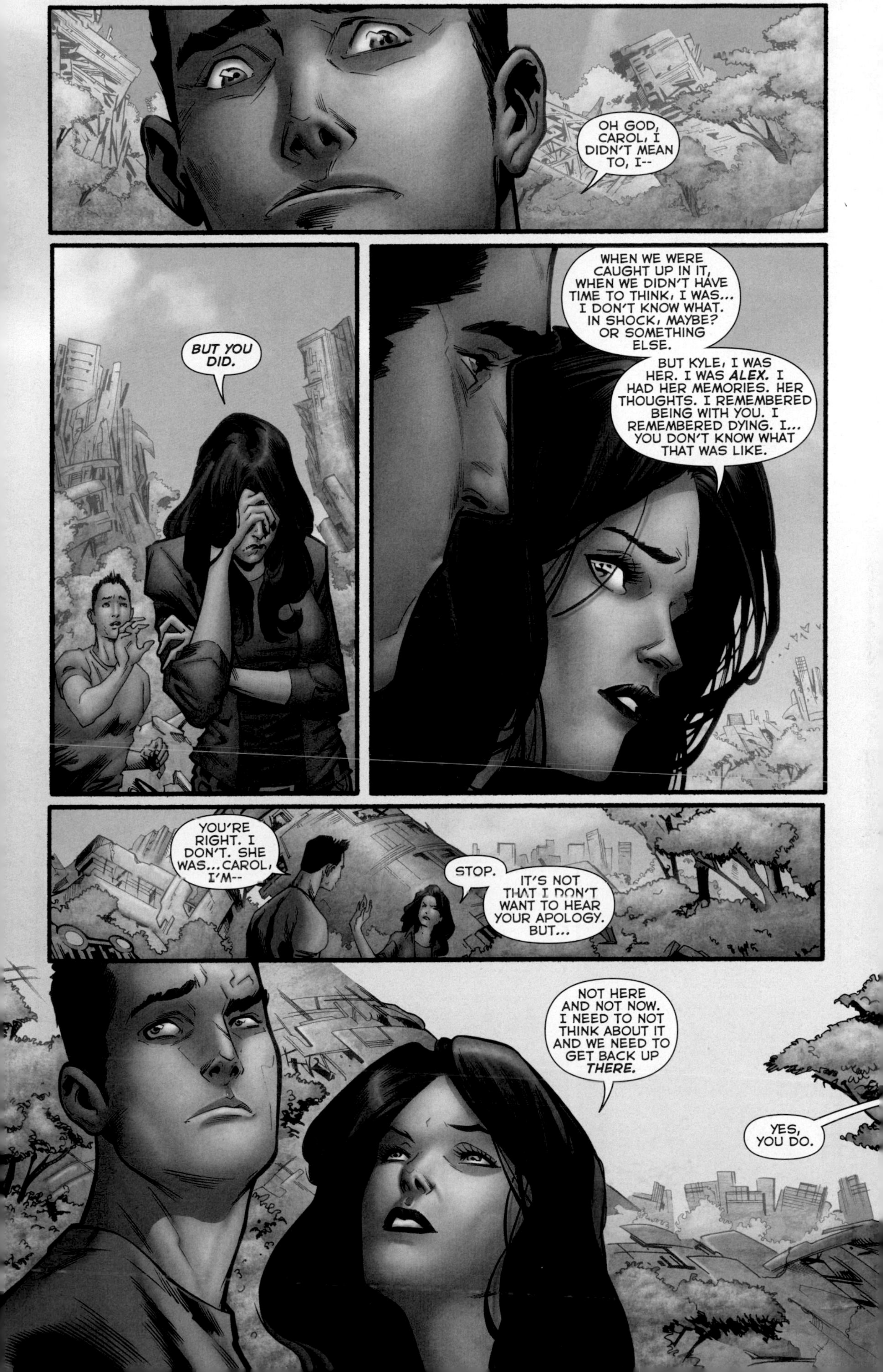
OH GOD, CAROL, I DIDN'T MEAN TO, I--
BUT YOU DID.
WHEN WE WERE CAUGHT UP IN IT, WHEN WE DIDN'T HAVE TIME TO THINK, I WAS... I DON'T KNOW WHAT. IN SHOCK, MAYBE? OR SOMETHING ELSE.
BUT KYLE, I WAS HER. I WAS ALEX. I HAD HER MEMORIES. HER THOUGHTS. I REMEMBERED BEING WITH YOU. I REMEMBERED DYING. I... YOU DON'T KNOW WHAT THAT WAS LIKE.
YOU'RE RIGHT. I DON'T. SHE WAS...CAROL, I'M--
STOP.
IT'S NOT THAT I DON'T WANT TO HEAR YOUR APOLOGY. BUT...
NOT HERE AND NOT NOW. I NEED TO NOT THINK ABOUT IT AND WE NEED TO GET BACK UP THERE.
YES, YOU DO.

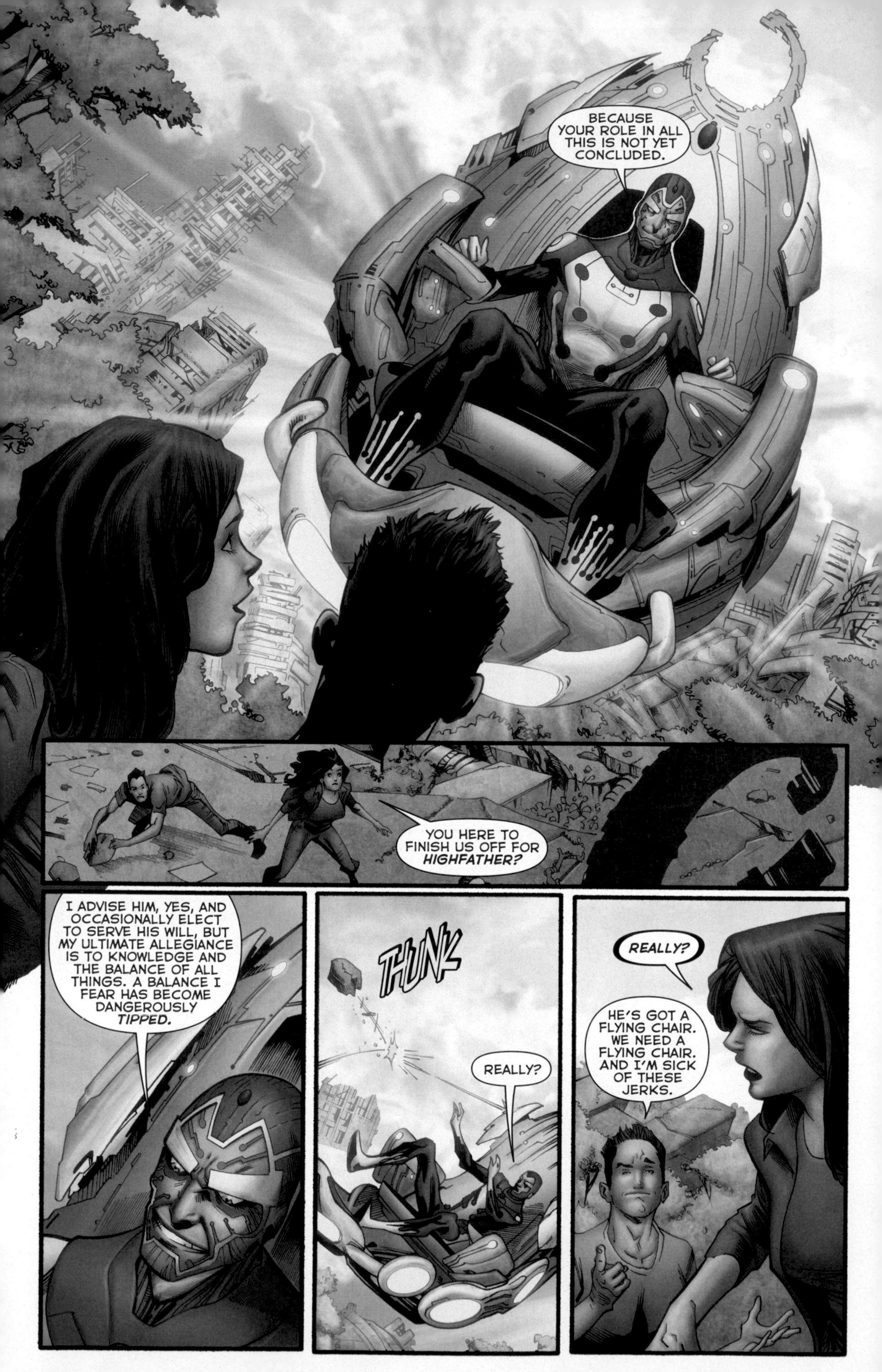
BECAUSE YOUR ROLE IN ALL THIS IS NOT YET CONCLUDED.
YOU HERE TO FINISH US OFF FOR HIGHFATHER?
I ADVISE HIM, YES, AND OCCASIONALLY ELECT TO SERVE HIS WILL, BUT MY ULTIMATE ALLEGIANCE IS TO KNOWLEDGE AND THE BALANCE OF ALL THINGS. A BALANCE I FEAR HAS BECOME DANGEROUSLY TIPPED.
THUNK
REALLY?
REALLY?
HE'S GOT A FLYING CHAIR. WE NEED A FLYING CHAIR. AND I'M SICK OF THESE JERKS.

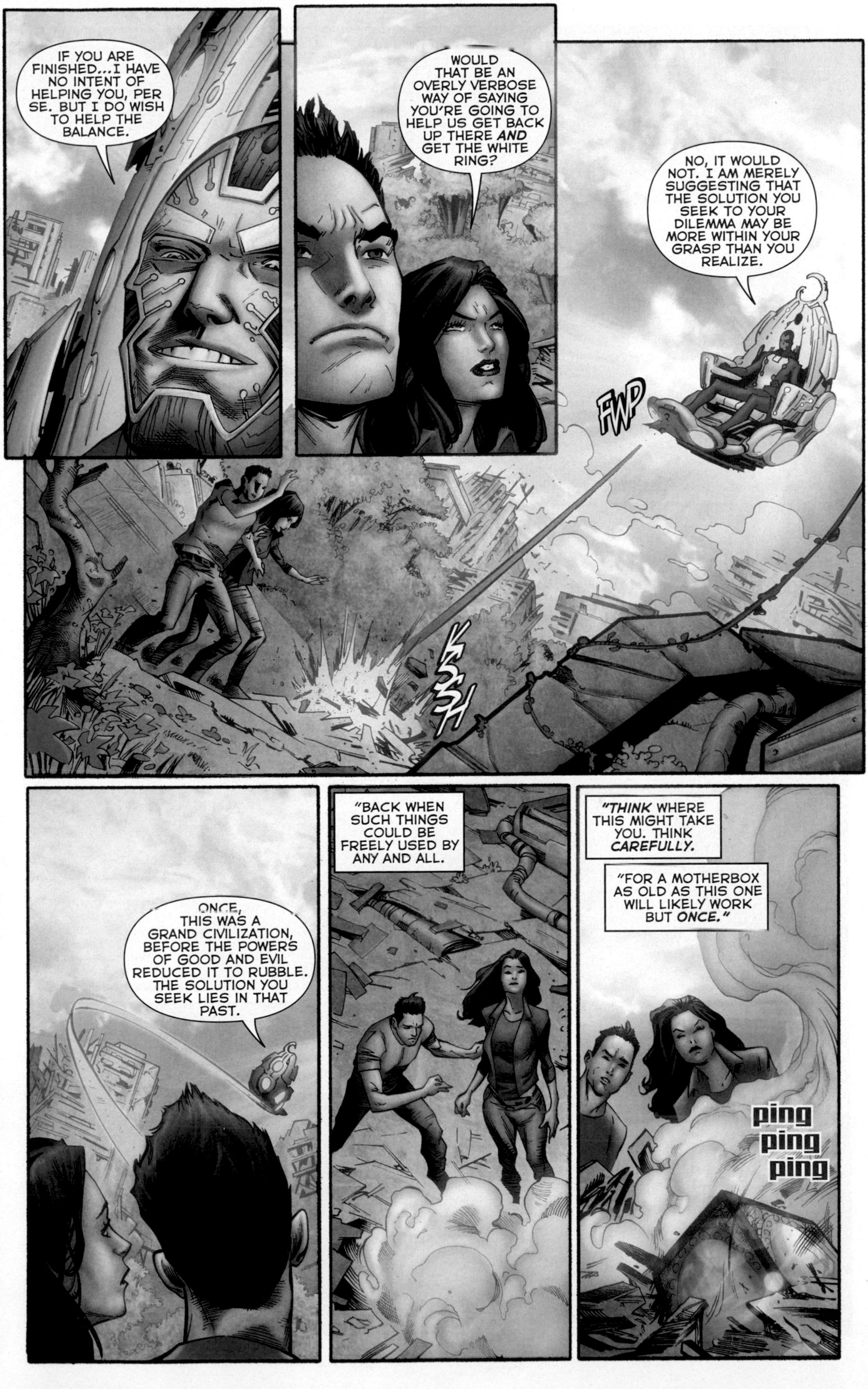
IF YOU ARE FINISHED...I HAVE NO INTENT OF HELPING YOU, PER SE. BUT I DO WISH TO HELP THE BALANCE.
WOULD THAT BE AN OVERLY VERBOSE WAY OF SAYING YOU'RE GOING TO HELP US GET BACK UP THERE AND GET THE WHITE RING?
NO, IT WOULD NOT. I AM MERELY SUGGESTING THAT THE SOLUTION YOU SEEK TO YOUR DILEMMA MAY BE MORE WITHIN YOUR GRASP THAN YOU REALIZE.
FWP
KSSH
ONCE, THIS WAS A GRAND CIVILIZATION, BEFORE THE POWERS OF GOOD AND EVIL REDUCED IT TO RUBBLE. THE SOLUTION YOU SEEK LIES IN THAT PAST.
"BACK WHEN SUCH THINGS COULD BE FREELY USED BY ANY AND ALL.
"THINK WHERE THIS MIGHT TAKE YOU. THINK CAREFULLY.
"FOR A MOTHERBOX AS OLD AS THIS ONE WILL LIKELY WORK BUT ONCE."
ping
ping
ping

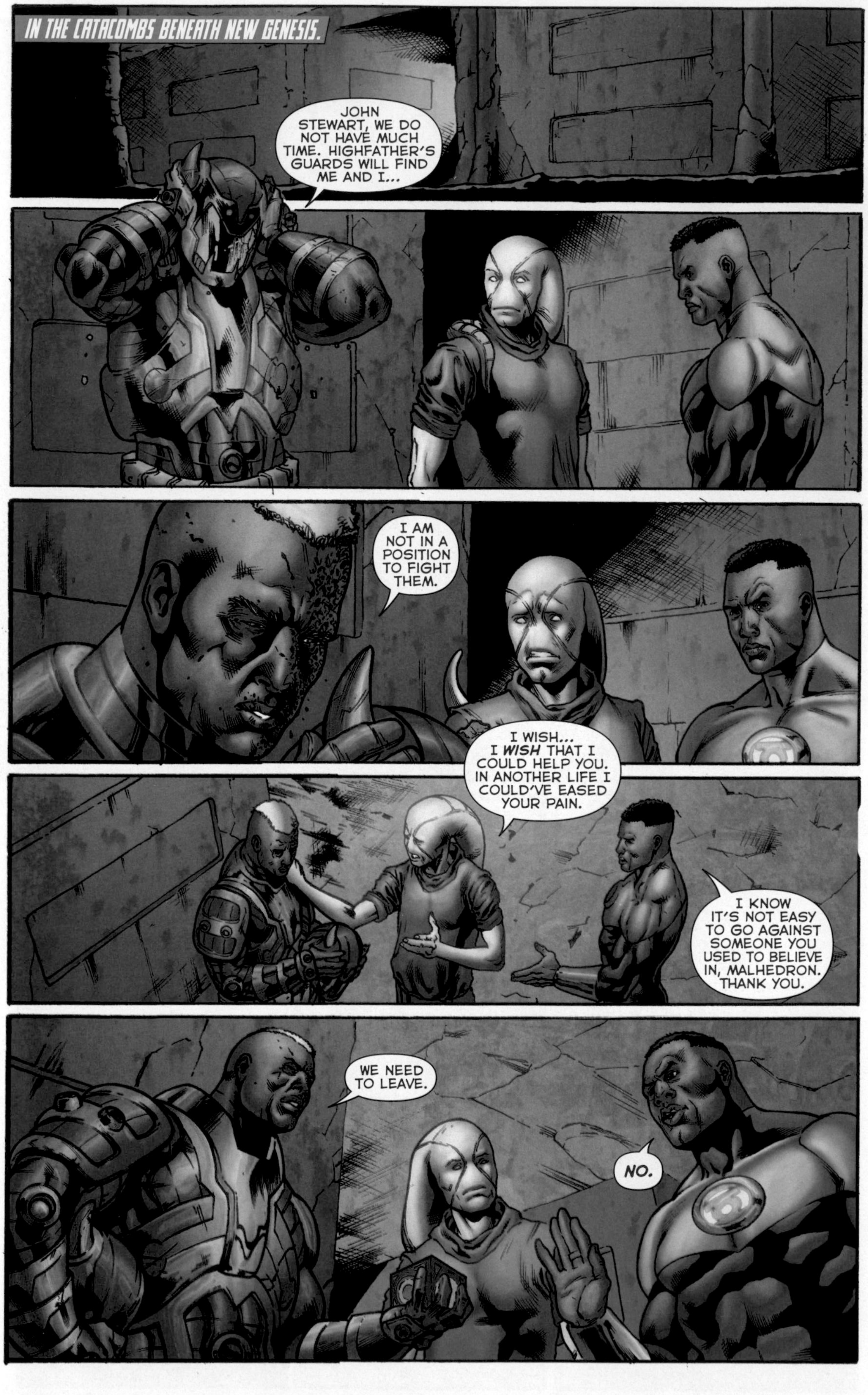

IN THE CATACOMBS BENEATH NEW GENESIS.
JOHN STEWART, WE DO NOT HAVE MUCH TIME. HIGHFATHER'S GUARDS WILL FIND ME AND I...
I AM NOT IN A POSITION TO FIGHT THEM.
I WISH... I WISH THAT I COULD HELP YOU. IN ANOTHER LIFE I COULD'VE EASED YOUR PAIN.
I KNOW IT'S NOT EASY TO GO AGAINST SOMEONE YOU USED TO BELIEVE IN, MALHEDRON. THANK YOU.
WE NEED TO LEAVE.
NO.

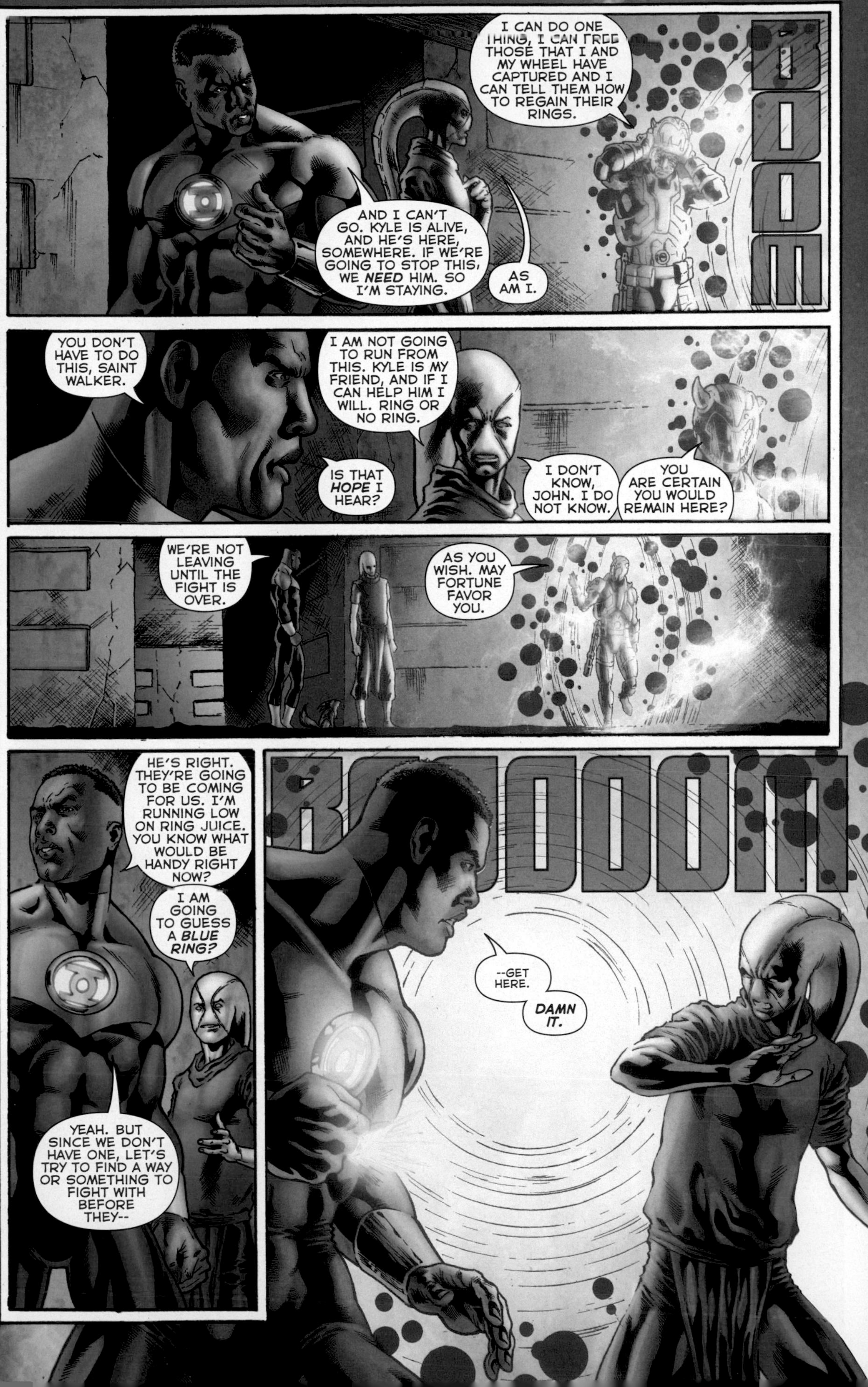
I CAN DO ONE THING, I CAN FREE THOSE THAT I AND MY WHEEL HAVE CAPTURED AND I CAN TELL THEM HOW TO REGAIN THEIR RINGS.
AND I CAN'T GO. KYLE IS ALIVE, AND HE'S HERE, SOMEWHERE. IF WE'RE GOING TO STOP THIS, WE *NEED* HIM. SO I'M STAYING.
AS AM I.
YOU DON'T HAVE TO DO THIS, SAINT WALKER.
I AM NOT GOING TO RUN FROM THIS. KYLE IS MY FRIEND, AND IF I CAN HELP HIM I WILL. RING OR NO RING.
IS THAT *HOPE* I HEAR?
I DON'T KNOW, JOHN. I DO NOT KNOW.
YOU ARE CERTAIN YOU WOULD REMAIN HERE?
WE'RE NOT LEAVING UNTIL THE FIGHT IS OVER.
AS YOU WISH. MAY FORTUNE FAVOR YOU.
HE'S RIGHT. THEY'RE GOING TO BE COMING FOR US. I'M RUNNING LOW ON RING JUICE. YOU KNOW WHAT WOULD BE HANDY RIGHT NOW?
I AM GOING TO GUESS A *BLUE RING?*
YEAH. BUT SINCE WE DON'T HAVE ONE, LET'S TRY TO FIND A WAY OR SOMETHING TO FIGHT WITH BEFORE THEY--
--GET HERE.
DAMN IT.

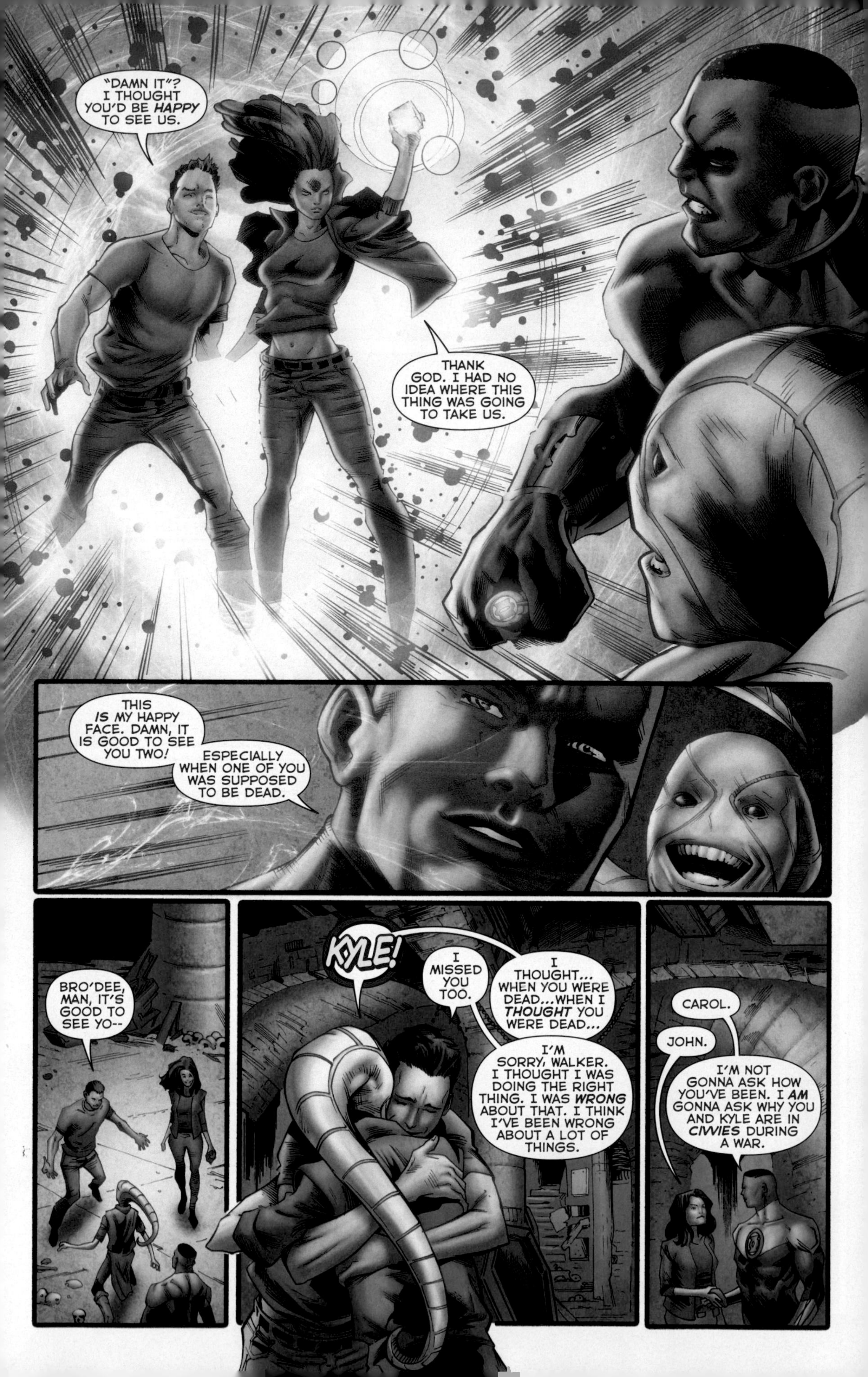
"DAMN IT"? I THOUGHT YOU'D BE HAPPY TO SEE US.
THANK GOD. I HAD NO IDEA WHERE THIS THING WAS GOING TO TAKE US.
THIS IS MY HAPPY FACE. DAMN, IT IS GOOD TO SEE YOU TWO!
ESPECIALLY WHEN ONE OF YOU WAS SUPPOSED TO BE DEAD.
BRO'DEE, MAN, IT'S GOOD TO SEE YO--
KYLE!
I MISSED YOU TOO.
I THOUGHT... WHEN YOU WERE DEAD...WHEN I THOUGHT YOU WERE DEAD...
I'M SORRY, WALKER. I THOUGHT I WAS DOING THE RIGHT THING. I WAS WRONG ABOUT THAT. I THINK I'VE BEEN WRONG ABOUT A LOT OF THINGS.
CAROL.
JOHN.
I'M NOT GONNA ASK HOW YOU'VE BEEN. I AM GONNA ASK WHY YOU AND KYLE ARE IN CIVVIES DURING A WAR.

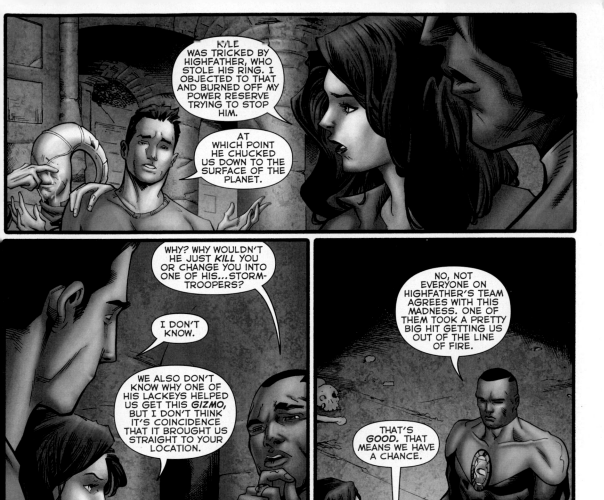

KYLE WAS TRICKED BY HIGHFATHER, WHO STOLE HIS RING. I OBJECTED TO THAT AND BURNED OFF MY POWER RESERVE TRYING TO STOP HIM.

AT WHICH POINT HE CHUCKED US DOWN TO THE SURFACE OF THE PLANET.

WHY? WHY WOULDN'T HE JUST *KILL* YOU OR CHANGE YOU INTO ONE OF HIS...STORM-TROOPERS?

I DON'T KNOW.

WE ALSO DON'T KNOW WHY ONE OF HIS LACKEYS HELPED US GET THIS *GIZMO*, BUT I DON'T THINK IT'S COINCIDENCE THAT IT BROUGHT US STRAIGHT TO YOUR LOCATION.

NO, NOT EVERYONE ON HIGHFATHER'S TEAM AGREES WITH THIS MADNESS. ONE OF THEM TOOK A PRETTY BIG HIT GETTING US OUT OF THE LINE OF FIRE.

THAT'S *GOOD*. THAT MEANS WE HAVE A CHANCE.

YOU HAVE A PLAN?

I HAVE AN *IDEA*.

THEN YOU'RE DOING BETTER THAN US.

?

KYLE, DOWN!

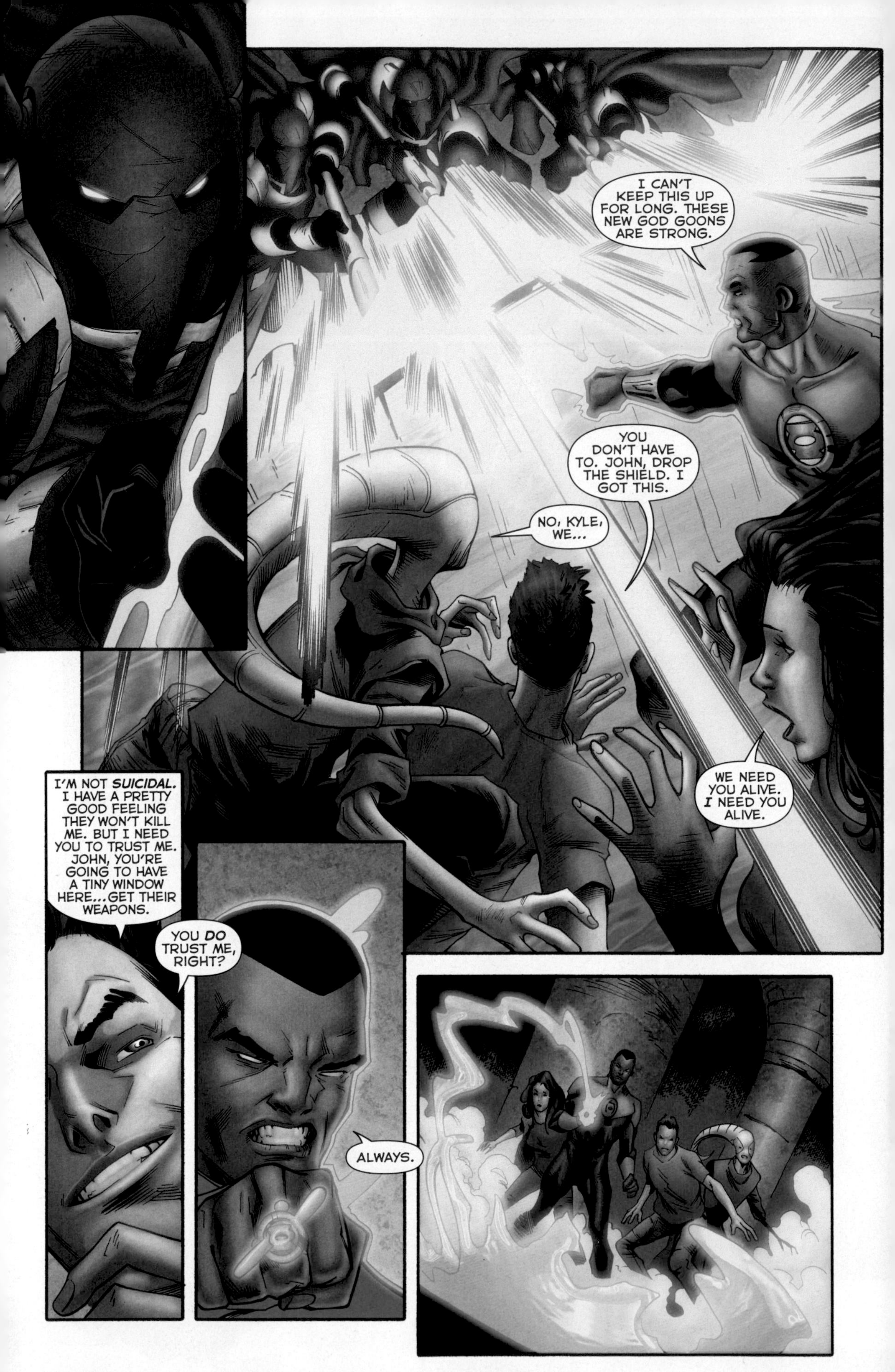
I CAN'T KEEP THIS UP FOR LONG. THESE NEW GOD GOONS ARE STRONG.
YOU DON'T HAVE TO. JOHN, DROP THE SHIELD. I GOT THIS.
NO, KYLE, WE...
WE NEED YOU ALIVE. I NEED YOU ALIVE.
I'M NOT SUICIDAL. I HAVE A PRETTY GOOD FEELING THEY WON'T KILL ME. BUT I NEED YOU TO TRUST ME. JOHN, YOU'RE GOING TO HAVE A TINY WINDOW HERE...GET THEIR WEAPONS.
YOU DO TRUST ME, RIGHT?
ALWAYS.

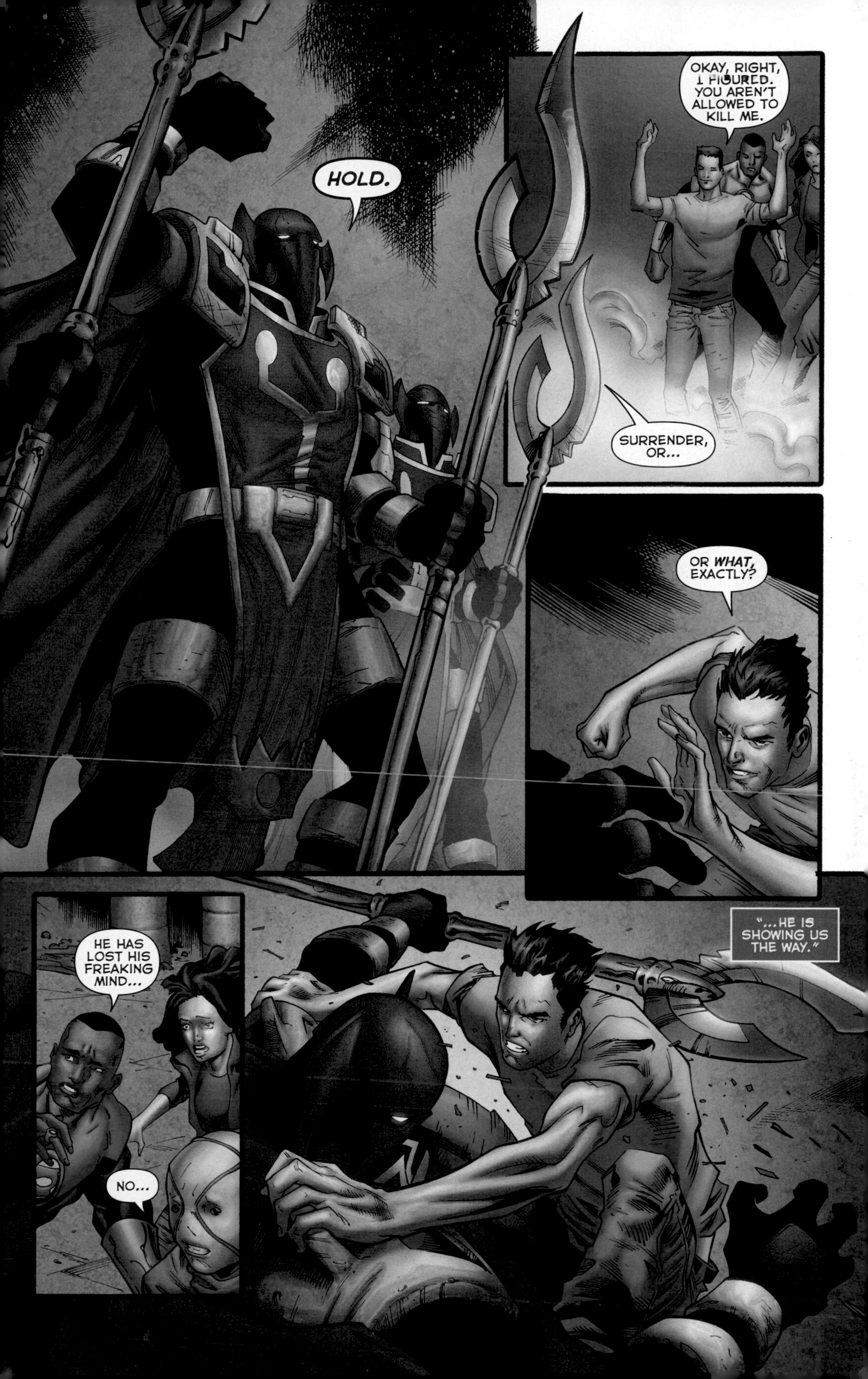
HOLD.
OKAY, RIGHT, I FIGURED. YOU AREN'T ALLOWED TO KILL ME.
SURRENDER, OR...
OR WHAT, EXACTLY?
"...HE IS SHOWING US THE WAY."
HE HAS LOST HIS FREAKING MIND...
NO...

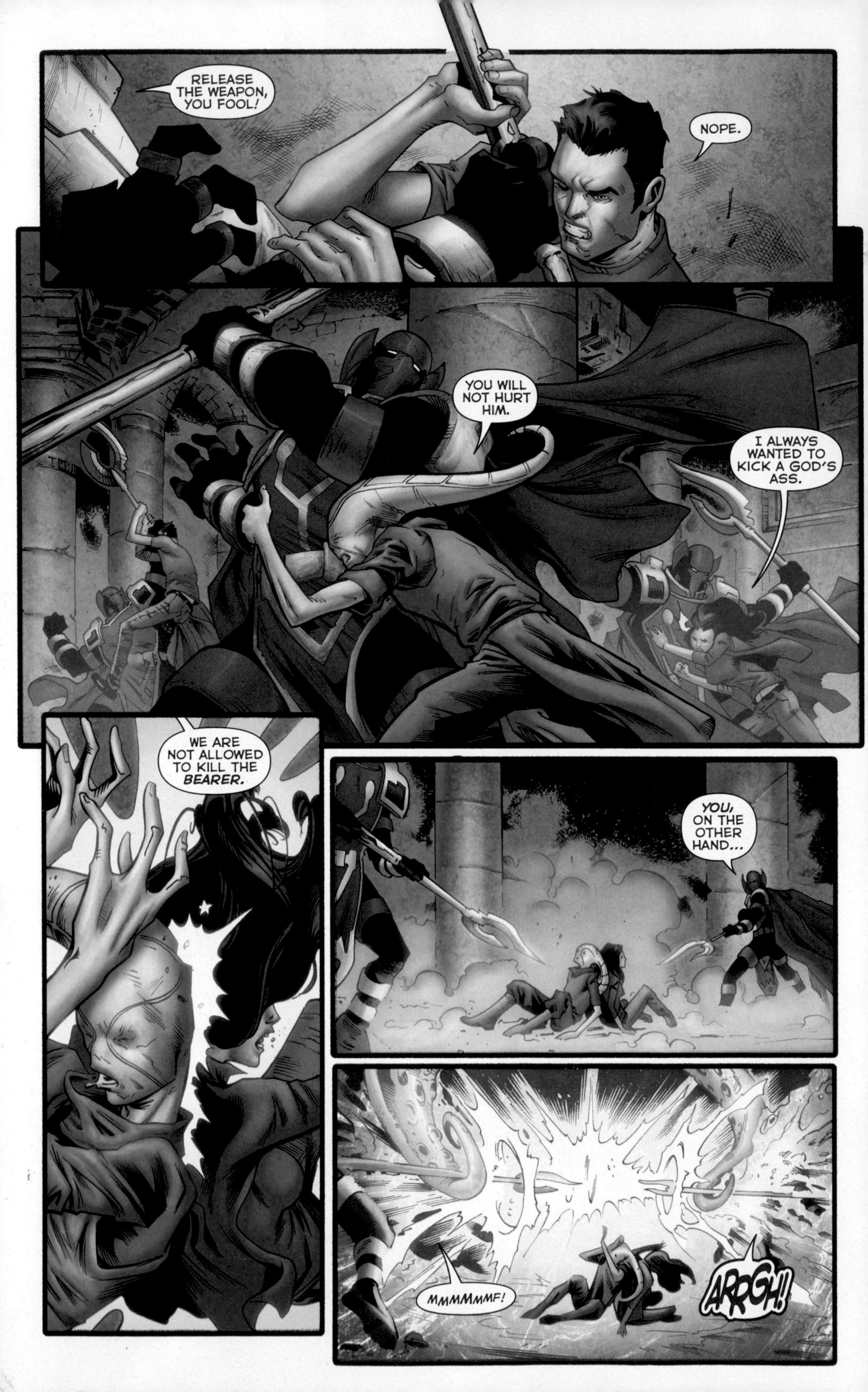
RELEASE THE WEAPON, YOU FOOL!
NOPE.
YOU WILL NOT HURT HIM.
I ALWAYS WANTED TO KICK A GOD'S ASS.
WE ARE NOT ALLOWED TO KILL THE *BEARER.*
YOU, ON THE OTHER HAND...
MMMMMMF!
ARRGH!

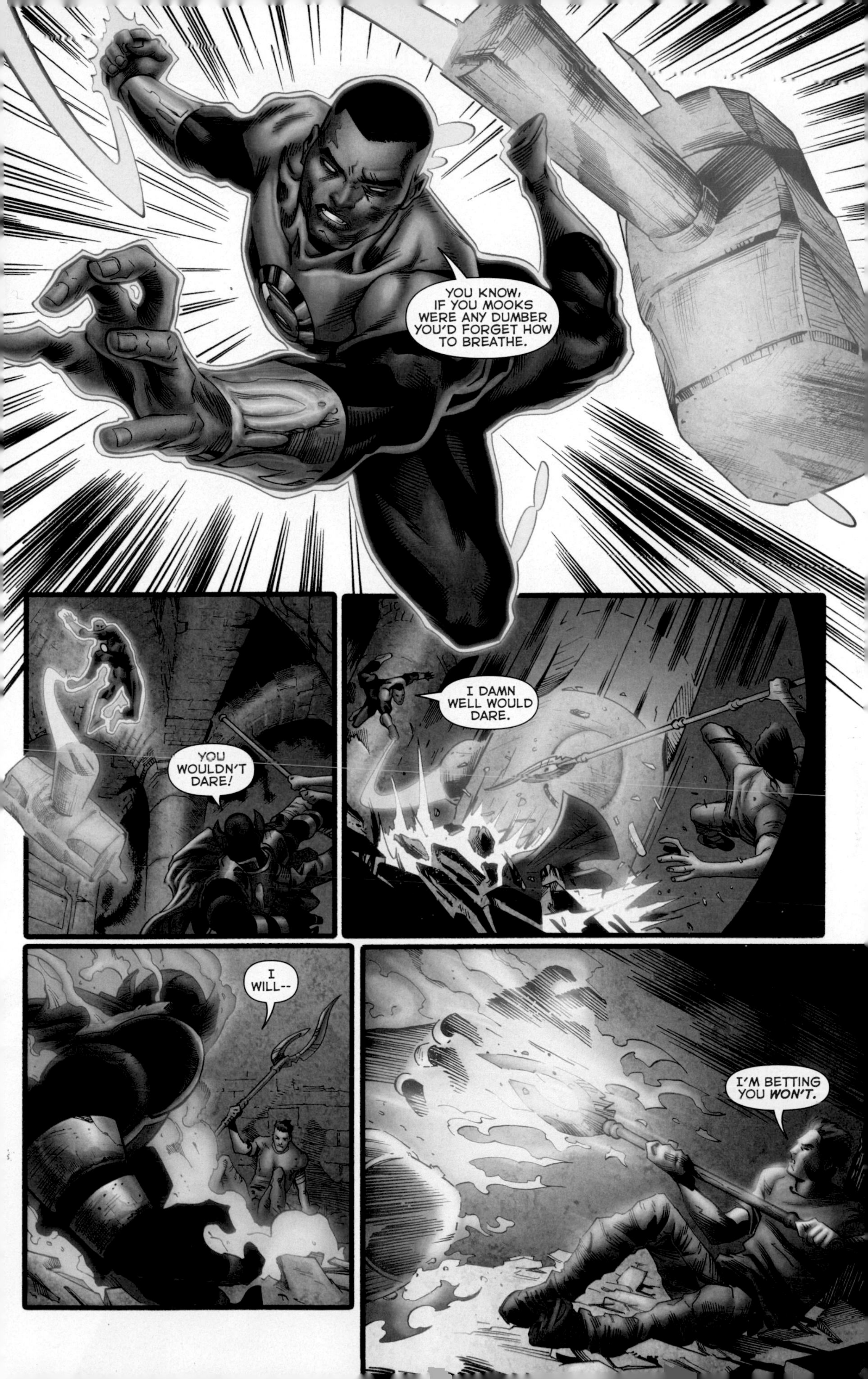
YOU KNOW, IF YOU MOOKS WERE ANY DUMBER YOU'D FORGET HOW TO BREATHE.
YOU WOULDN'T DARE!
I DAMN WELL WOULD DARE.
I WILL--
I'M BETTING YOU *WON'T*.

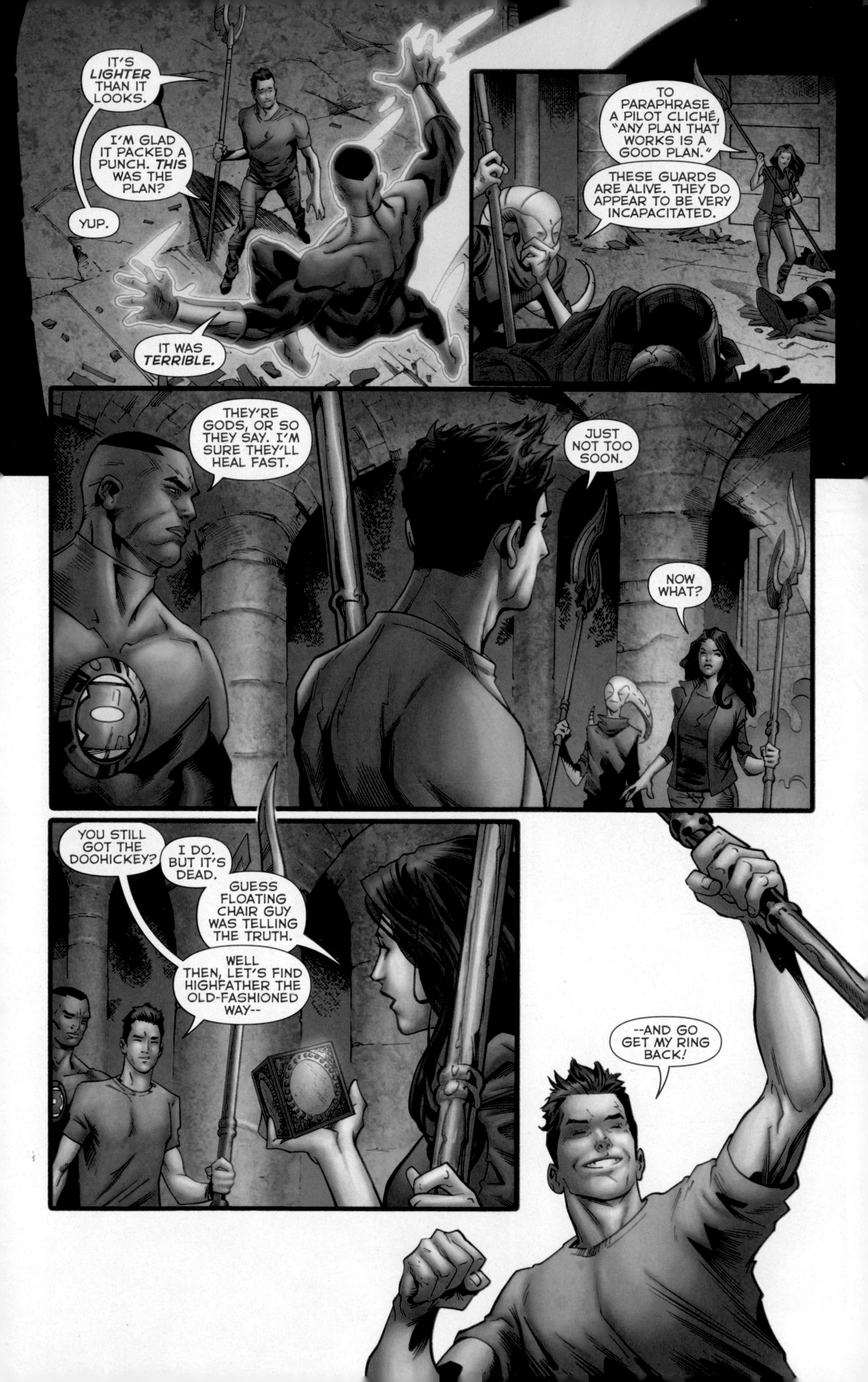
IT'S *LIGHTER* THAN IT LOOKS.
I'M GLAD IT PACKED A PUNCH. *THIS* WAS THE PLAN?
YUP.
IT WAS *TERRIBLE.*
TO PARAPHRASE A PILOT CLICHÉ, "ANY PLAN THAT WORKS IS A GOOD PLAN."
THESE GUARDS ARE ALIVE. THEY DO APPEAR TO BE VERY INCAPACITATED.
THEY'RE GODS, OR SO THEY SAY. I'M SURE THEY'LL HEAL FAST.
JUST NOT TOO SOON.
NOW WHAT?
YOU STILL GOT THE DOOHICKEY?
I DO. BUT IT'S DEAD.
GUESS FLOATING CHAIR GUY WAS TELLING THE TRUTH.
WELL THEN, LET'S FIND HIGHFATHER THE OLD-FASHIONED WAY--
--AND GO GET MY RING BACK!

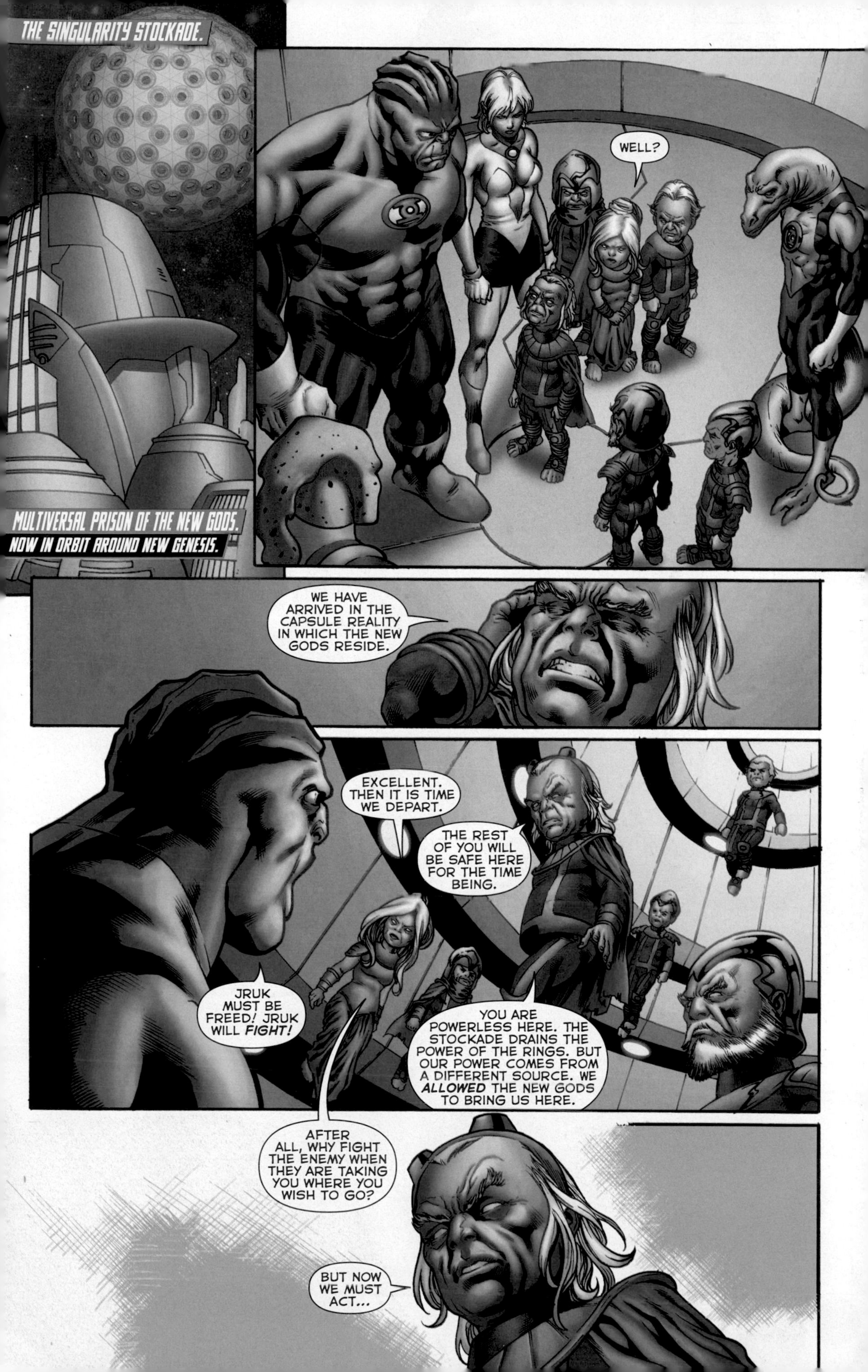
THE SINGULARITY STOCKADE.
MULTIVERSAL PRISON OF THE NEW GODS. NOW IN ORBIT AROUND NEW GENESIS.
WELL?
WE HAVE ARRIVED IN THE CAPSULE REALITY IN WHICH THE NEW GODS RESIDE.
EXCELLENT. THEN IT IS TIME WE DEPART.
THE REST OF YOU WILL BE SAFE HERE FOR THE TIME BEING.
JRUK MUST BE FREED! JRUK WILL FIGHT!
YOU ARE POWERLESS HERE. THE STOCKADE DRAINS THE POWER OF THE RINGS. BUT OUR POWER COMES FROM A DIFFERENT SOURCE. WE ALLOWED THE NEW GODS TO BRING US HERE.
AFTER ALL, WHY FIGHT THE ENEMY WHEN THEY ARE TAKING YOU WHERE YOU WISH TO GO?
BUT NOW WE MUST ACT...

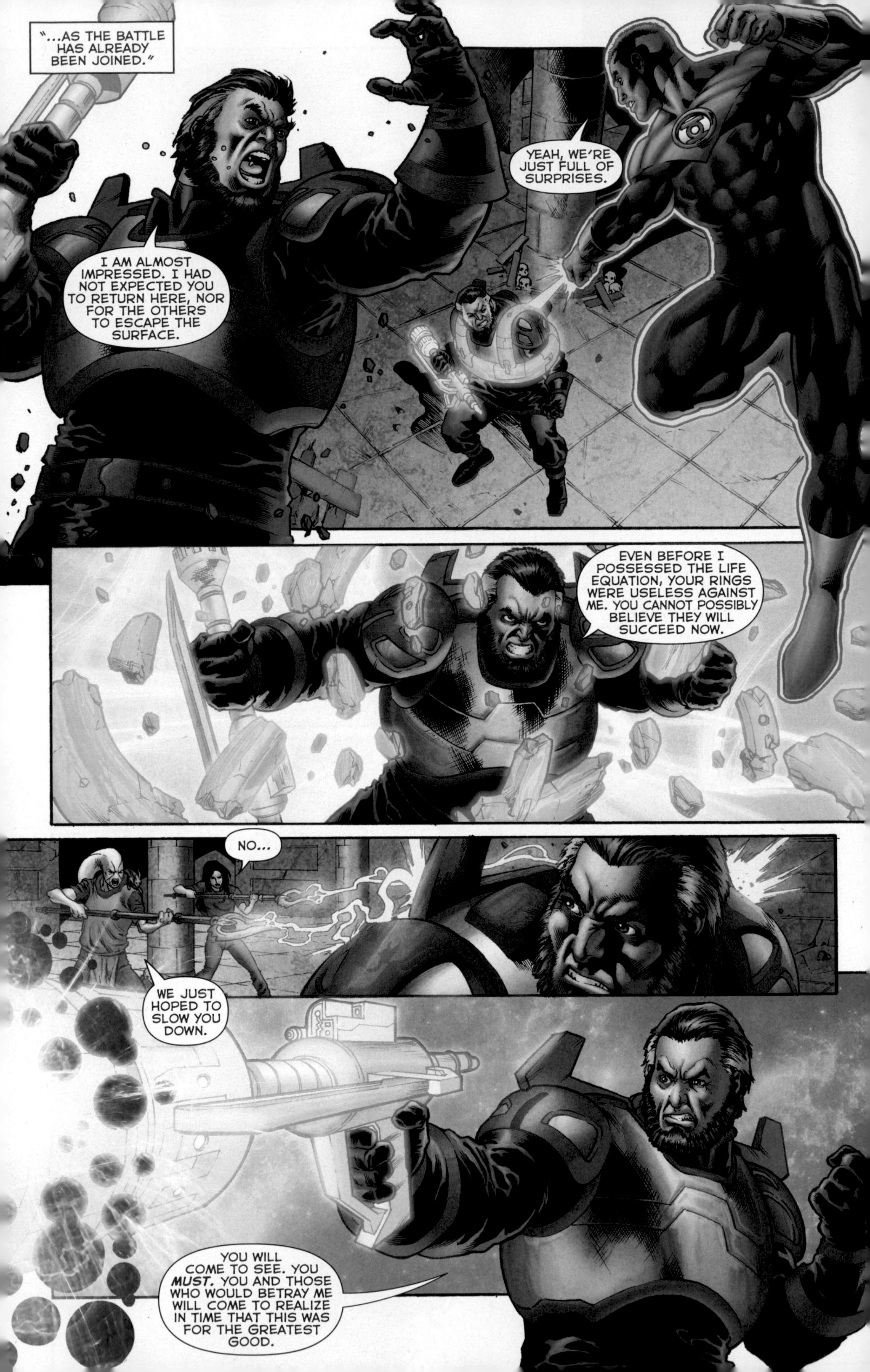
"...AS THE BATTLE HAS ALREADY BEEN JOINED."
YEAH, WE'RE JUST FULL OF SURPRISES.
I AM ALMOST IMPRESSED. I HAD NOT EXPECTED YOU TO RETURN HERE, NOR FOR THE OTHERS TO ESCAPE THE SURFACE.
EVEN BEFORE I POSSESSED THE LIFE EQUATION, YOUR RINGS WERE USELESS AGAINST ME. YOU CANNOT POSSIBLY BELIEVE THEY WILL SUCCEED NOW.
NO...
WE JUST HOPED TO SLOW YOU DOWN.
YOU WILL COME TO SEE. YOU MUST. YOU AND THOSE WHO WOULD BETRAY ME WILL COME TO REALIZE IN TIME THAT THIS WAS FOR THE GREATEST GOOD.

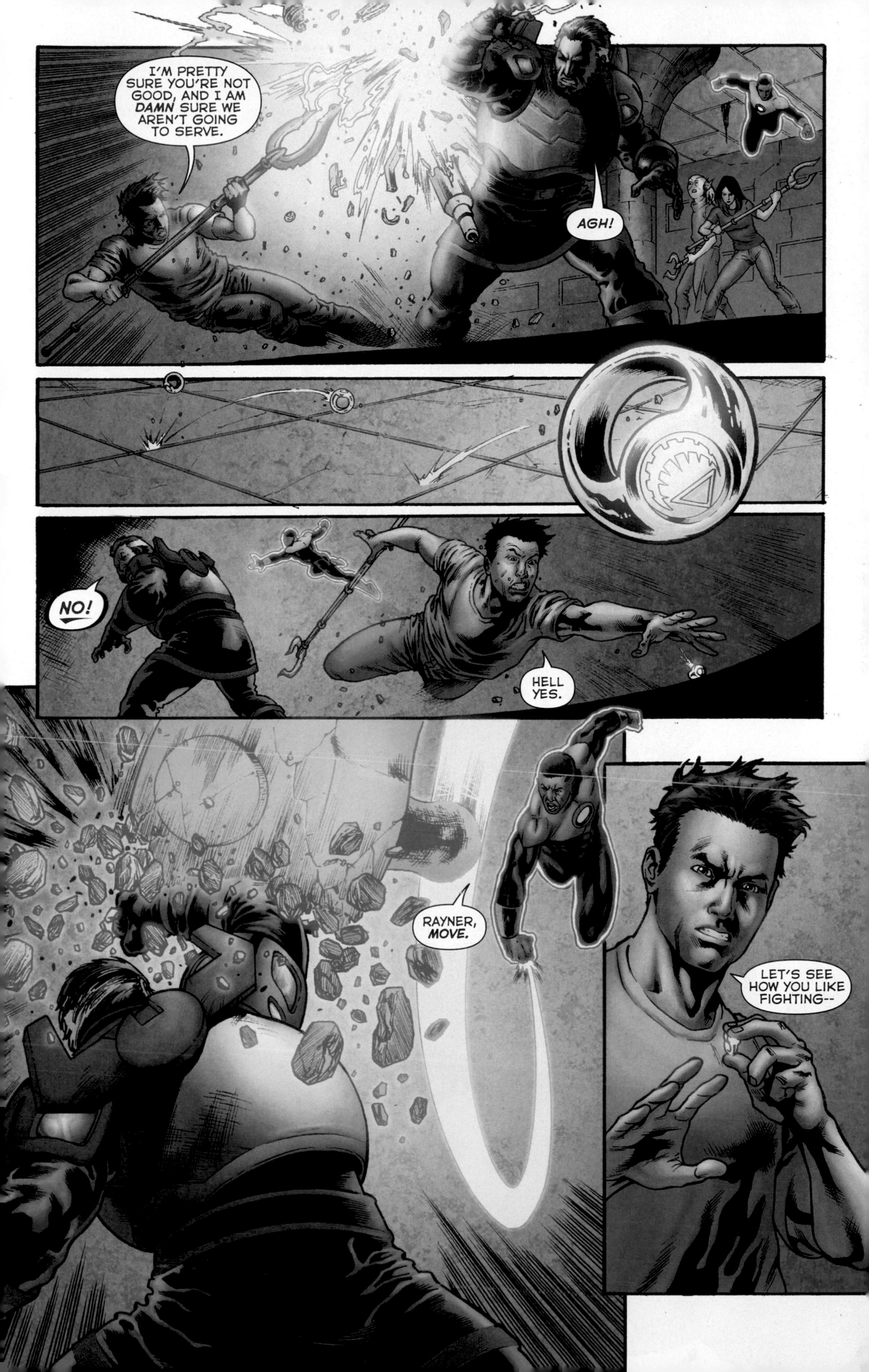
I'M PRETTY SURE YOU'RE NOT GOOD, AND I AM DAMN SURE WE AREN'T GOING TO SERVE.
AGH!
NO!
HELL YES.
RAYNER, MOVE.
LET'S SEE HOW YOU LIKE FIGHTING--

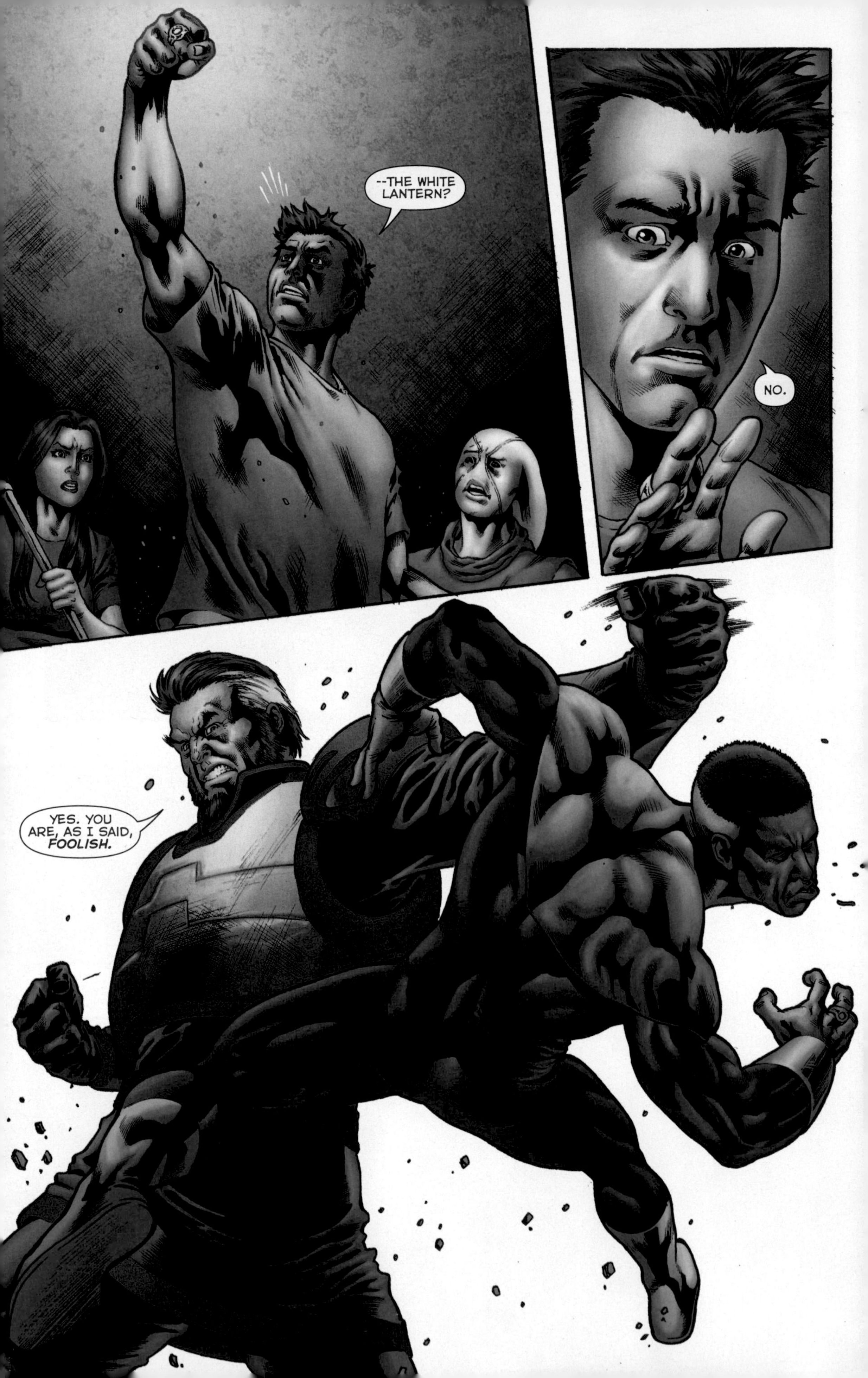
--THE WHITE LANTERN?
NO.
YES. YOU ARE, AS I SAID, FOOLISH.

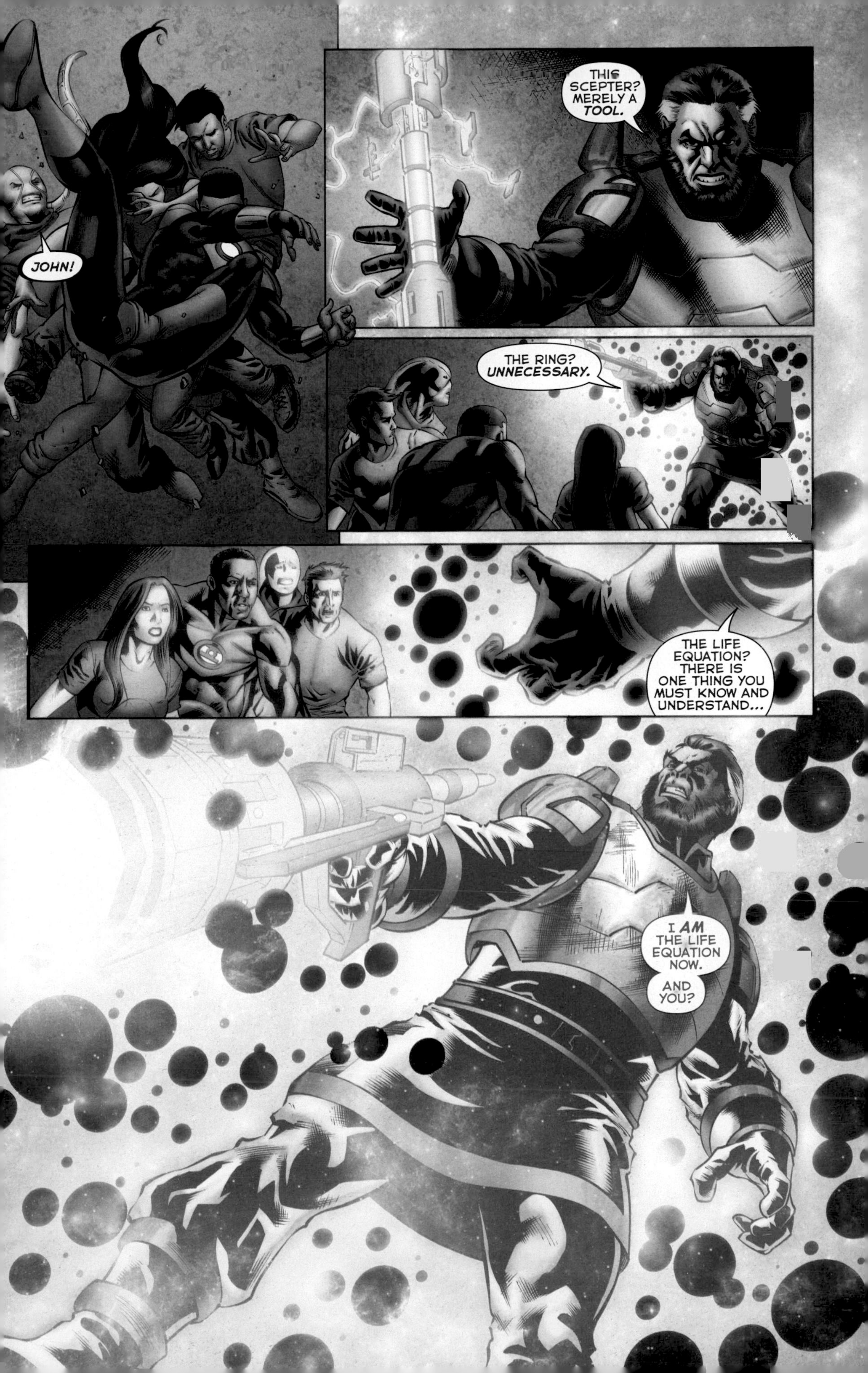
JOHN!
THIS SCEPTER? MERELY A TOOL.
THE RING? UNNECESSARY.
THE LIFE EQUATION? THERE IS ONE THING YOU MUST KNOW AND UNDERSTAND...
I AM THE LIFE EQUATION NOW.
AND YOU?

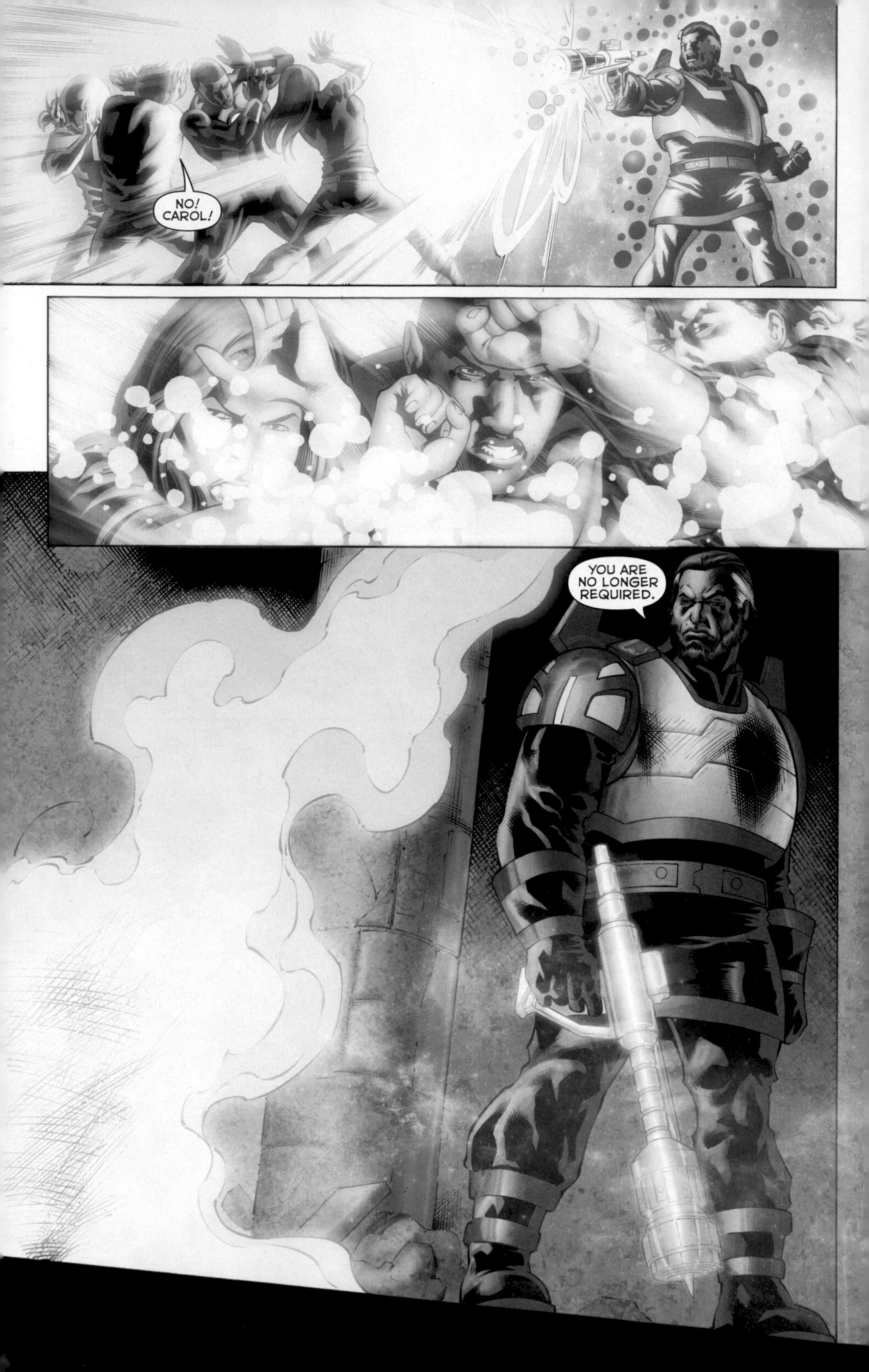
NO! CAROL!
YOU ARE NO LONGER REQUIRED.

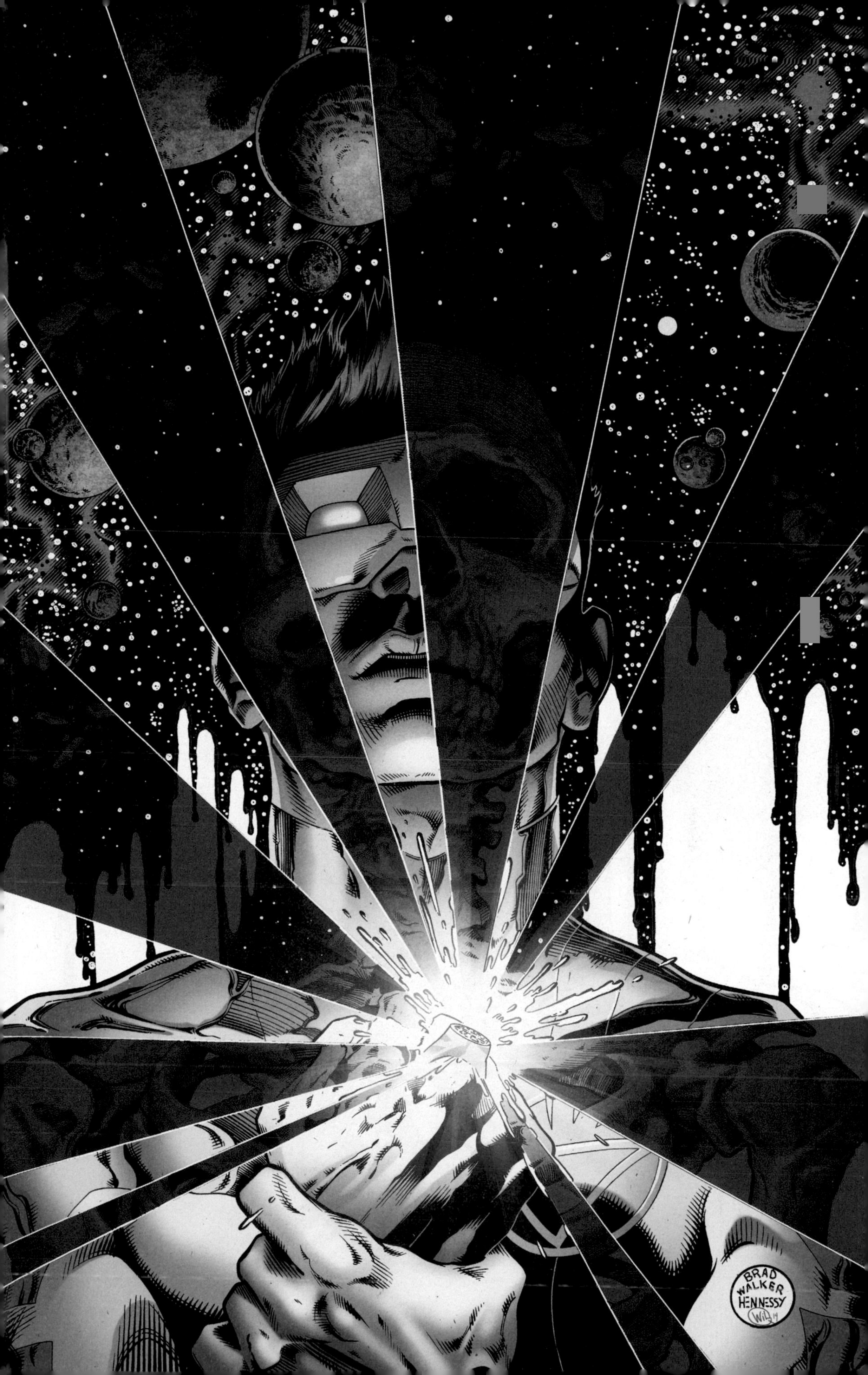
BRAD WALKER HENNESSY

IT ALL ENDS HERE: PART 1

JUSTIN JORDAN writer **DIOGENES NEVES RONAN CLIQUET** pencillers **MARC DEERING RONAN CLIQUET** inkers **WIL QUINTANA ANDREW DALHOUSE** colorists **DAVE SHARPE** letterer cover art by **WALKER, HENNESSY** and **QUINTANA**

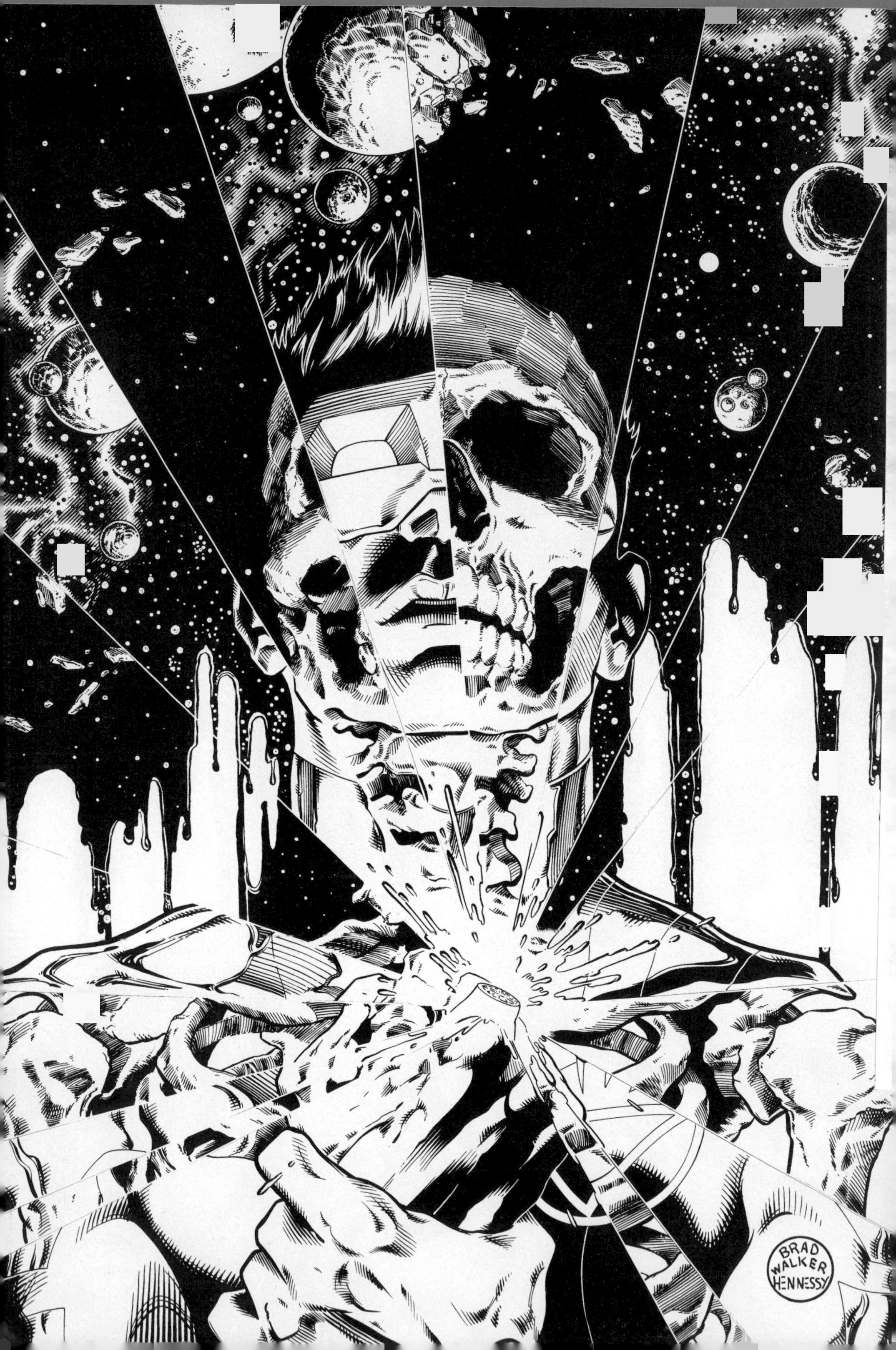
BRAD WALKER HENNESSY

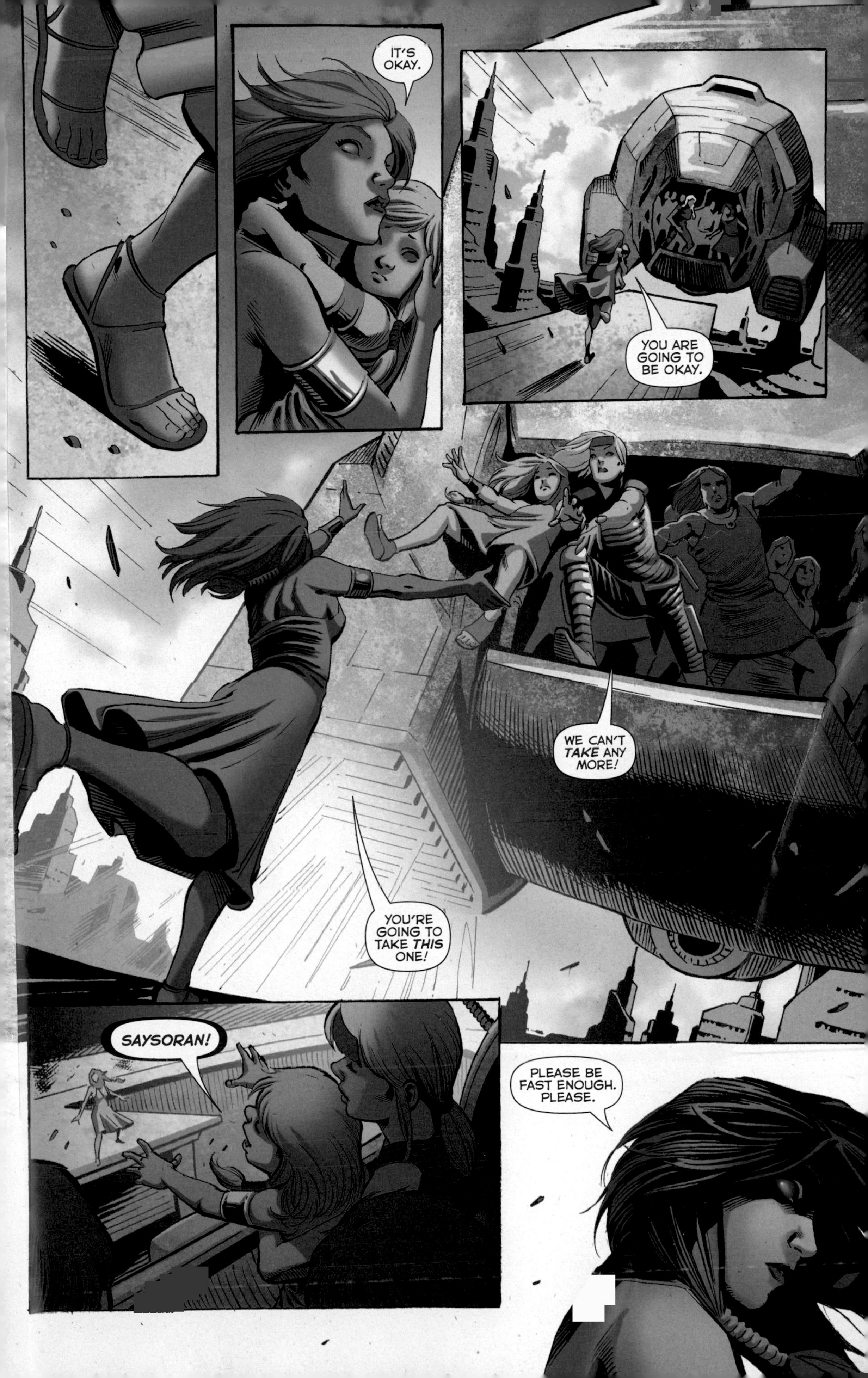
IT'S OKAY.
YOU ARE GOING TO BE OKAY.
WE CAN'T *TAKE* ANY MORE!
YOU'RE GOING TO TAKE *THIS* ONE!
SAYSORAN!
PLEASE BE FAST ENOUGH. PLEASE.

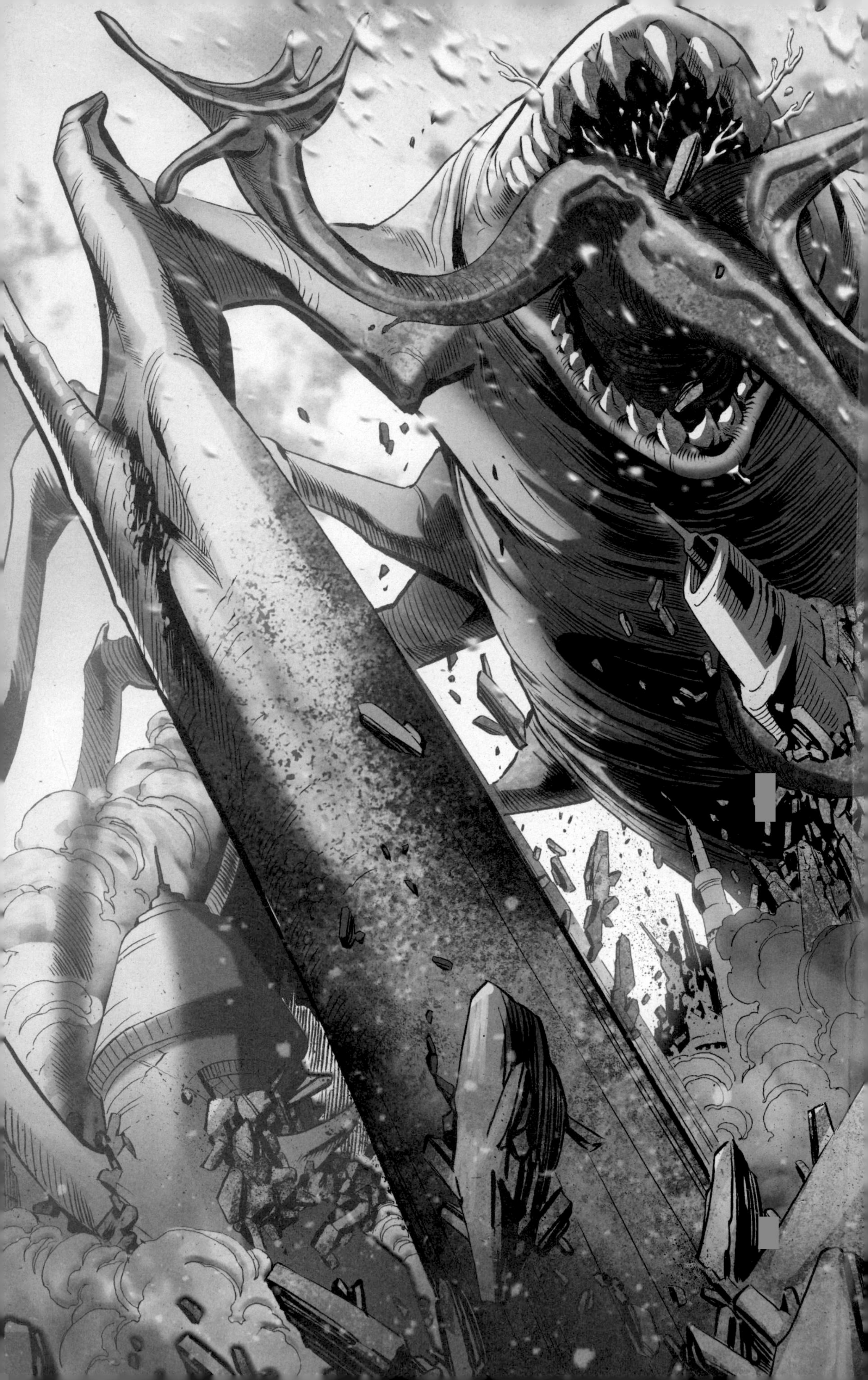

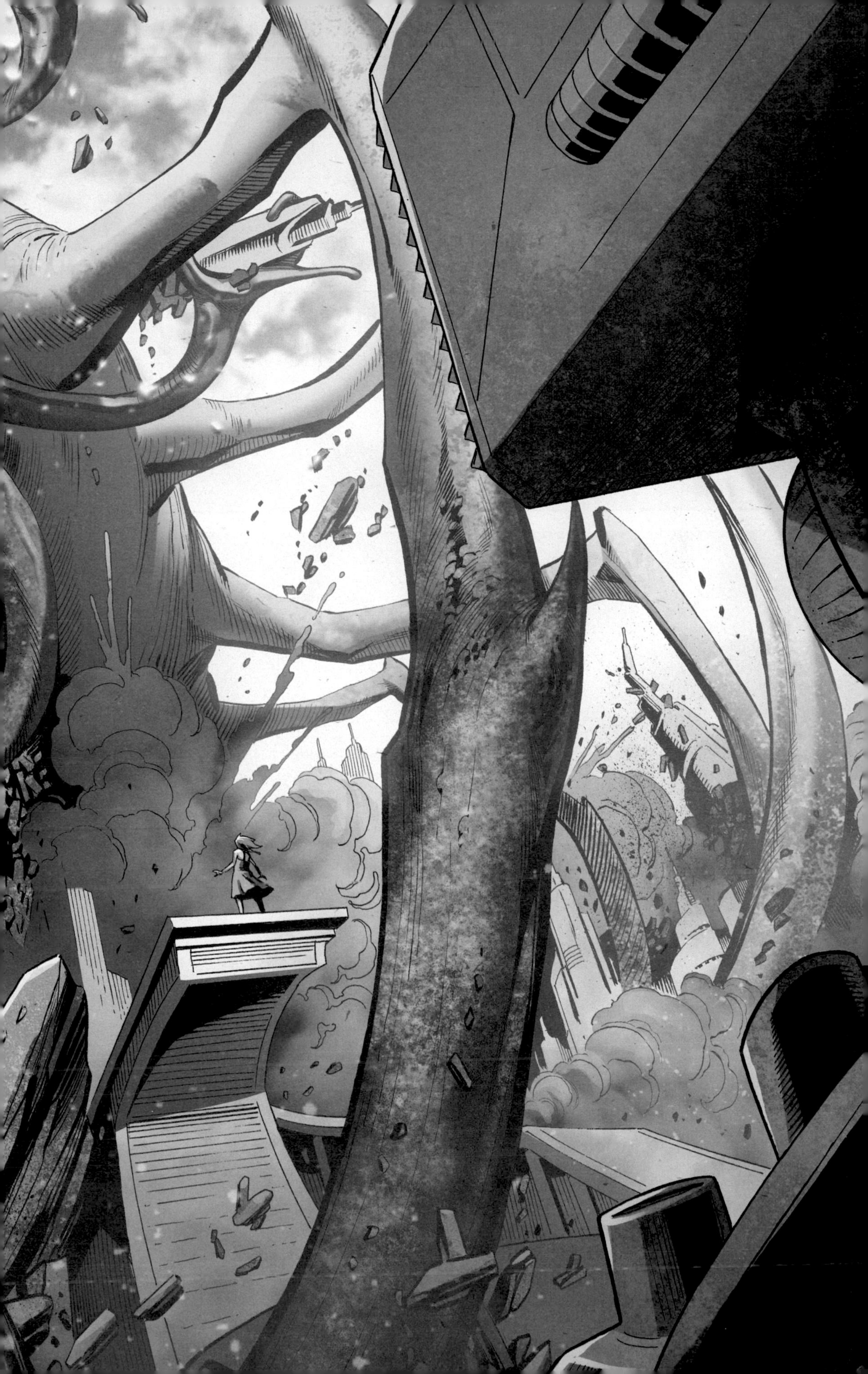

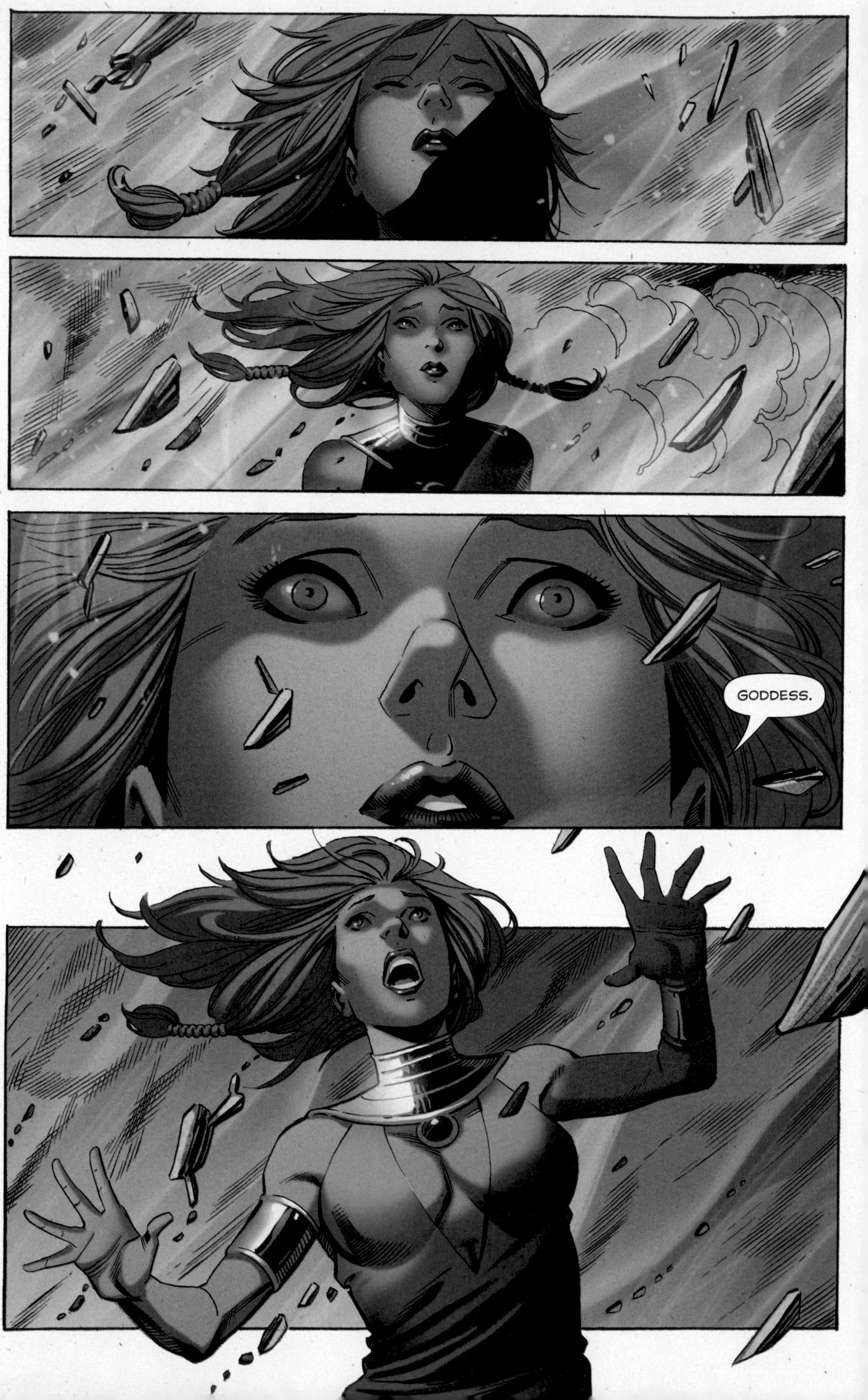
GODDESS.

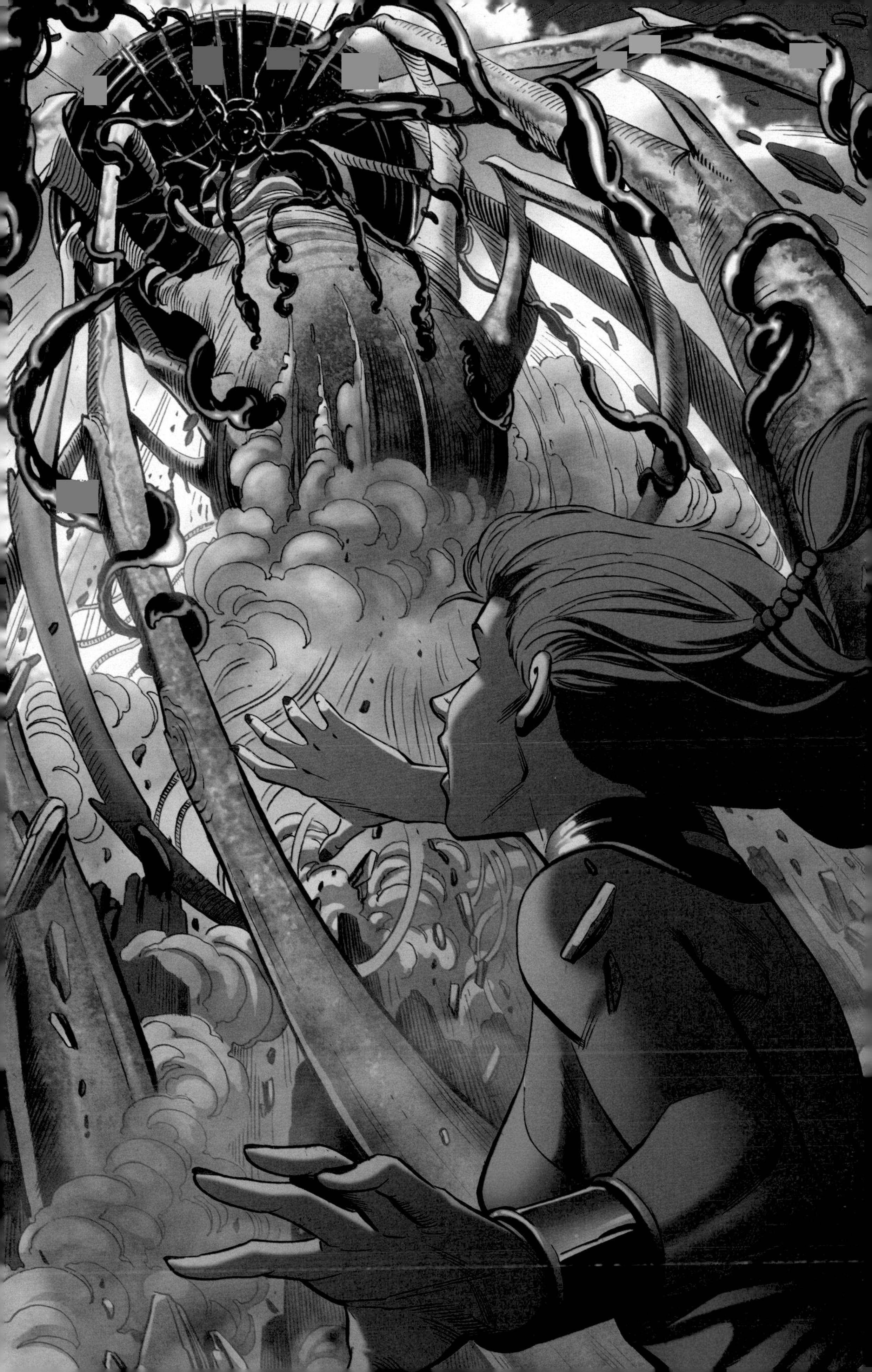

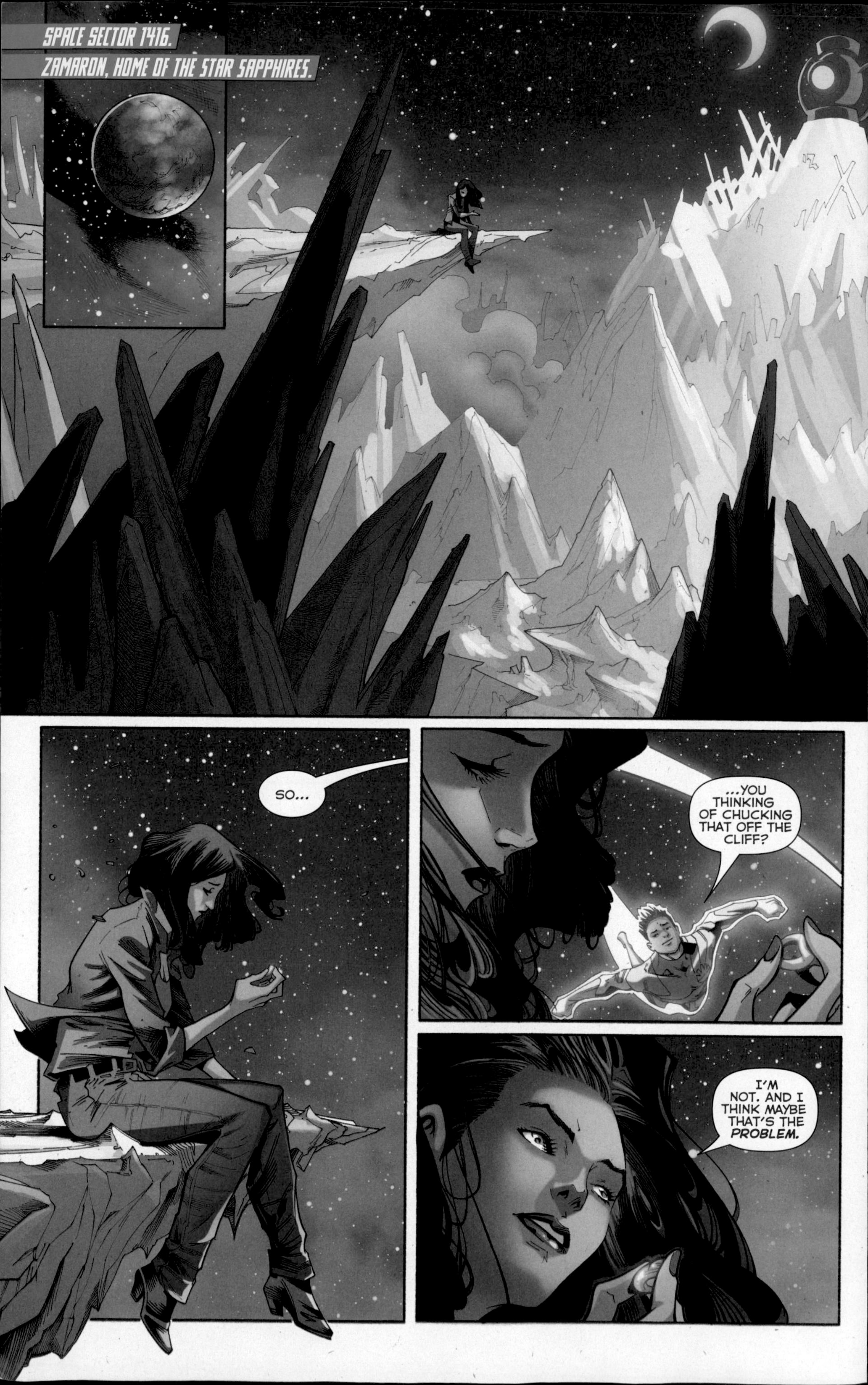
SPACE SECTOR 1416.
ZAMARON, HOME OF THE STAR SAPPHIRES.
SO...
...YOU THINKING OF CHUCKING THAT OFF THE CLIFF?
I'M NOT. AND I THINK MAYBE THAT'S THE PROBLEM.

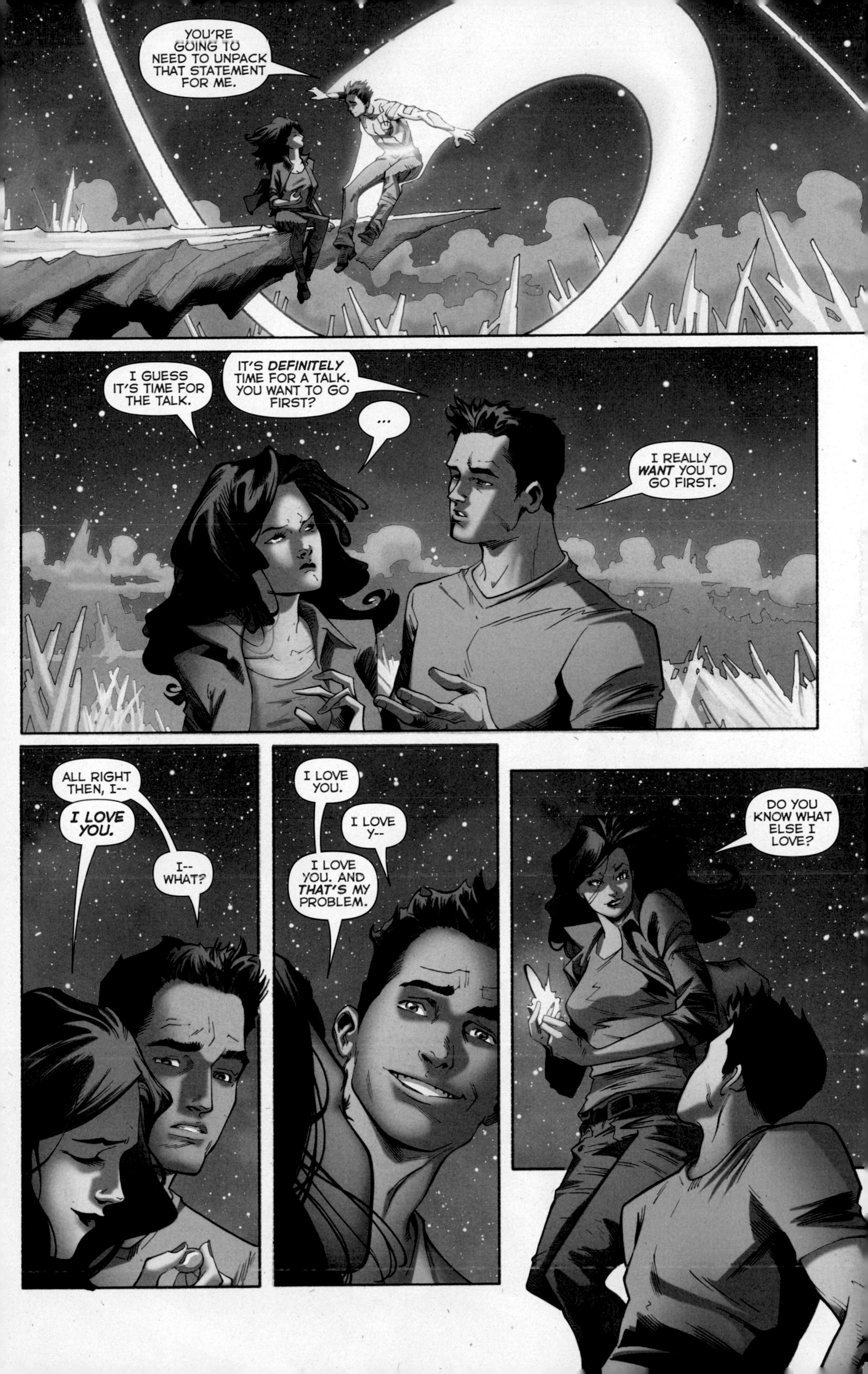
YOU'RE GOING TO NEED TO UNPACK THAT STATEMENT FOR ME.
I GUESS IT'S TIME FOR THE TALK.
IT'S *DEFINITELY* TIME FOR A TALK. YOU WANT TO GO FIRST?
...
I REALLY *WANT* YOU TO GO FIRST.
ALL RIGHT THEN, I--
I LOVE YOU.
I-- WHAT?
I LOVE YOU.
I LOVE Y--
I LOVE YOU. AND *THAT'S* MY PROBLEM.
DO YOU KNOW WHAT ELSE I LOVE?

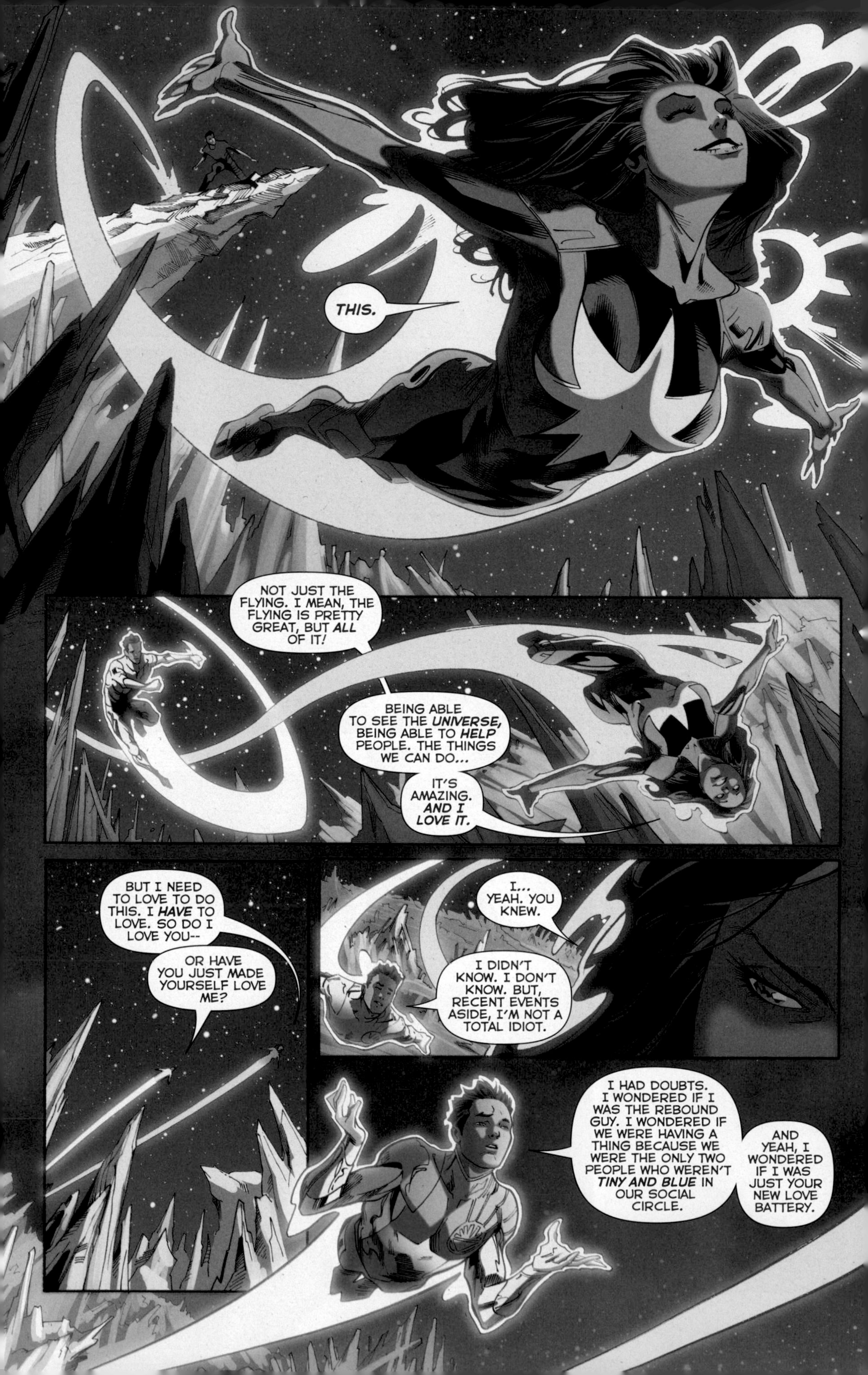
THIS.
NOT JUST THE FLYING. I MEAN, THE FLYING IS PRETTY GREAT, BUT ALL OF IT!
BEING ABLE TO SEE THE UNIVERSE, BEING ABLE TO HELP PEOPLE. THE THINGS WE CAN DO...
IT'S AMAZING. AND I LOVE IT.
BUT I NEED TO LOVE TO DO THIS. I HAVE TO LOVE. SO DO I LOVE YOU--
OR HAVE YOU JUST MADE YOURSELF LOVE ME?
I... YEAH. YOU KNEW.
I DIDN'T KNOW. I DON'T KNOW. BUT, RECENT EVENTS ASIDE, I'M NOT A TOTAL IDIOT.
I HAD DOUBTS. I WONDERED IF I WAS THE REBOUND GUY. I WONDERED IF WE WERE HAVING A THING BECAUSE WE WERE THE ONLY TWO PEOPLE WHO WEREN'T TINY AND BLUE IN OUR SOCIAL CIRCLE.
AND YEAH, I WONDERED IF I WAS JUST YOUR NEW LOVE BATTERY.

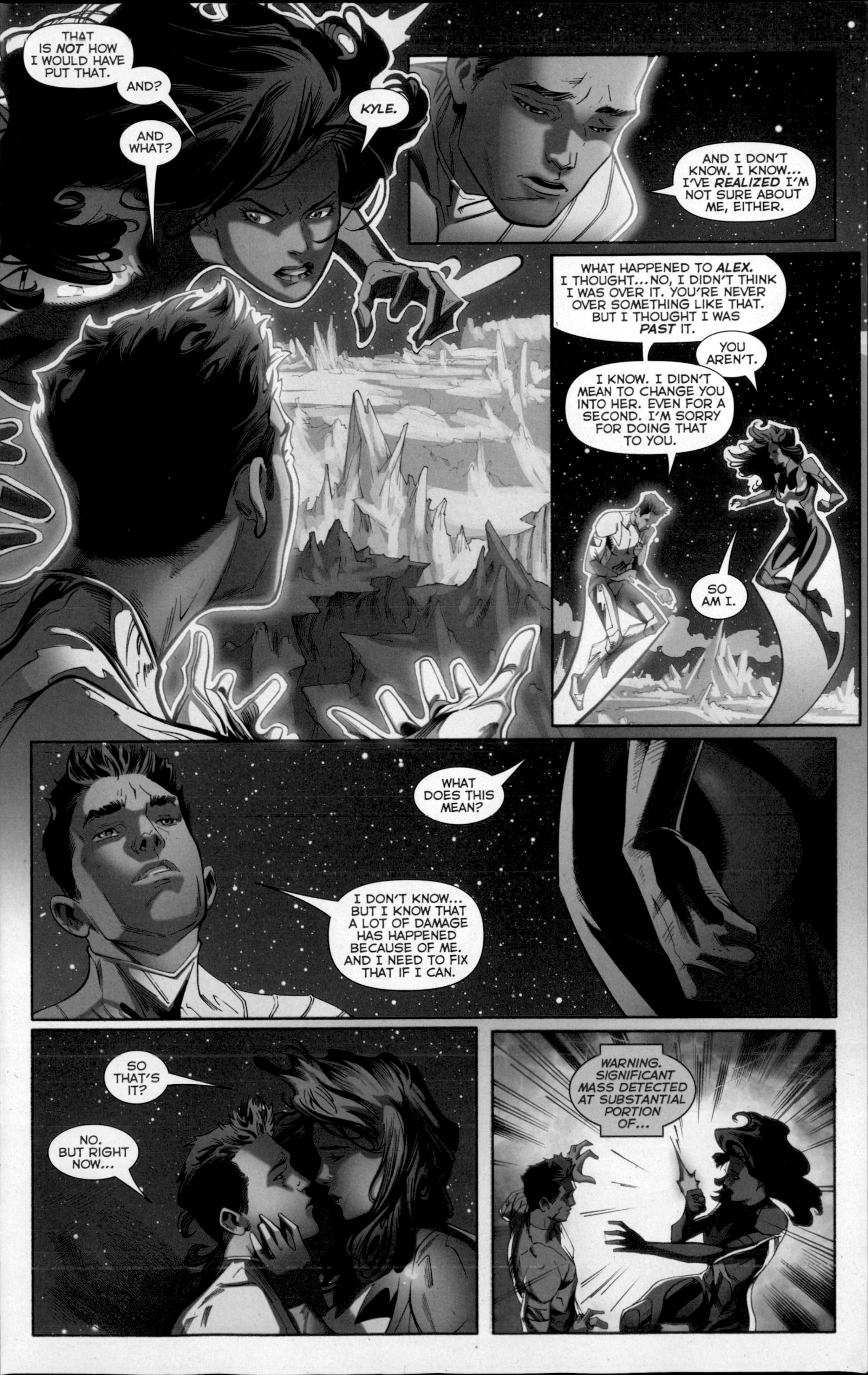

THAT IS NOT HOW I WOULD HAVE PUT THAT.
AND?
AND WHAT?
KYLE.
AND I DON'T KNOW. I KNOW... I'VE REALIZED I'M NOT SURE ABOUT ME, EITHER.
WHAT HAPPENED TO ALEX. I THOUGHT...NO, I DIDN'T THINK I WAS OVER IT. YOU'RE NEVER OVER SOMETHING LIKE THAT. BUT I THOUGHT I WAS PAST IT.
YOU AREN'T.
I KNOW. I DIDN'T MEAN TO CHANGE YOU INTO HER. EVEN FOR A SECOND. I'M SORRY FOR DOING THAT TO YOU.
SO AM I.
WHAT DOES THIS MEAN?
I DON'T KNOW... BUT I KNOW THAT A LOT OF DAMAGE HAS HAPPENED BECAUSE OF ME. AND I NEED TO FIX THAT IF I CAN.
SO THAT'S IT?
NO. BUT RIGHT NOW...
WARNING. SIGNIFICANT MASS DETECTED AT SUBSTANTIAL PORTION OF...

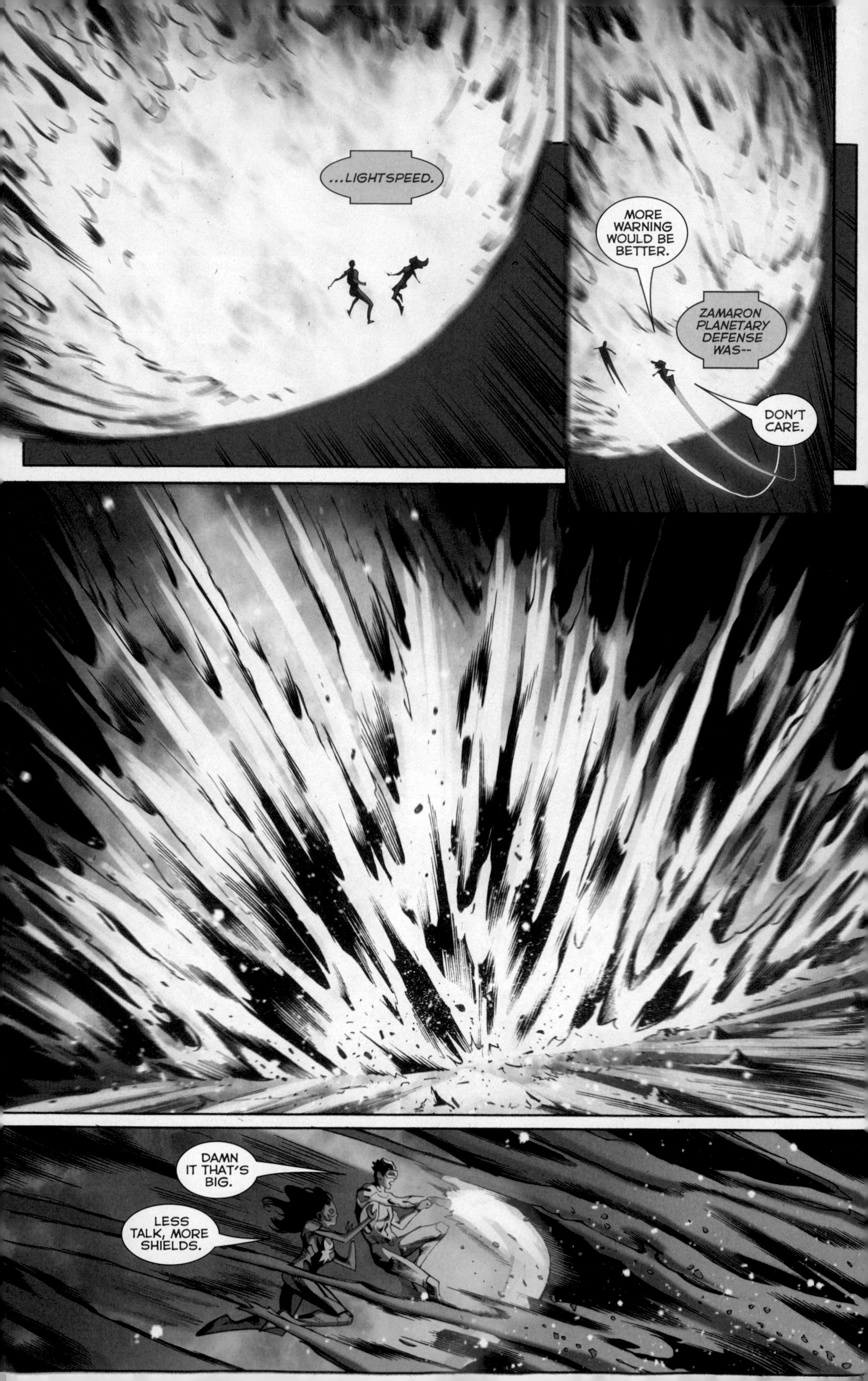
...LIGHTSPEED.
MORE WARNING WOULD BE BETTER.
ZAMARON PLANETARY DEFENSE WAS--
DON'T CARE.
DAMN IT THAT'S BIG.
LESS TALK, MORE SHIELDS.

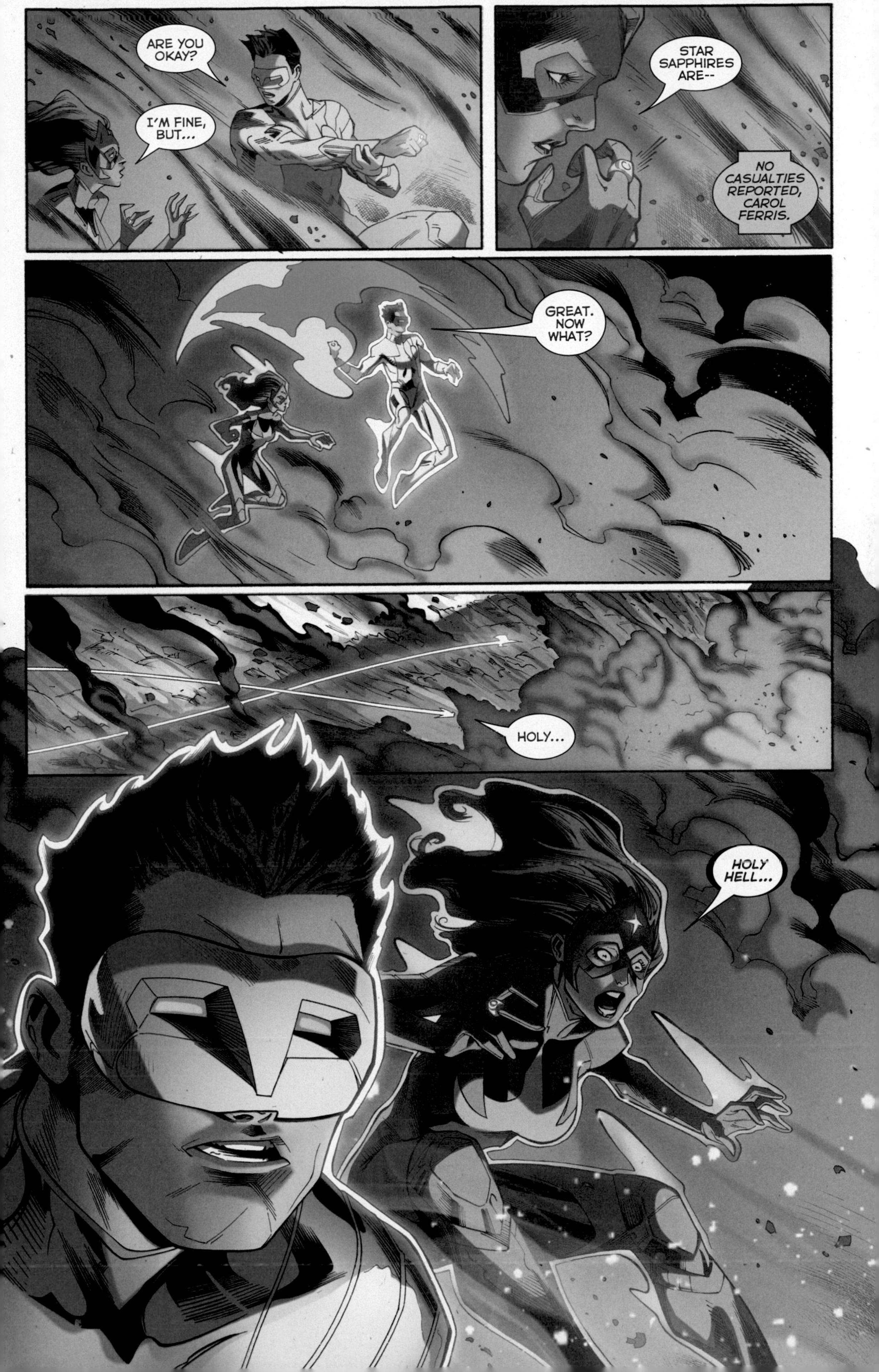
ARE YOU OKAY?
I'M FINE, BUT...
STAR SAPPHIRES ARE--
NO CASUALTIES REPORTED, CAROL FERRIS.
GREAT. NOW WHAT?
HOLY...
HOLY HELL...

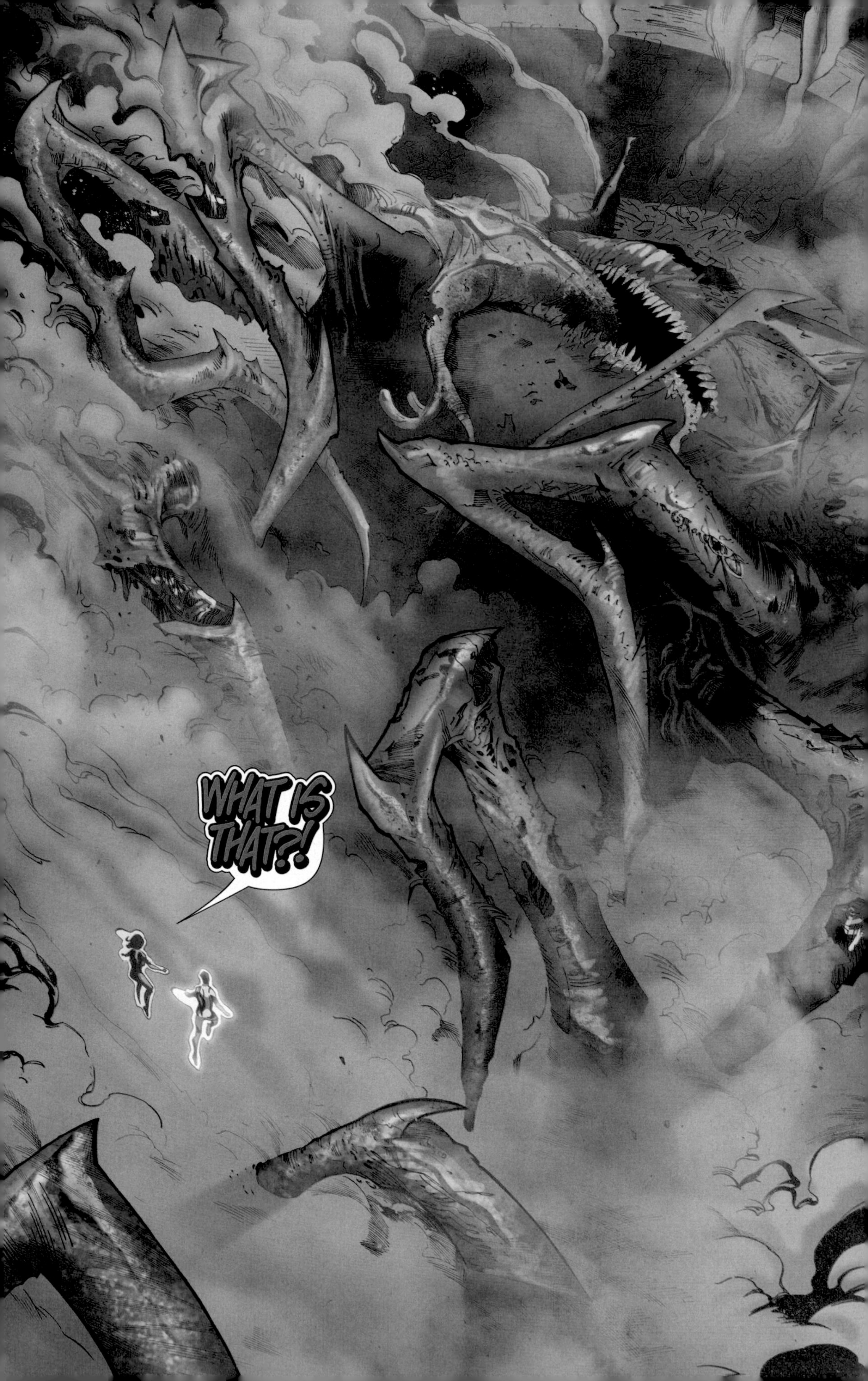
WHAT IS THAT?!

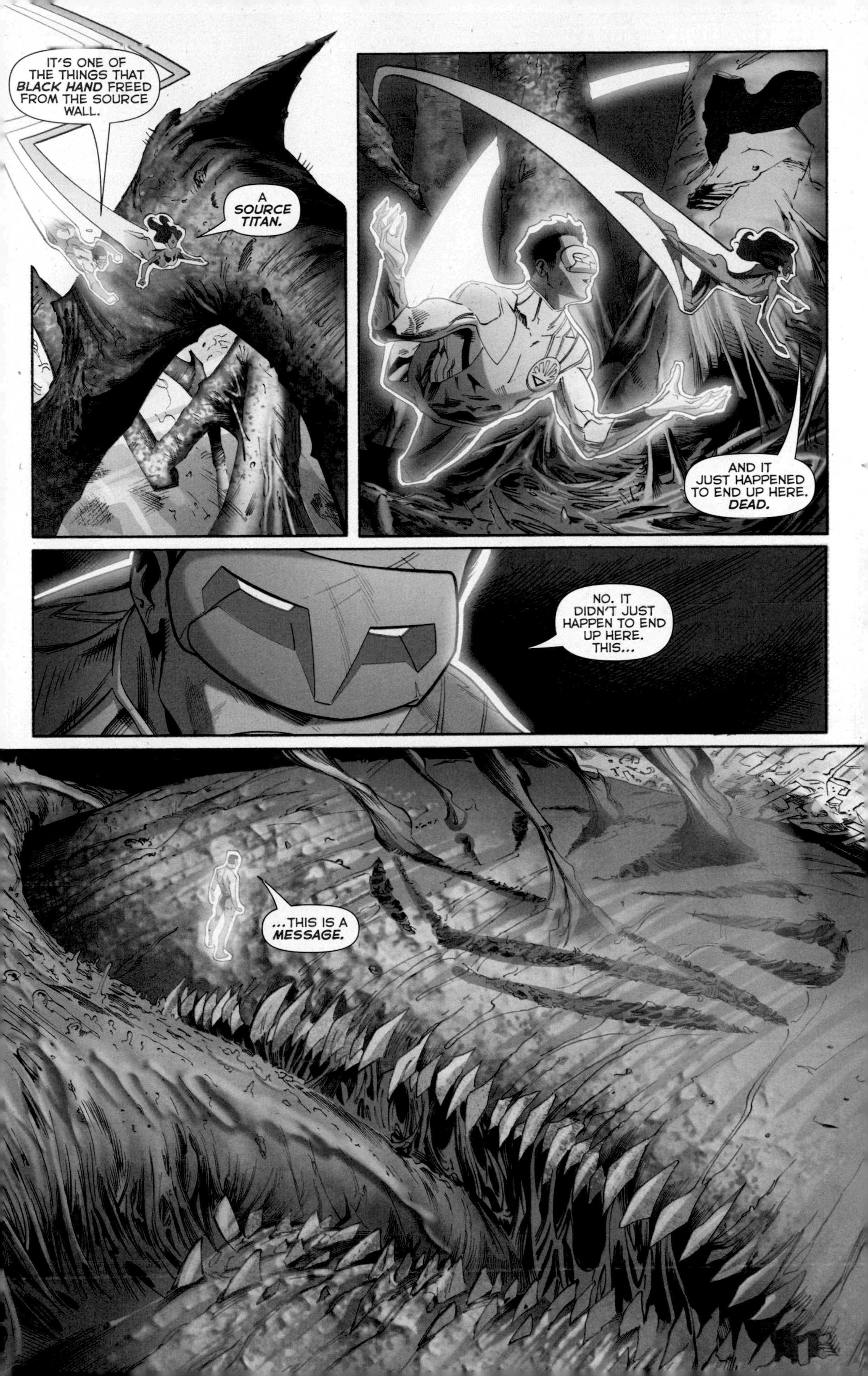

IT'S ONE OF THE THINGS THAT BLACK HAND FREED FROM THE SOURCE WALL.
A SOURCE TITAN.
AND IT JUST HAPPENED TO END UP HERE. DEAD.
NO. IT DIDN'T JUST HAPPEN TO END UP HERE. THIS...
...THIS IS A MESSAGE.

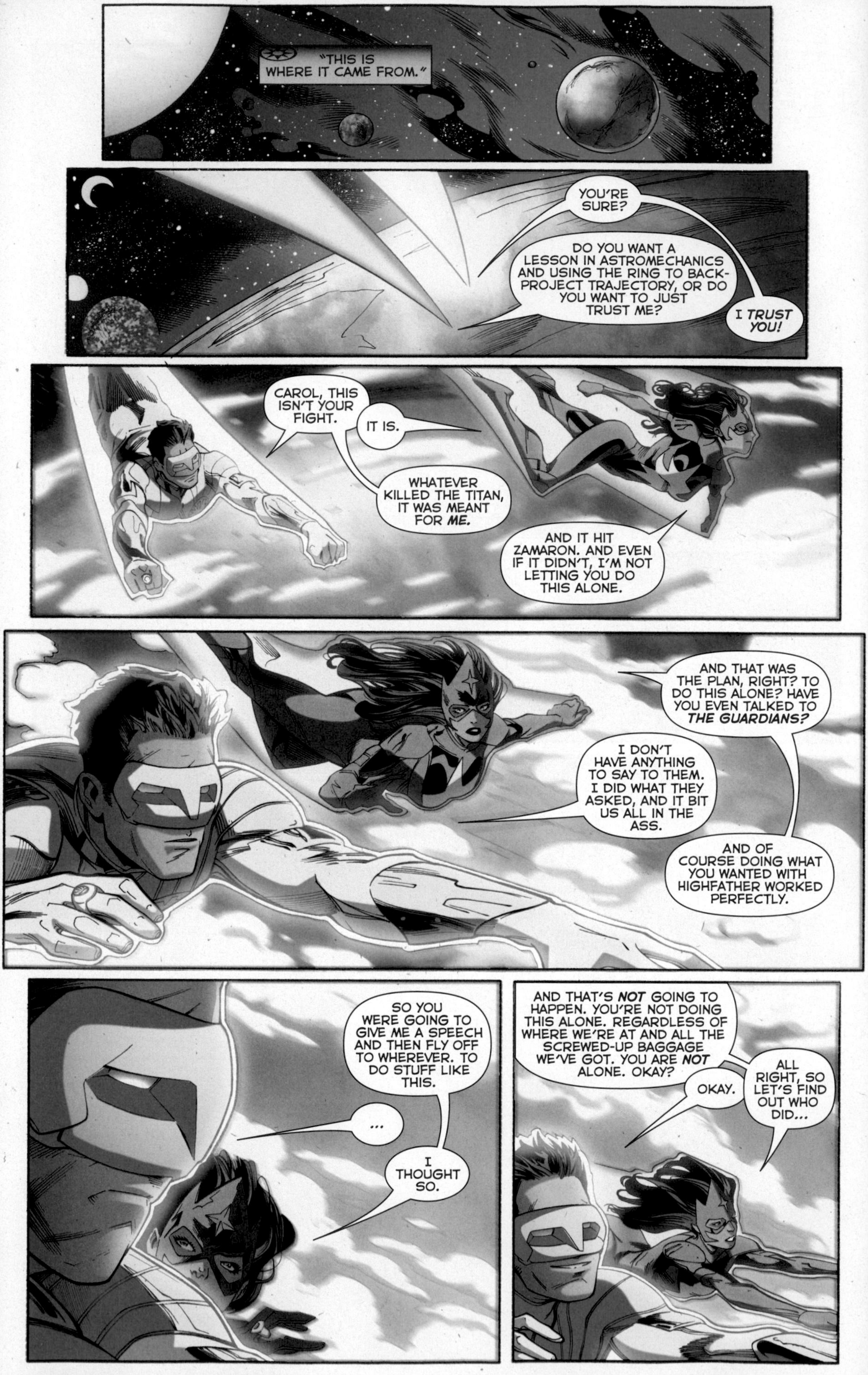
"THIS IS WHERE IT CAME FROM."
YOU'RE SURE?
DO YOU WANT A LESSON IN ASTROMECHANICS AND USING THE RING TO BACK-PROJECT TRAJECTORY, OR DO YOU WANT TO JUST TRUST ME?
I *TRUST YOU!*
CAROL, THIS ISN'T YOUR FIGHT.
IT IS.
WHATEVER KILLED THE TITAN, IT WAS MEANT FOR *ME.*
AND IT HIT ZAMARON. AND EVEN IF IT DIDN'T, I'M NOT LETTING YOU DO THIS ALONE.
AND THAT WAS THE PLAN, RIGHT? TO DO THIS ALONE? HAVE YOU EVEN TALKED TO *THE GUARDIANS?*
I DON'T HAVE ANYTHING TO SAY TO THEM. I DID WHAT THEY ASKED, AND IT BIT US ALL IN THE ASS.
AND OF COURSE DOING WHAT YOU WANTED WITH HIGHFATHER WORKED PERFECTLY.
SO YOU WERE GOING TO GIVE ME A SPEECH AND THEN FLY OFF TO WHEREVER. TO DO STUFF LIKE THIS.
...
I THOUGHT SO.
AND THAT'S *NOT* GOING TO HAPPEN. YOU'RE NOT DOING THIS ALONE. REGARDLESS OF WHERE WE'RE AT AND ALL THE SCREWED-UP BAGGAGE WE'VE GOT. YOU ARE *NOT* ALONE. OKAY?
OKAY.
ALL RIGHT, SO LET'S FIND OUT WHO DID...

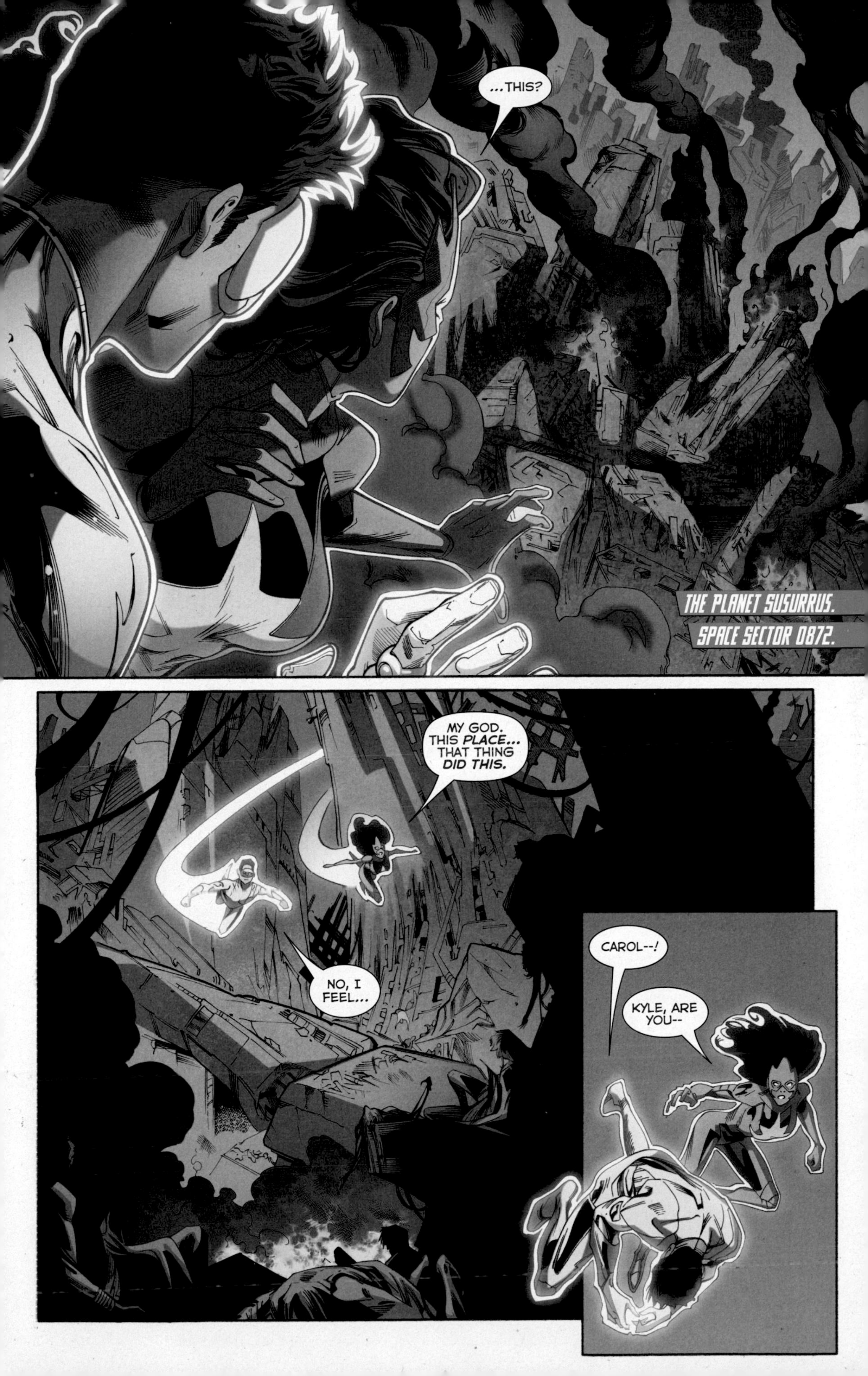
...THIS?
THE PLANET SUSURRUS.
SPACE SECTOR 0872.
MY GOD. THIS PLACE... THAT THING DID THIS.
NO, I FEEL...
CAROL--!
KYLE, ARE YOU--

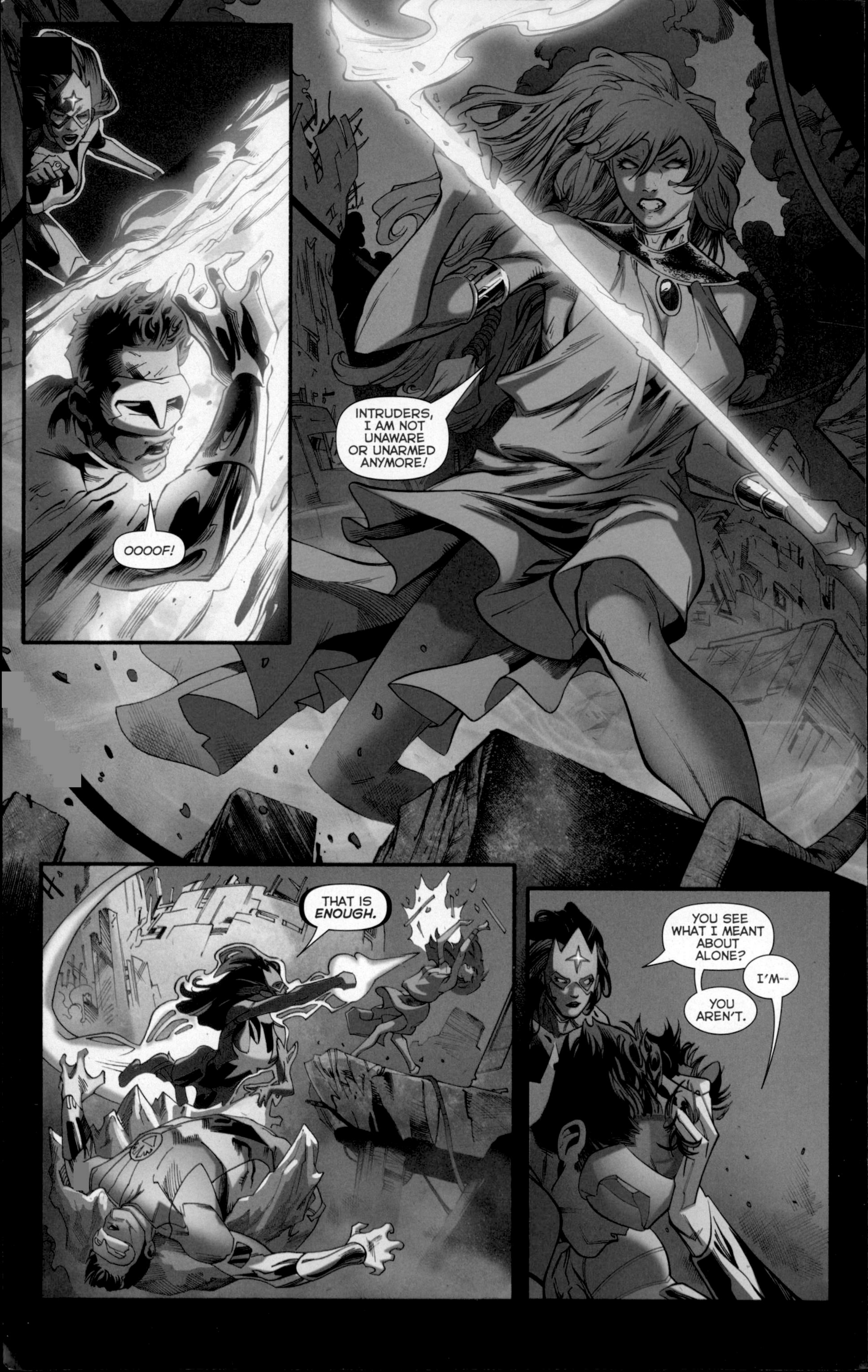
OOOOF!
INTRUDERS, I AM NOT UNAWARE OR UNARMED ANYMORE!
THAT IS ENOUGH.
YOU SEE WHAT I MEANT ABOUT ALONE?
I'M--
YOU AREN'T.

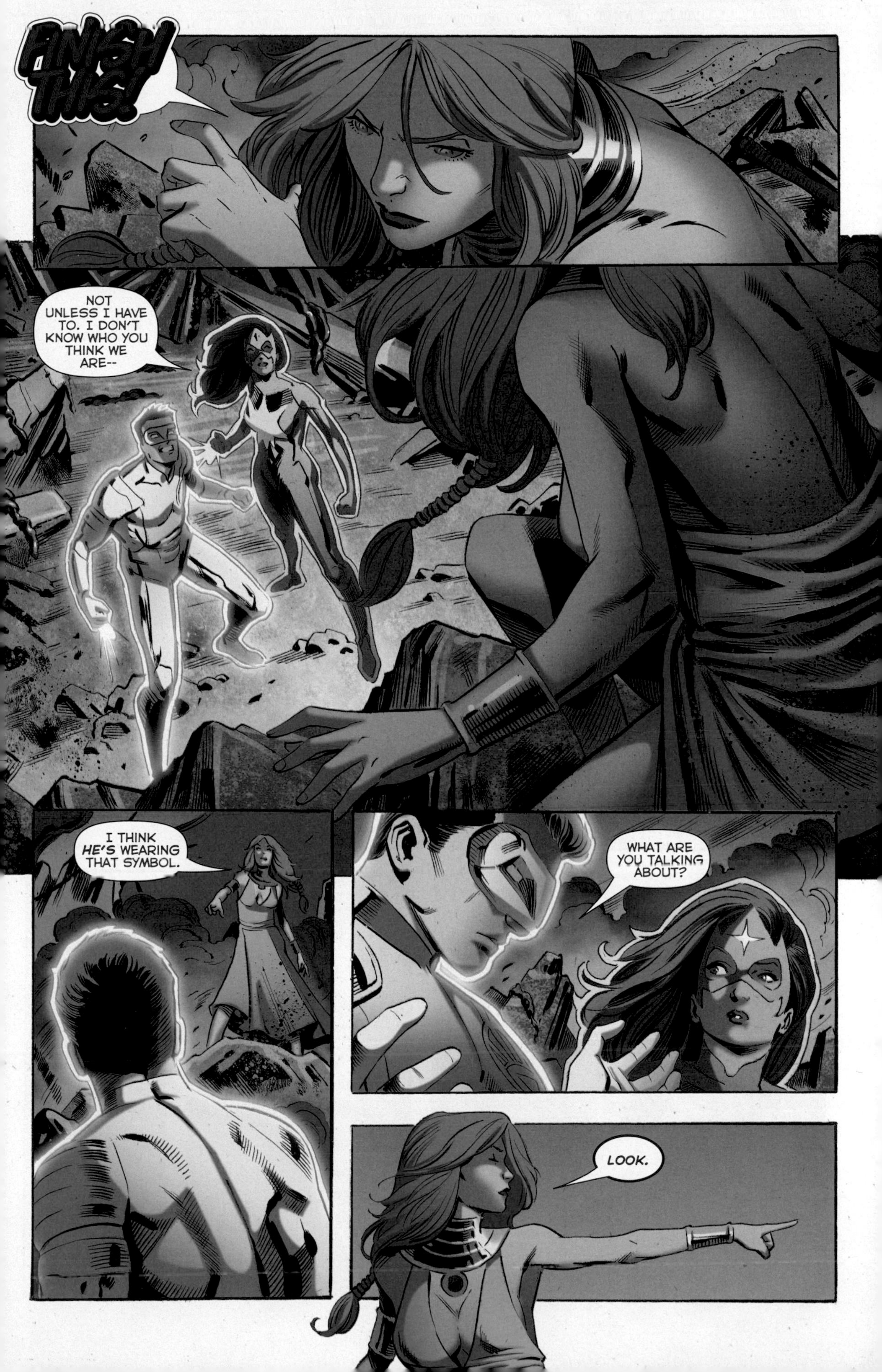
FINISH THIS!
NOT UNLESS I HAVE TO. I DON'T KNOW WHO YOU THINK WE ARE--
I THINK *HE'S* WEARING THAT SYMBOL.
WHAT ARE YOU TALKING ABOUT?
LOOK.

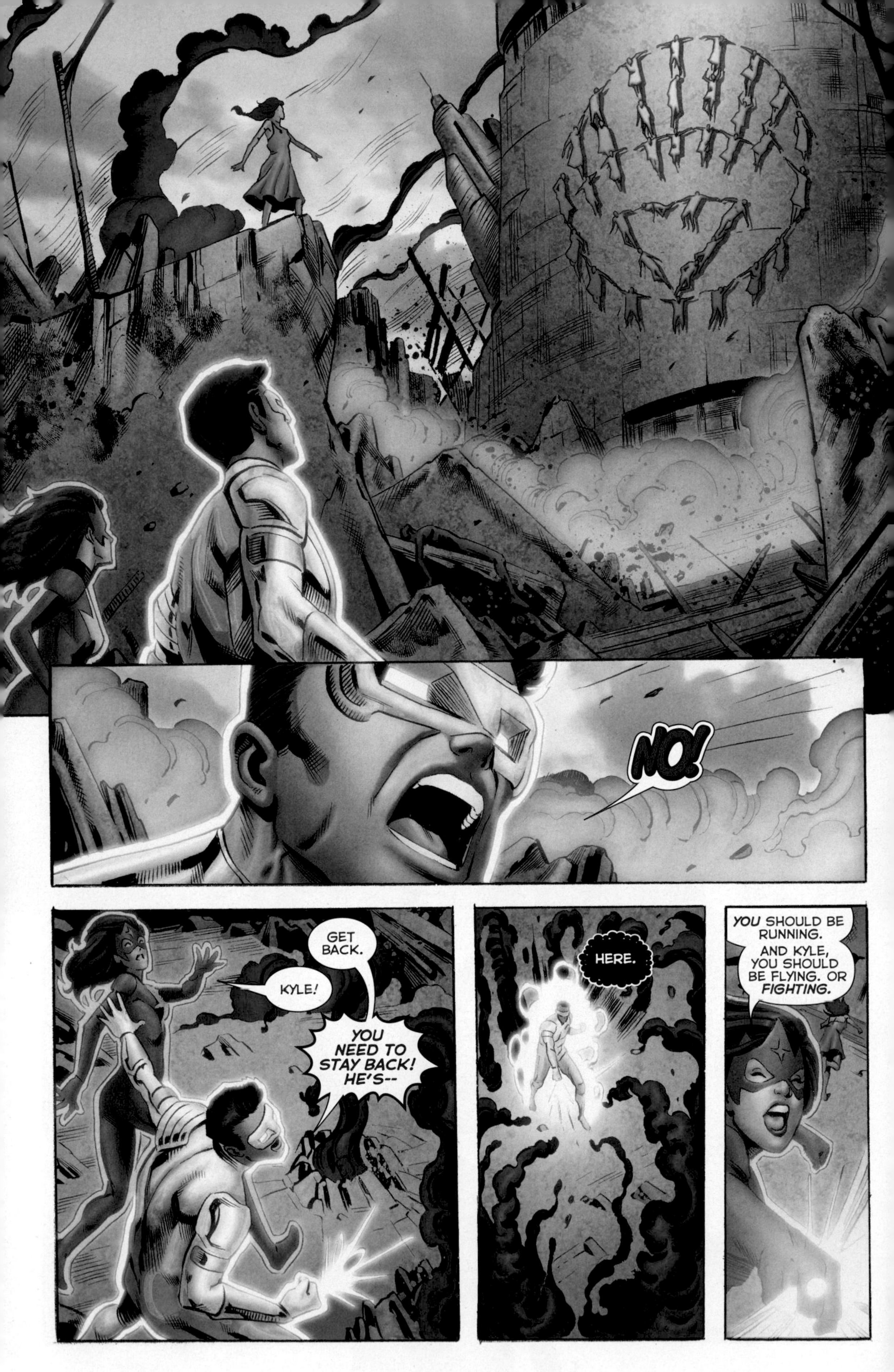
NO!
GET BACK.
KYLE!
YOU NEED TO STAY BACK! HE'S--
HERE.
YOU SHOULD BE RUNNING.
AND KYLE, YOU SHOULD BE FLYING. OR FIGHTING.

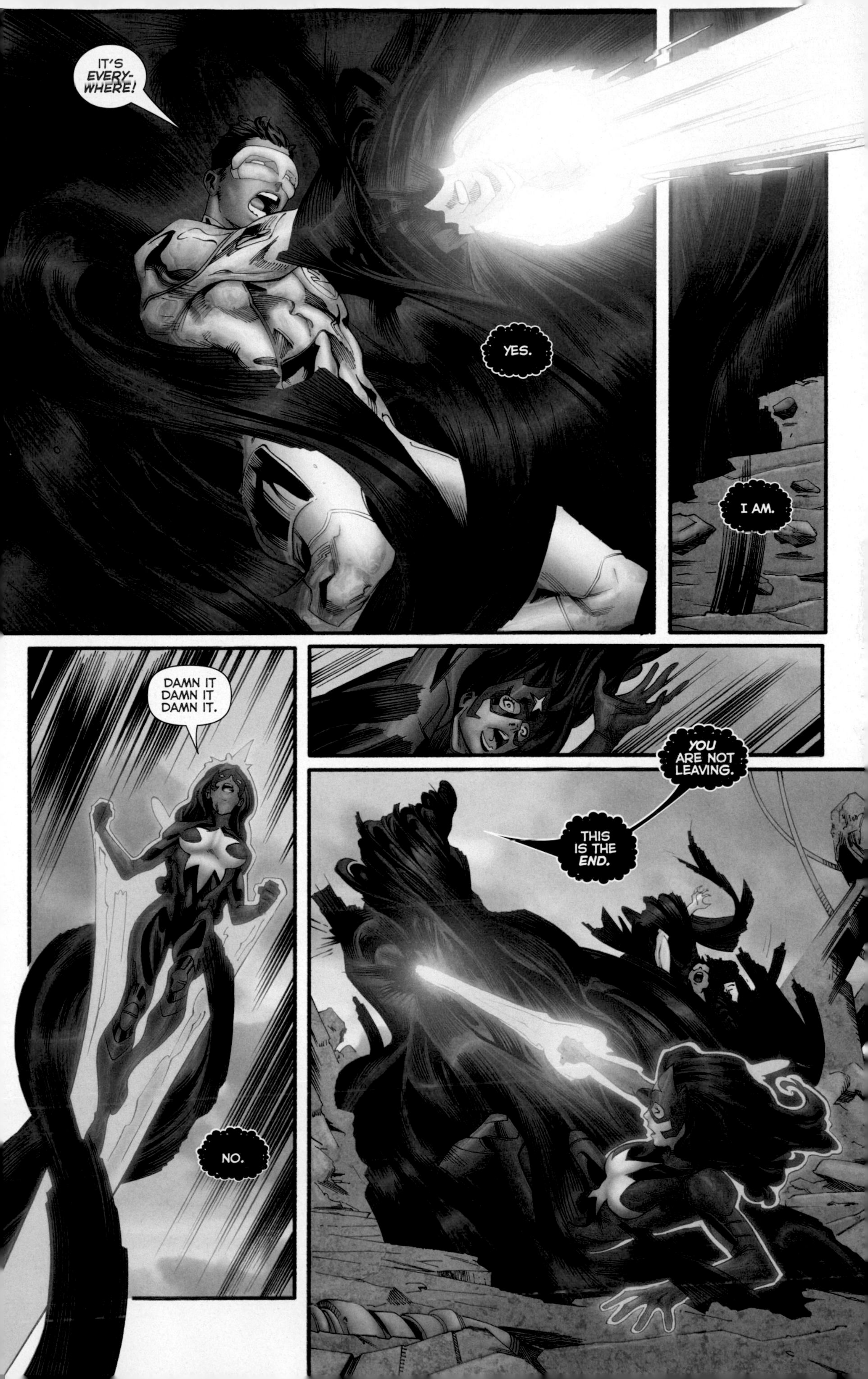
IT'S EVERY-WHERE!
YES.
I AM.
DAMN IT DAMN IT DAMN IT.
NO.
YOU ARE NOT LEAVING.
THIS IS THE END.

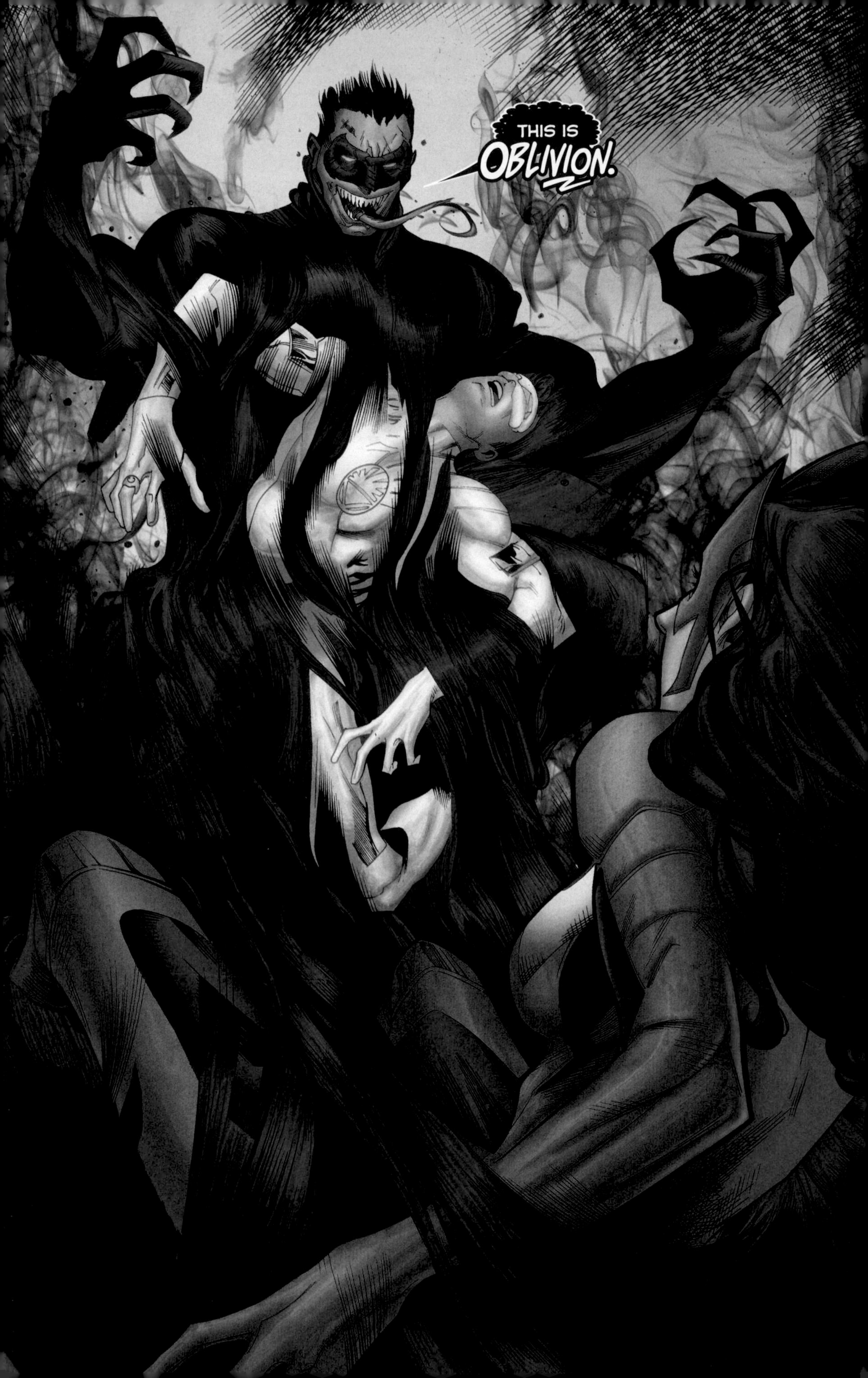
THIS IS OBLIVION.

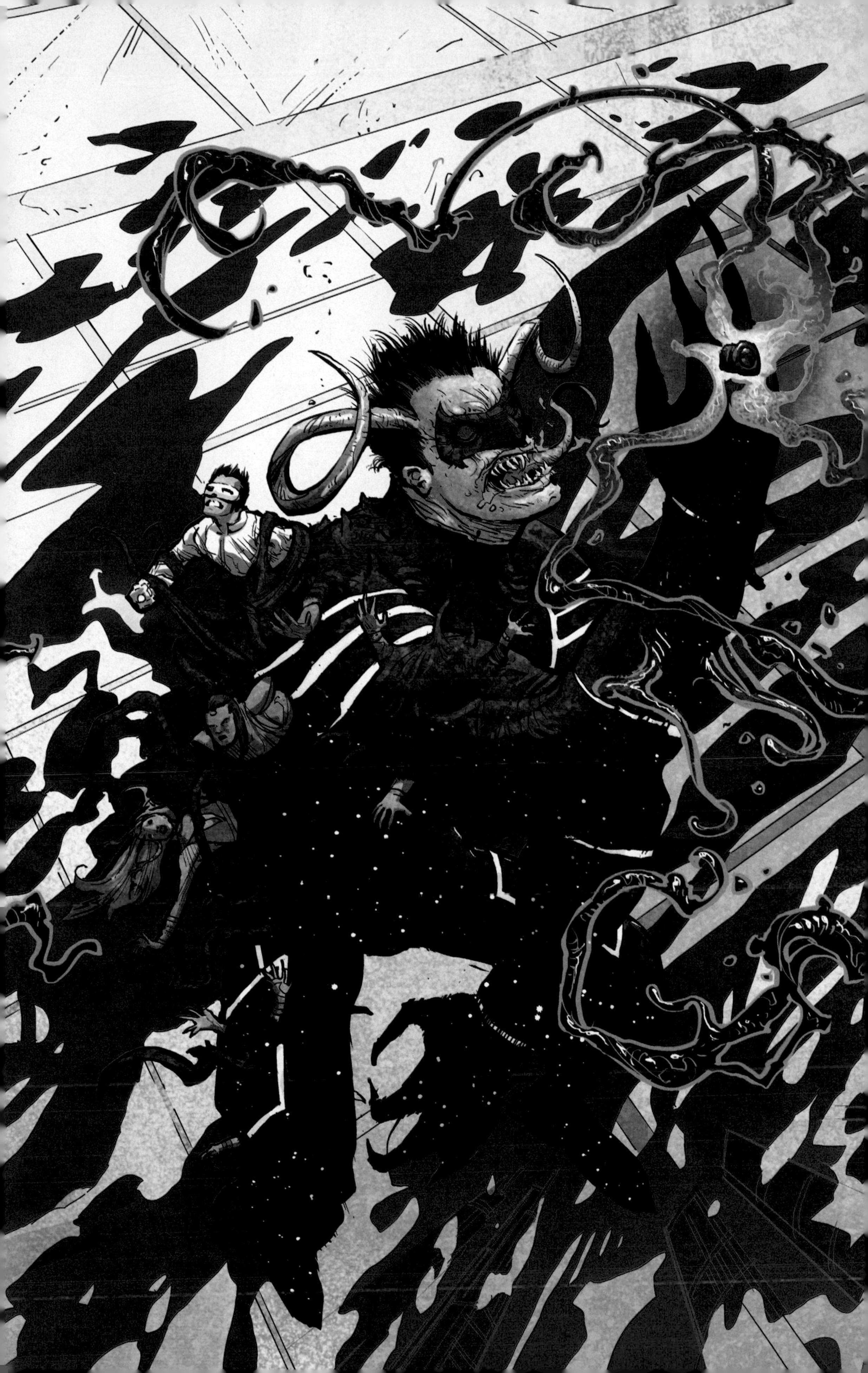

IT ALL ENDS HERE: PART 2

JUSTIN JORDAN writer **DIOGENES NEVES** penciller **MARC DEERING** inker **WIL QUINTANA** colorist **DAVE SHARPE** letterer
cover art by **KYLE STRAHM** and **FELIPE SOBREIRO**

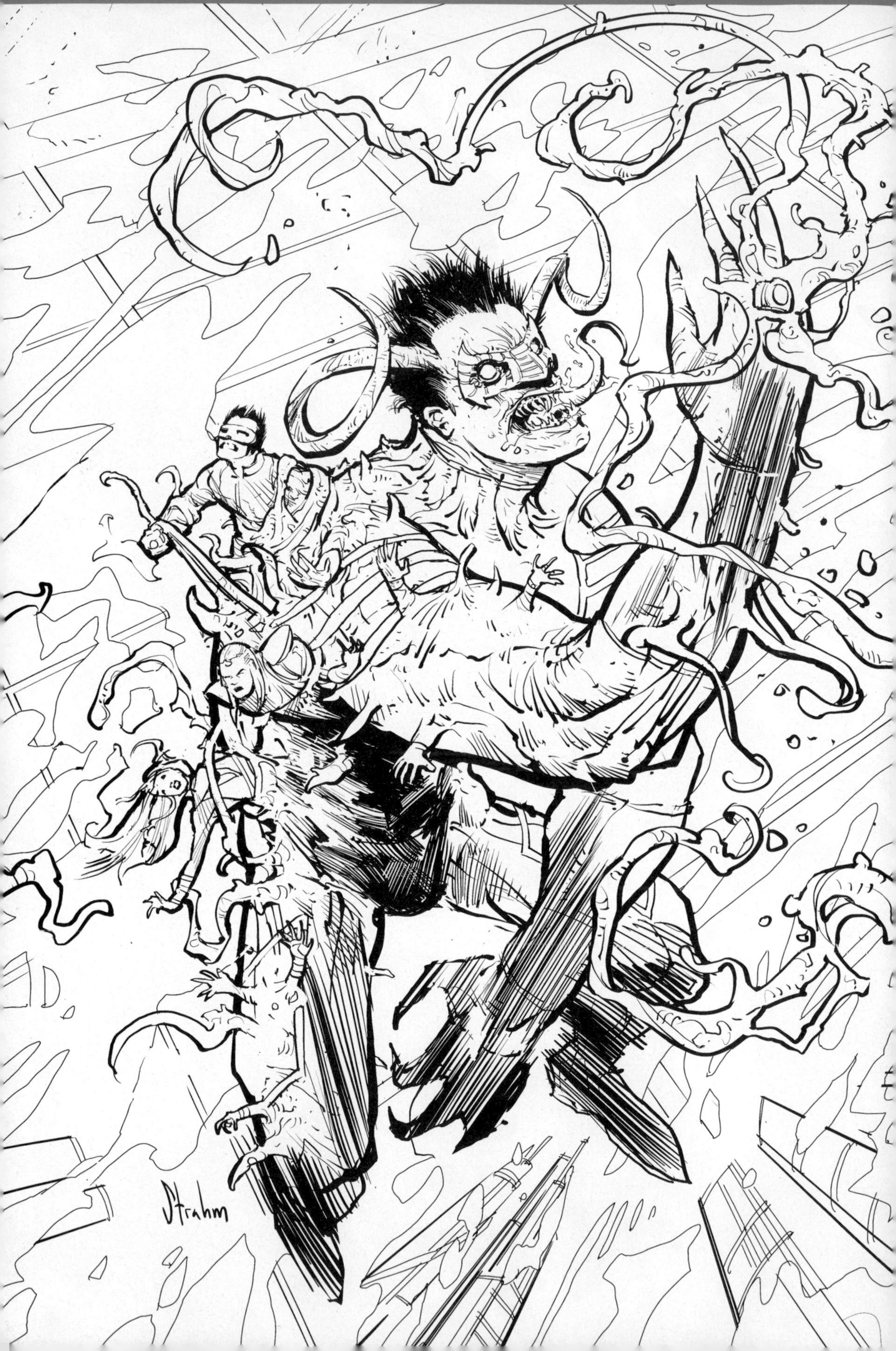

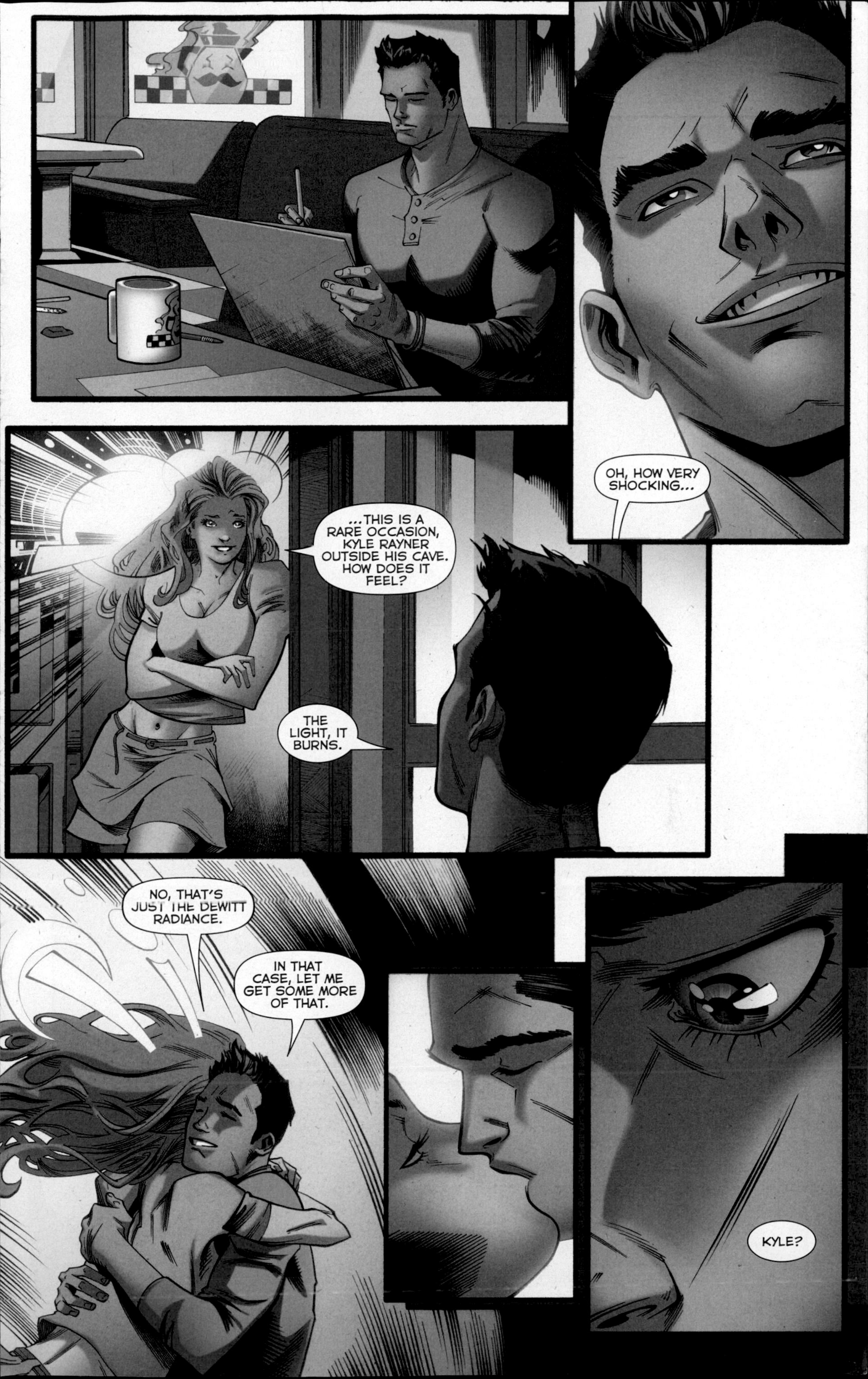
OH, HOW VERY SHOCKING...
...THIS IS A RARE OCCASION, KYLE RAYNER OUTSIDE HIS CAVE. HOW DOES IT FEEL?
THE LIGHT, IT BURNS.
NO, THAT'S JUST THE DEWITT RADIANCE.
IN THAT CASE, LET ME GET SOME MORE OF THAT.
KYLE?

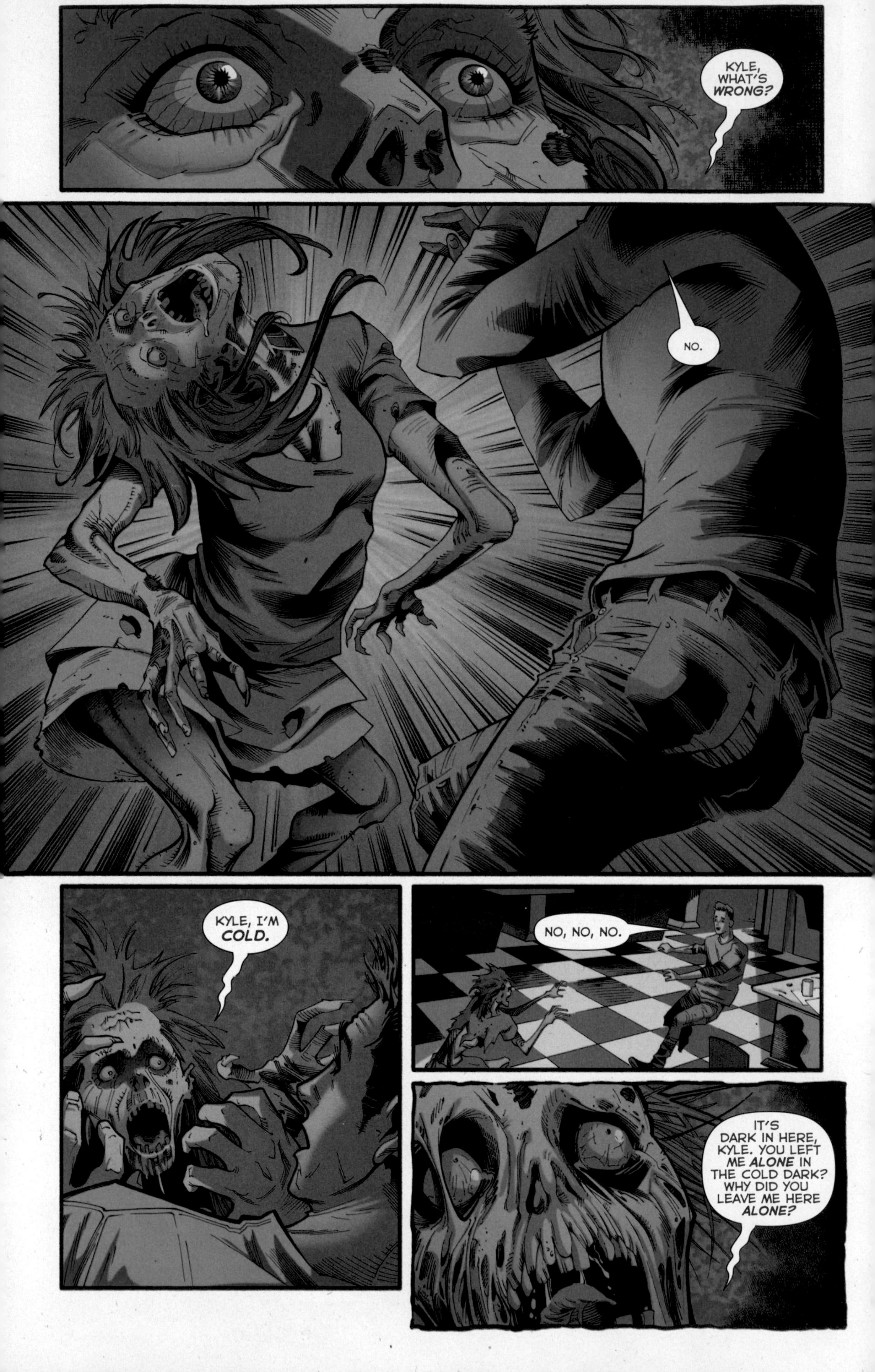
KYLE, WHAT'S **WRONG?**
NO.
KYLE, I'M **COLD.**
NO, NO, NO.
IT'S DARK IN HERE, KYLE. YOU LEFT ME **ALONE** IN THE COLD DARK? WHY DID YOU LEAVE ME HERE **ALONE?**

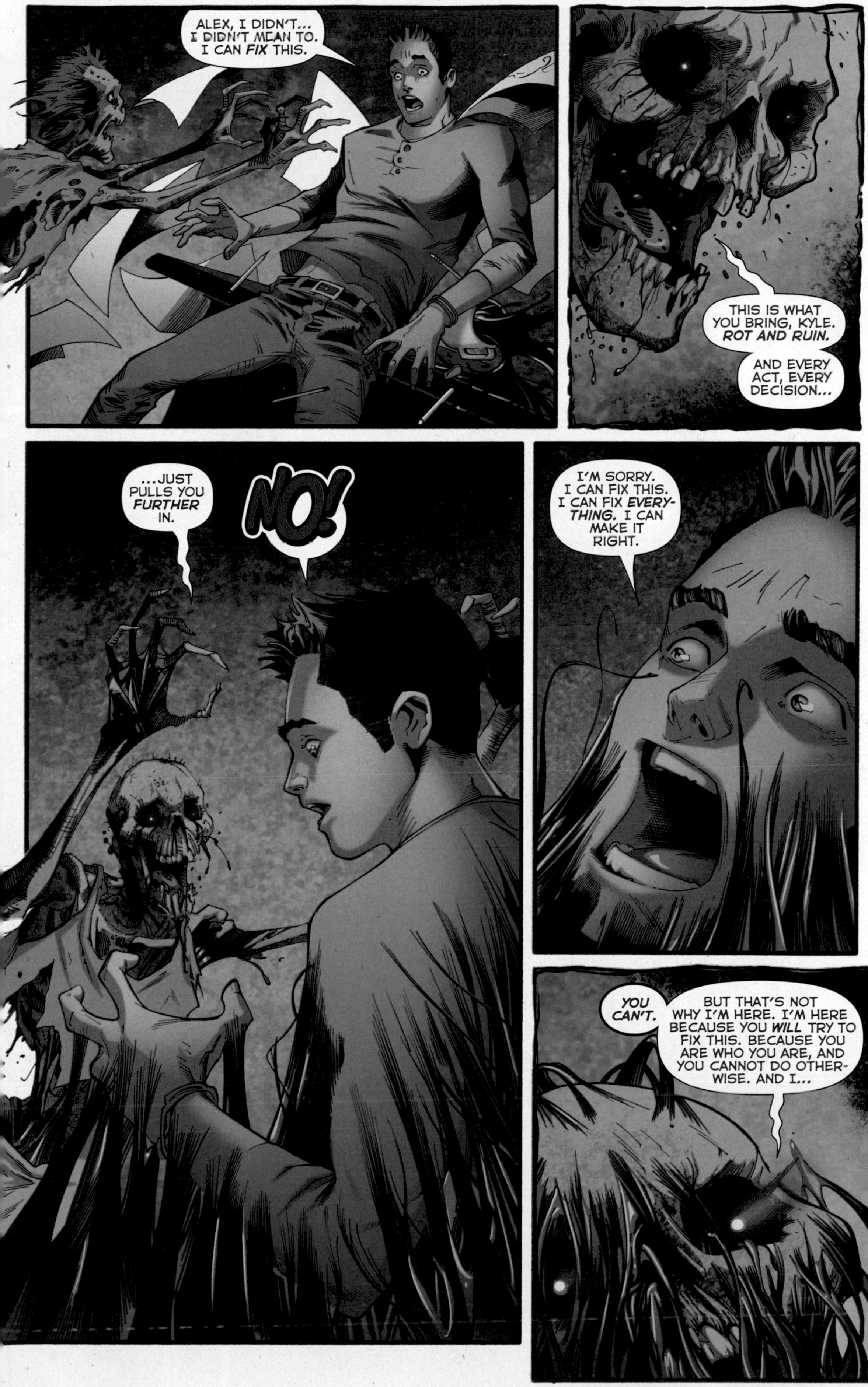

ALEX, I DIDN'T... I DIDN'T MEAN TO. I CAN *FIX* THIS.
THIS IS WHAT YOU BRING, KYLE. ***ROT AND RUIN.***
AND EVERY ACT, EVERY DECISION...
...JUST PULLS YOU ***FURTHER*** IN.
NO!
I'M SORRY. I CAN FIX THIS. I CAN FIX ***EVERY-THING.*** I CAN MAKE IT RIGHT.
YOU CAN'T.
BUT THAT'S NOT WHY I'M HERE. I'M HERE BECAUSE YOU ***WILL*** TRY TO FIX THIS. BECAUSE YOU ARE WHO YOU ARE, AND YOU CANNOT DO OTHER-WISE. AND I...

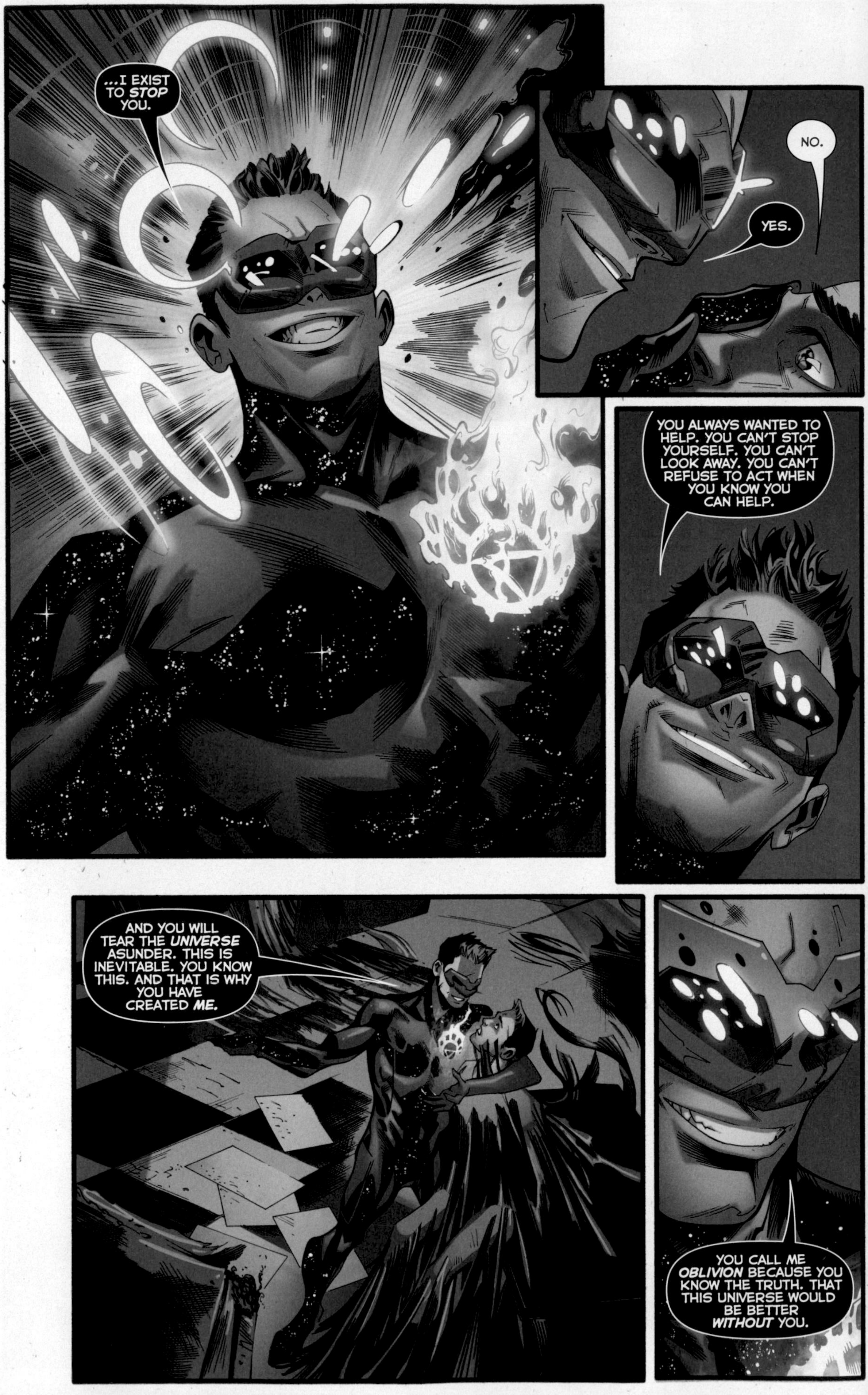
...I EXIST TO STOP YOU.
NO.
YES.
YOU ALWAYS WANTED TO HELP. YOU CAN'T STOP YOURSELF. YOU CAN'T LOOK AWAY. YOU CAN'T REFUSE TO ACT WHEN YOU KNOW YOU CAN HELP.
AND YOU WILL TEAR THE UNIVERSE ASUNDER. THIS IS INEVITABLE. YOU KNOW THIS. AND THAT IS WHY YOU HAVE CREATED ME.
YOU CALL ME OBLIVION BECAUSE YOU KNOW THE TRUTH. THAT THIS UNIVERSE WOULD BE BETTER WITHOUT YOU.

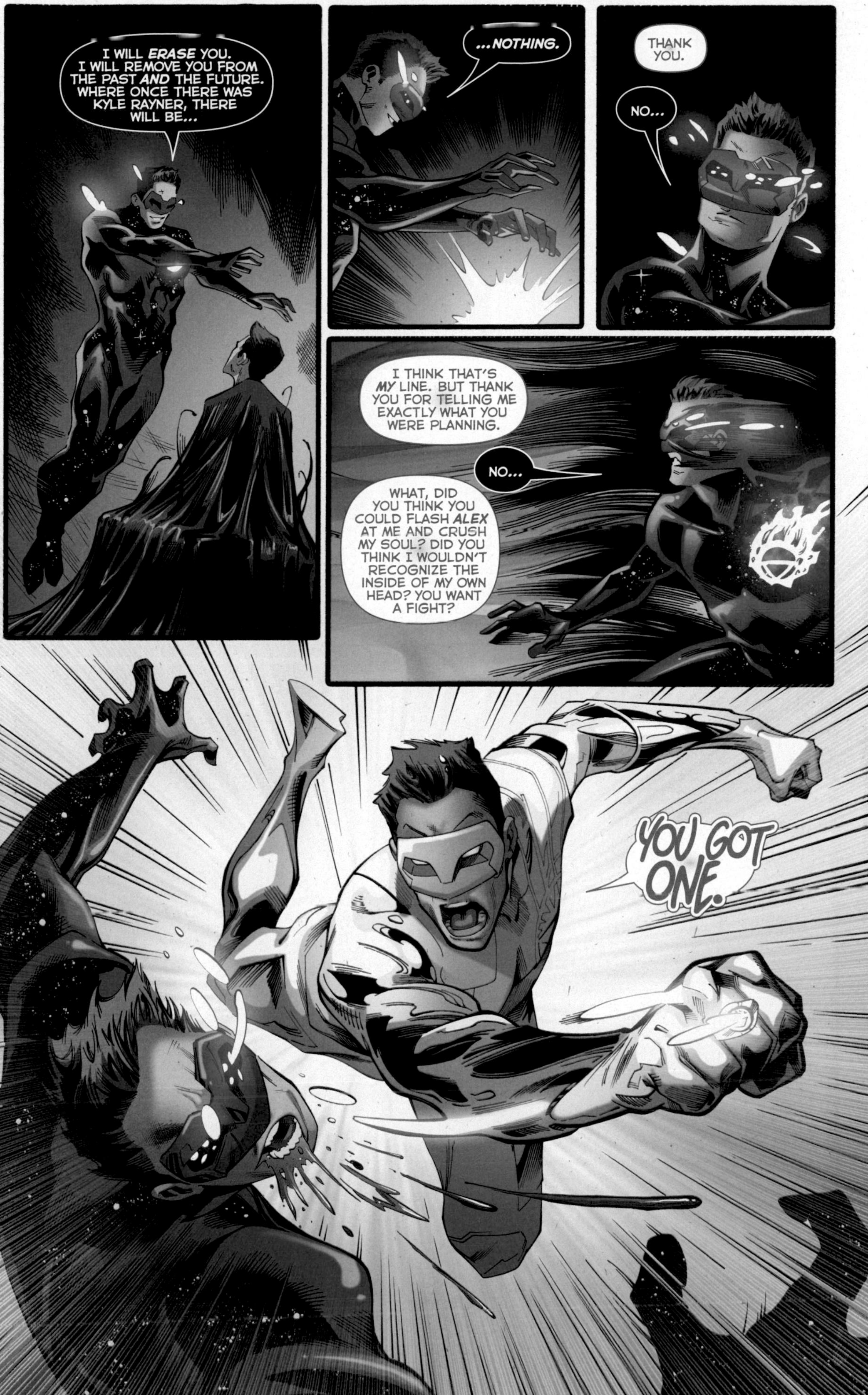
I WILL ERASE YOU. I WILL REMOVE YOU FROM THE PAST AND THE FUTURE. WHERE ONCE THERE WAS KYLE RAYNER, THERE WILL BE...
...NOTHING.
THANK YOU.
NO...
I THINK THAT'S MY LINE. BUT THANK YOU FOR TELLING ME EXACTLY WHAT YOU WERE PLANNING.
NO...
WHAT, DID YOU THINK YOU COULD FLASH ALEX AT ME AND CRUSH MY SOUL? DID YOU THINK I WOULDN'T RECOGNIZE THE INSIDE OF MY OWN HEAD? YOU WANT A FIGHT?
YOU GOT ONE.

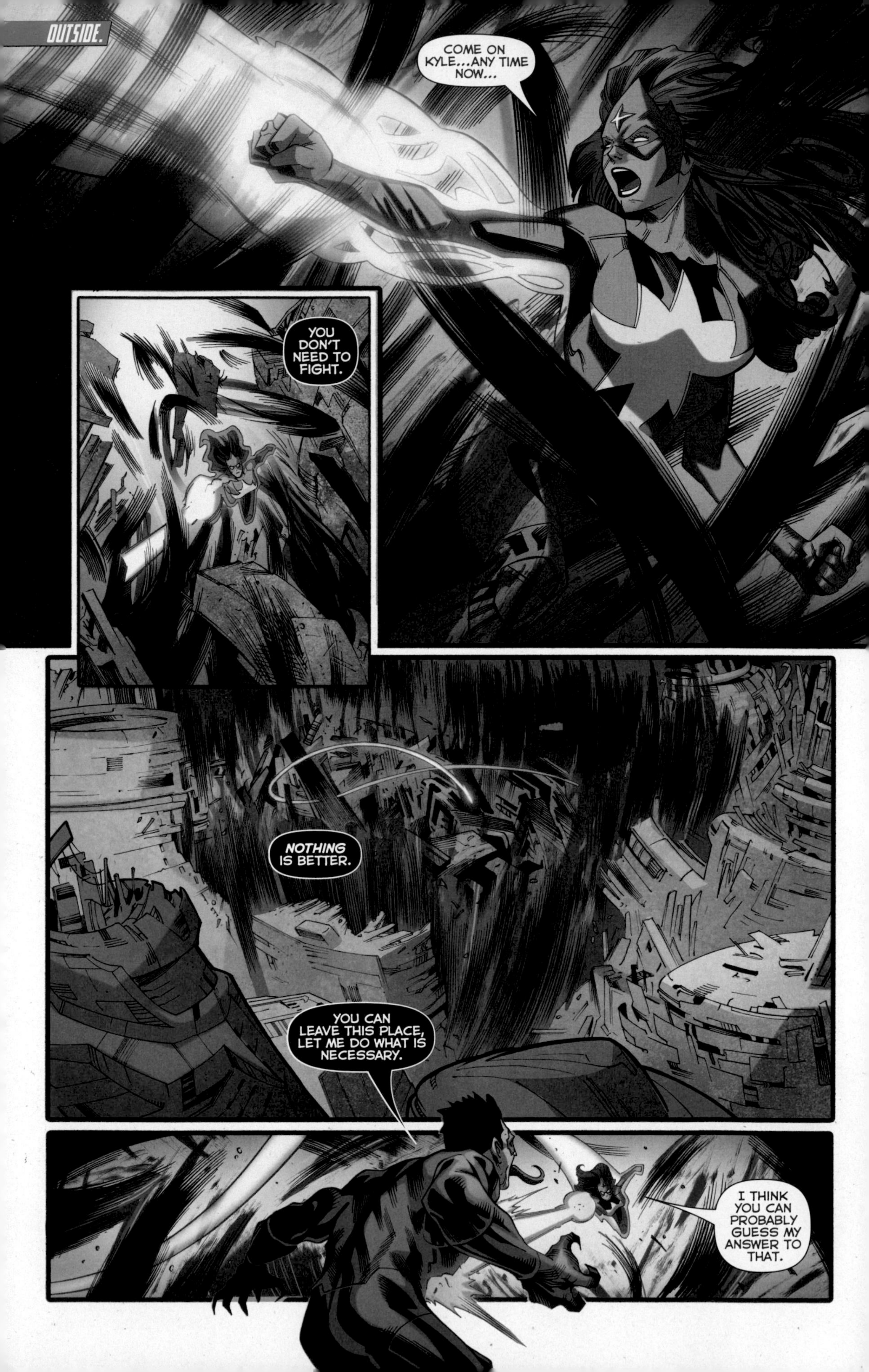
OUTSIDE.
COME ON KYLE...ANY TIME NOW...
YOU DON'T NEED TO FIGHT.
NOTHING IS BETTER.
YOU CAN LEAVE THIS PLACE, LET ME DO WHAT IS NECESSARY.
I THINK YOU CAN PROBABLY GUESS MY ANSWER TO THAT.

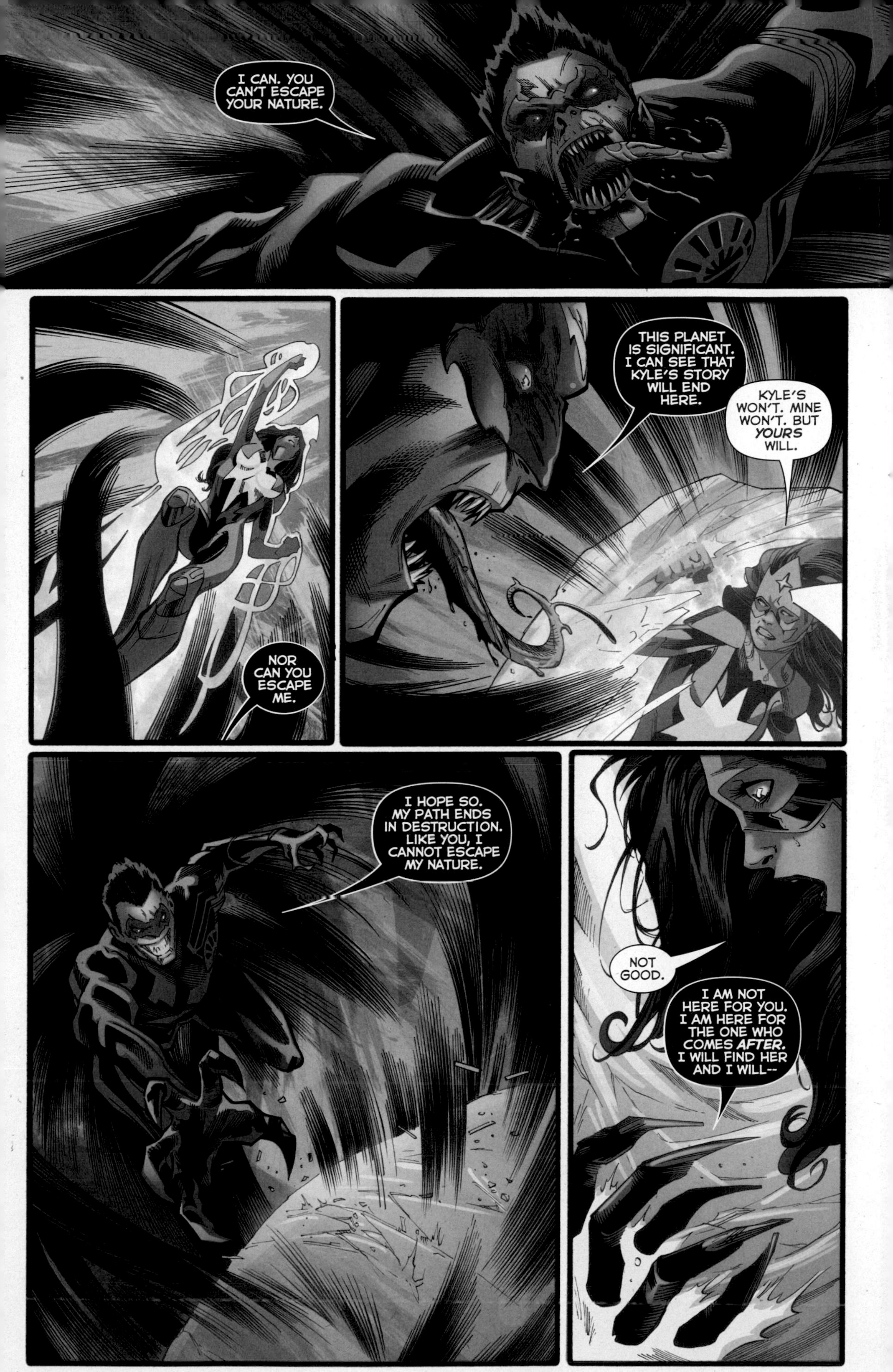
I CAN. YOU CAN'T ESCAPE YOUR NATURE.
NOR CAN YOU ESCAPE ME.
THIS PLANET IS SIGNIFICANT. I CAN SEE THAT KYLE'S STORY WILL END HERE.
KYLE'S WON'T. MINE WON'T. BUT *YOURS* WILL.
I HOPE SO. MY PATH ENDS IN DESTRUCTION. LIKE YOU, I CANNOT ESCAPE MY NATURE.
NOT GOOD.
I AM NOT HERE FOR YOU. I AM HERE FOR THE ONE WHO COMES *AFTER*. I WILL FIND HER AND I WILL--

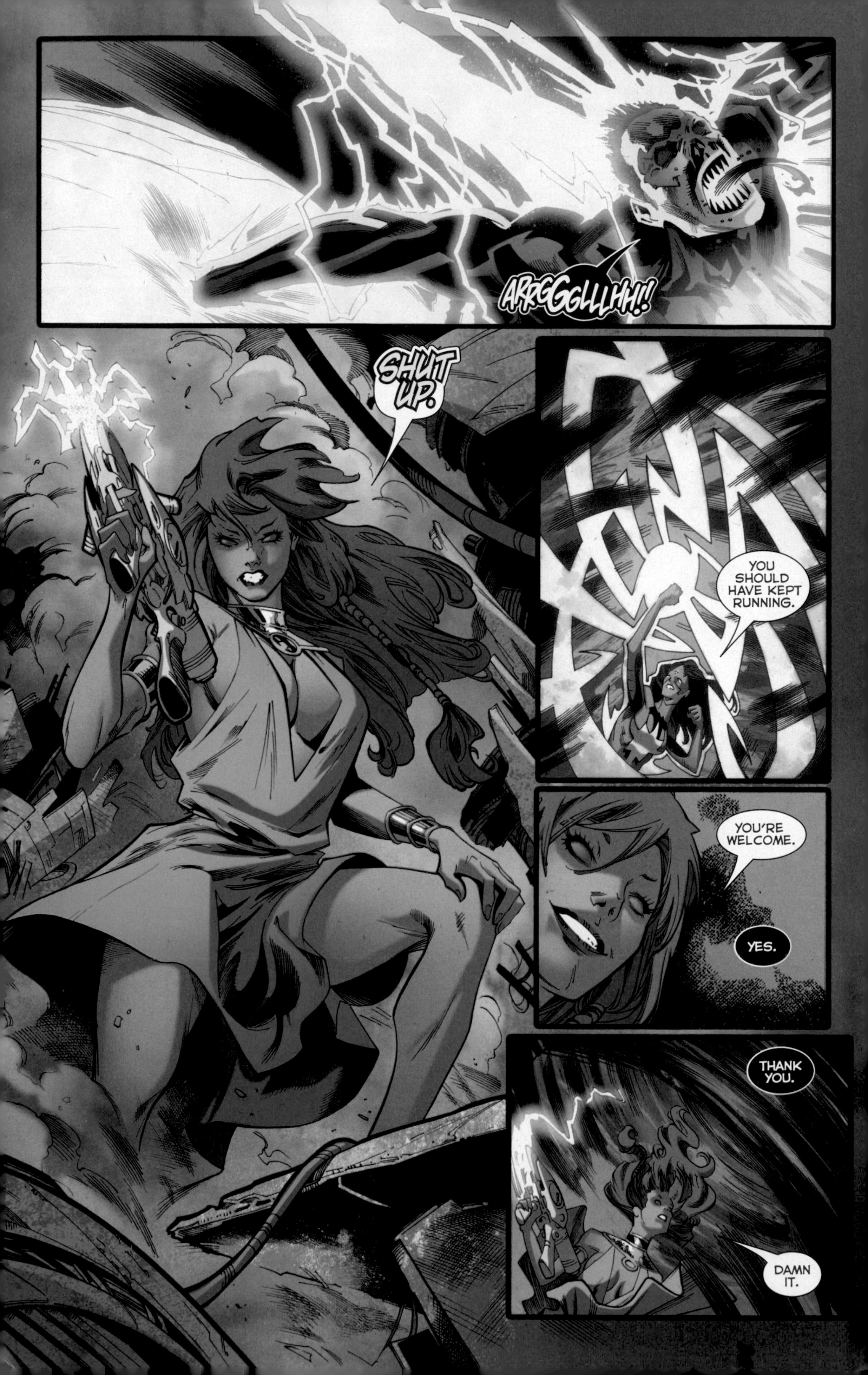
ARRGGGLLLHH!!
SHUT UP.
YOU SHOULD HAVE KEPT RUNNING.
YOU'RE WELCOME.
YES.
THANK YOU.
DAMN IT.

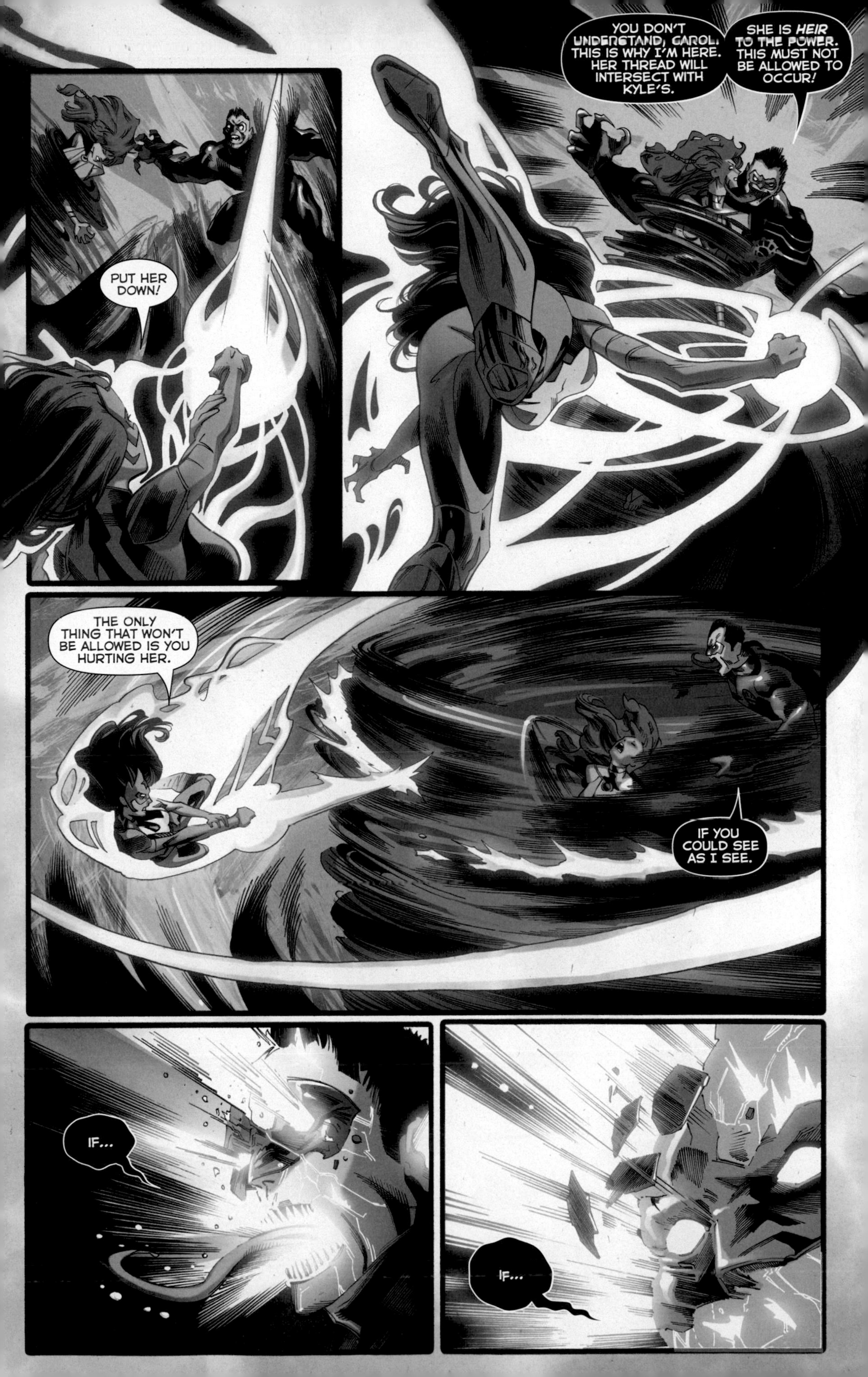
PUT HER DOWN!
YOU DON'T UNDERSTAND, CAROL! THIS IS WHY I'M HERE. HER THREAD WILL INTERSECT WITH KYLE'S.
SHE IS HEIR TO THE POWER. THIS MUST NOT BE ALLOWED TO OCCUR!
THE ONLY THING THAT WON'T BE ALLOWED IS YOU HURTING HER.
IF YOU COULD SEE AS I SEE.
IF...
IF...

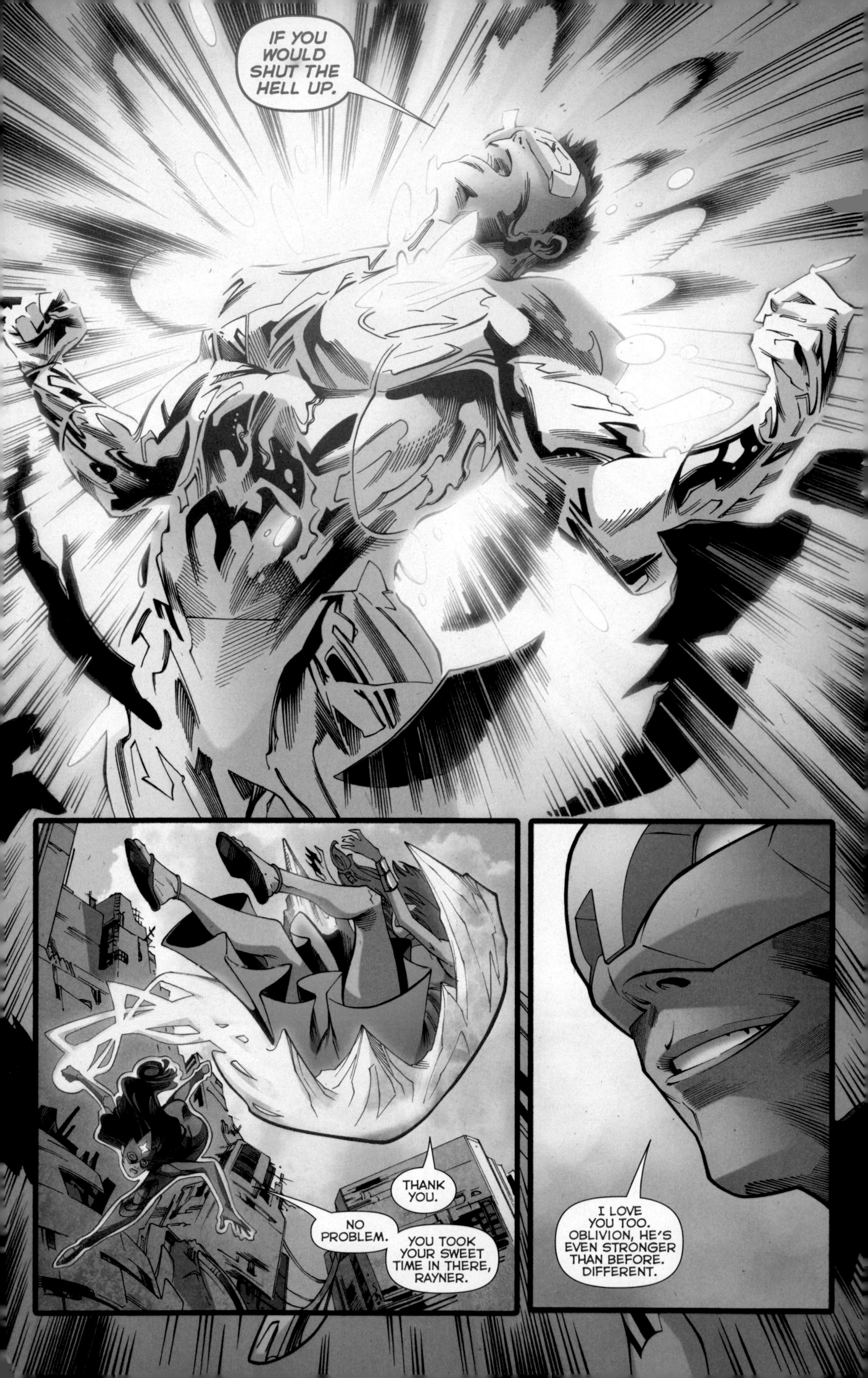
IF YOU WOULD SHUT THE HELL UP.
THANK YOU.
NO PROBLEM.
YOU TOOK YOUR SWEET TIME IN THERE, RAYNER.
I LOVE YOU TOO. OBLIVION, HE'S EVEN STRONGER THAN BEFORE. DIFFERENT.

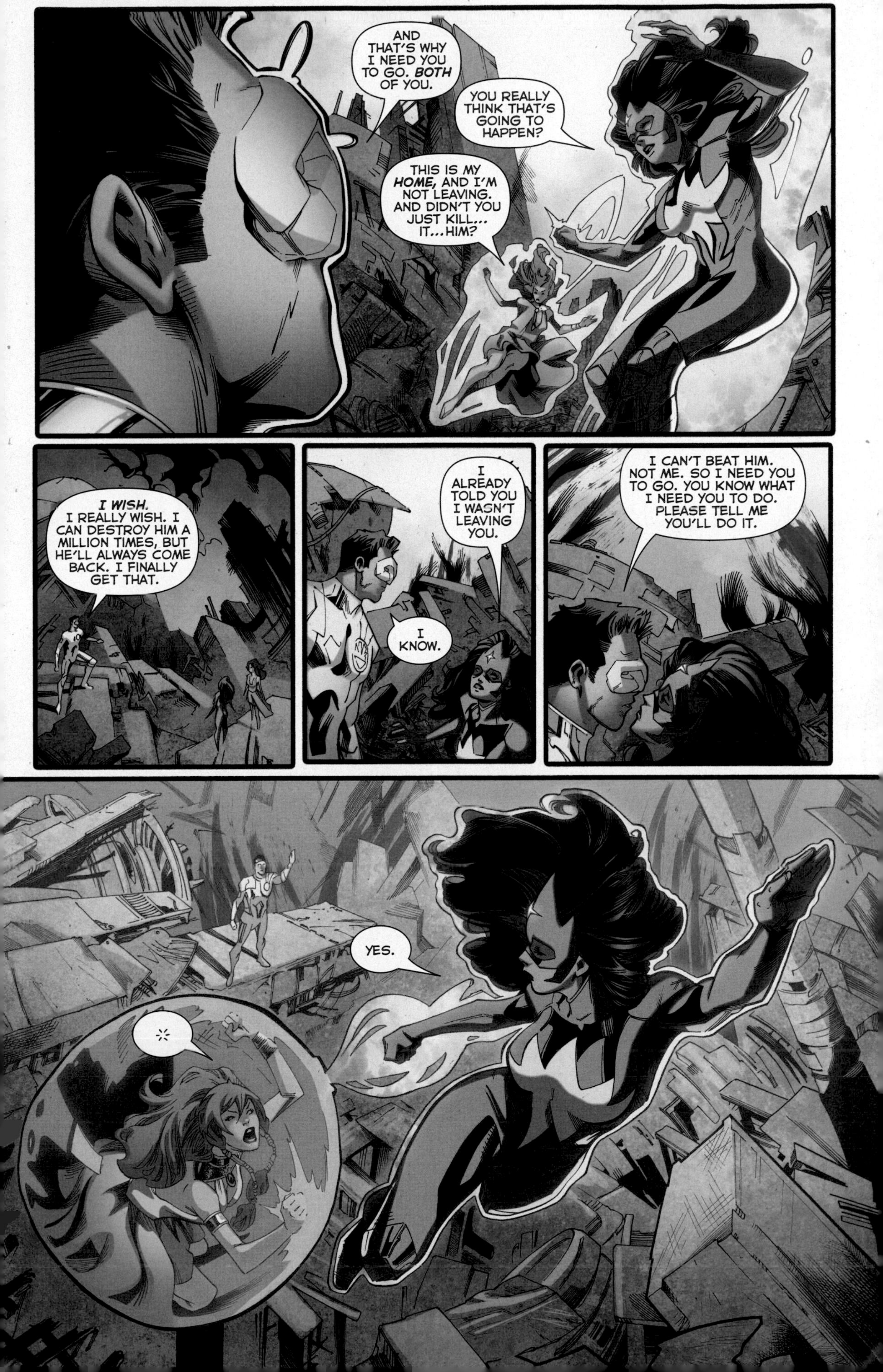
AND THAT'S WHY I NEED YOU TO GO. BOTH OF YOU.
YOU REALLY THINK THAT'S GOING TO HAPPEN?
THIS IS MY HOME, AND I'M NOT LEAVING. AND DIDN'T YOU JUST KILL... IT...HIM?
I WISH. I REALLY WISH. I CAN DESTROY HIM A MILLION TIMES, BUT HE'LL ALWAYS COME BACK. I FINALLY GET THAT.
I ALREADY TOLD YOU I WASN'T LEAVING YOU.
I KNOW.
I CAN'T BEAT HIM. NOT ME. SO I NEED YOU TO GO. YOU KNOW WHAT I NEED YOU TO DO. PLEASE TELL ME YOU'LL DO IT.
YES.

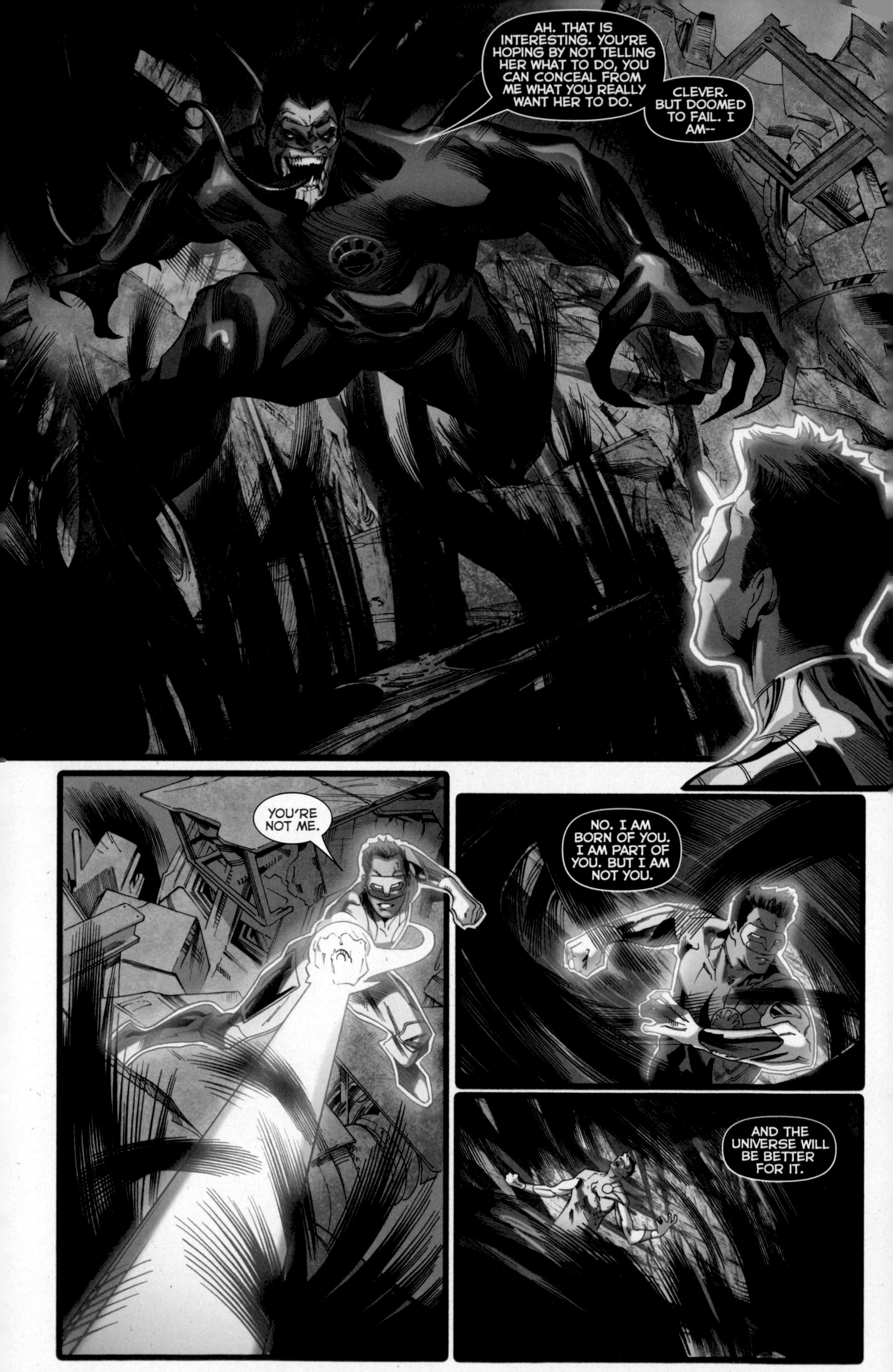
AH. THAT IS INTERESTING. YOU'RE HOPING BY NOT TELLING HER WHAT TO DO, YOU CAN CONCEAL FROM ME WHAT YOU REALLY WANT HER TO DO.
CLEVER. BUT DOOMED TO FAIL. I AM--
YOU'RE NOT ME.
NO. I AM BORN OF YOU. I AM PART OF YOU. BUT I AM NOT YOU.
AND THE UNIVERSE WILL BE BETTER FOR IT.

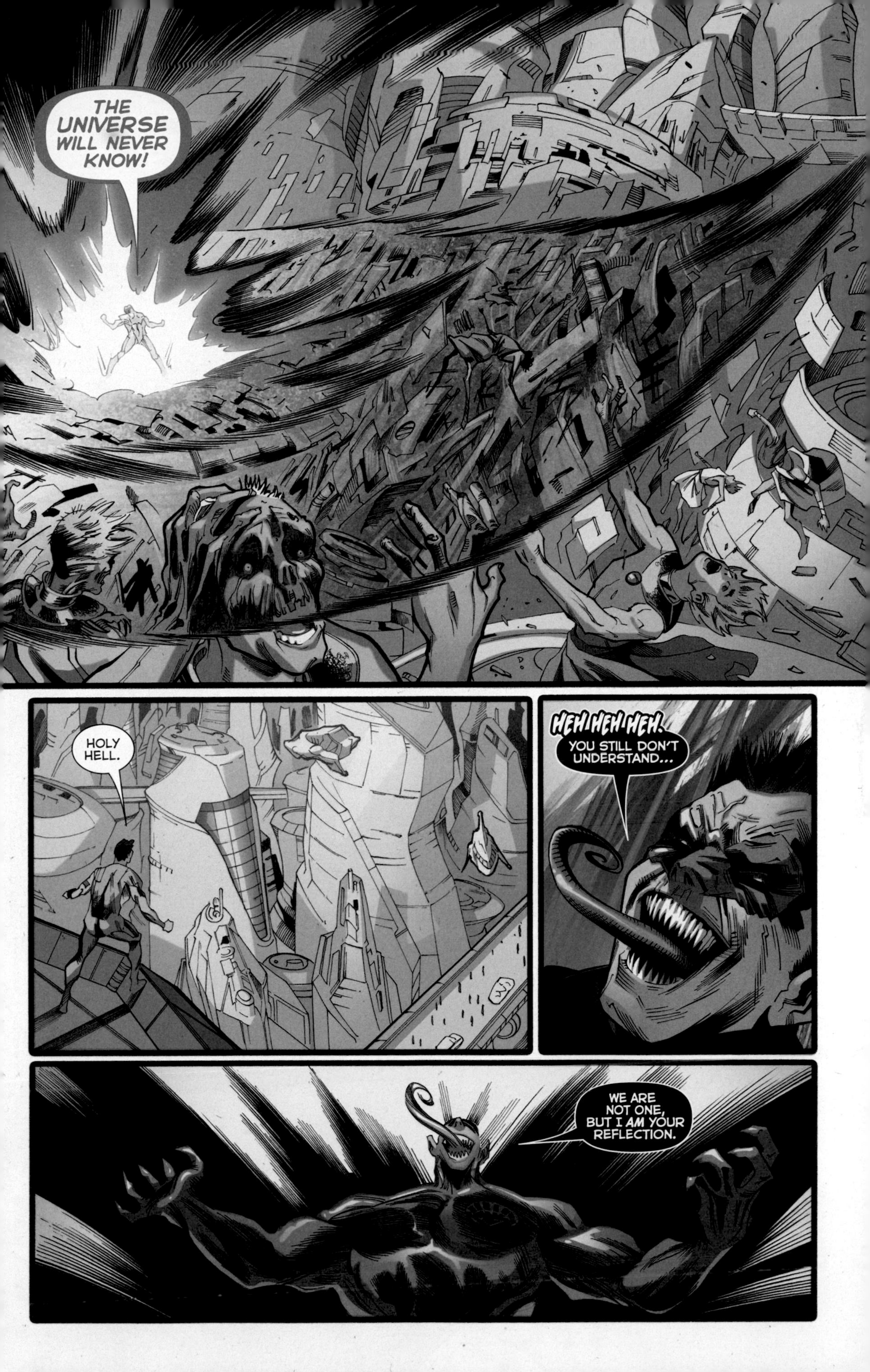
THE UNIVERSE WILL NEVER KNOW!
HOLY HELL.
HEH HEH HEH!
YOU STILL DON'T UNDERSTAND...
WE ARE NOT ONE, BUT I AM YOUR REFLECTION.

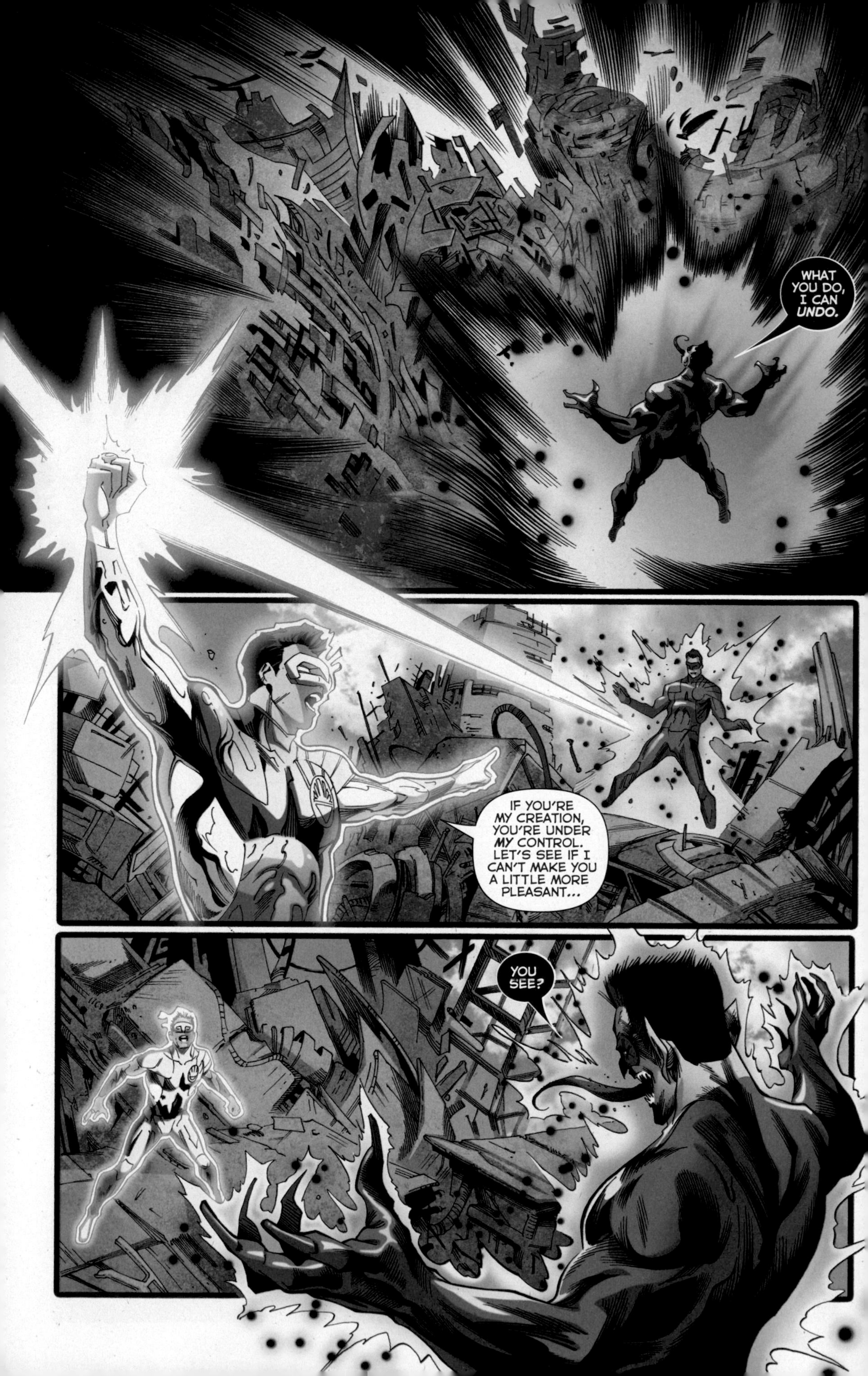
WHAT YOU DO, I CAN UNDO.
IF YOU'RE MY CREATION, YOU'RE UNDER MY CONTROL. LET'S SEE IF I CAN'T MAKE YOU A LITTLE MORE PLEASANT...
YOU SEE?

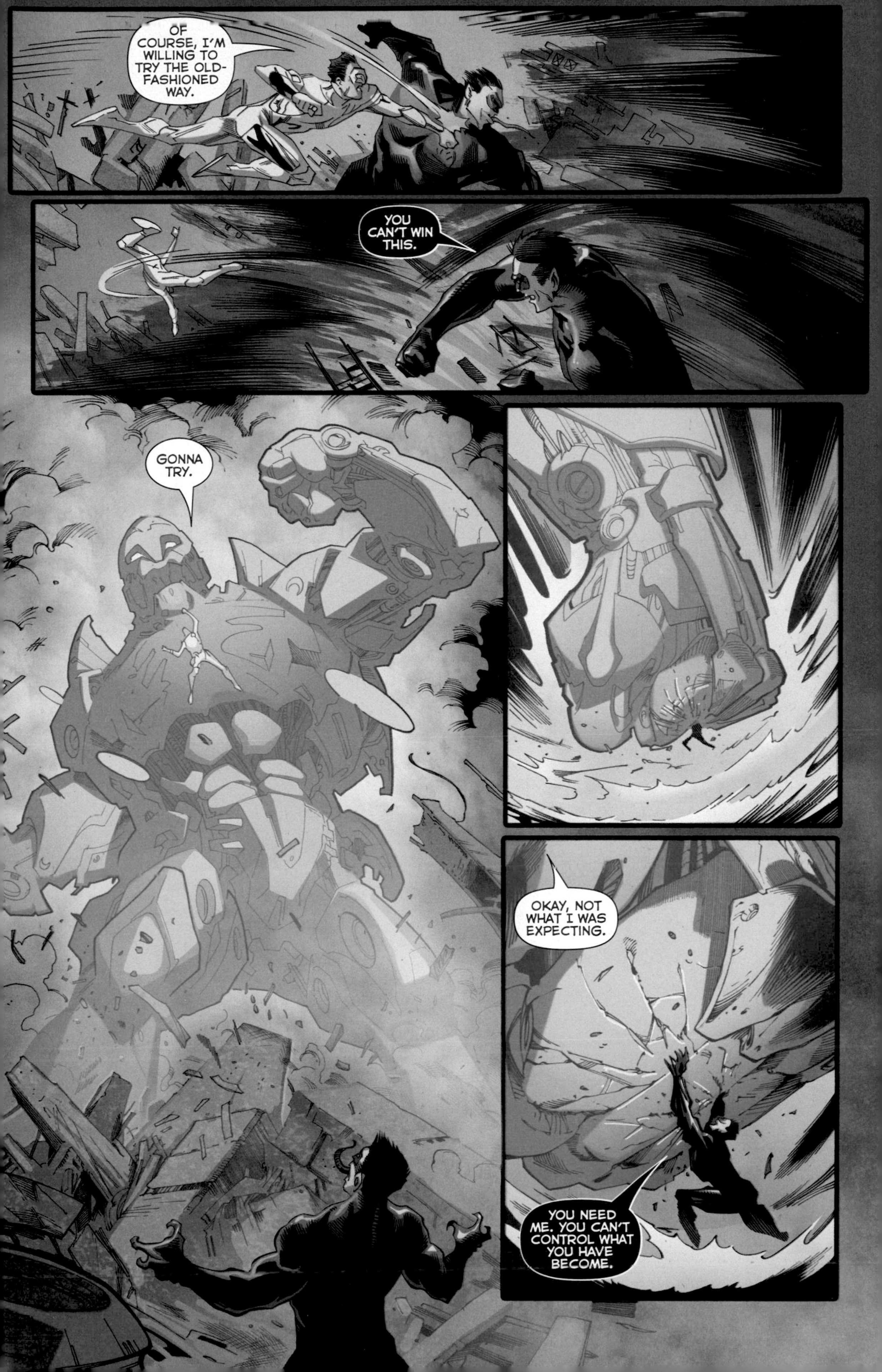
OF COURSE, I'M WILLING TO TRY THE OLD-FASHIONED WAY.
YOU CAN'T WIN THIS.
GONNA TRY.
OKAY, NOT WHAT I WAS EXPECTING.
YOU NEED ME. YOU CAN'T CONTROL WHAT YOU HAVE BECOME.

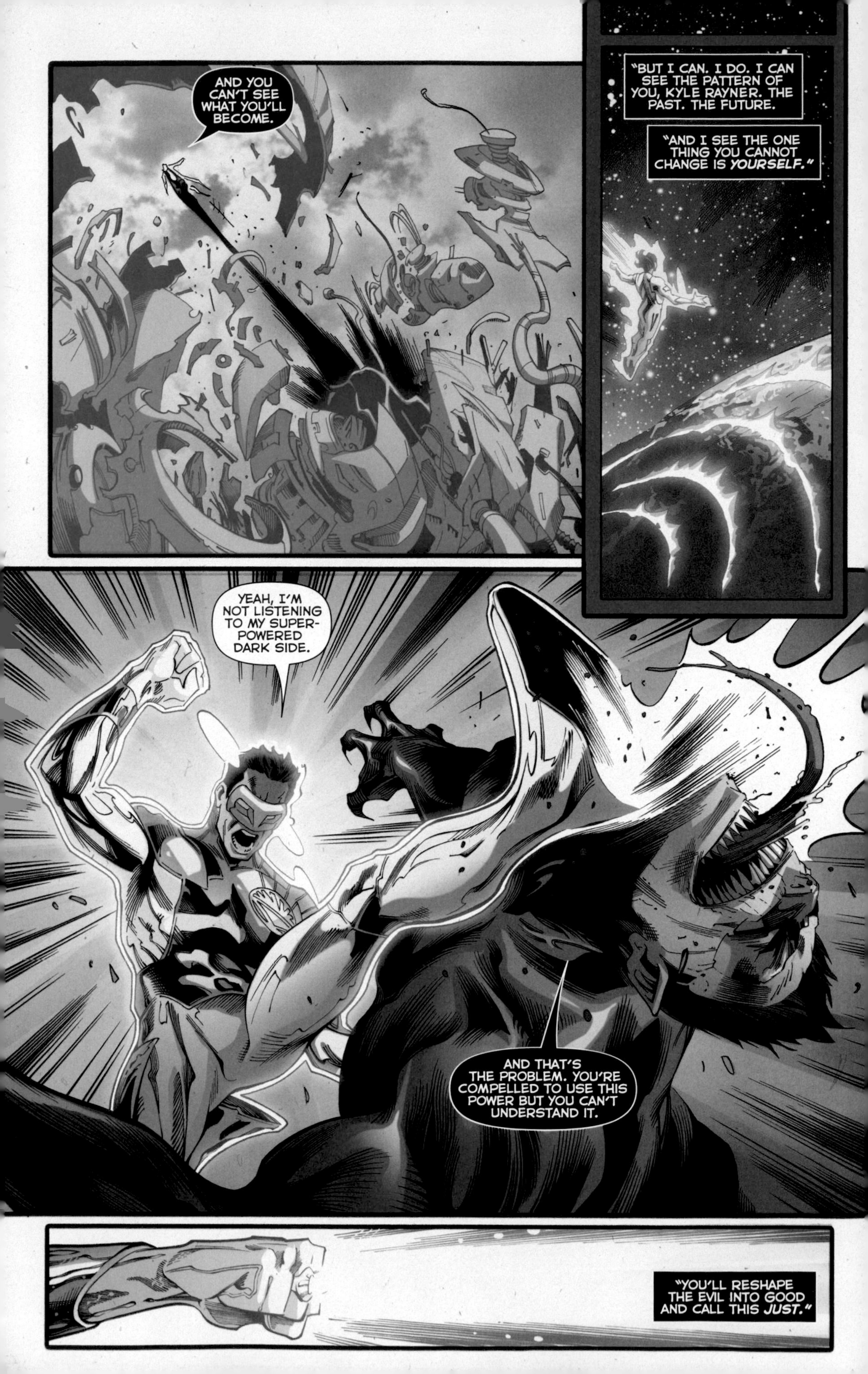
AND YOU CAN'T SEE WHAT YOU'LL BECOME.
"BUT I CAN. I DO. I CAN SEE THE PATTERN OF YOU, KYLE RAYNER. THE PAST. THE FUTURE.
"AND I SEE THE ONE THING YOU CANNOT CHANGE IS *YOURSELF.*"
YEAH, I'M NOT LISTENING TO MY SUPER-POWERED DARK SIDE.
AND THAT'S THE PROBLEM. YOU'RE COMPELLED TO USE THIS POWER BUT YOU CAN'T UNDERSTAND IT.
"YOU'LL RESHAPE THE EVIL INTO GOOD AND CALL THIS *JUST.*"

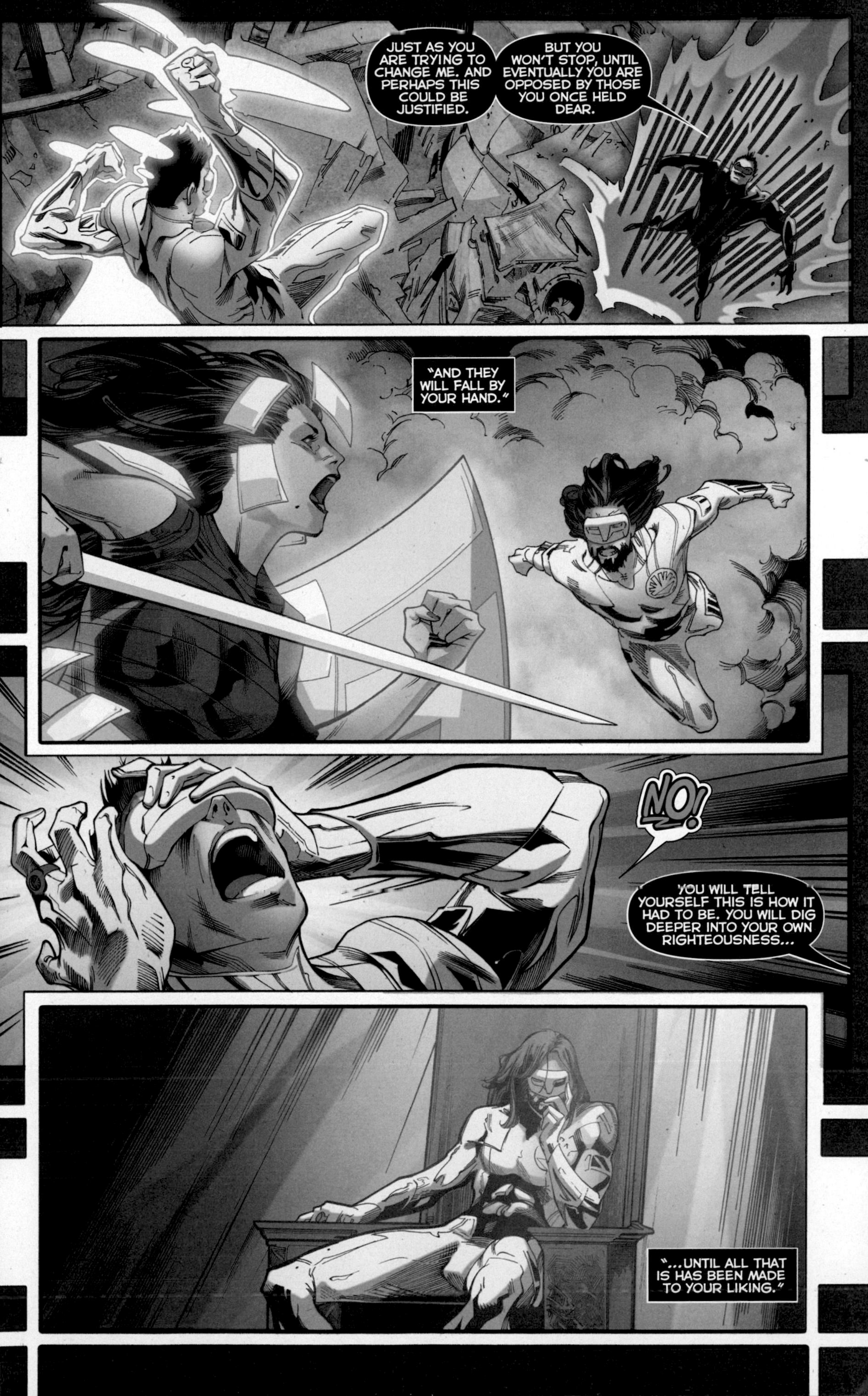
JUST AS YOU ARE TRYING TO CHANGE ME. AND PERHAPS THIS COULD BE JUSTIFIED.
BUT YOU WON'T STOP, UNTIL EVENTUALLY YOU ARE OPPOSED BY THOSE YOU ONCE HELD DEAR.
"AND THEY WILL FALL BY YOUR HAND."
NO!
YOU WILL TELL YOURSELF THIS IS HOW IT HAD TO BE. YOU WILL DIG DEEPER INTO YOUR OWN RIGHTEOUSNESS...
"...UNTIL ALL THAT IS HAS BEEN MADE TO YOUR LIKING."

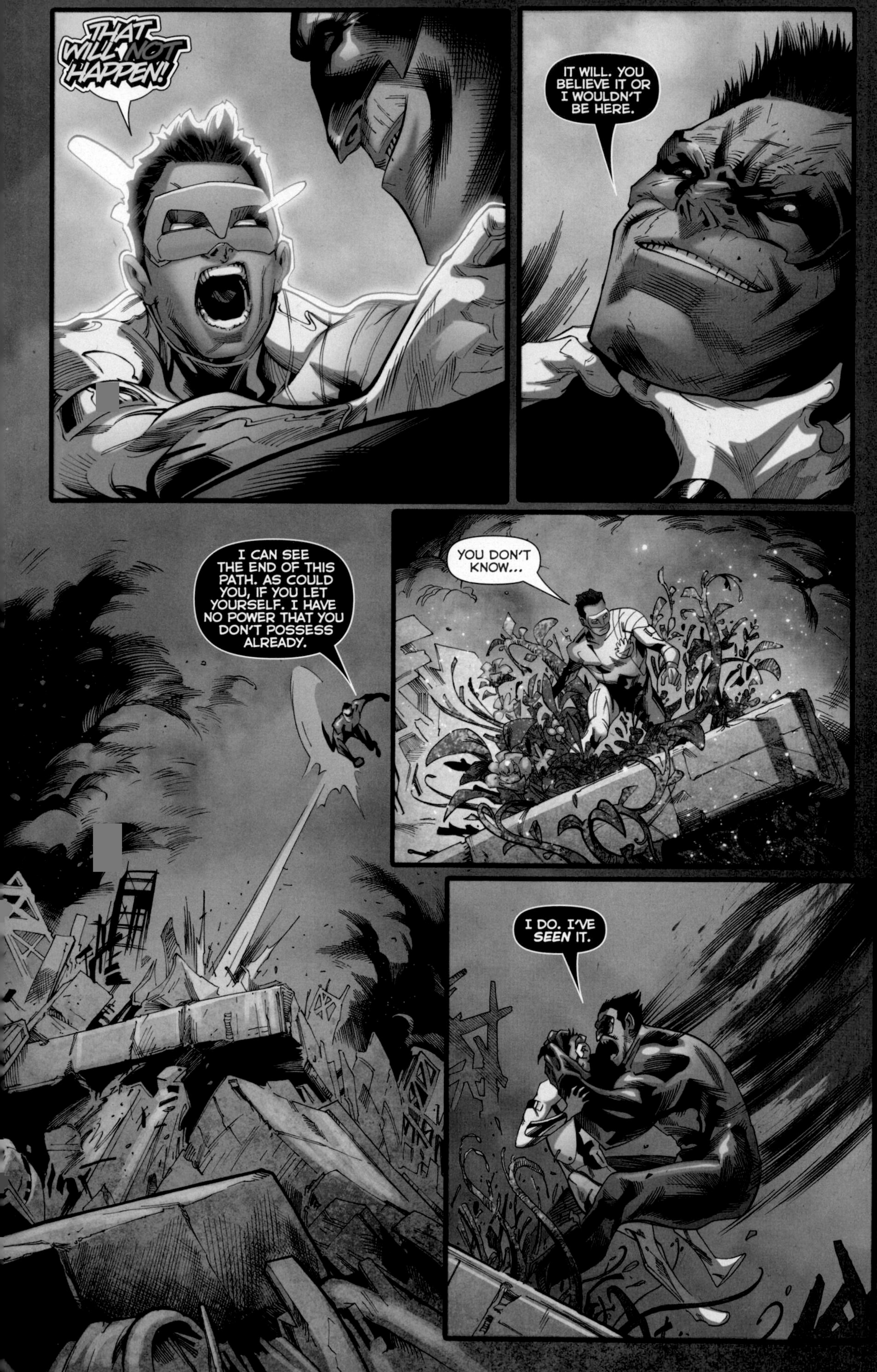
THAT WILL NOT HAPPEN!
IT WILL. YOU BELIEVE IT OR I WOULDN'T BE HERE.
I CAN SEE THE END OF THIS PATH. AS COULD YOU, IF YOU LET YOURSELF. I HAVE NO POWER THAT YOU DON'T POSSESS ALREADY.
YOU DON'T KNOW...
I DO. I'VE SEEN IT.

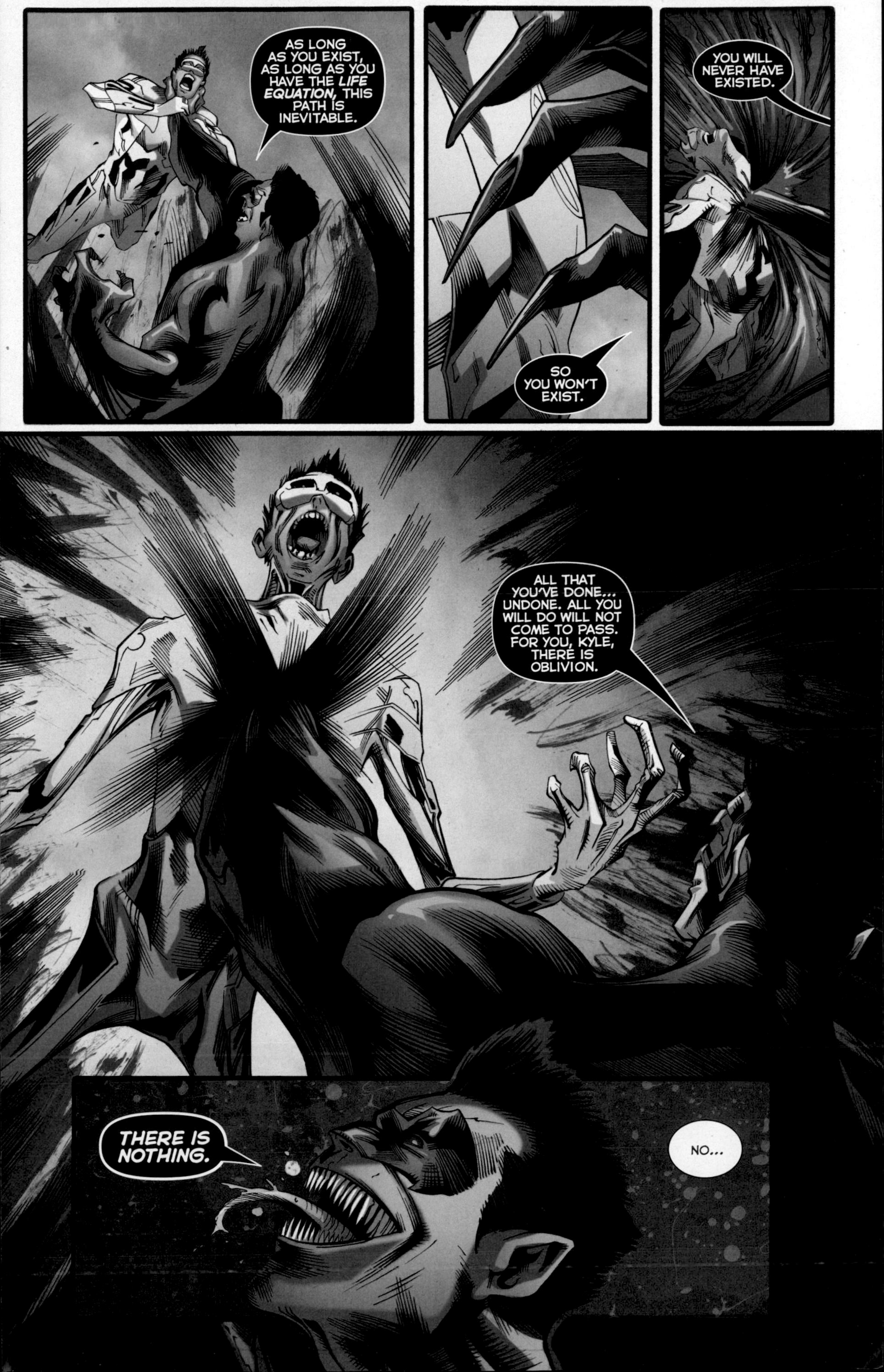
AS LONG AS YOU EXIST, AS LONG AS YOU HAVE THE *LIFE EQUATION,* THIS PATH IS INEVITABLE.
SO YOU WON'T EXIST.
YOU WILL NEVER HAVE EXISTED.
ALL THAT YOU'VE DONE... UNDONE. ALL YOU WILL DO WILL NOT COME TO PASS. FOR YOU, KYLE, THERE IS OBLIVION.
THERE IS NOTHING.
NO...

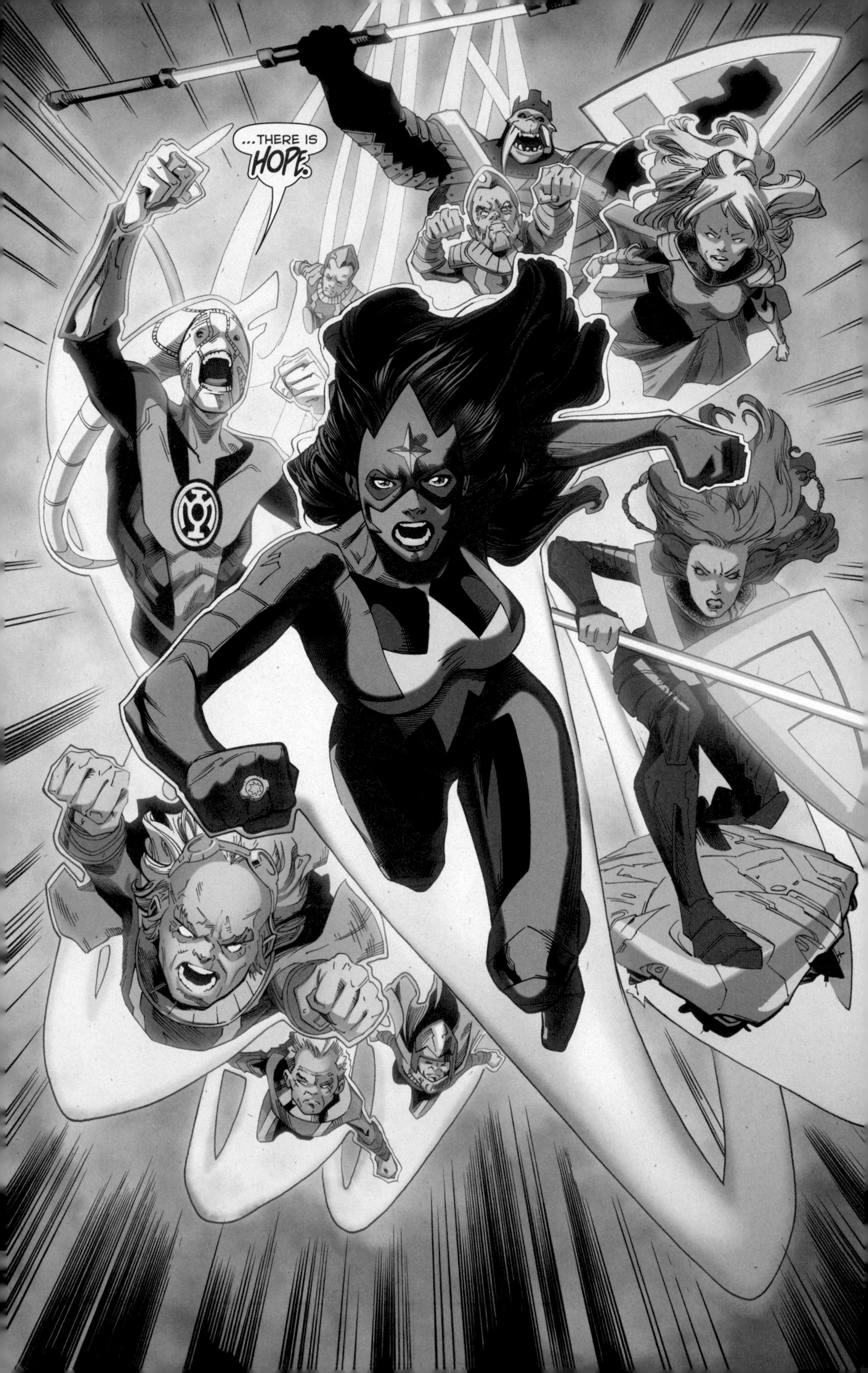
...THERE IS HOPE.

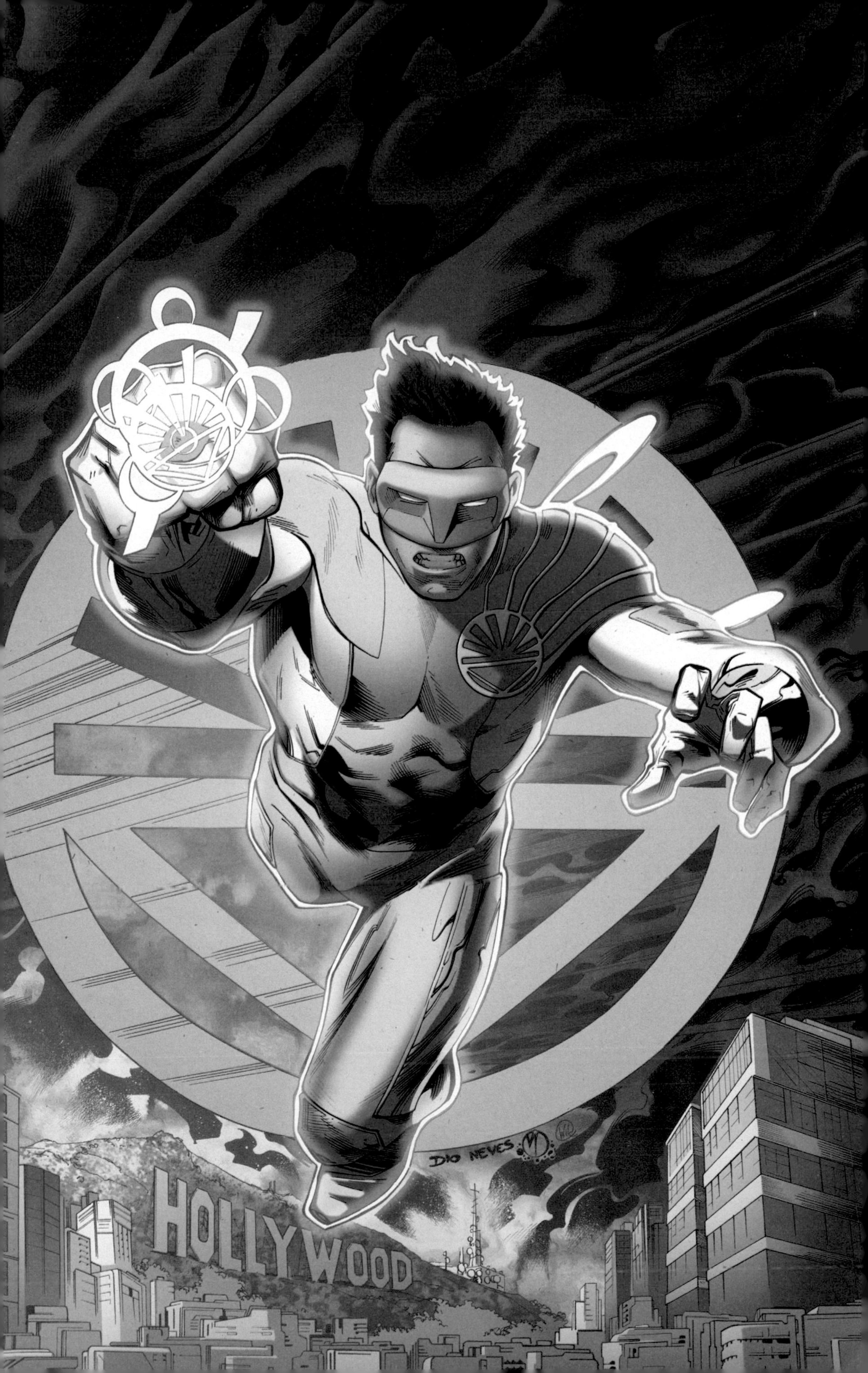
DIO NEVES
HOLLYWOOD

IT ALL ENDS HERE: CONCLUSION

JUSTIN JORDAN writer **DIOGENES NEVES ROGE ANTONIO** pencillers **MARC DEERING DANIEL HENRIQUES ROGE ANTONIO** inkers
WIL QUINTANA colorist **DAVE SHARPE** letterer cover art by **NEVES, DEERING** and **QUINTANA**

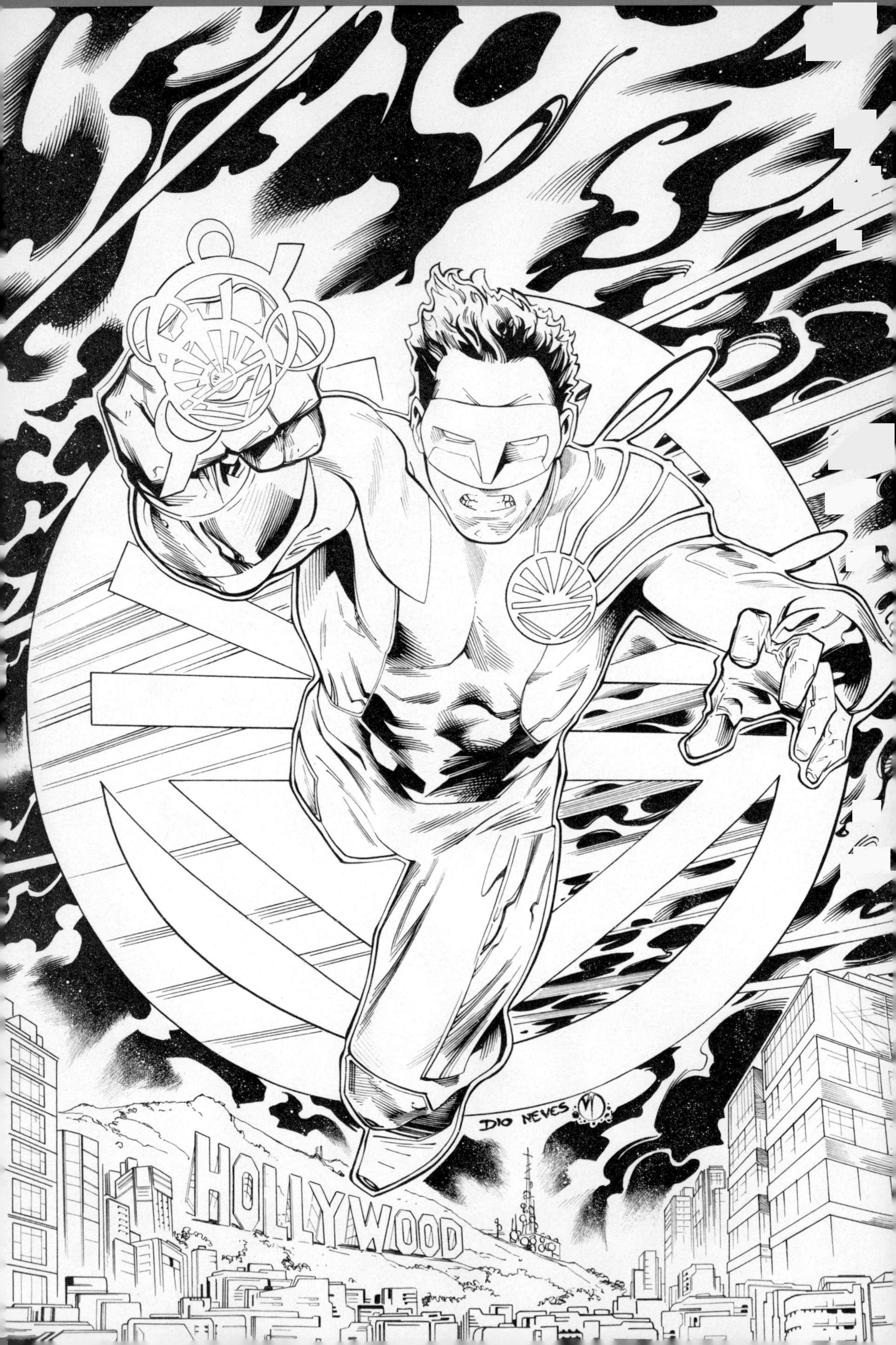
DIO NEVES
HOLLYWOOD

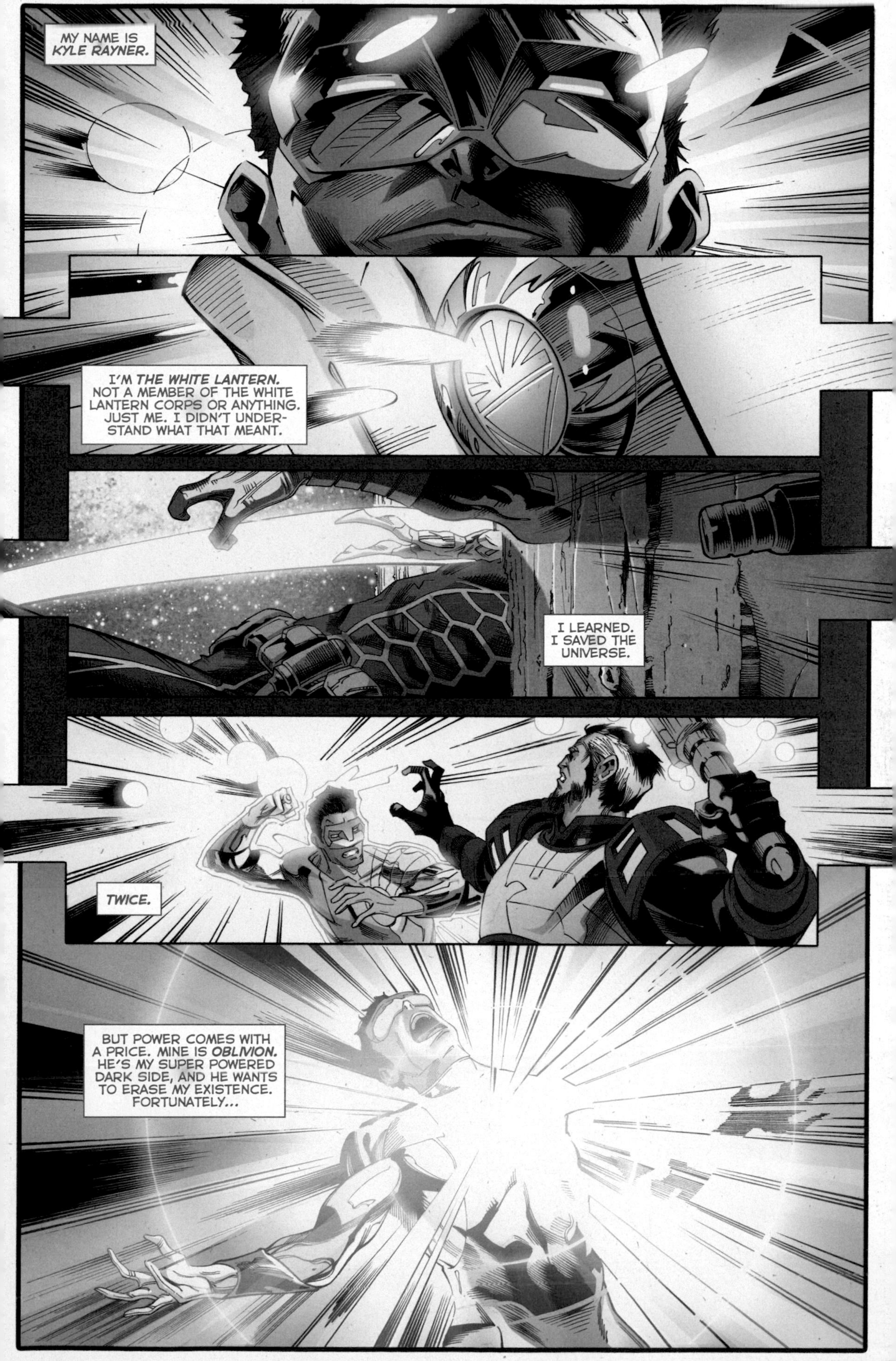
MY NAME IS KYLE RAYNER.
I'M THE WHITE LANTERN. NOT A MEMBER OF THE WHITE LANTERN CORPS OR ANYTHING. JUST ME. I DIDN'T UNDERSTAND WHAT THAT MEANT.
I LEARNED. I SAVED THE UNIVERSE.
TWICE.
BUT POWER COMES WITH A PRICE. MINE IS OBLIVION. HE'S MY SUPER POWERED DARK SIDE, AND HE WANTS TO ERASE MY EXISTENCE. FORTUNATELY...

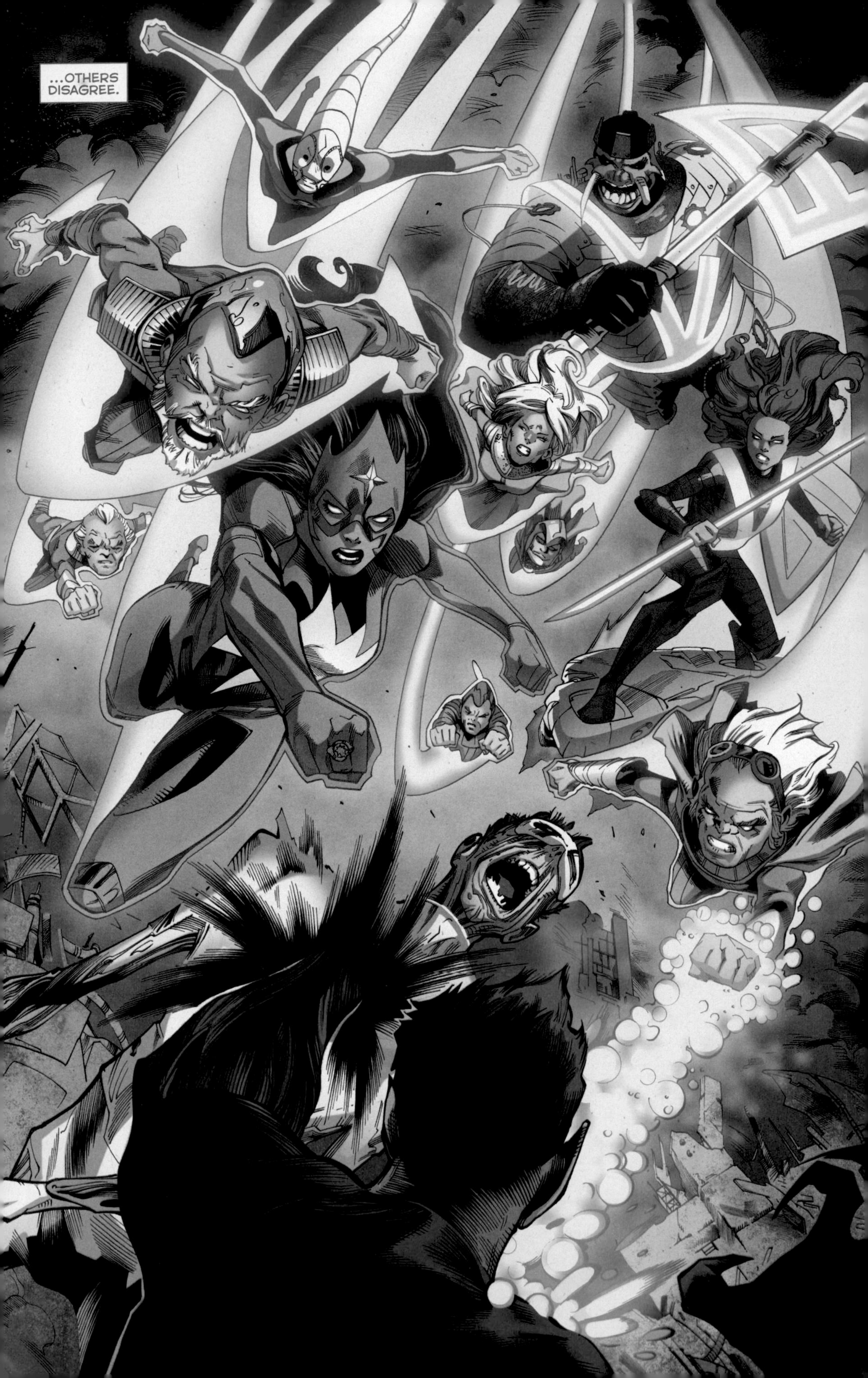
...OTHERS DISAGREE.

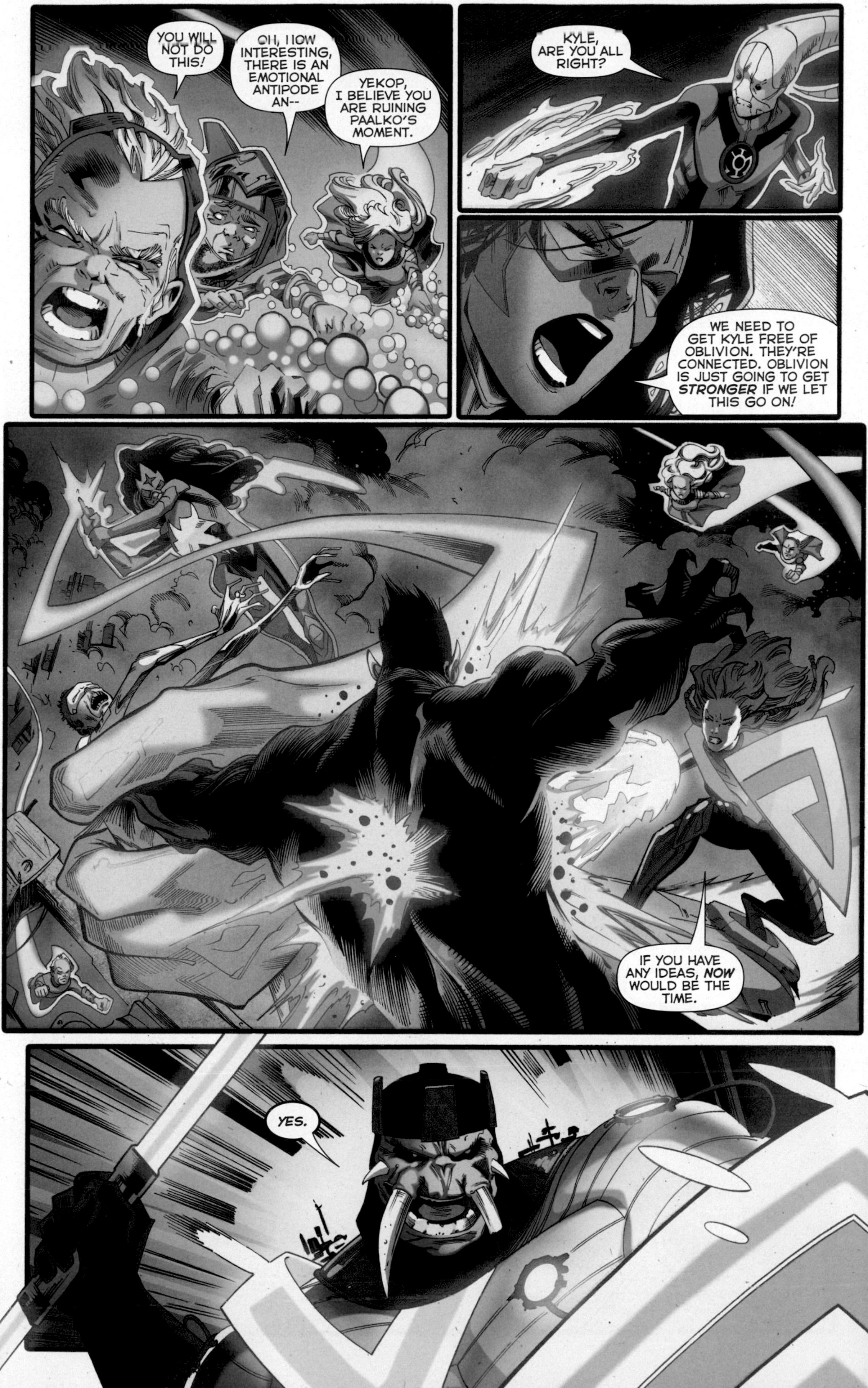
YOU WILL NOT DO THIS!
OH, HOW INTERESTING, THERE IS AN EMOTIONAL ANTIPODE AN--
YEKOP, I BELIEVE YOU ARE RUINING PAALKO'S MOMENT.
KYLE, ARE YOU ALL RIGHT?
WE NEED TO GET KYLE FREE OF OBLIVION. THEY'RE CONNECTED. OBLIVION IS JUST GOING TO GET *STRONGER* IF WE LET THIS GO ON!
IF YOU HAVE ANY IDEAS, *NOW* WOULD BE THE TIME.
YES.

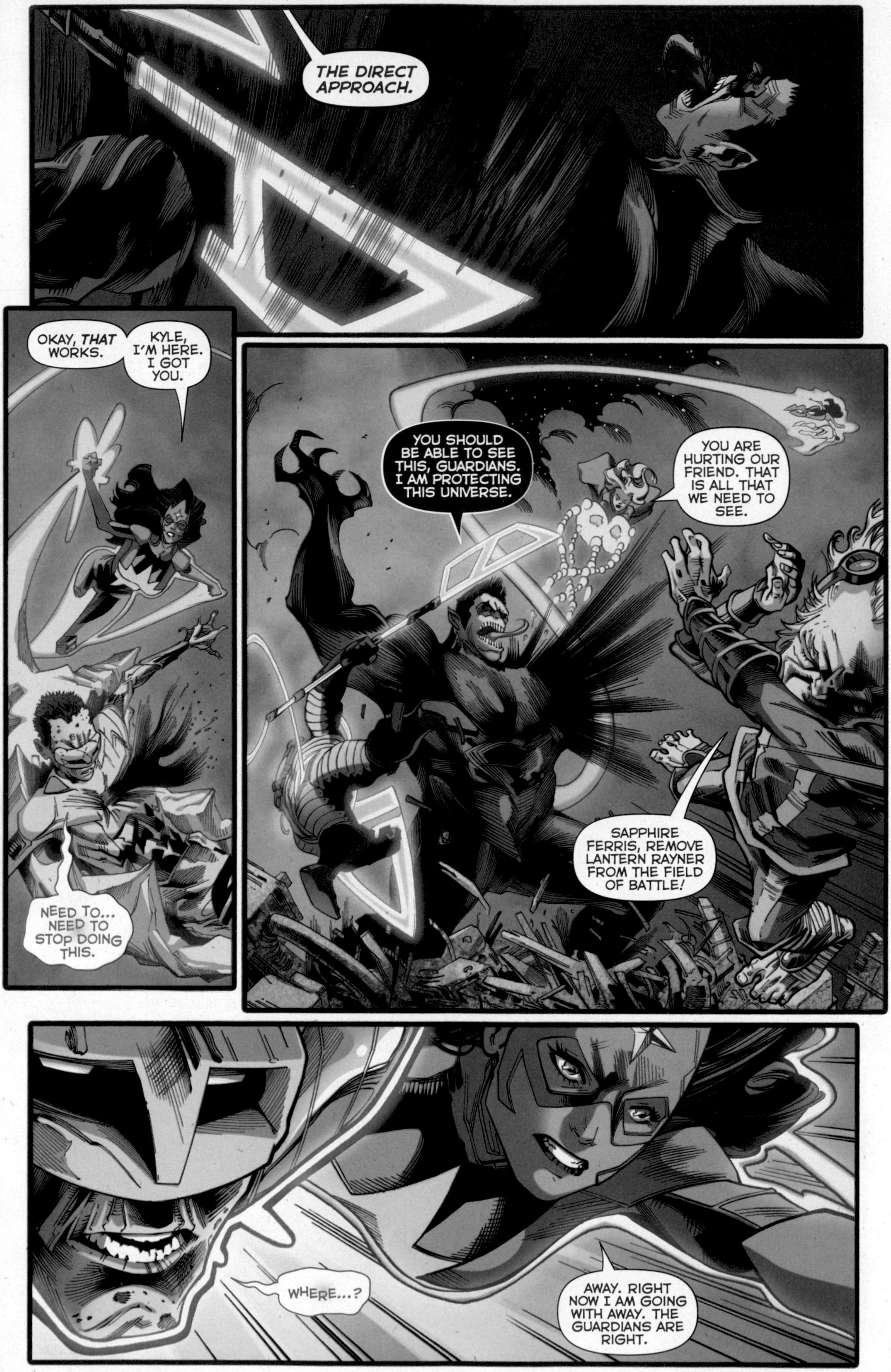
THE DIRECT APPROACH.
OKAY, *THAT* WORKS.
KYLE, I'M HERE. I GOT YOU.
NEED TO... NEED TO STOP DOING THIS.
YOU SHOULD BE ABLE TO SEE THIS, GUARDIANS. I AM PROTECTING THIS UNIVERSE.
YOU ARE HURTING OUR FRIEND. THAT IS ALL THAT WE NEED TO SEE.
SAPPHIRE FERRIS, REMOVE LANTERN RAYNER FROM THE FIELD OF BATTLE!
WHERE...?
AWAY. RIGHT NOW I AM GOING WITH AWAY. THE GUARDIANS ARE RIGHT.

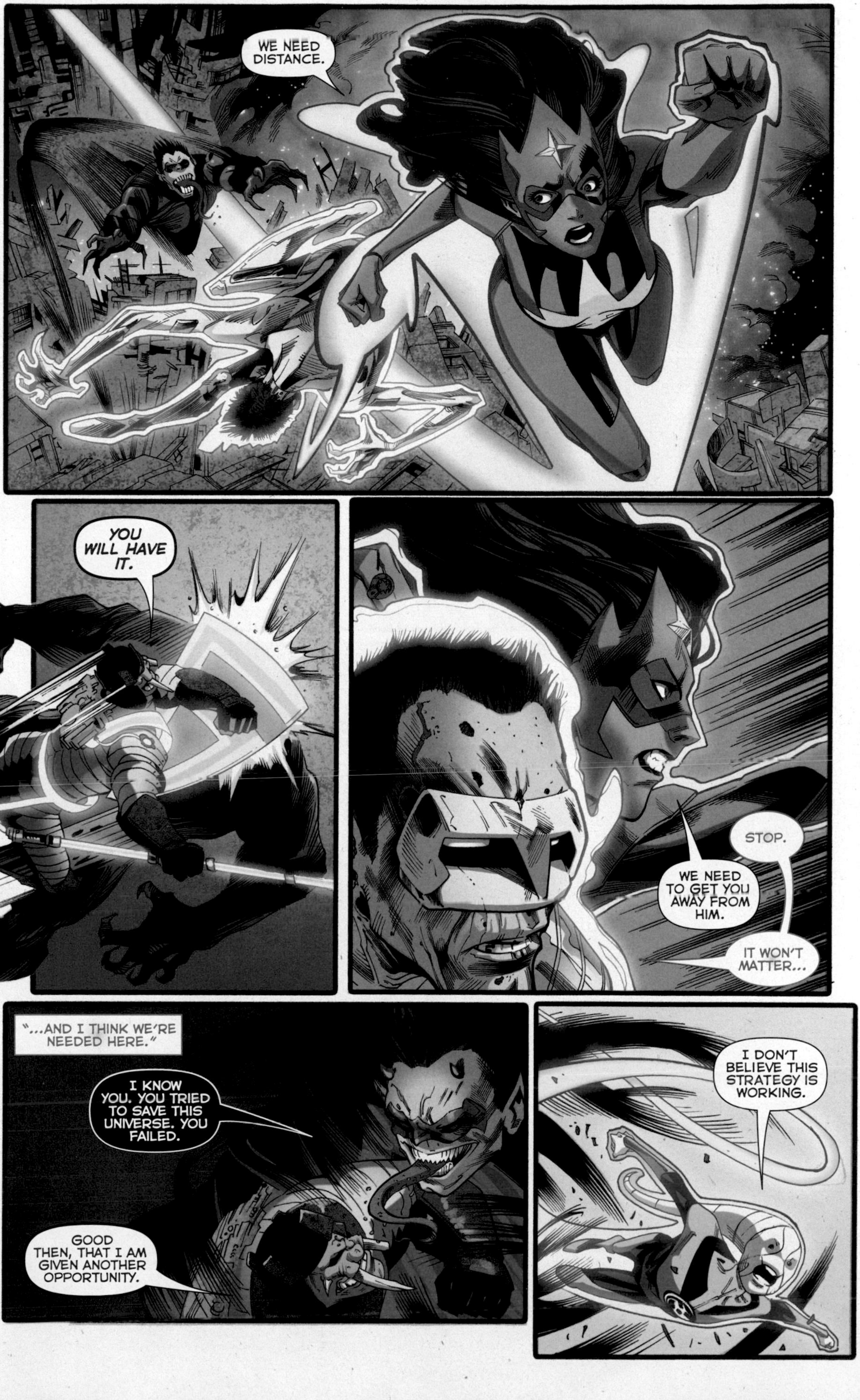

WE NEED DISTANCE.
YOU WILL HAVE IT.
STOP.
WE NEED TO GET YOU AWAY FROM HIM.
IT WON'T MATTER...
"...AND I THINK WE'RE NEEDED HERE."
I KNOW YOU. YOU TRIED TO SAVE THIS UNIVERSE. YOU FAILED.
GOOD THEN, THAT I AM GIVEN ANOTHER OPPORTUNITY.
I DON'T BELIEVE THIS STRATEGY IS WORKING.

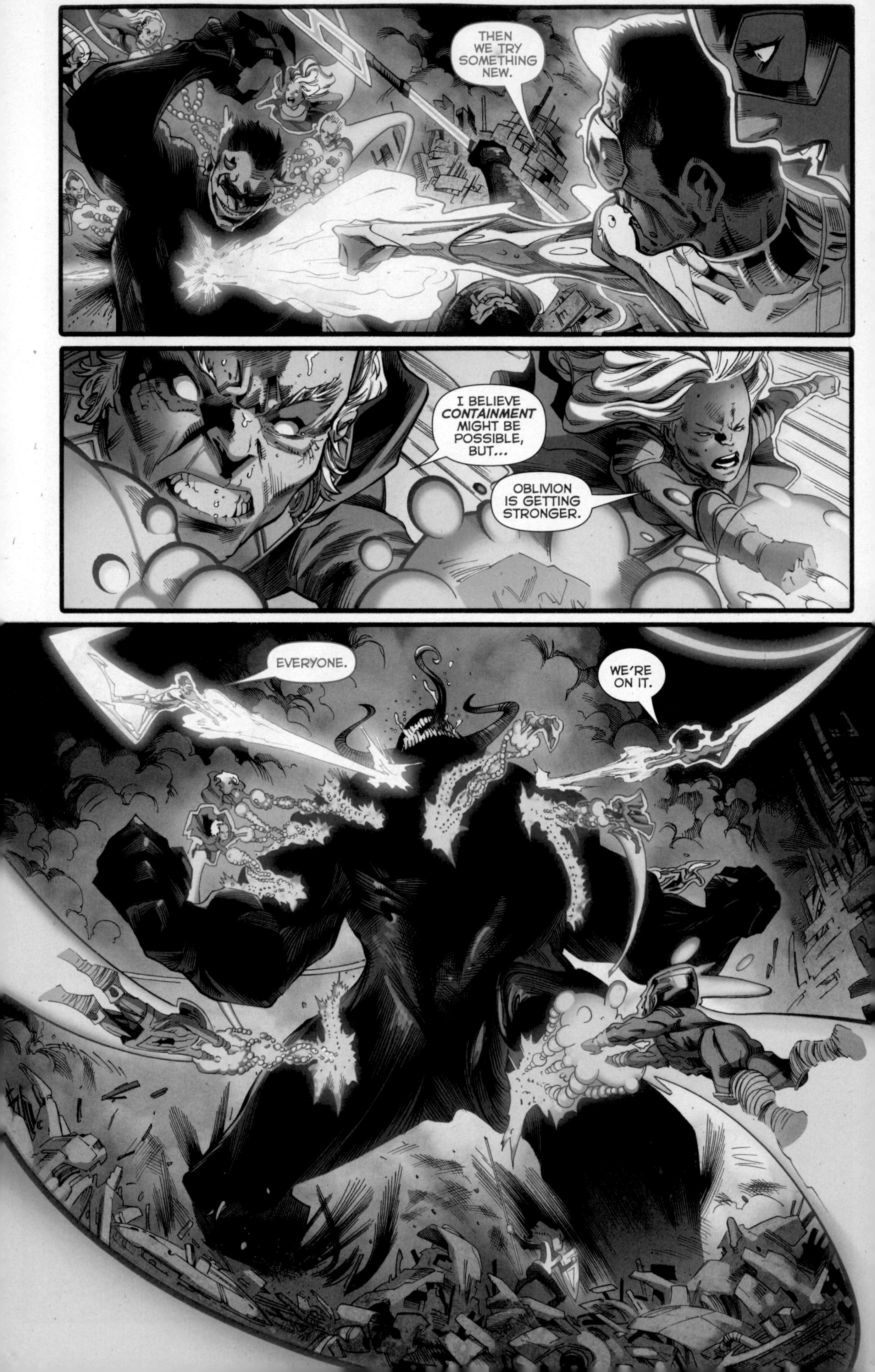
THEN WE TRY SOMETHING NEW.
I BELIEVE *CONTAINMENT* MIGHT BE POSSIBLE, BUT...
OBLIVION IS GETTING STRONGER.
EVERYONE.
WE'RE ON IT.

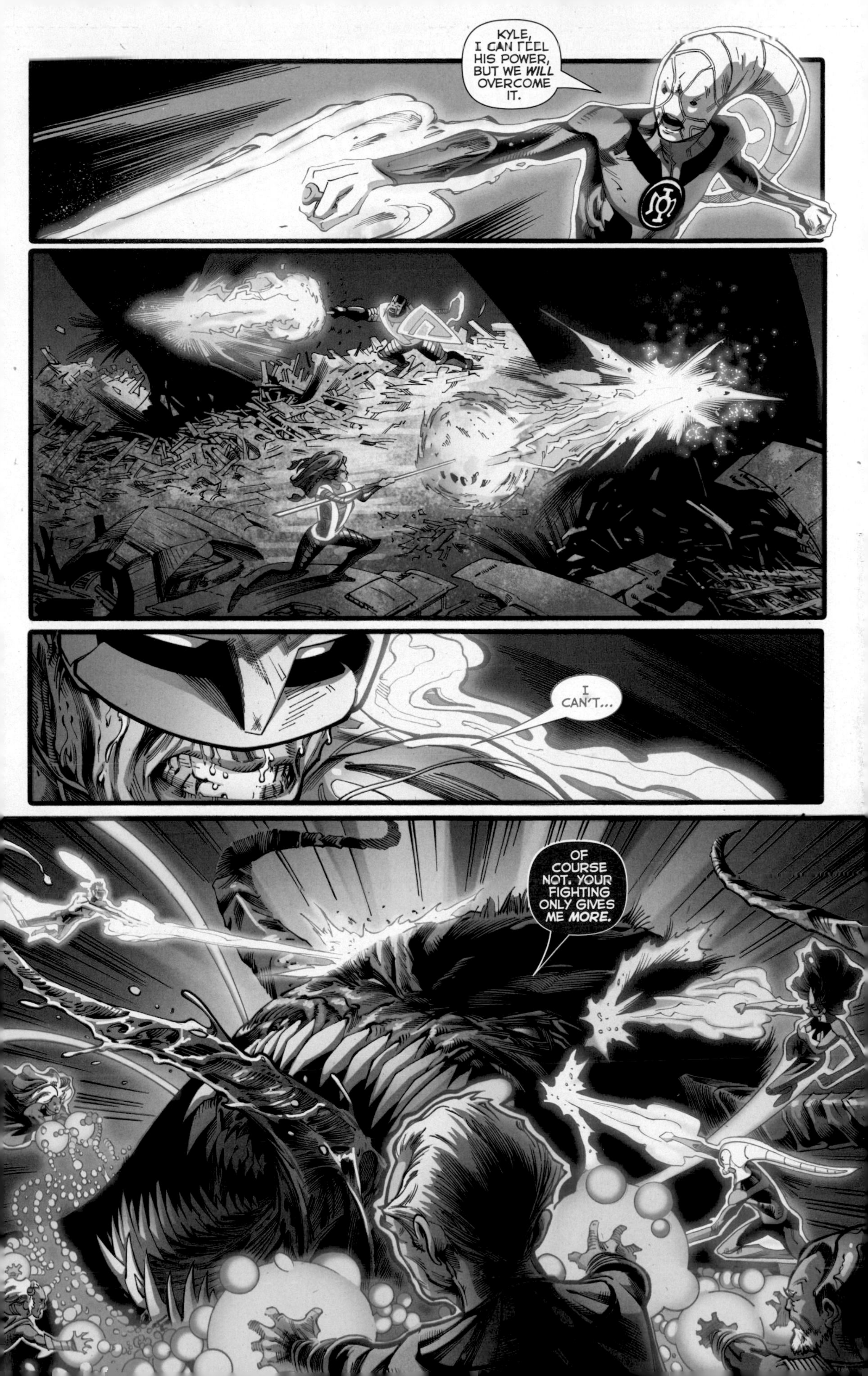
KYLE, I CAN FEEL HIS POWER, BUT WE WILL OVERCOME IT.
I CAN'T...
OF COURSE NOT. YOUR FIGHTING ONLY GIVES ME MORE.

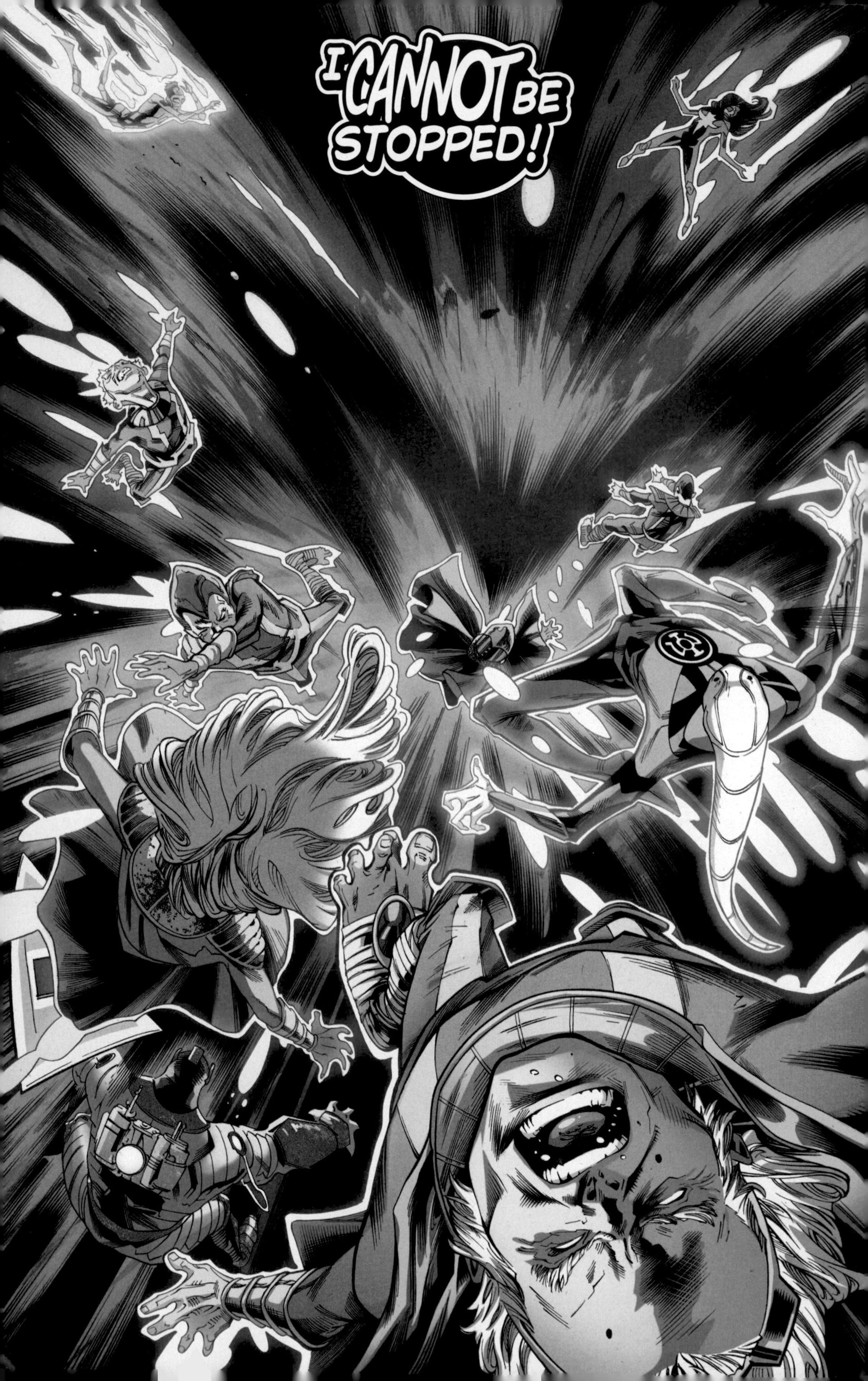
I CANNOT BE STOPPED!

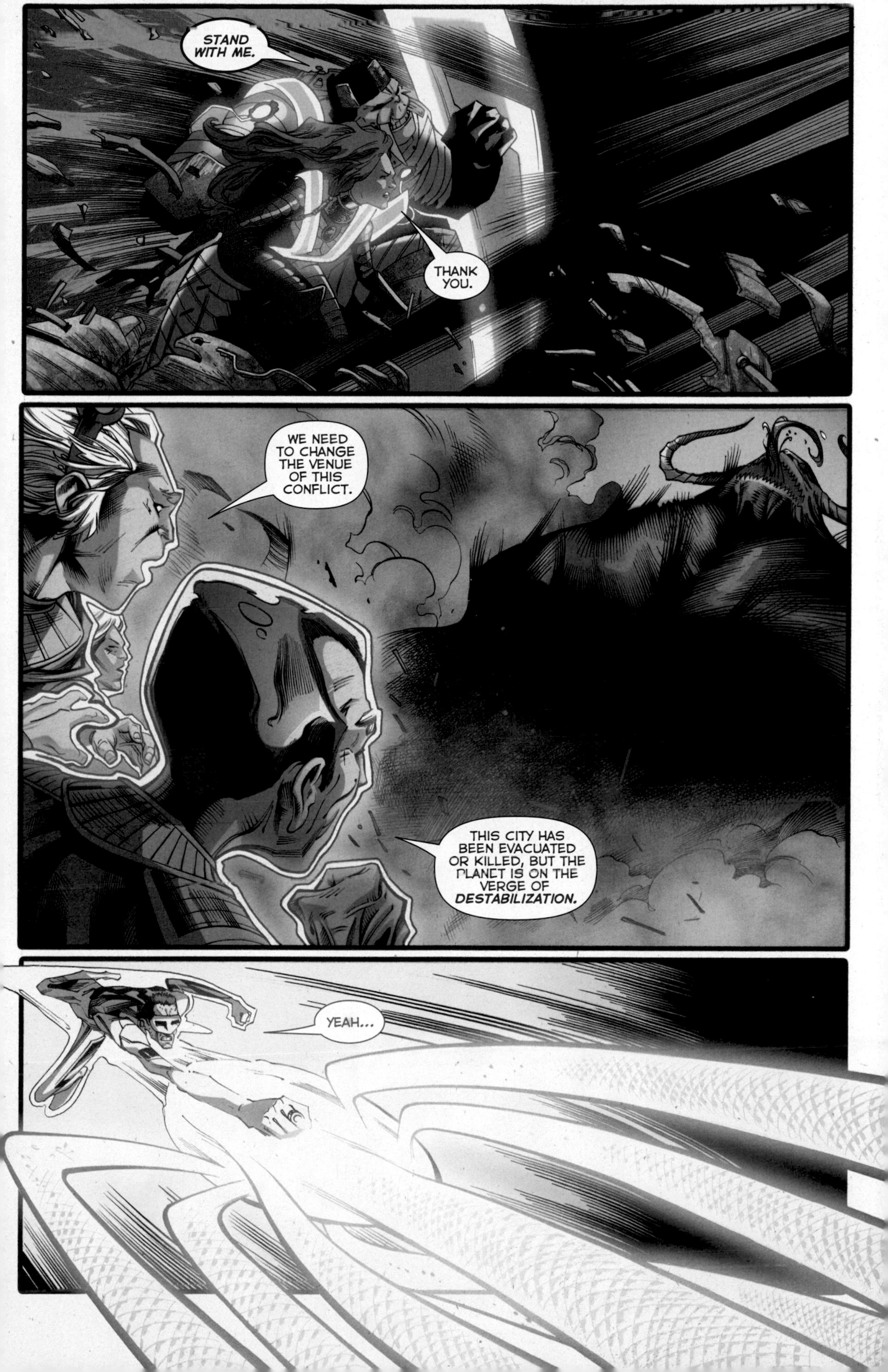
STAND WITH ME.
THANK YOU.
WE NEED TO CHANGE THE VENUE OF THIS CONFLICT.
THIS CITY HAS BEEN EVACUATED OR KILLED, BUT THE PLANET IS ON THE VERGE OF *DESTABILIZATION.*
YEAH...

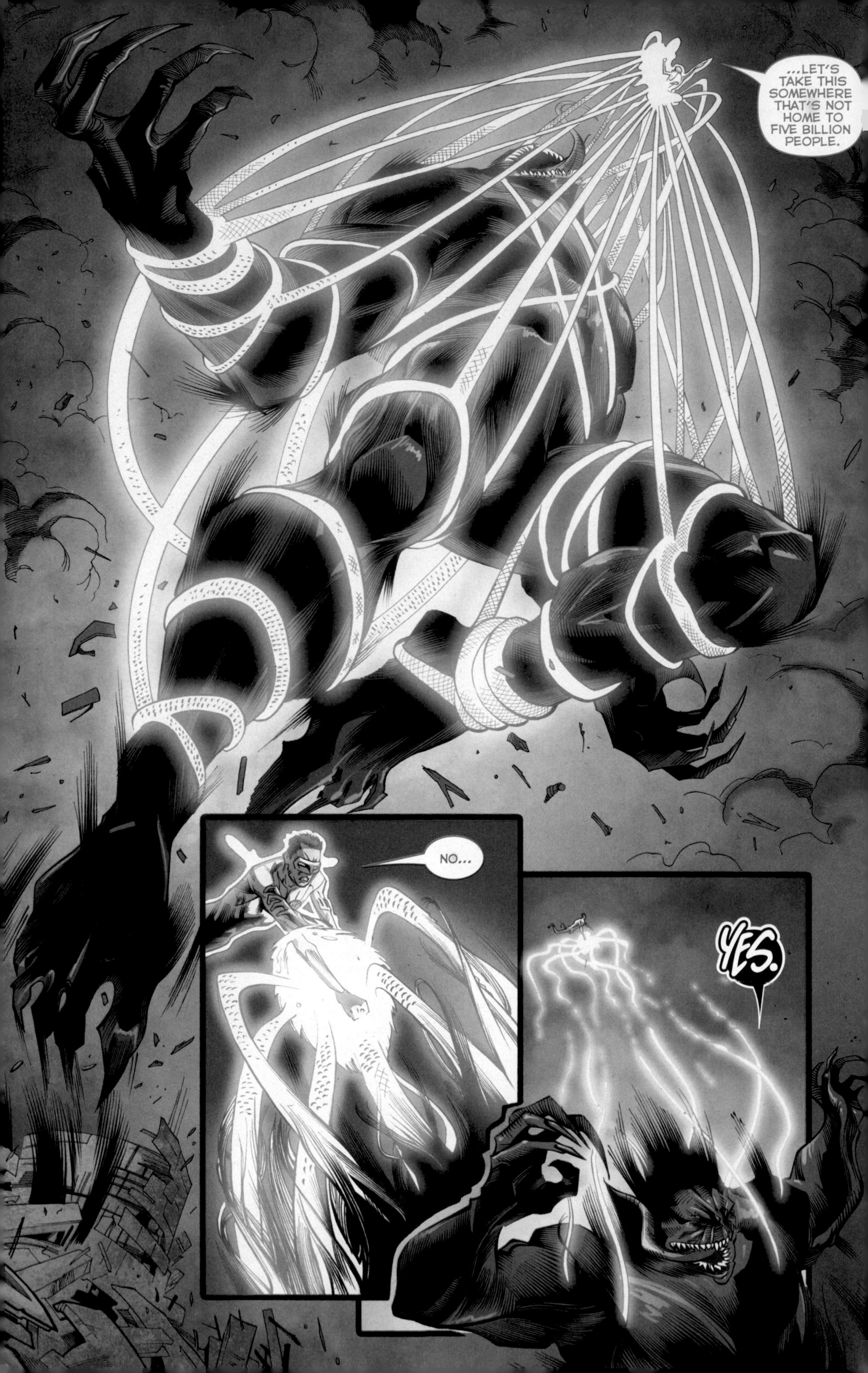
...LET'S TAKE THIS SOMEWHERE THAT'S NOT HOME TO FIVE BILLION PEOPLE.
NO...
YES.

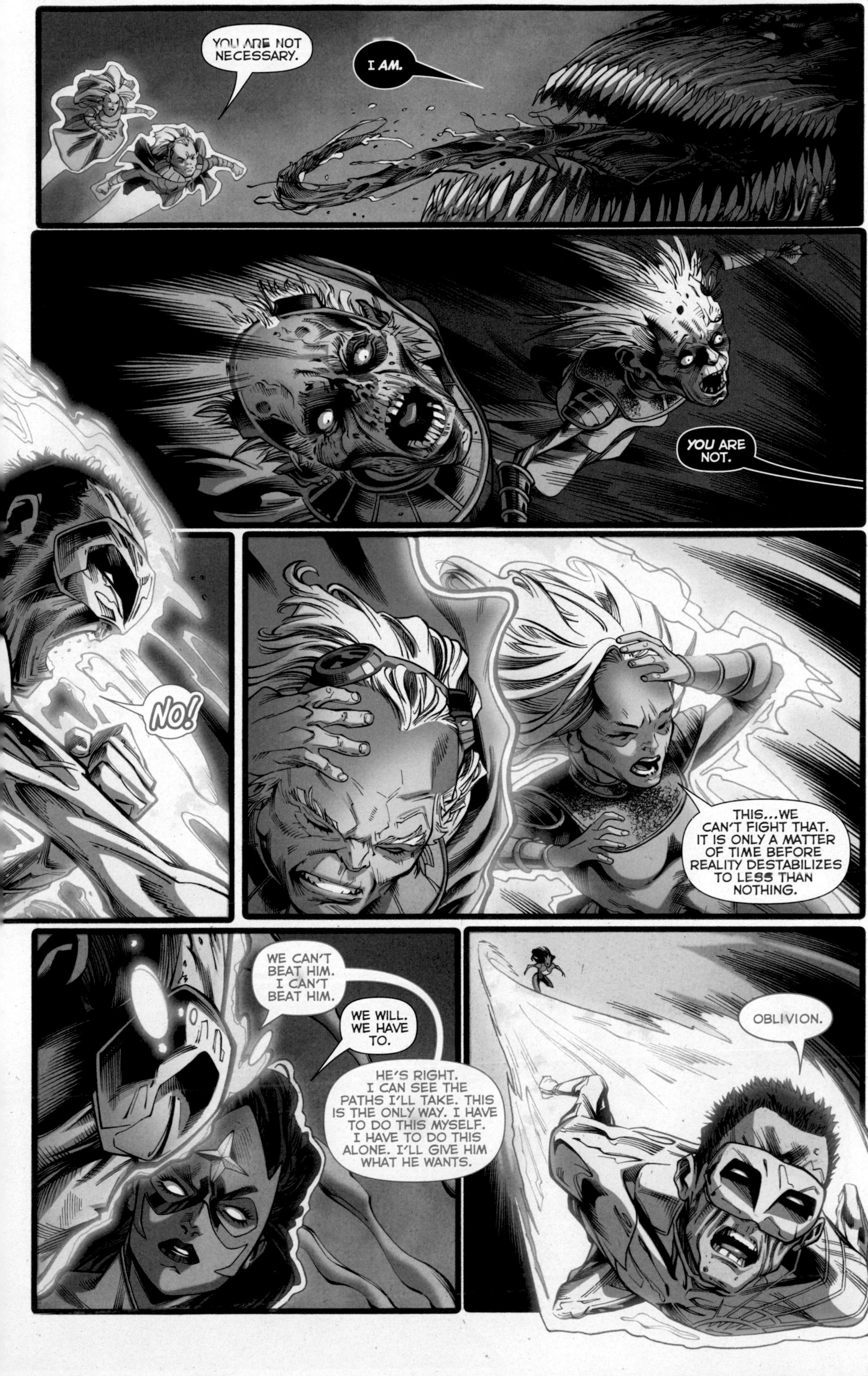
YOU ARE NOT NECESSARY.
I AM.
YOU ARE NOT.
NO!
THIS...WE CAN'T FIGHT THAT. IT IS ONLY A MATTER OF TIME BEFORE REALITY DESTABILIZES TO LESS THAN NOTHING.
WE CAN'T BEAT HIM. I CAN'T BEAT HIM.
WE WILL. WE HAVE TO.
HE'S RIGHT. I CAN SEE THE PATHS I'LL TAKE. THIS IS THE ONLY WAY. I HAVE TO DO THIS MYSELF. I HAVE TO DO THIS ALONE. I'LL GIVE HIM WHAT HE WANTS.
OBLIVION.

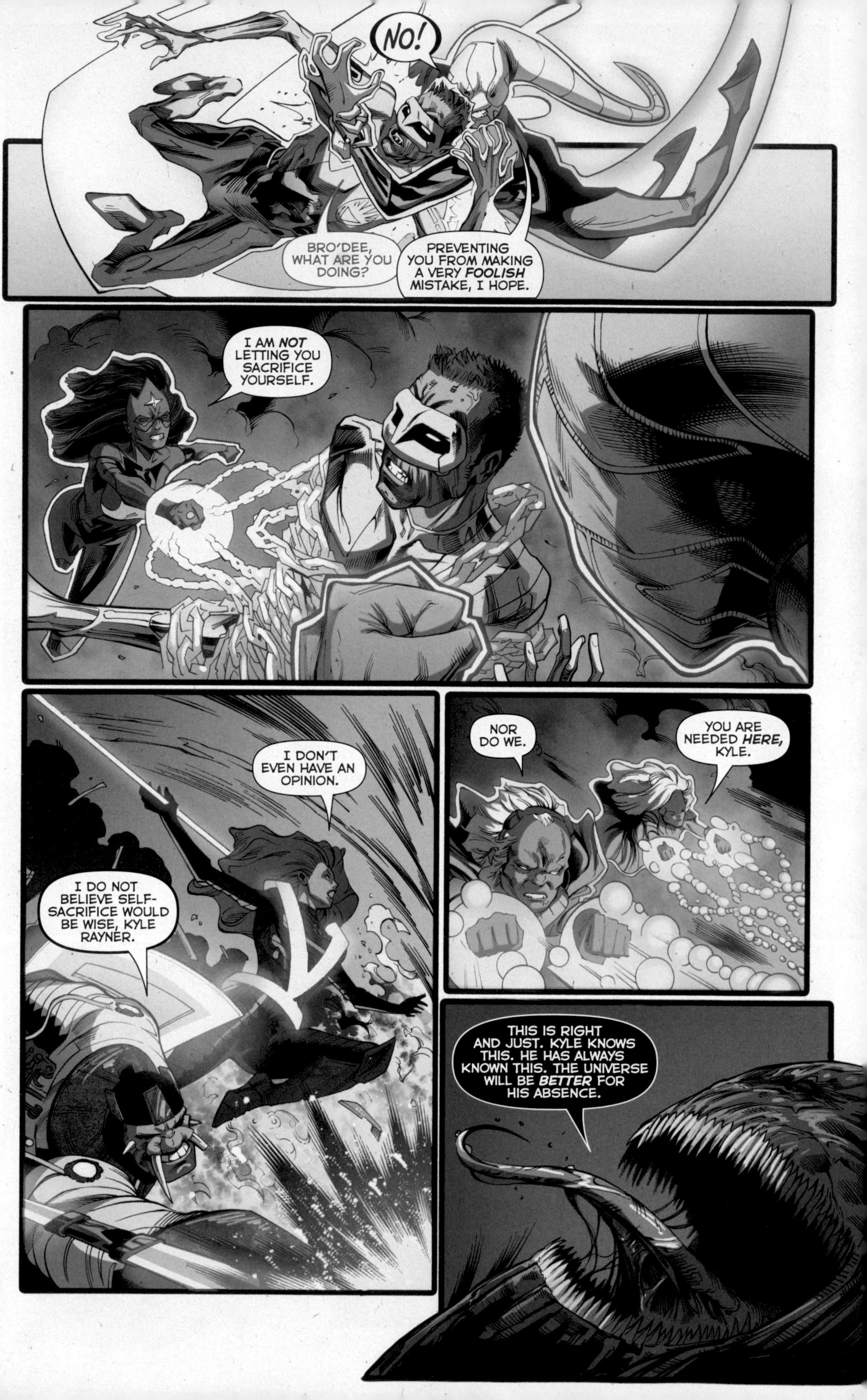
NO!
BRO'DEE, WHAT ARE YOU DOING?
PREVENTING YOU FROM MAKING A VERY *FOOLISH* MISTAKE, I HOPE.
I AM *NOT* LETTING YOU SACRIFICE YOURSELF.
I DON'T EVEN HAVE AN OPINION.
I DO NOT BELIEVE SELF-SACRIFICE WOULD BE WISE, KYLE RAYNER.
NOR DO WE.
YOU ARE NEEDED *HERE,* KYLE.
THIS IS RIGHT AND JUST. KYLE KNOWS THIS. HE HAS ALWAYS KNOWN THIS. THE UNIVERSE WILL BE *BETTER* FOR HIS ABSENCE.

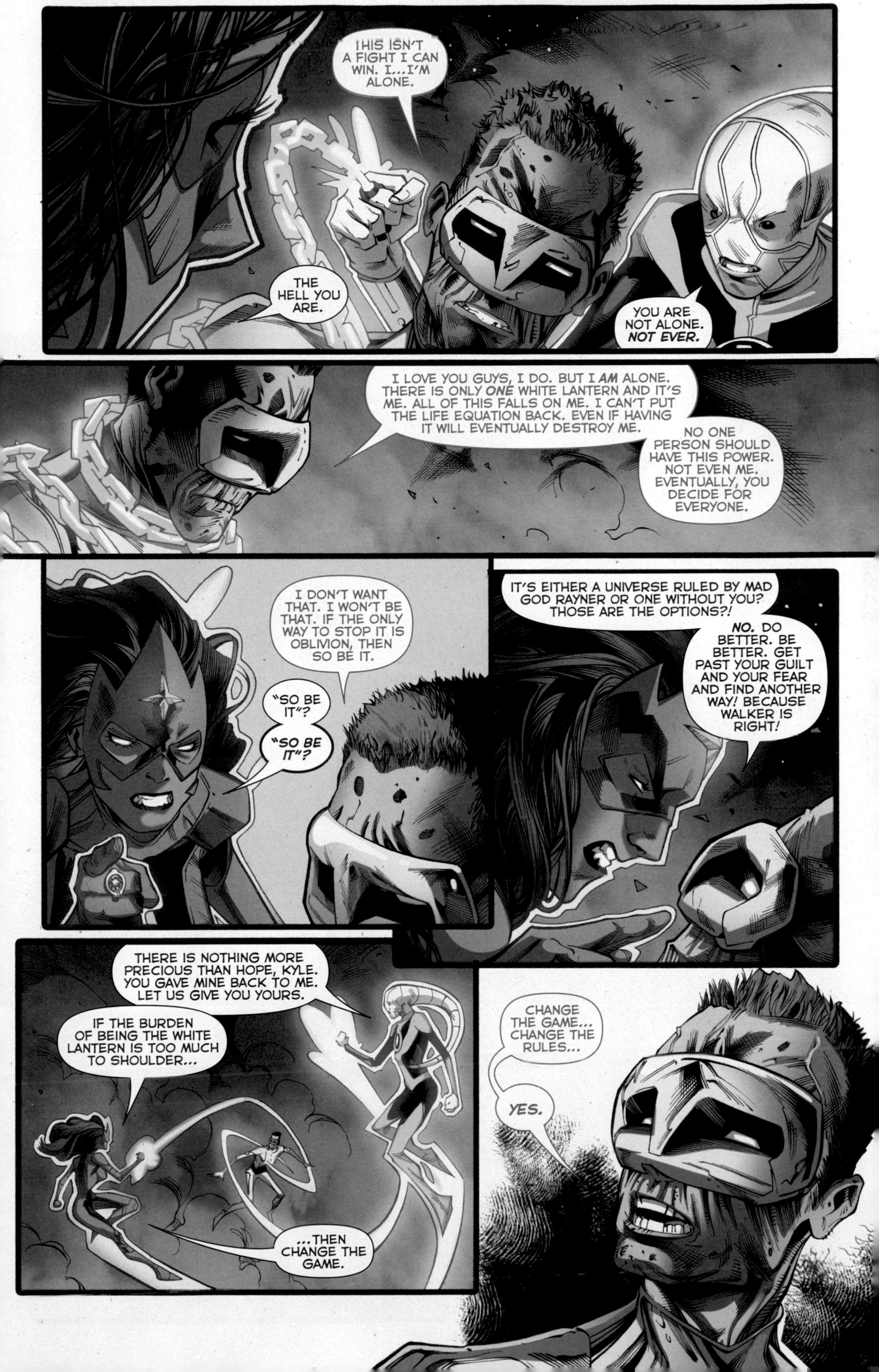
THIS ISN'T A FIGHT I CAN WIN. I...I'M ALONE.
THE HELL YOU ARE.
YOU ARE NOT ALONE. NOT EVER.
I LOVE YOU GUYS, I DO. BUT I AM ALONE. THERE IS ONLY ONE WHITE LANTERN AND IT'S ME. ALL OF THIS FALLS ON ME. I CAN'T PUT THE LIFE EQUATION BACK. EVEN IF HAVING IT WILL EVENTUALLY DESTROY ME.
NO ONE PERSON SHOULD HAVE THIS POWER. NOT EVEN ME. EVENTUALLY, YOU DECIDE FOR EVERYONE.
I DON'T WANT THAT. I WON'T BE THAT. IF THE ONLY WAY TO STOP IT IS OBLIVION, THEN SO BE IT.
"SO BE IT"?
"SO BE IT"?
IT'S EITHER A UNIVERSE RULED BY MAD GOD RAYNER OR ONE WITHOUT YOU? THOSE ARE THE OPTIONS?!
NO. DO BETTER. BE BETTER. GET PAST YOUR GUILT AND YOUR FEAR AND FIND ANOTHER WAY! BECAUSE WALKER IS RIGHT!
THERE IS NOTHING MORE PRECIOUS THAN HOPE, KYLE. YOU GAVE MINE BACK TO ME. LET US GIVE YOU YOURS.
IF THE BURDEN OF BEING THE WHITE LANTERN IS TOO MUCH TO SHOULDER...
...THEN CHANGE THE GAME.
CHANGE THE GAME... CHANGE THE RULES...
YES.

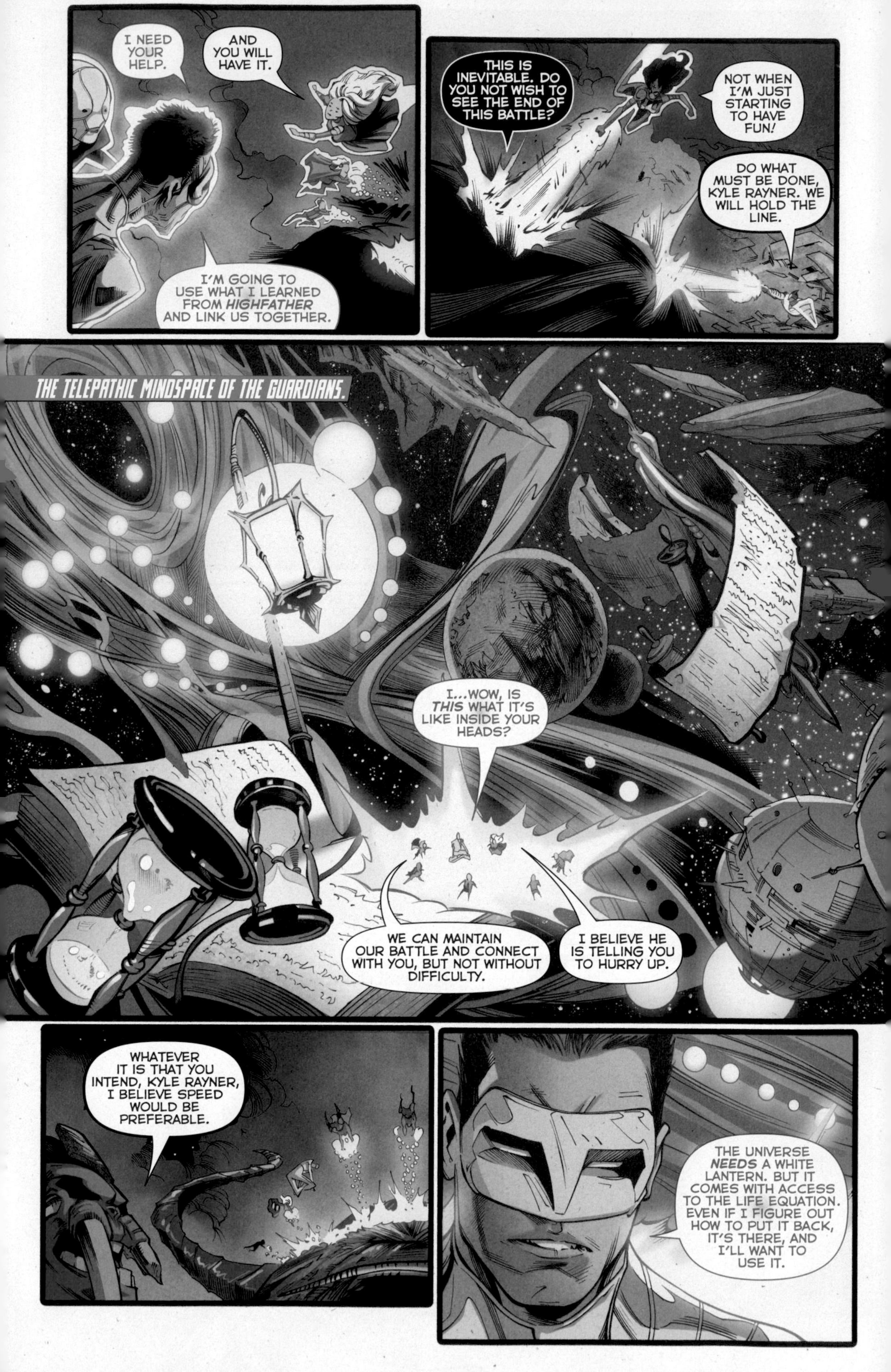
I NEED YOUR HELP.
AND YOU WILL HAVE IT.
I'M GOING TO USE WHAT I LEARNED FROM *HIGHFATHER* AND LINK US TOGETHER.
THIS IS INEVITABLE. DO YOU NOT WISH TO SEE THE END OF THIS BATTLE?
NOT WHEN I'M JUST STARTING TO HAVE FUN!
DO WHAT MUST BE DONE, KYLE RAYNER. WE WILL HOLD THE LINE.
THE TELEPATHIC MINDSPACE OF THE GUARDIANS.
I...WOW, IS *THIS* WHAT IT'S LIKE INSIDE YOUR HEADS?
WE CAN MAINTAIN OUR BATTLE AND CONNECT WITH YOU, BUT NOT WITHOUT DIFFICULTY.
I BELIEVE HE IS TELLING YOU TO HURRY UP.
WHATEVER IT IS THAT YOU INTEND, KYLE RAYNER, I BELIEVE SPEED WOULD BE PREFERABLE.
THE UNIVERSE *NEEDS* A WHITE LANTERN. BUT IT COMES WITH ACCESS TO THE LIFE EQUATION. EVEN IF I FIGURE OUT HOW TO PUT IT BACK, IT'S THERE, AND I'LL WANT TO USE IT.

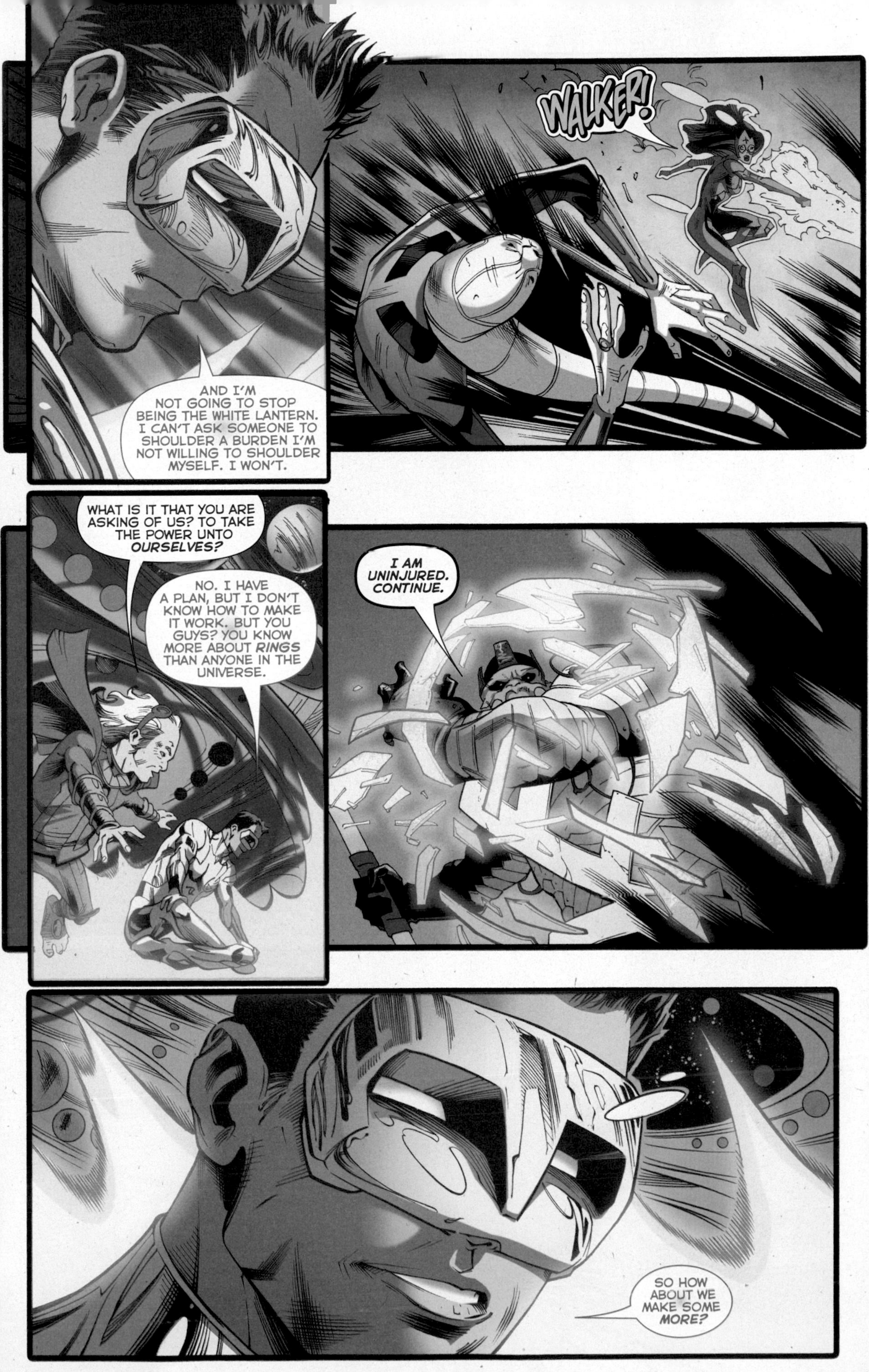

AND I'M NOT GOING TO STOP BEING THE WHITE LANTERN. I CAN'T ASK SOMEONE TO SHOULDER A BURDEN I'M NOT WILLING TO SHOULDER MYSELF. I WON'T.
WALKER!
WHAT IS IT THAT YOU ARE ASKING OF US? TO TAKE THE POWER UNTO *OURSELVES?*
NO. I HAVE A PLAN, BUT I DON'T KNOW HOW TO MAKE IT WORK. BUT YOU GUYS? YOU KNOW MORE ABOUT *RINGS* THAN ANYONE IN THE UNIVERSE.
I AM UNINJURED. CONTINUE.
SO HOW ABOUT WE MAKE SOME *MORE?*

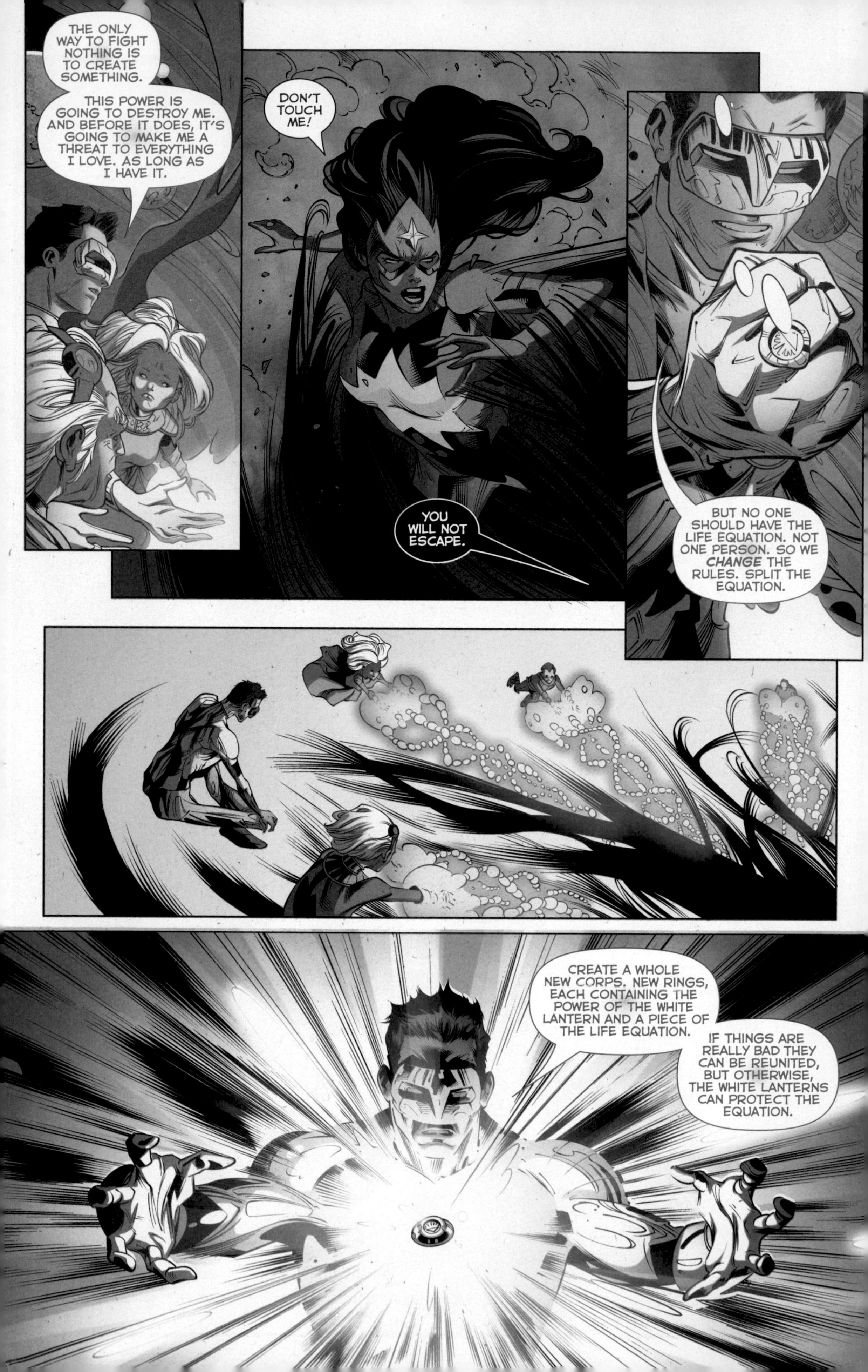
THE ONLY WAY TO FIGHT NOTHING IS TO CREATE SOMETHING.
THIS POWER IS GOING TO DESTROY ME. AND BEFORE IT DOES, IT'S GOING TO MAKE ME A THREAT TO EVERYTHING I LOVE. AS LONG AS I HAVE IT.
DON'T TOUCH ME!
YOU WILL NOT ESCAPE.
BUT NO ONE SHOULD HAVE THE LIFE EQUATION. NOT ONE PERSON. SO WE *CHANGE* THE RULES. SPLIT THE EQUATION.
CREATE A WHOLE NEW CORPS. NEW RINGS, EACH CONTAINING THE POWER OF THE WHITE LANTERN AND A PIECE OF THE LIFE EQUATION.
IF THINGS ARE REALLY BAD THEY CAN BE REUNITED, BUT OTHERWISE, THE WHITE LANTERNS CAN PROTECT THE EQUATION.

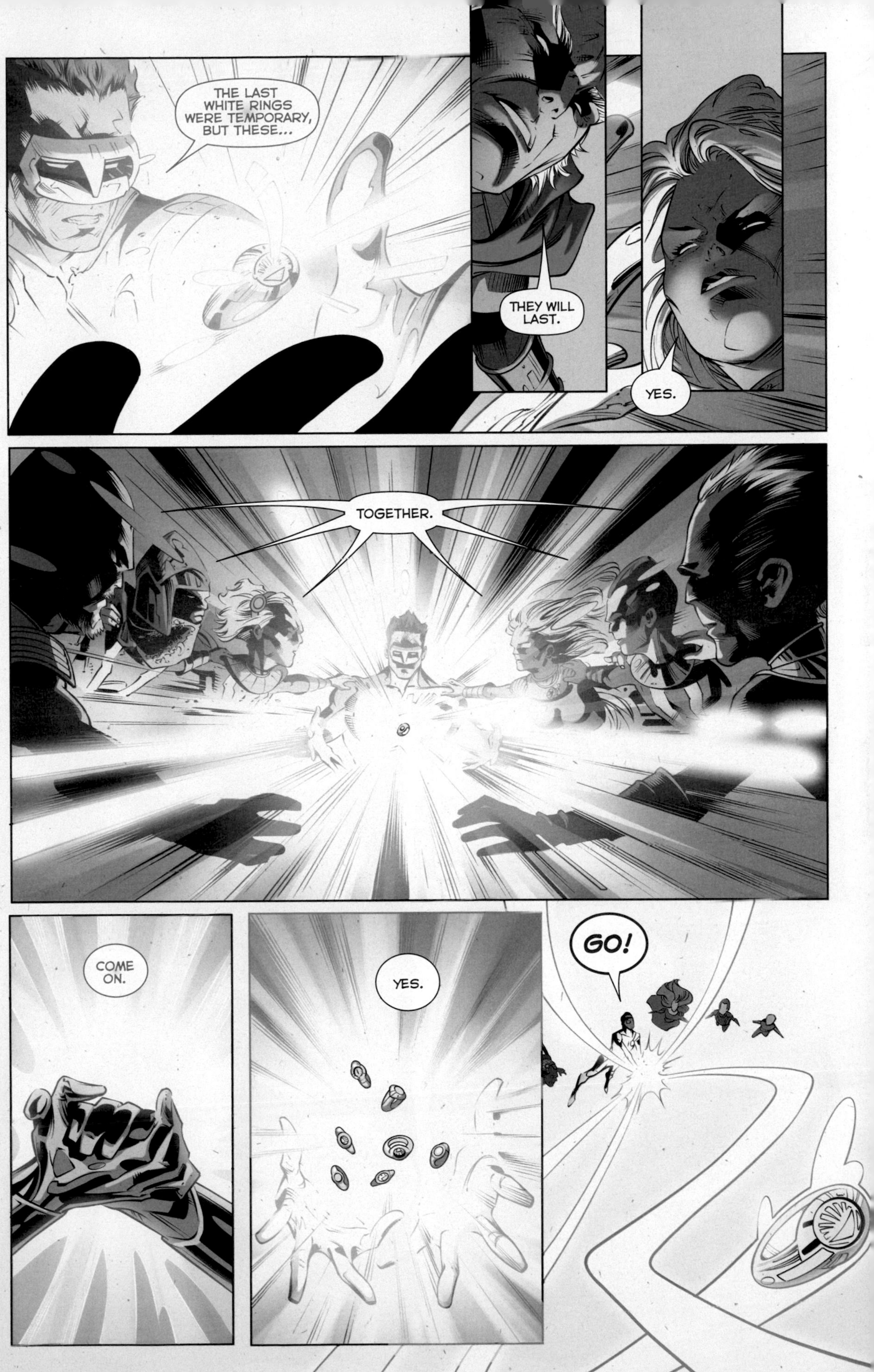
THE LAST WHITE RINGS WERE TEMPORARY, BUT THESE...
THEY WILL LAST.
YES.
TOGETHER.
COME ON.
YES.
GO!

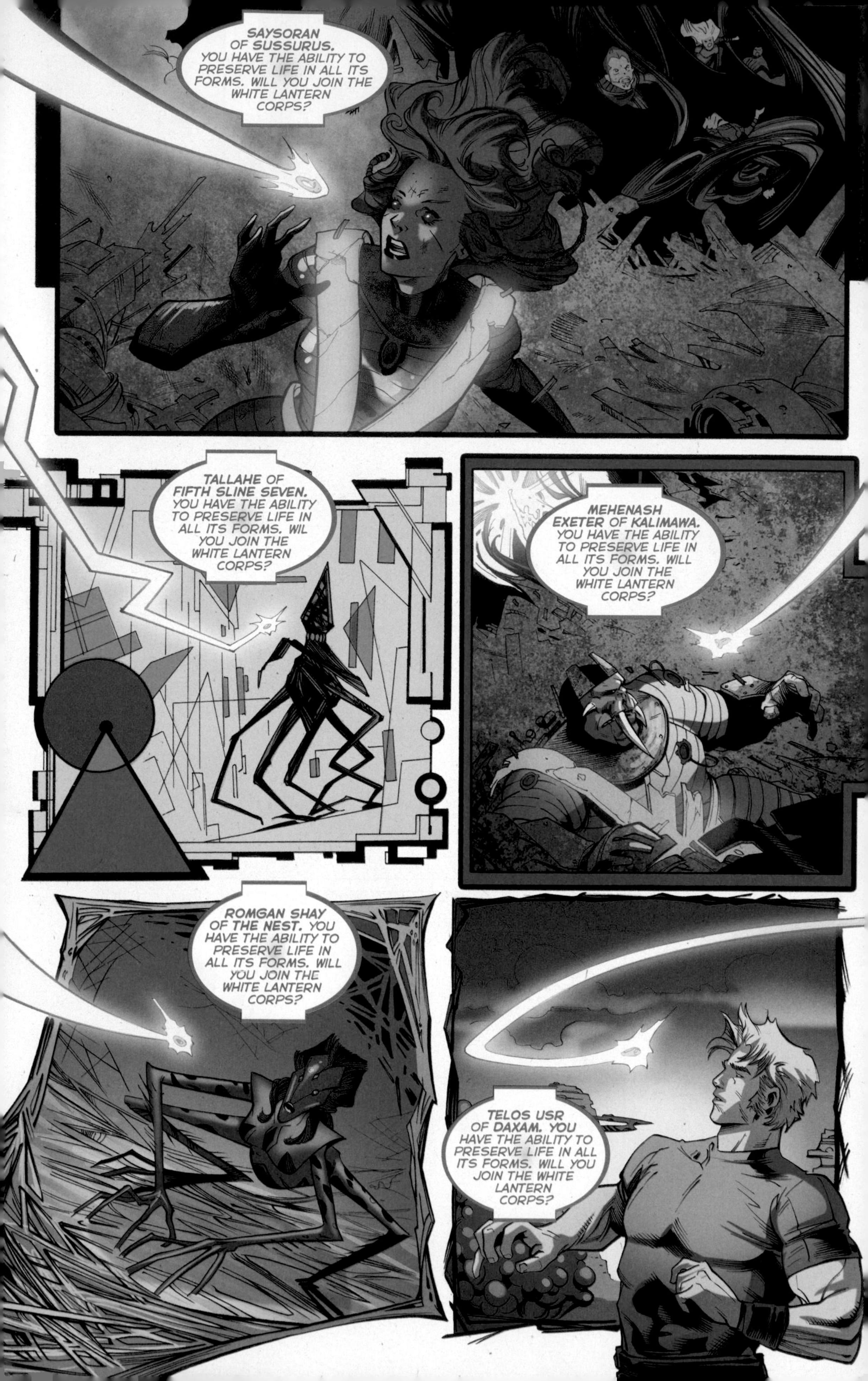
SAYSORAN OF SUSSURUS. YOU HAVE THE ABILITY TO PRESERVE LIFE IN ALL ITS FORMS. WILL YOU JOIN THE WHITE LANTERN CORPS?
TALLAHE OF FIFTH SLINE SEVEN. YOU HAVE THE ABILITY TO PRESERVE LIFE IN ALL ITS FORMS. WIL YOU JOIN THE WHITE LANTERN CORPS?
MEHENASH EXETER OF KALIMAWA. YOU HAVE THE ABILITY TO PRESERVE LIFE IN ALL ITS FORMS. WILL YOU JOIN THE WHITE LANTERN CORPS?
ROMGAN SHAY OF THE NEST. YOU HAVE THE ABILITY TO PRESERVE LIFE IN ALL ITS FORMS. WILL YOU JOIN THE WHITE LANTERN CORPS?
TELOS USR OF DAXAM. YOU HAVE THE ABILITY TO PRESERVE LIFE IN ALL ITS FORMS. WILL YOU JOIN THE WHITE LANTERN CORPS?

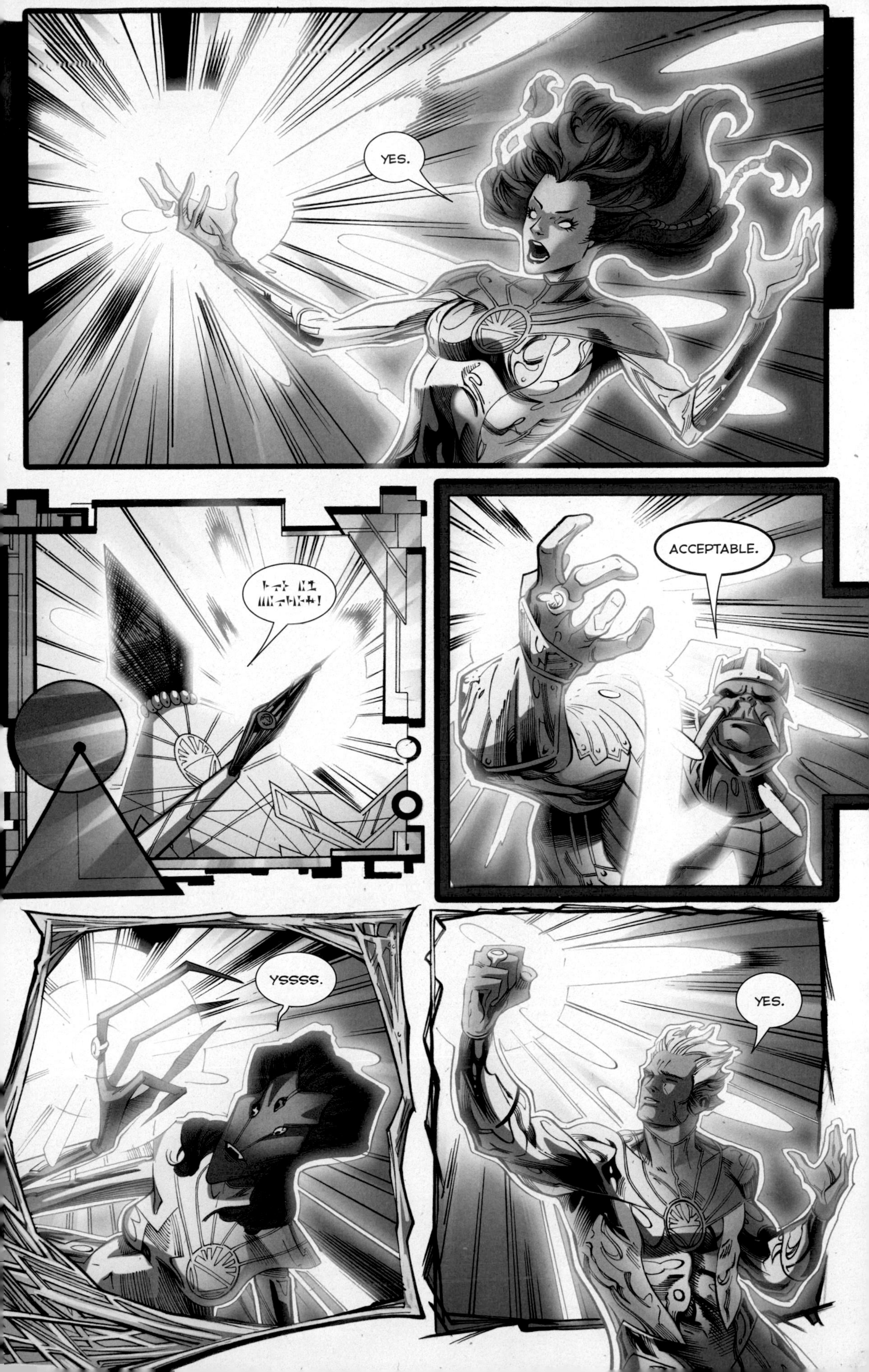
YES.
ACCEPTABLE.
YSSSS.
YES.

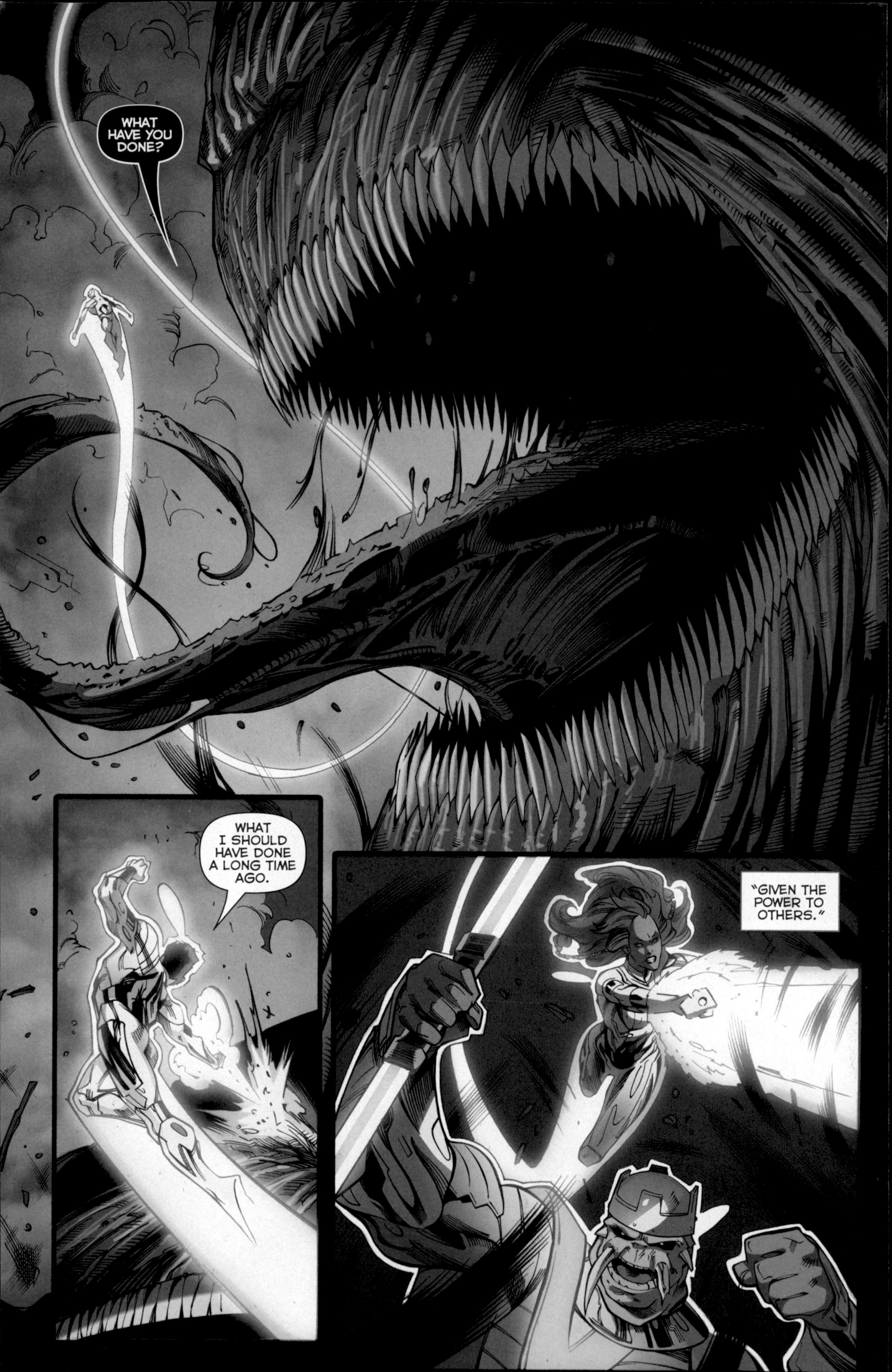
WHAT HAVE YOU DONE?
WHAT I SHOULD HAVE DONE A LONG TIME AGO.
"GIVEN THE POWER TO OTHERS."

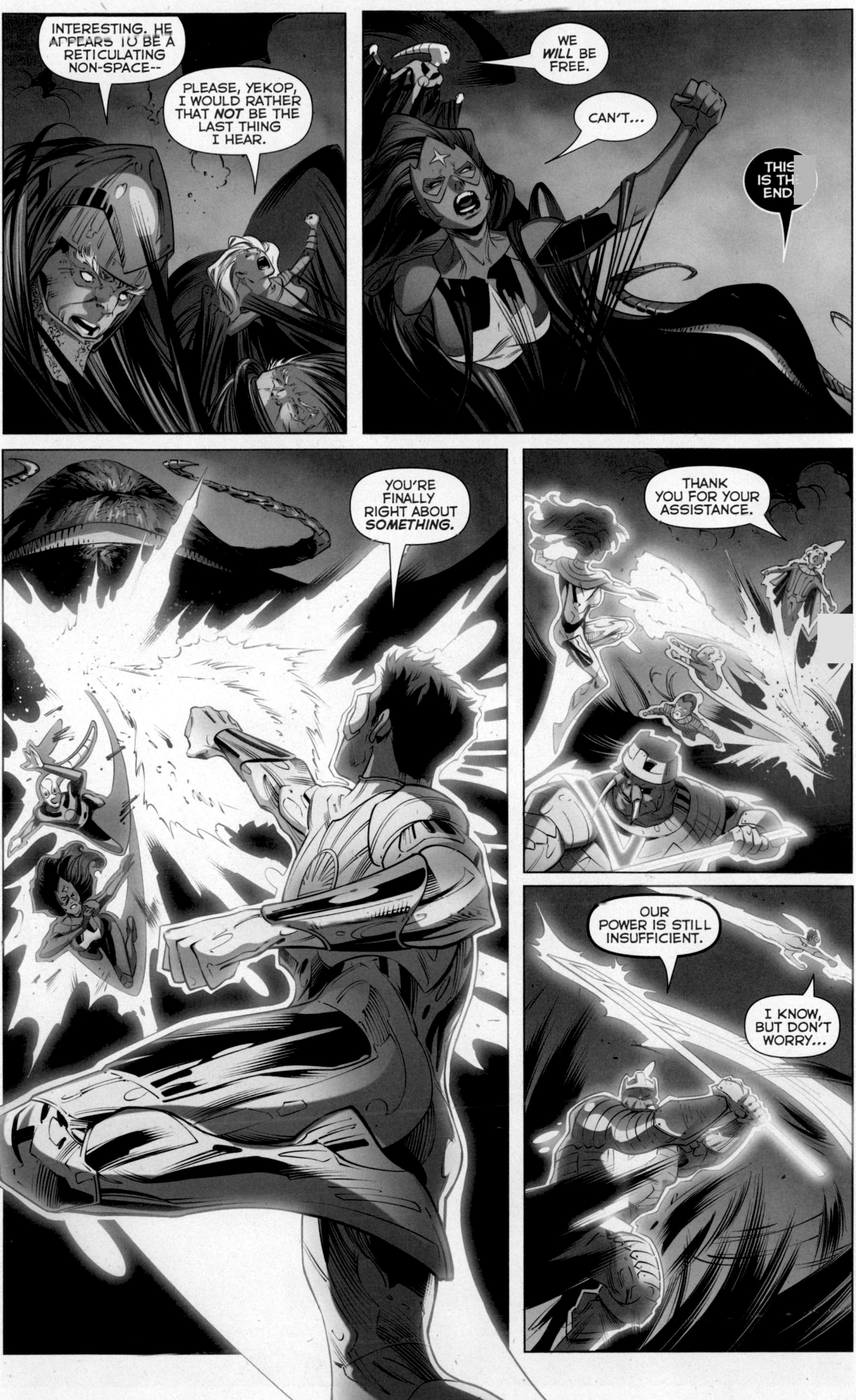
INTERESTING. HE APPEARS TO BE A RETICULATING NON-SPACE--
PLEASE, YEKOP, I WOULD RATHER THAT NOT BE THE LAST THING I HEAR.
WE WILL BE FREE.
CAN'T...
THIS IS TH END
YOU'RE FINALLY RIGHT ABOUT SOMETHING.
THANK YOU FOR YOUR ASSISTANCE.
OUR POWER IS STILL INSUFFICIENT.
I KNOW, BUT DON'T WORRY...

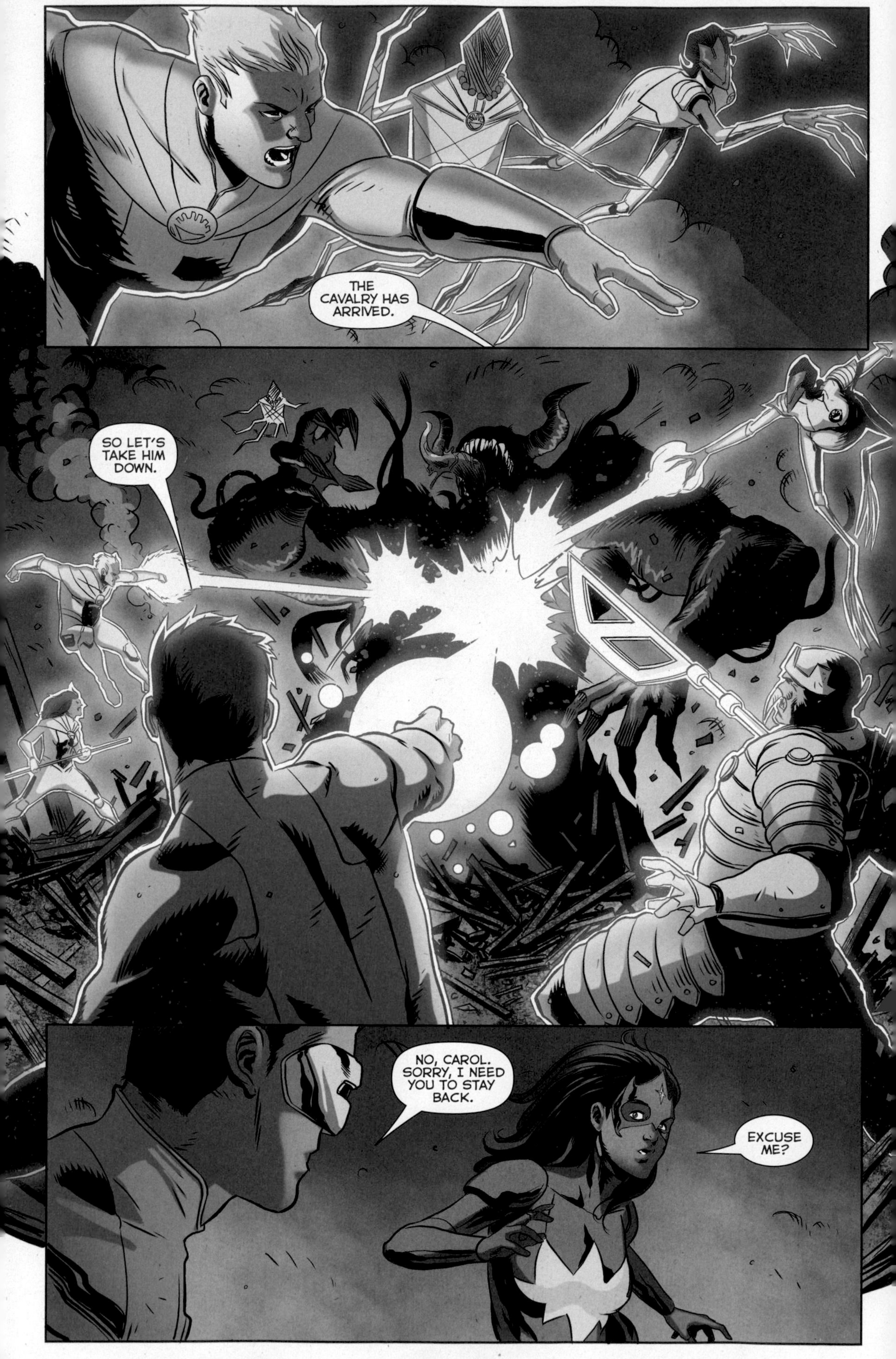
THE CAVALRY HAS ARRIVED.
SO LET'S TAKE HIM DOWN.
NO, CAROL. SORRY, I NEED YOU TO STAY BACK.
EXCUSE ME?

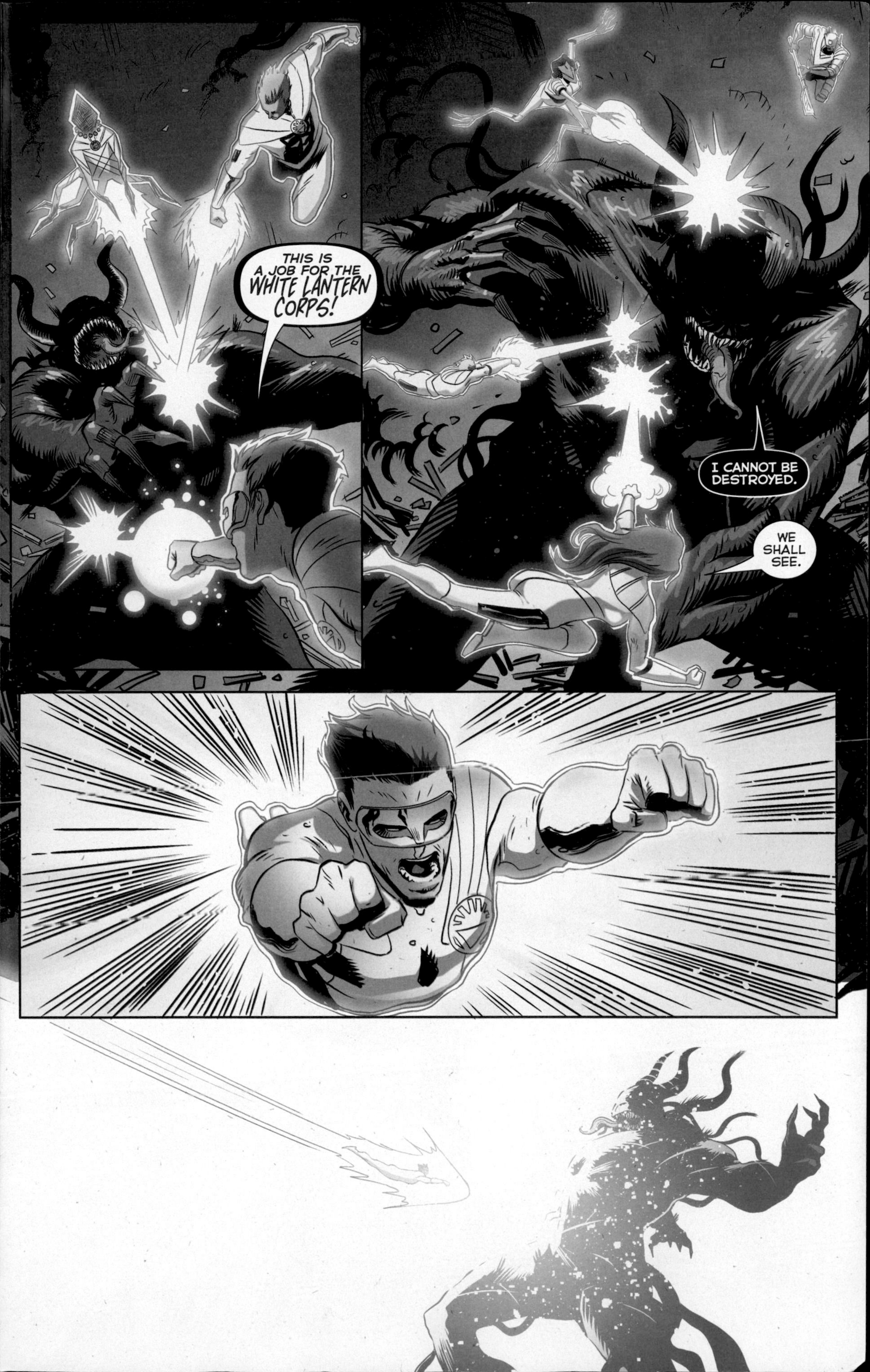
THIS IS A JOB FOR THE WHITE LANTERN CORPS!
I CANNOT BE DESTROYED.
WE SHALL SEE.

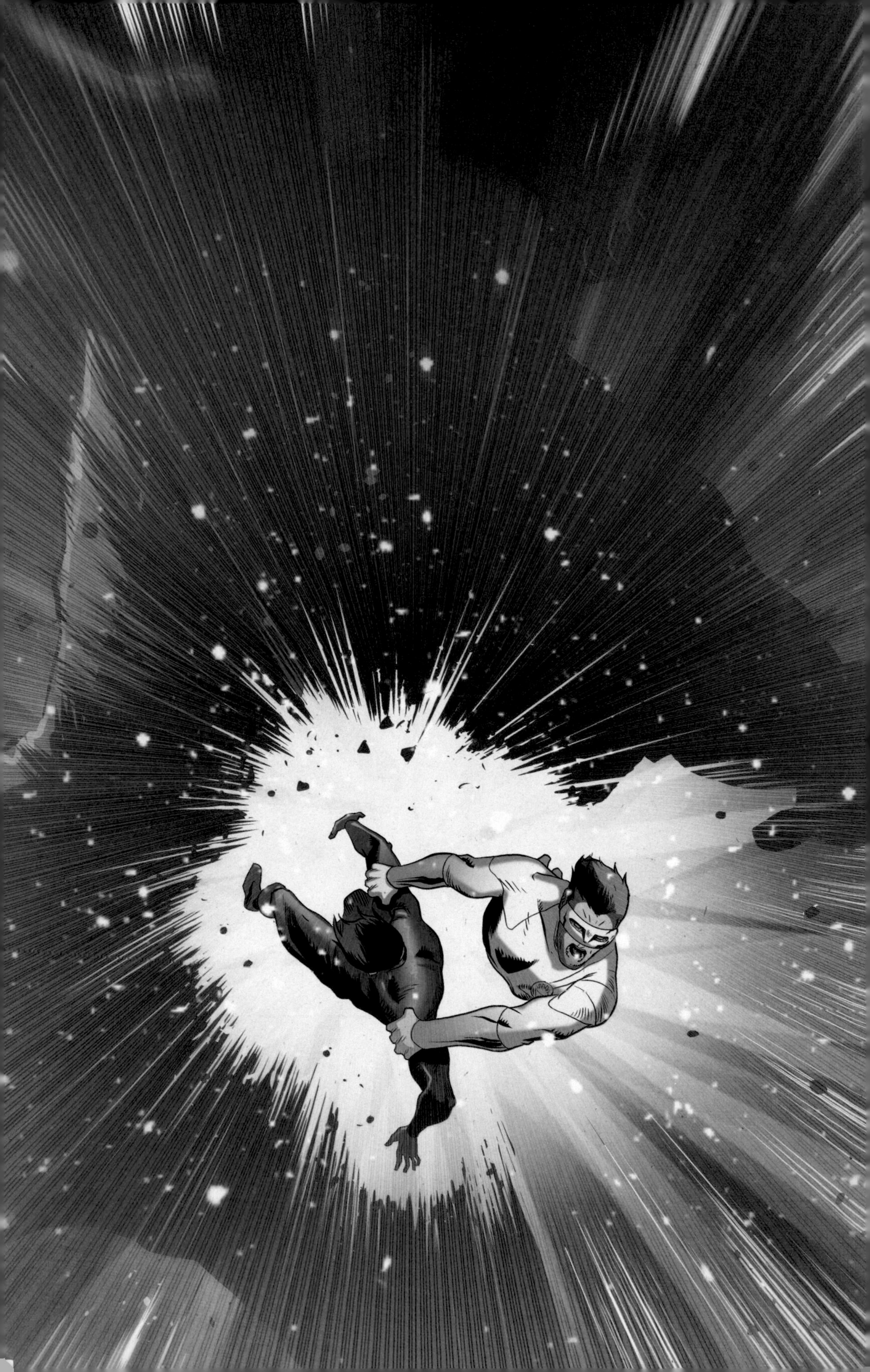

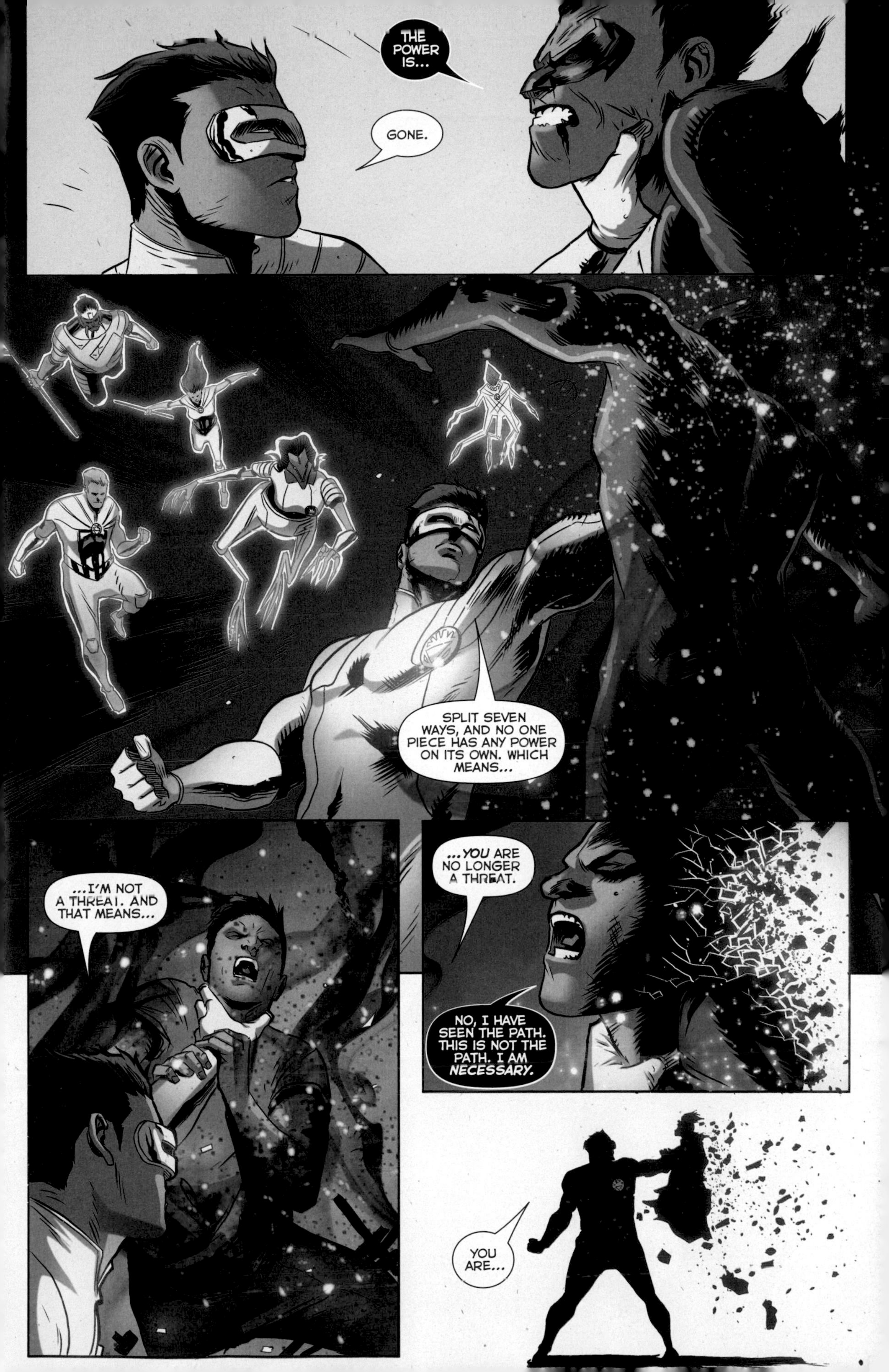

THE POWER IS...
GONE.
SPLIT SEVEN WAYS, AND NO ONE PIECE HAS ANY POWER ON ITS OWN. WHICH MEANS...
...I'M NOT A THREAT. AND THAT MEANS...
...YOU ARE NO LONGER A THREAT.
NO, I HAVE SEEN THE PATH. THIS IS NOT THE PATH. I AM NECESSARY.
YOU ARE...

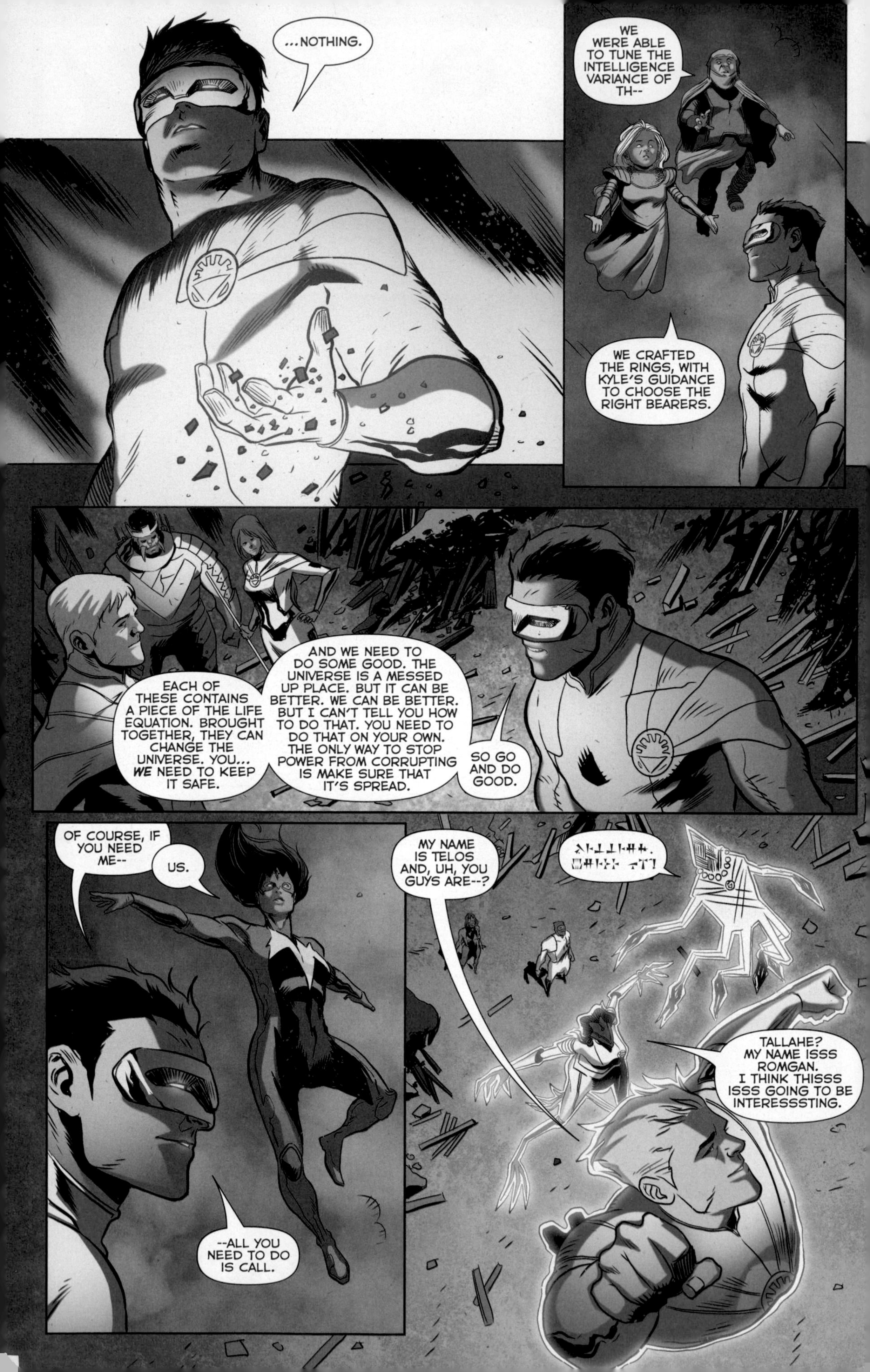
...NOTHING.
WE WERE ABLE TO TUNE THE INTELLIGENCE VARIANCE OF TH--
WE CRAFTED THE RINGS, WITH KYLE'S GUIDANCE TO CHOOSE THE RIGHT BEARERS.
EACH OF THESE CONTAINS A PIECE OF THE LIFE EQUATION. BROUGHT TOGETHER, THEY CAN CHANGE THE UNIVERSE. YOU... *WE* NEED TO KEEP IT SAFE.
AND WE NEED TO DO SOME GOOD. THE UNIVERSE IS A MESSED UP PLACE. BUT IT CAN BE BETTER. WE CAN BE BETTER. BUT I CAN'T TELL YOU HOW TO DO THAT. YOU NEED TO DO THAT ON YOUR OWN. THE ONLY WAY TO STOP POWER FROM CORRUPTING IS MAKE SURE THAT IT'S SPREAD.
SO GO AND DO GOOD.
OF COURSE, IF YOU NEED ME--
US.
--ALL YOU NEED TO DO IS CALL.
MY NAME IS TELOS AND, UH, YOU GUYS ARE--?
TALLAHE? MY NAME ISSS ROMGAN. I THINK THISSS ISSS GOING TO BE INTERESSSTING.

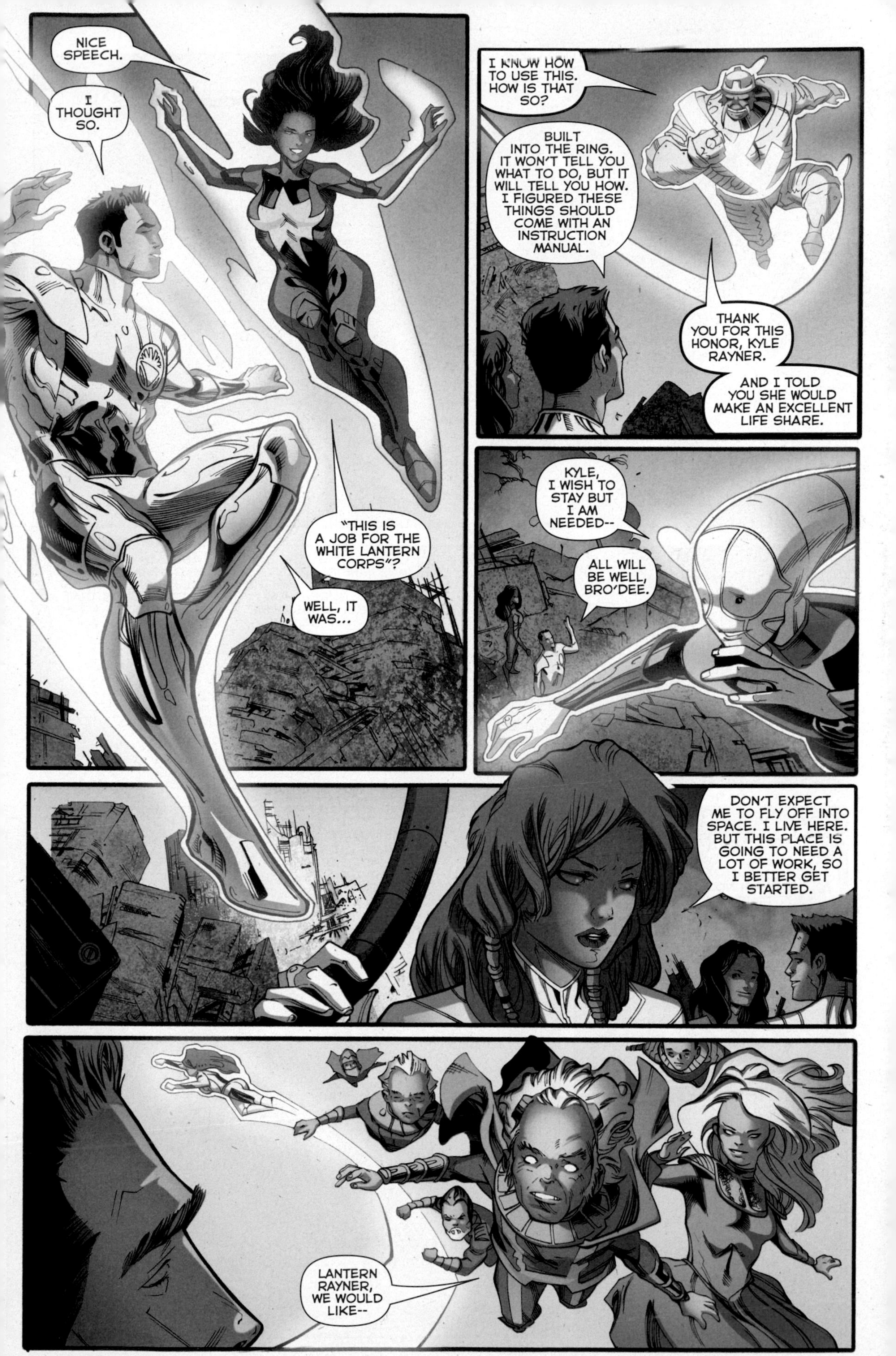
NICE SPEECH.
I THOUGHT SO.
"THIS IS A JOB FOR THE WHITE LANTERN CORPS"?
WELL, IT WAS...
I KNOW HOW TO USE THIS. HOW IS THAT SO?
BUILT INTO THE RING. IT WON'T TELL YOU WHAT TO DO, BUT IT WILL TELL YOU HOW. I FIGURED THESE THINGS SHOULD COME WITH AN INSTRUCTION MANUAL.
THANK YOU FOR THIS HONOR, KYLE RAYNER.
AND I TOLD YOU SHE WOULD MAKE AN EXCELLENT LIFE SHARE.
KYLE, I WISH TO STAY BUT I AM NEEDED--
ALL WILL BE WELL, BRO'DEE.
DON'T EXPECT ME TO FLY OFF INTO SPACE. I LIVE HERE. BUT THIS PLACE IS GOING TO NEED A LOT OF WORK, SO I BETTER GET STARTED.
LANTERN RAYNER, WE WOULD LIKE--

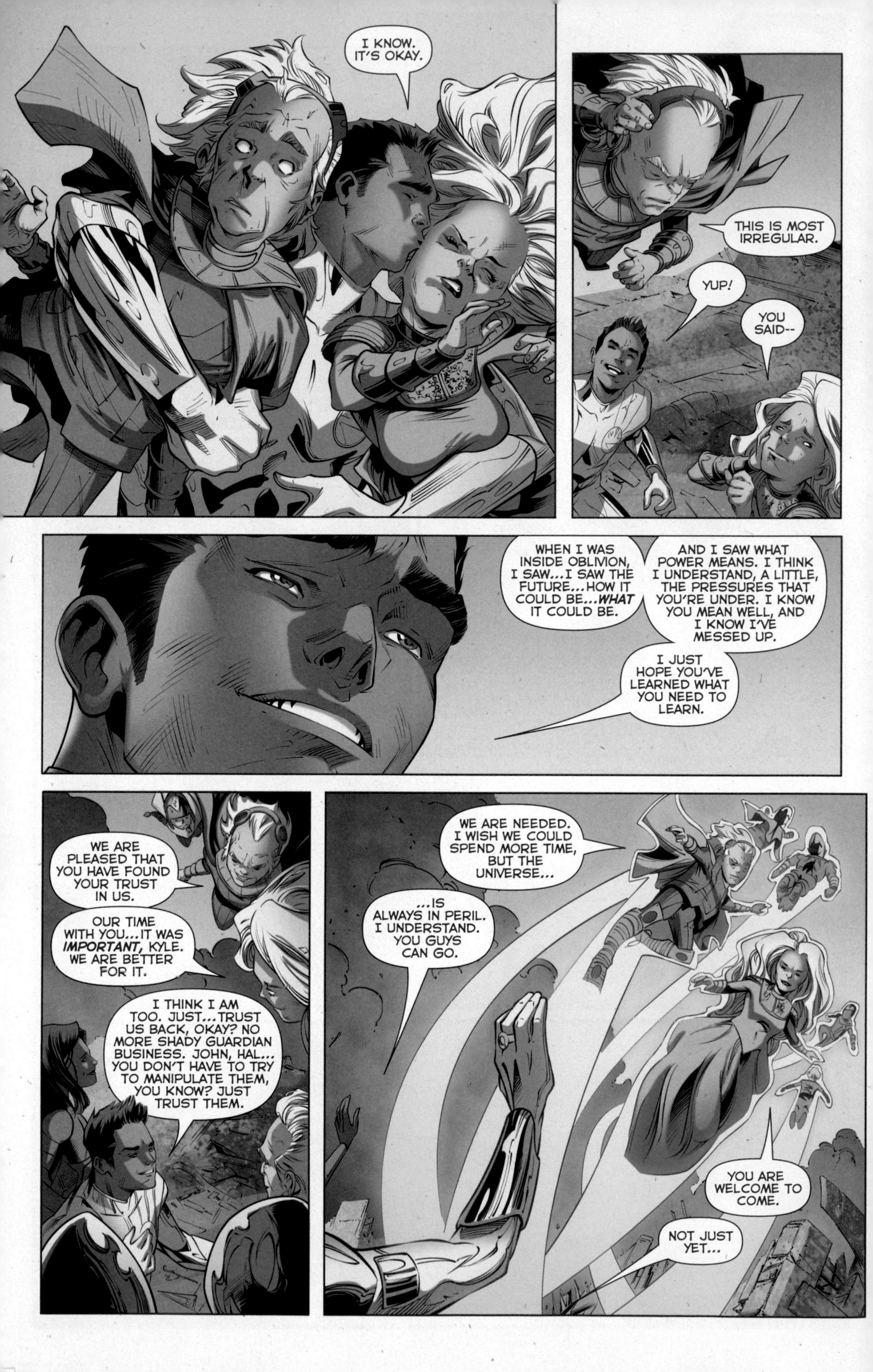
I KNOW. IT'S OKAY.
THIS IS MOST IRREGULAR.
YUP!
YOU SAID--
WHEN I WAS INSIDE OBLIVION, I SAW...I SAW THE FUTURE...HOW IT COULD BE...WHAT IT COULD BE.
AND I SAW WHAT POWER MEANS. I THINK I UNDERSTAND, A LITTLE, THE PRESSURES THAT YOU'RE UNDER. I KNOW YOU MEAN WELL, AND I KNOW I'VE MESSED UP.
I JUST HOPE YOU'VE LEARNED WHAT YOU NEED TO LEARN.
WE ARE PLEASED THAT YOU HAVE FOUND YOUR TRUST IN US.
OUR TIME WITH YOU...IT WAS IMPORTANT, KYLE. WE ARE BETTER FOR IT.
I THINK I AM TOO. JUST...TRUST US BACK, OKAY? NO MORE SHADY GUARDIAN BUSINESS. JOHN, HAL... YOU DON'T HAVE TO TRY TO MANIPULATE THEM, YOU KNOW? JUST TRUST THEM.
WE ARE NEEDED. I WISH WE COULD SPEND MORE TIME, BUT THE UNIVERSE...
...IS ALWAYS IN PERIL. I UNDERSTAND. YOU GUYS CAN GO.
YOU ARE WELCOME TO COME.
NOT JUST YET...

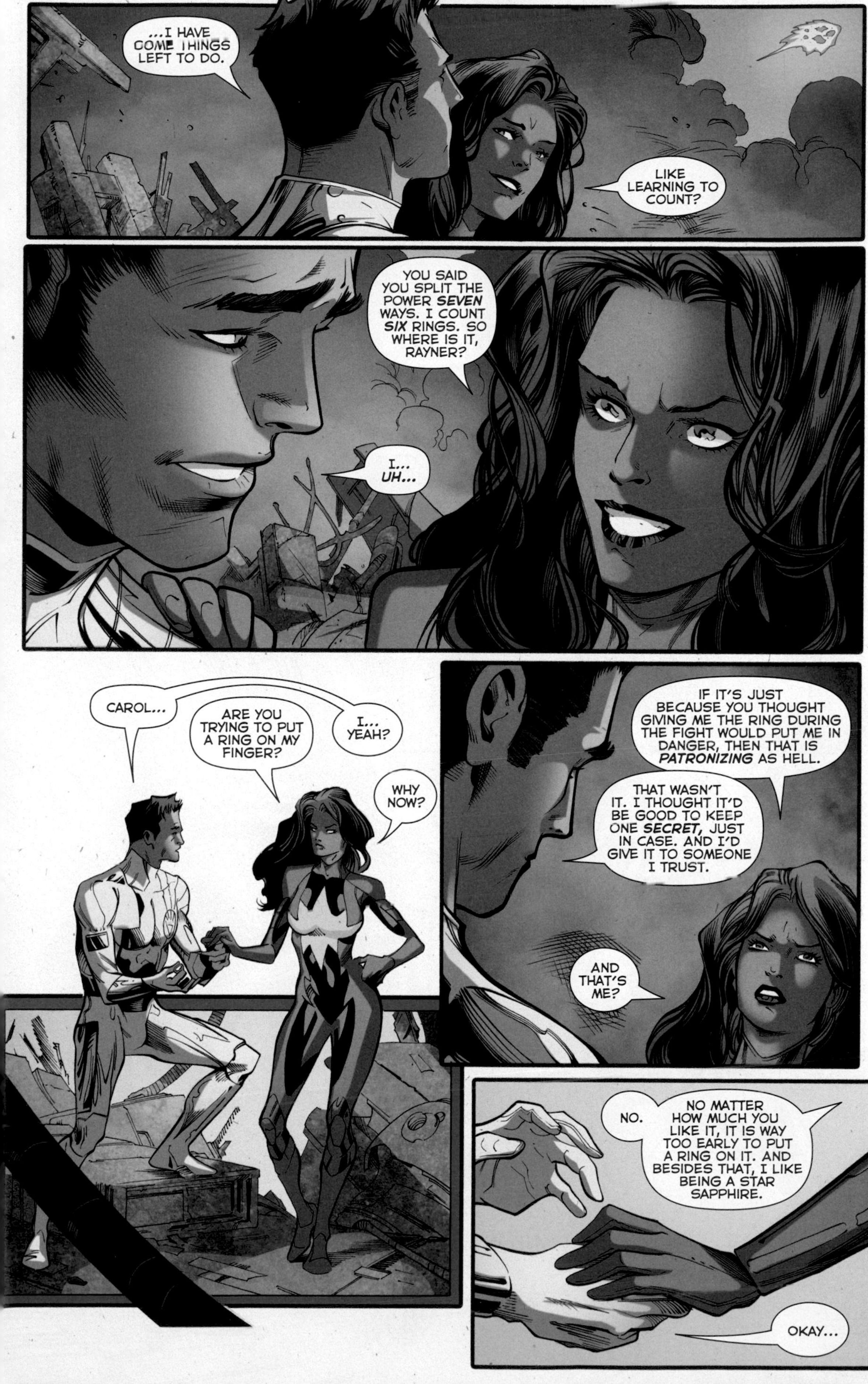
...I HAVE SOME THINGS LEFT TO DO.
LIKE LEARNING TO COUNT?
YOU SAID YOU SPLIT THE POWER SEVEN WAYS. I COUNT SIX RINGS. SO WHERE IS IT, RAYNER?
I... UH...
CAROL...
ARE YOU TRYING TO PUT A RING ON MY FINGER?
I... YEAH?
WHY NOW?
IF IT'S JUST BECAUSE YOU THOUGHT GIVING ME THE RING DURING THE FIGHT WOULD PUT ME IN DANGER, THEN THAT IS PATRONIZING AS HELL.
THAT WASN'T IT. I THOUGHT IT'D BE GOOD TO KEEP ONE SECRET, JUST IN CASE. AND I'D GIVE IT TO SOMEONE I TRUST.
AND THAT'S ME?
NO.
NO MATTER HOW MUCH YOU LIKE IT, IT IS WAY TOO EARLY TO PUT A RING ON IT. AND BESIDES THAT, I LIKE BEING A STAR SAPPHIRE.
OKAY...

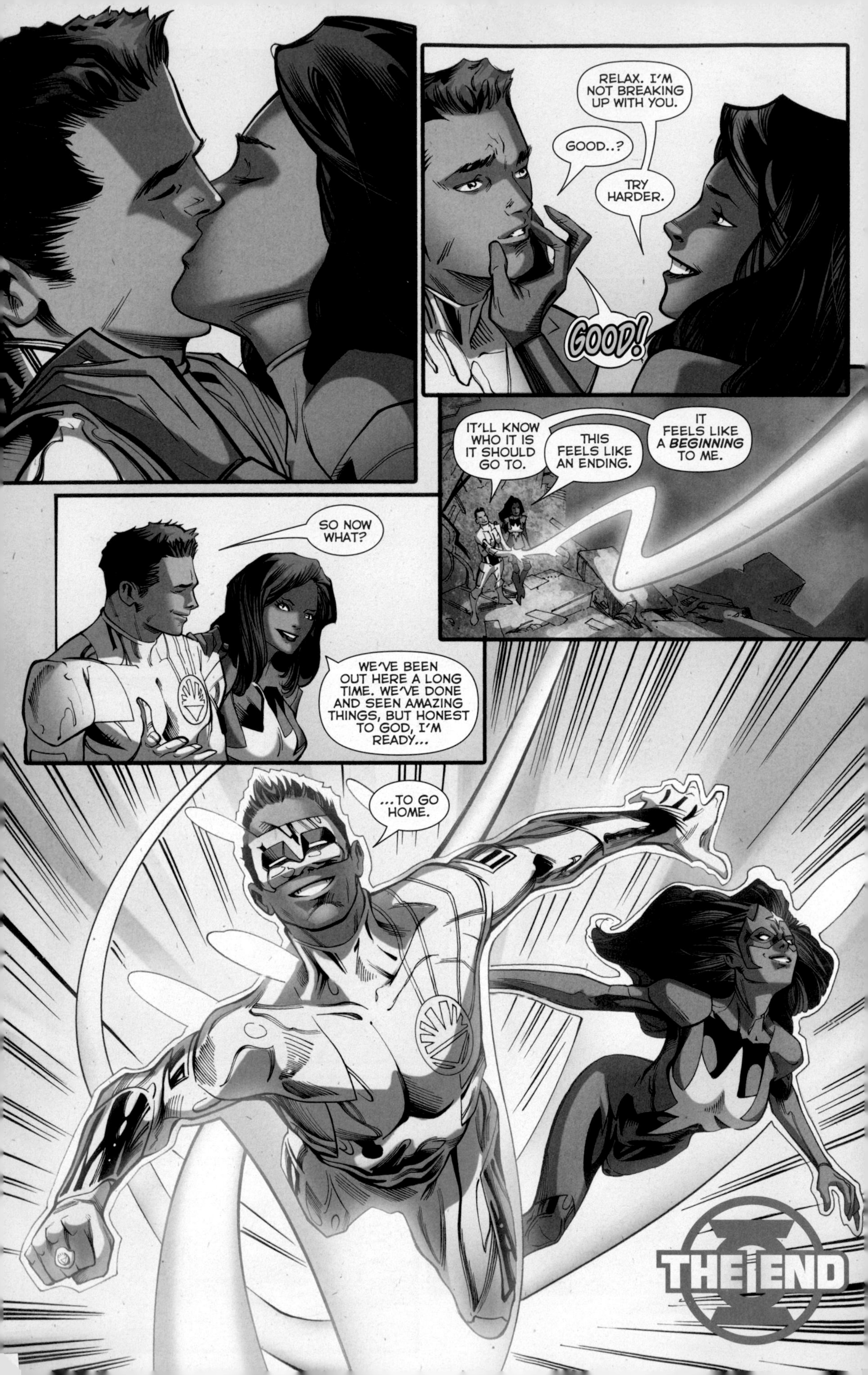
RELAX. I'M NOT BREAKING UP WITH YOU.
GOOD..?
TRY HARDER.
GOOD!
IT'LL KNOW WHO IT IS IT SHOULD GO TO.
THIS FEELS LIKE AN ENDING.
IT FEELS LIKE A *BEGINNING* TO ME.
SO NOW WHAT?
WE'VE BEEN OUT HERE A LONG TIME. WE'VE DONE AND SEEN AMAZING THINGS, BUT HONEST TO GOD, I'M READY...
...TO GO HOME.
THE END

GREEN LANTERN – NEW GUARDIANS #40 pencils by Diogenes Neves

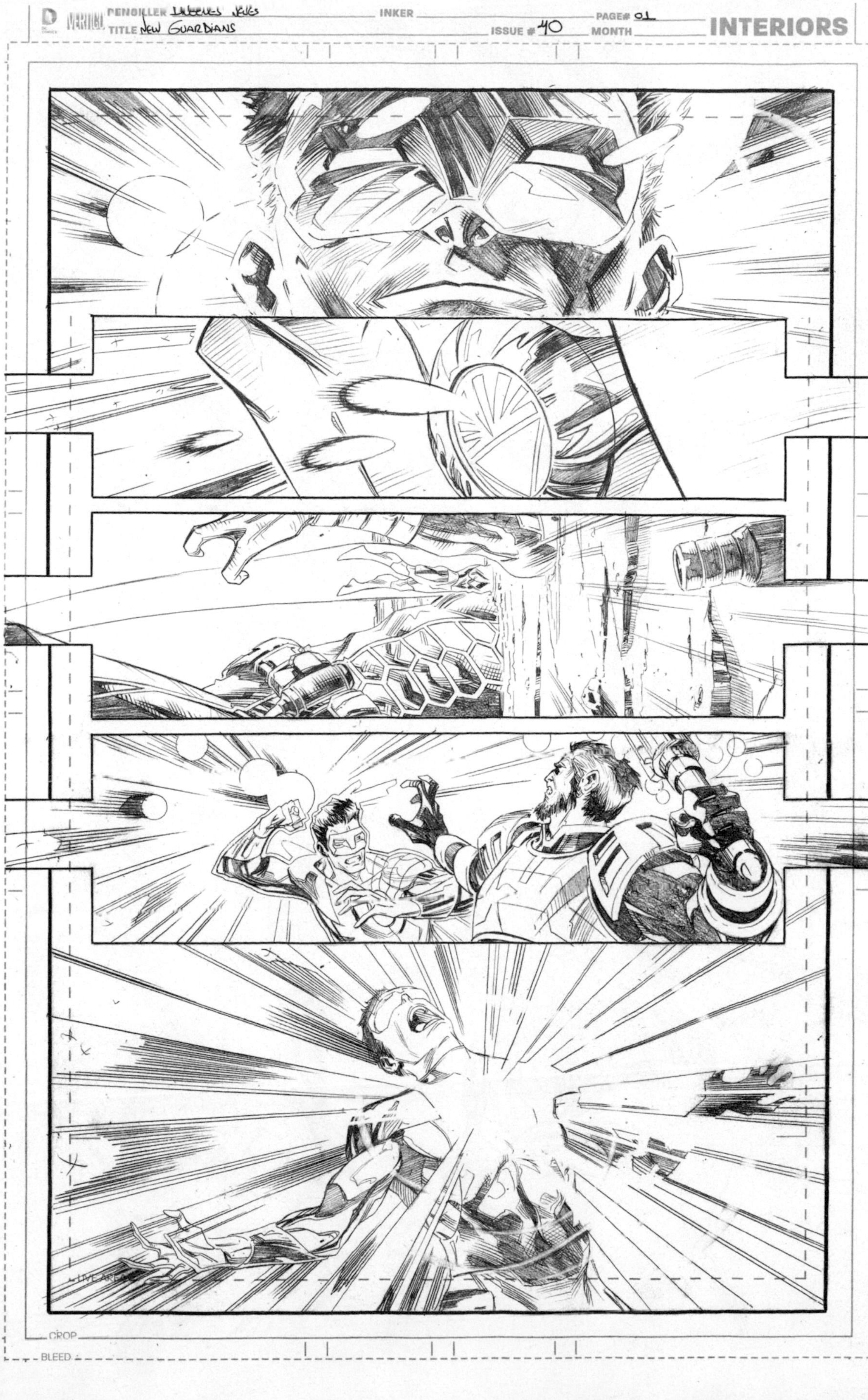
PENCILLER
INKER
PAGE# 01
TITLE NEW GUARDIANS
ISSUE # 40
MONTH
INTERIORS
CROP
BLEED

PENCILLER Diogenes Neves INKER PAGE# 02

TITLE New Guardians ISSUE # 40 MONTH

INTERIORS

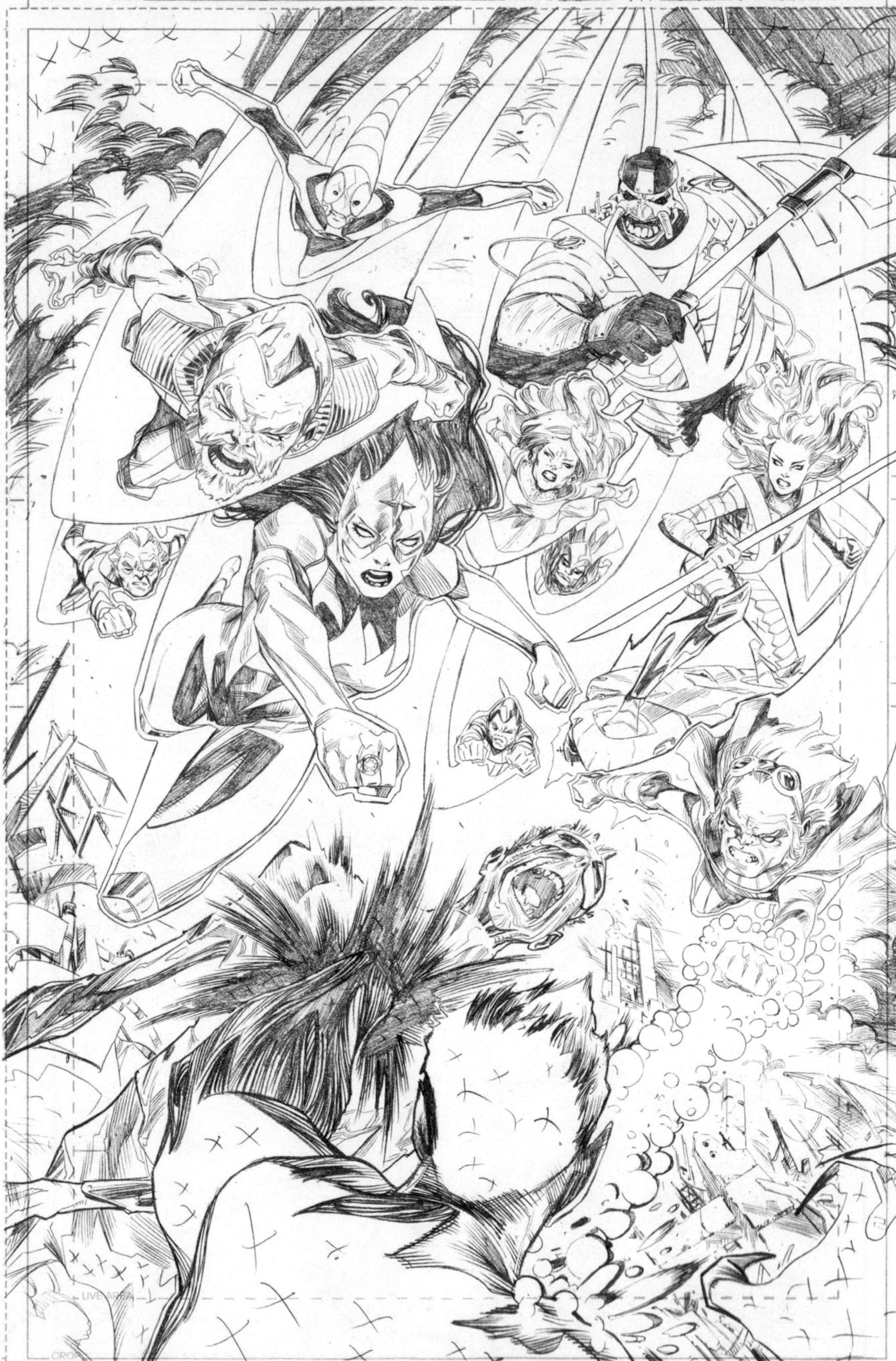
LIVE AREA
CROP
BLEED

PENCILLER DIOGENES NEVES INKER PAGE# UJ **INTERIORS**
TITLE NEW GUARDIANS ISSUE # 40 MONTH

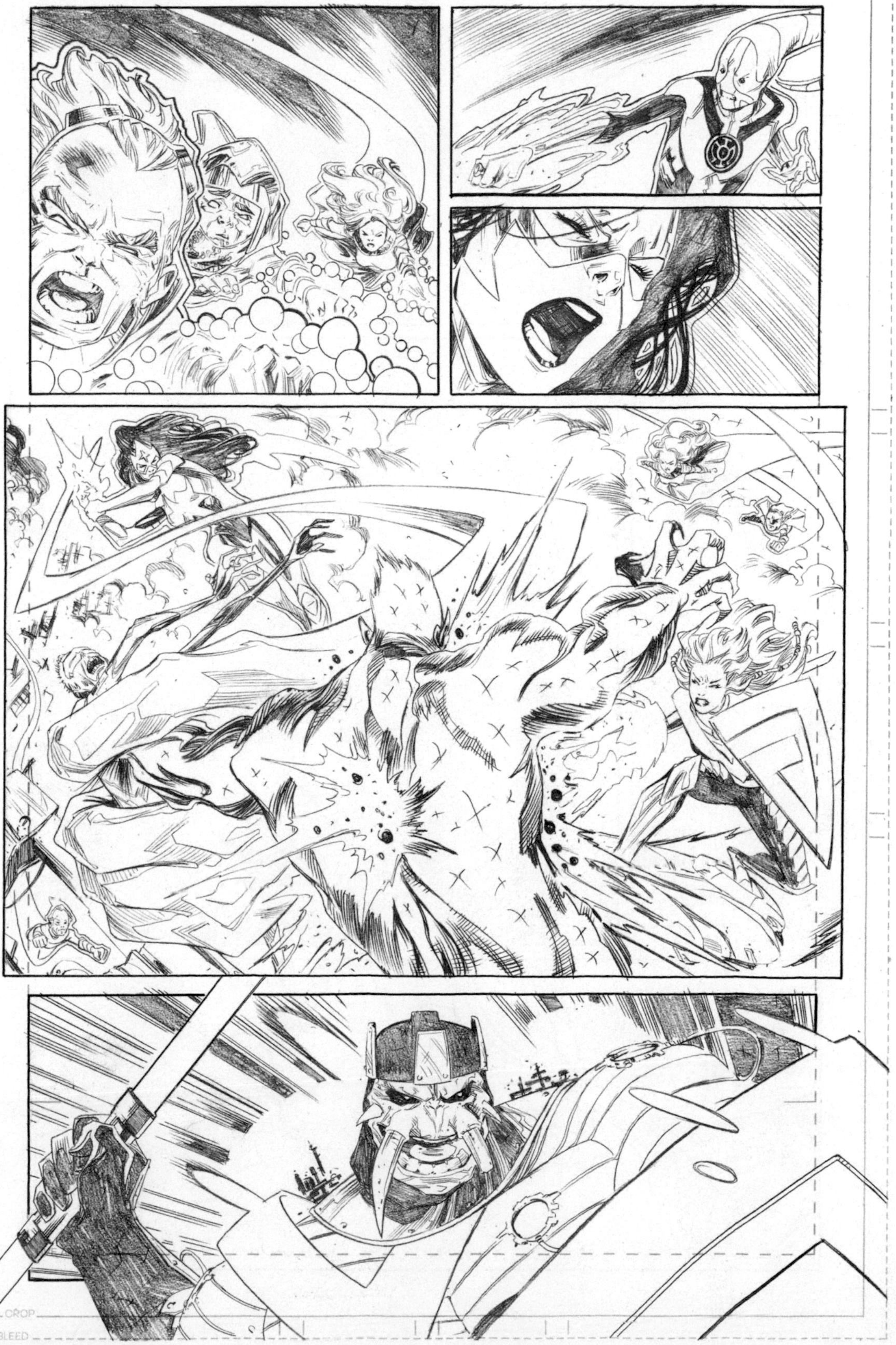

CROP
BLEED

PENCILLER Diogenes Neves INKER PAGE# 04

TITLE New Guardians ISSUE # 40 MONTH

INTERIORS

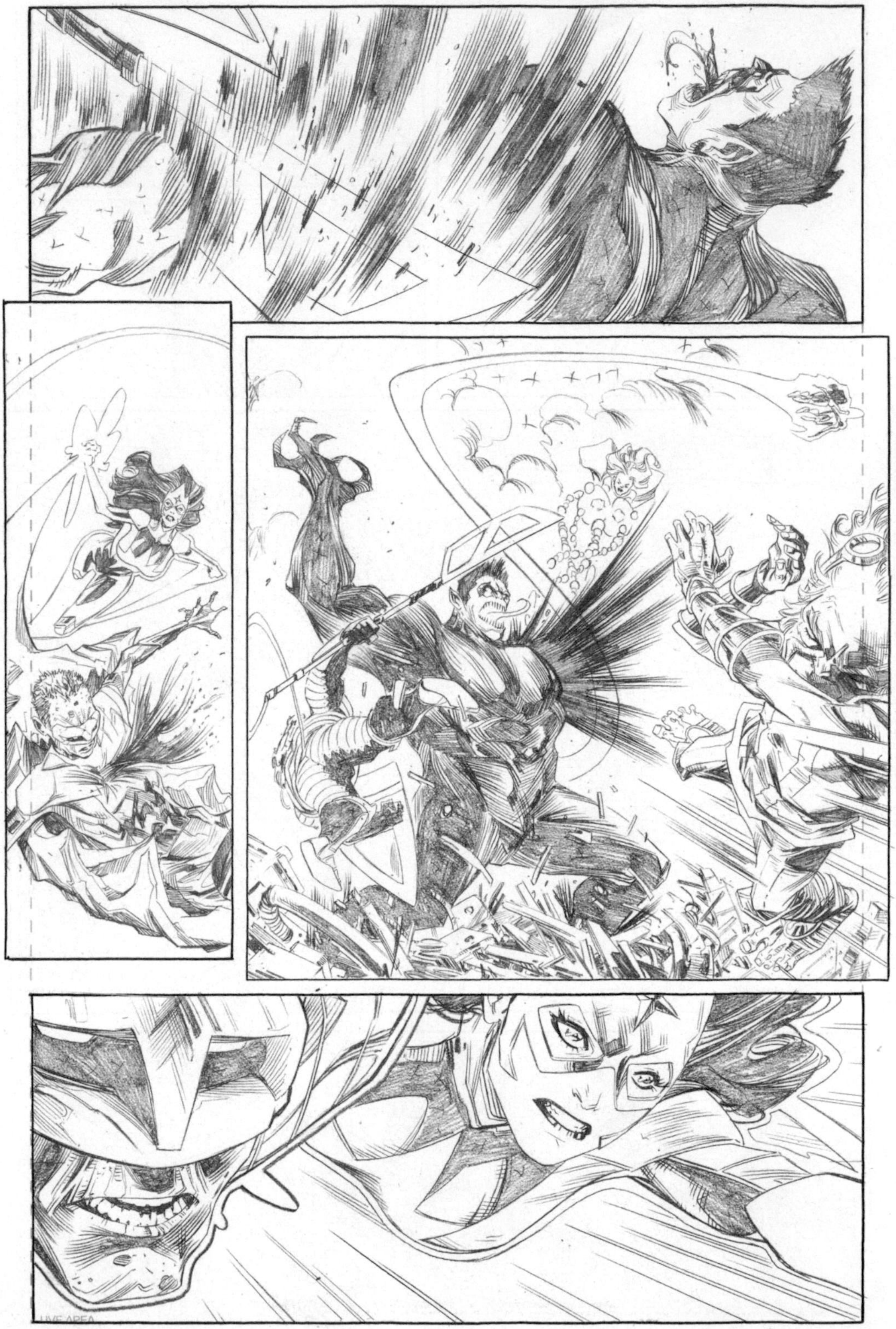

CROP

BLEED

PENCILLER Diogenes Neves INKER PAGE# 05
TITLE New Guardians ISSUE # 40 MONTH
INTERIORS

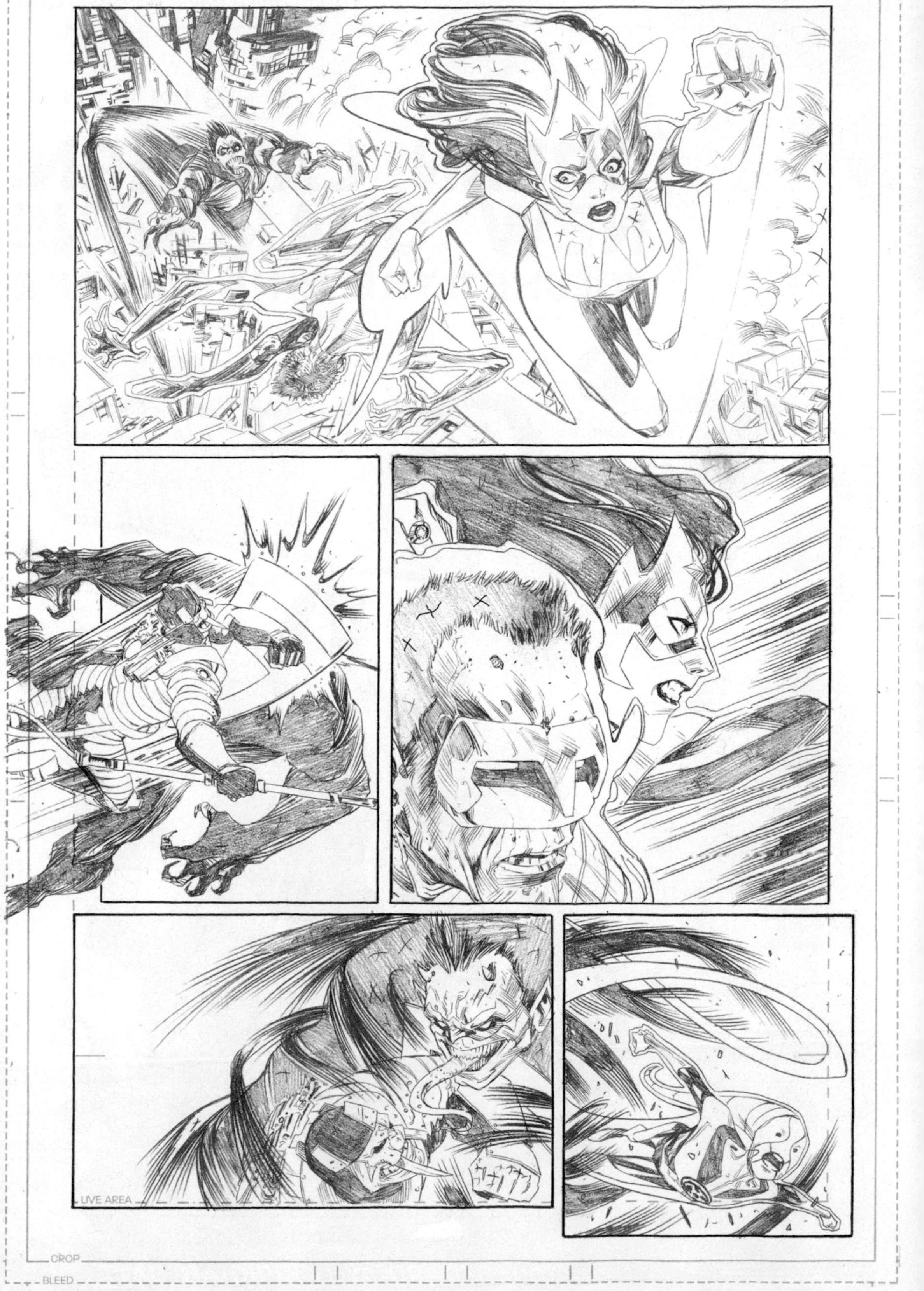

DC COMICS™

"It's bright and shiny and the most interesting ringslingin' goin' these days."—CRAVE ONLINE

START AT THE BEGINNING!

GREEN LANTERN: NEW GUARDIANS

VOLUME 1: THE RING BEARER

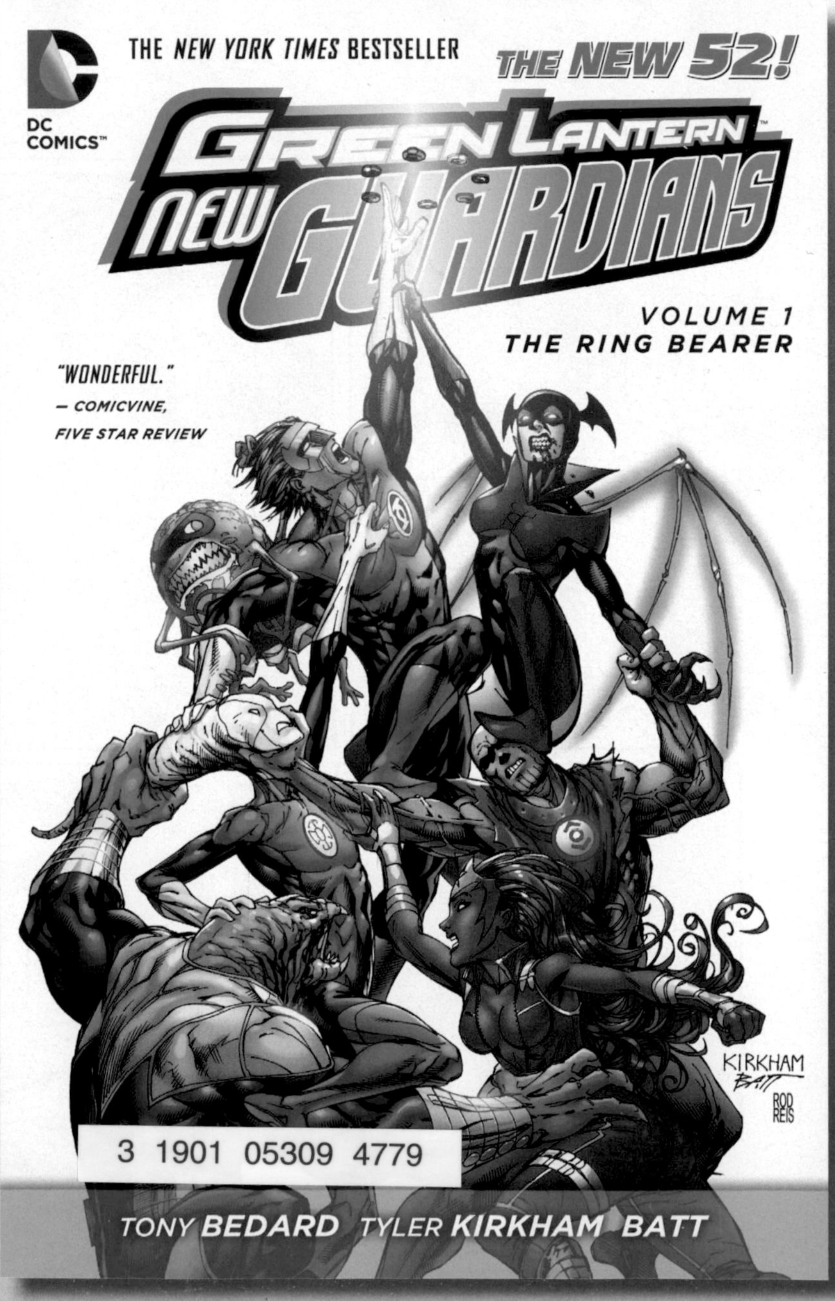

DC COMICS™
THE NEW YORK TIMES BESTSELLER
THE NEW 52!
GREEN LANTERN NEW GUARDIANS
VOLUME 1
THE RING BEARER
"WONDERFUL."
— COMICVINE,
FIVE STAR REVIEW
KIRKHAM
BATT
ROD REIS
3 1901 05309 4779
TONY BEDARD TYLER KIRKHAM BATT

GREEN LANTERN: NEW GUARDIANS VOL. 2: BEYOND HOPE

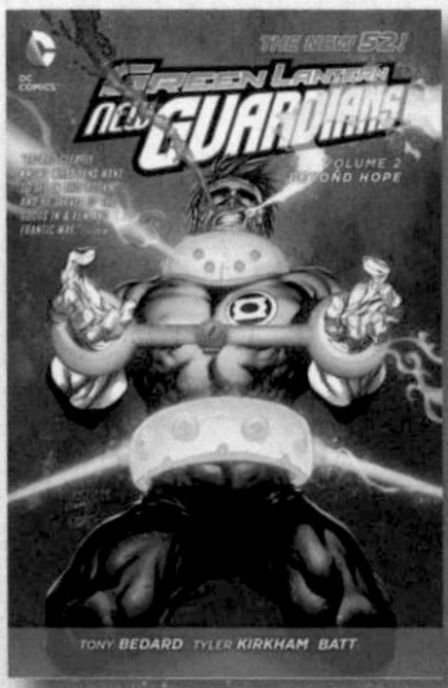

THE NEW 52!
GREEN LANTERN NEW GUARDIANS
VOLUME 2 BEYOND HOPE
TONY BEDARD TYLER KIRKHAM BATT

GREEN LANTERN: NEW GUARDIANS VOL. 3: LOVE AND DEATH

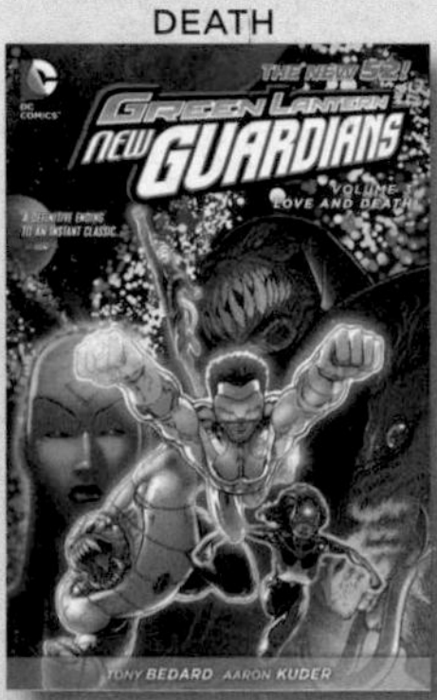

THE NEW 52!
GREEN LANTERN NEW GUARDIANS
LOVE AND DEATH
TONY BEDARD AARON KUDER

GREEN LANTERN: WRATH OF THE FIRST LANTERN

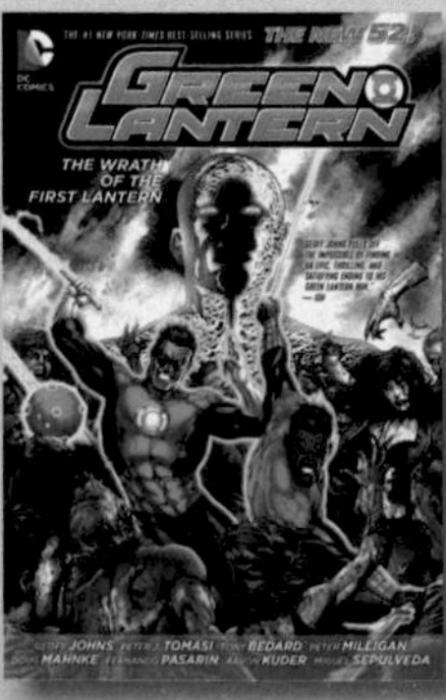

THE NEW 52!
GREEN LANTERN
THE WRATH OF THE FIRST LANTERN